REINVENTING
REVOLUTION

SOCIALISM AND
SOCIAL MOVEMENTS

Series Editor: Mark Selden

REINVENTING REVOLUTION
New Social Movements and the Socialist Tradition in India
Gail Omvedt

CHINA'S TRANSITION FROM SOCIALISM
Statist Legacies and Market Reform, 1980-1990
Dorothy J. Solinger

THE POLITICAL ECONOMY OF CHINESE DEVELOPMENT
Mark Selden

THE HIGHLANDERS OF CENTRAL CHINA
A History, 1895-1937
Jerome Ch'en

BUKHARIN IN RETROSPECT
Edited by Theodor Bergmann, Gert Schaefer, and Mark Selden
Introduction by Moshe Lewin

THE CHINESE STATE IN THE ERA OF ECONOMIC REFORM
Edited by Gordon White

MARXISM AND THE CHINESE EXPERIENCE
Issues in Contemporary Chinese Socialism
Edited by Arlif Dirlik and Maurice Meisner

STALINISM AND THE SEEDS OF SOVIET REFORM
The Debates of the 1960s
Moshe Lewin

REINVENTING REVOLUTION

New Social Movements and the Socialist Tradition in

INDIA

Gail Omvedt

An East Gate Book

M.E. Sharpe
ARMONK, NEW YORK
LONDON, ENGLAND

An East Gate Book

Library of Congress Cataloging-in-Publication Data

Omvedt, Gail
Reinventing revolution : new social movements and the socialist tradition in India /
Gail Omvedt.
p.   cm.—(Socialism and social movements)
Includes bibliographical references and index
ISBN 0-87332-784-5.—ISBN 0-87332-785-3 (pbk)
1. Social movements—India. 2. Socialism—India.
3. India—Social conditions—1947-. 4. Feminism—India. 5. Caste—India.
6. Green movement—India. 7. Peasant uprisings—India.
I. Title. II. Series.
HC683.5.O49   1993
303.48′4′0954—dc20
92-46911
CIP

Printed in the United States of America

Contents

Part IV: Toward a New Vision, 1985–1991

List of Tables

Comrade

by Prabhakar Gangurde
Astitva, Aurangabad, 1978

Don't expect revolution
from those living corpses,
comrade.
First you
become their beacon.
The revolution that
will flash like lightning
and not be extinguished in any storm
is still far far
away.
Don't be in a hurry for revolution.
You are still very small;
your ability to resist
the atrocities, boycotts and rapes
that go on every moment
has become nil,
comrade.
Tomorrow's sun is yet to rise;
sleep undisturbed until then.
Take the fantasy out of
your daydreams.
What will happen
from simply waving the red flag
over the many colors of reality?
In showing the way to violent revolution
take care
of your own existence, comrade.
I'm worried about you,
not knowing
what will happen tomorrow.
The sun will set.
Where are you going
with your existence in the dark,
comrade?

Don't be so impatient,
there are some boundaries to sacrifice.
From a thousand sacrifices
what will be accomplished?
This is the
story of each generation.
Why give to one generation only
the sacrifice of all generations?
Comrade don't be so anxious,
don't worry about me.
Now I have awakened,
I am moving in blazing sunlight.
Come ...
You won't come with me
you won't embrace me.
I have tiger claws scattered
all over my body.
They won't pierce you.
If they pierce you it is
certainly not for your sacrifice
comrade.

(Dalit poem of the late 1970s; translated by Gail Omvedt and Bharat Patankar. The ''tiger claws'' in the last section refer to the weapons used by the Maratha king Shivaji to kill the Muslim chief Afzal Khan in an embrace at a meeting in which both were planning treachery.)

Introduction

"LONG YEARS ago we made a tryst with destiny, and now the time comes when we shall redeem our.pledge, not wholly or in full measure, but very substantially. At the stroke of the midnight hour, when the world sleeps, India will awake to life and freedom."

These were the words with which Jawaharlal Nehru, a leader of India's dominant Congress party and the first prime minister of the country, hailed its independence in 1947.[1] Nehru, the aristocratic scion of a long line of Kashmiri brahmans, was himself to be a virtual dynastic founder, with his daughter (Indira) and grandson (Rajiv) to follow him. Nevertheless, he and other Congress leaders had led a long, often militant if nonviolent struggle under the leadership of Mohandas Karamchand Gandhi, and with planning and public ownership accepted even by the Indian bourgeoisie, the country seemed set on at least a semisocialistic path. Nehru had some basis to proclaim his achievements.

But others were not so optimistic. Dr. B. R. Ambedkar, "Babasaheb," son of an untouchable minor military officer, educated to heights that would have been unimaginable for any earlier generation, leader of his people and a vociferous opponent of Nehru's Congress party as the "party of brahmans and the bourgeoisie," had nevertheless been chosen to draft the constitution of the newly independent nation. "On 26 January, 1950," warned Ambedkar before the constituent assembly, referring to the day celebrated as "Republic Day," "we are going to enter into a life of contradictions. In politics we shall have equality and in social and economic life we will have inequality. . . . We must remove this contradiction at the earliest possible moment or else those who suffer from inequality will blow up the structure of political democracy which we have so laboriously built up."[2]

If atrocities against untouchables did not stop, thundered Ambedkar on subsequent occasions to his impoverished and oppressed followers, "I myself will burn the constitution."

Over four decades later, it is Ambedkar's centenary that is celebrated with tumultuous mass meetings rather than Nehru's, and it is the explosions and contradictions he prophesied that appear to be overwhelming Nehru's promises. Even more striking, they are not the explosions of the "class struggle" of traditional Marxism but rather have been revolving around the kind of issues—of caste, gender, community, and ethnicity—represented by people like Ambedkar.

These are the issues of what are beginning to be called, as they exert their force in countries throughout the world, the "new social movements." By the end of the 1980s they were the questions defining Indian politics. Workers' struggles persist, but calls for "nationalization" are no longer heard, and it is instead demands for higher prices for farm products and debt relief that are part of the agenda of every political party. "Agrarian reform" is still a slogan, but only in small pockets are there serious efforts to capture land from big landlords; instead, determined popular struggles have emerged throughout the country to save land being lost for the construction of dams or other government projects, with an increasing call for "alternative development." The urban and rural poor have responded with only moderate enthusiasm to "class demands" such as struggles for employment, while proposals to give members of their castes and communities reservations in public service have shaken up the country and emerged as the central slogan of the "left and democratic" forces. And, while "armed struggle" clearly remained on some people's agenda, it is not the armed struggle of revolutionary upsurge, but more often religion dominated "liberation movements" for autonomy or independence in the peripheral regions of the subcontinent, shaking not only Kashmir and the hill tribes of the northeast, but also Punjab, Assam, and, in different ways, Tamilnadu.

By the late 1980s the predominant features of Indian politics had become the "new social movements" of women, dalits and low castes, peasants, farmers, and tribals as well as ethnicity-based struggles for autonomy or independence on the periphery and the violence-ridden assertion of religious fundamentalism. The hegemony of the Congress party has been decisively broken; "Nehruvian" models of development are discredited. The major "centrist" alternative to the Congress, the Janata Dal, has been defined in terms of at least some of the issues represented by the new movements. The Communist parties have survived, better than in most countries in the world, but only by taking up the same issues. The main theme of the Janata Dal left-regional party campaign in the 1991 elections was in fact a major demand of the movement led for so long by Ambedkar, that is, the implementation of reservations in public service for dalits and low castes, under the slogan of "social justice."

Have the new social movements then "arrived"? Hardly, for the caste oppression, patriarchy, loot of peasants' labor and natural resources, drought, and environmental destruction that they have protested against goes on. The parties, left and center, keep backtracking and "betraying" their promises, and the movements can get no direct representation in the party structure and have failed to form an alternative political front of their own. The ideological hegemony of the Congress party has been broken along with its political hammerlock on the center, and the preeminence of traditional Marxism among the opposition has been shaken up by the slogans and theories raised by the activists of the new movements; yet no new alternative, no differently articulated version of socialism has as yet emerged as a political force. The new social movements have thus arrived on the threshhold of an alternative model of politics and development, but they are as yet unable to cross it, while the unmapped terrain beyond is barely discernible.

This book focuses on the four major new social movements in India—the women's movement, the anticaste movement of dalits and other low or "shudra" castes, the environmental movement, and the farmers' movement of peasants struggling over issues of market production. Based on participant observation, documentation from the movements themselves and from newspaper and journal reports, and academic studies, it describes the process of their rise from the early 1970s to their arrival on the threshhold of the 1990s.

It is also concerned with the great debate surrounding these movements. This is a debate that has taken place largely within the context of Marxism, since Marxism has been the main ideology of those struggling for relief from oppression and exploitation in India, and as people have begun to struggle in new ways and formulate new theories and ideologies, they have done so, quite often, in confrontation with what I describe as "traditional Marxism." It is important to note that this debate has included academics as well as activists, and that academics, as upper castes, as males, as members of an urban elite, are often confronted by the movements. For this reason I have treated the studies and theoretical positions of intellectuals regarding the social movements as part of the ongoing ideological debate in and about the movements, conditioned by their own social position and related to the hegemonic ideological structures of the society—not as theories that should be used to analyze the movements or which are to be tested with reference to the movements. In other words, this is a book about the movements themselves, not an effort to give a full analysis of the social system that has generated them. To give an example, I am concerned, at this point, not so much to refute or confirm interpretations of the women's movement as "bourgeois feminism" or of the farmers' movement as representing a "kulak lobby," but rather to understand the significance of the fact that they are understood in this way by specific groups of people.

Nevertheless, some major distinctions with important studies of Indian political economy should be mentioned. Overwhelmingly, those who work with some kind of "class" model of Indian politics, indeed any notion of a "political economy," whether it is the Rudolphs, Francine Frankel, other European Marxists, the traditional Marxists of the "mode of production" debate, or the new Marxists of the "subaltern studies" group, or for that matter left-identified scholars such as Atul Kohli, define "class" in terms of private property and overlook the relations of exploitation and surplus extraction between toilers (for instance, landowning small peasants) and those controlling other conditions of production, the market, or the state itself. That is, they may see the state as backing up a system of exploitation and maintaining "domination" (with more or less autonomy), but they do not see it as a direct agent of exploitation, and they do not see state powerholders as exploiters. "Class/caste" conflicts are thus defined as centering on the village or local level, whether within the enterprise between capitalists and workers, or within the locality between rich farmers and laborers, landlords or moneylenders and peasants, landholding "dominant castes" and low castes/dalits. Outside of this are "political" relations only. The exploitation of nonwage laborers, with petty commodity producers, sellers of minor forest produce, or subsistence producers, is missed, and so are the processes of surplus extraction of nature's products that are linked to the destruction of nature.

Thus the Rudolphs can see Indian politics as "centrist" in spite of struggles mounted by small peasants, precisely because they define these as petty-bourgeois commodity producers ("bullock capitalists") and not as exploited toilers.[3] Similarly, Atul Kohli can argue in his latest book that "The socioeconomic forces at work are well understood by development scholars and require only brief mention. . . . What looms even larger . . . is a series of political variables" only because he, like the "development scholars" who presumably thoroughly understand them, defines "socioeconomic forces" exclusive of relations between the state and workers or peasants.[4] For that matter, in spite of the brilliant contributions of the "subaltern studies" school with regard to the colonial period, its practitioners have hardly made a stab at dealing with the postcolonial period, partly because of the dilemmas in defining "subaltern." (Was Ambedkar subaltern? Are upper class women subaltern?) Those who do so, such as Partha Chatterjee, still use "traditional Marxist" frameworks that see the peasantry as necessarily differentiating, so that the maintenance of "community" is seen as now illegitimate. Nearly all interpretations of social movements, new or old, are within this framework.[5] Only a few recent studies and analyses, for instance Tornquist on India and Indonesia or van Schendal on India and Burma, have begun to look at relations of exploitation and surplus extraction between the centers of national and world capitalism and the rural localities,[6] and there are even fewer that deal with new social movements.

Within India, there has not been much conceptualization of the "new social movements" as such. In the early 1980s Rajni Kothari and others connected with the Lokayan group brought forward the concept of "nonparty political formations," which brought together new women's organizations, nonparty mass organizations such as the Jharkhand Mukti Morcha, and funded "voluntary agencies" to contrast them with traditional left parties and their mass organizations. But funded organizations (though sometimes connected with movements) are neither "political" nor movements, and it is more accurate to treat specific women's organizations and groups like the JMM as "people's organizations" and the movements they are connected with as "social movements." Many Marxists have suggested the term "popular movements," but this tends to imply a privileged (and vanguard) position for "working class" movements, a position that the new movements themselves reject in theory and ignore in practice.

Finally, there is an increasingly popular conceptualization of the new movements as "grass roots" movements. A recent article, "Nine Theses on Social Movements" by André Gunter Frank and Marta Fuentes, describes new movements generally as basically "grass roots" and apolitical. This has been criticized by D. N. Dhanagare and J. John as "essentialist," arguing that "Frank and Fuentes conspire theoretically to take away political consciousness from the exploited classes and bestow upon them an apolitical force of morality and social power."[7] The point is well taken. Frank and Fuentes are essentialist, for instance, when they claim that "similarly to the women's movement, the very notion of state or even political party power for them [individually small-scale community-based movements] would negate most of their grass roots aims and essence."[8] This rests on defining movements in such a way as to exclude those that are "political." Yet, in India, the anticaste movement has had political power as a core thrust; the farmers' movement has consciously sought to organize a political impact even while shying away from politics in the traditional sense, and even the women's movement has enthusiastically taken up political aims at the local and regional levels. Similarly, the new movements are no more "grass roots" than "old" social movements based on workers and peasants. Yet most discussions of "new social movements" appear to be influenced by the "grass roots" conceptualization, and usually exclude discussion of the anticaste movement and the farmers' movement. Thus, while using the concept of "new social movements," it is necessary to differentiate the analysis from "Theses" such as these, which are too much under the impact of NGO-generated ideologizations of social movements.

The "new social movements" have the following characteristics:

1. They are "social movements" in the sense of having a broad overall organization, structure, and ideology aiming at social change.

2. They are "new" in that they themselves, through the ideologies they generate, define their exploitation and oppression, the system that generates these, and the way to end this exploitation and oppression, in "new" terms—related to traditional Marxism but having clear differences with it. They cannot, in other words, be seen as simply "popular movements" of sections willing to follow along under the vanguardship of the working class and its parties or accept working class ideology; they consciously reject this kind of relationship and question the ideology as they have experienced it.

3. They are movements of groups that were either ignored as exploited by traditional Marxism (women, dalits, and shudras) or who are exploited in ways related to the new processes of contemporary capitalism (peasants forced to produce for capital through market exploitation managed by the state, peasants and forest dwellers victimized by environmental degradation) but left unconceptualized by a preoccupation with "private property" and wage labor.

4. The full analysis of their position requires thus a modified Marxist, that is, a historical materialist analysis of the contemporary capitalist system.

As noted, this report focuses on four major new social movements. It will deal with them in their relation to Indian society and the state, and to the Marxism of the existing left parties and Indian intellectuals.

Following a background section in part I, the four chapters of part II describe the emergence of these movements in the period between 1972 and 1985. Part III examines the relationship of the movements with the working class movement and traditional Marxism (both the Marxism of the intellectuals and the Marxism of the Communist parties); it looks at their interaction with the politics of the period, including the issues raised by the ethnic-nationality movements (e.g., those of Assam and Punjab); the problems of the rising of religious fundamentalism, or "communalism" as it is called in the Indian context (referring to the defining of religious communities as the relevant unit of action); and the responses of the political elite. Part IV takes up the period from 1985 to the present, one of the intermingling of the movements at the base (spearheaded in some ways by developments in the women's movement, particularly among organizations based on rural women) and a move to formulate models of and struggle for aspects of "alternative development," an emerging concept implying an "alternative socialism."

The approach offered here is that the movements are revolutionary in their aspirations and antisystemic in their impact; they have been oriented as single-issue ("one-point program," in Indian terminology) efforts to bring about change, but, because they have grown in a period in which the solutions of "traditional socialism" are so overwhelmingly discredited, they are faced, in spite of this "single-issue" orientation, with the task of "reinventing revolution."

The basic framework of the approach used here is that while Marxism has been called the historical materialism of the proletariat, what is needed today is a historical materialism of not only industrial factory workers, but also of peasants, women, tribals, dalits and low castes, and oppressed nationalities. It can no longer be assumed that a theory that (apparently) serves the needs of the industrial working class is adequate for the liberatory struggles of the whole society. An analysis of capitalism will be insufficient, even erroneous, if it does not move out of the sphere of commodity production and exchange in which value is defined in terms of abstract labor time and capital accumulation is defined through the appropriation of surplus value only.

Domestic labor produces surplus labor (but not as surplus value) necessary for capital accumulation; "nature" is the source of wealth (but not of exchange-value) and thus also contributes to capital accumulation even while being kept outside the sphere of valorization. Finally, the thesis of "primitive accumulation" points to the way in which the sphere of commodity production and exchange ("capitalism" in the narrow sense) is embedded in a larger society in which production relations and accumulation are defined in terms of force and violence exerted against nonwage laborers. All of these have to be taken together to produce a unified theory, for the sphere of capital accumulation and its processes is wider than the sphere of commodity production and exchange as normally defined.

And so, revolution itself has to be defined in broader terms: it can no longer consist of the "proletariat" in commodity production taking over the "means of production," for this will only yield a state-managed system of wider exploitation. The fate of the East European statist societies has sufficiently shown this. Redefining revolution, then, is the need of the time, and the beginning of this process can be seen in India's new social movements.

This study owes its origin to the innumerable movement activists and participants with whom I have interacted, debated, and argued; who have given me their time and hospitality and passed on something of their fervor for change. Their names are too numerous to mention here; many of them appear in the following pages. I owe a great debt to the Centre for Social Studies in Surat for providing the facilities and time necessary to carry through the production of a viable manuscript: a library and computer room open twenty-four hours a day and gracious and helpful colleagues and staff have made all the differences.

And for moral support and inspiration I owe gratitude to the entire "Patankar-Nikam" family, most especially of course to Bharat Patankar. Of them, I would like to dedicate this book to Surya, whose own special moral support and inspiration was tragically too brief.

REINVENTING
REVOLUTION

Part I
Historical Background

1

The National Movement and the Roots of Socialism

We with our own hands have spread the coals beneath our feet,
We have run till we fainted on the path of our ideals,
We have never paused for rest, we have never looked behind,
We have let neither love nor fame be shackles to bind,
A single star before us, the burning coals beneath—
Shout victory, victory to the revolution! Shout victory!

Why, mother, do your eyes fill with tears? your future is bright,
The dawn of tomorrow comes out of the womb of the night,
Today it is our corpses that blaze upon the funeral pyre,
Out of that blaze will come revolution's leaders of tomorrow
Then the shackles on your feet will shatter with a clang,
Shout victory, victory to the revolution! Shout victory!
—Nationalist song by "Kusumagraj," Marathi

THE "REVOLUTION" referred to in this song, one inspiring many generations of youth, is the nationalist one—the most famous of India's "social movements." It was this movement that gave birth to the main trend of socialism in India, and when the "Hindu" definition of Indian identity came to overshadow nationalism it also affected the socialist movement. Nationalism, however, was not the only movement of its time in India; there were others, movements of middle and low castes, peasants and tribals often defining themselves in ways contradictory to and often in opposition to those of the national movements. These also helped to give birth to a socialist tradition, one that is only beginning to flower in the new social movements of the 1970s and 1980s. This chapter, then, will examine the preindependence roots of both "old" and "new" social movements, "traditional" and "alternative" socialism.

"Swaraj Is My Birthright"

In 1885 a British civil servant, Allan Hume, helped a group of English-educated Indians to form an organization that he hoped would prove an effective mediating agency between the British and the vast empire they ruled. But this organization, aspiringly named the Indian National Congress, went beyond Hume's expectations, and beyond the expectations of the polite and moderate Indians who gathered for its early three-day sessions of political debate and the passing of resolutions; it went from demanding more scope for Indians in governing the empire to asking that the empire itself be scrapped. Within two decades the Congress had come under control of the group called "Extremists" who were attempting mass contact and mobilization campaigns, who had contacts with dedicated bands of youthful bomb-throwers, and whose rhetoric was moving away from the polite accusation that imperial rule was "un-British" to the forthright claim of B. G. Tilak that "Swaraj is my birthright, and I will have it."

The term *raj* or *rajya* means "rule, regime, kingdom" and is widely used in Indian languages, so that *swaraj* (self-rule), Hindu *raj* (Hindu rule, regime of Hindus), *Ram-rajya* (the regime of Ram), *gram raj* (village rule), *kisan-mazdur raj* (the rule of peasants and workers) and *Bali-rajya* (the kingdom of Bali or regime of Bali) came to describe varying versions of an ideal society. When Tilak used the term *swaraj* or "self-rule," he changed the framework of debate completely; the Congress simply had to add a small adjective, *purna swaraj*, "full independence," to signify its radical opposition to foreign rule. It did so only in 1929—forty-four years after its founding—but by then its sessions were mass events marked by huge rallies and backed by growing struggles of workers and peasants throughout the country; its membership was in the hundreds of thousands, and beyond it lay more radical organizations. For "terrorism" had also developed in India, from small sectarian bands of bomb-throwers to efforts at mass organizing. Bhagat Singh, the most famous of these early revolutionaries, had led a group that united activists from many parts of India. It had an open youth organization along with its underground activities, and with the name "Hindustan Socialist Republican Army" it proclaimed its goal of a total change in society. The youthful hero (only twenty-three at the time of his death) proclaimed himself an atheist and a socialist and declared at his trial,

> Revolution is the inalienable right of mankind. Freedom is the imprescriptible birthright of all. The labourer is the real sustainer of society. . . . To the altar of this revolution we have brought our youth as incense, for no sacrifice is too great for so magnificent a cause. We are content, we await the advent of revolution. Inquilab Zindabad![1]

Swaraj was not only anti-imperialist; it was giving birth to socialism. The dominant socialist tradition in India arose out of this fervent nationalism of the Indian intelligentsia.

Even more ominous to the British than the development of militant opposition by this English-educated elite was the fact that the masses of people themselves were moving to make the same kind of linkage. Tribal peasants may have had little connection with Congress leaders, may even have directed their first struggles against local moneylenders and bureaucrats—but it was British armies they came up against, and they were even readier than the elite to assert their rights to freedom. Nontribal peasants were slower to pick up the meaning of freedom, accustomed as they were to centuries of looting, known as rule, by Indian rulers and feudatories, but they also fought exploitation, and some linked with the Congress in resisting landlord depredations or the state's imposition of land revenue and the destruction of their forests. And a new class was growing in the textile and jute factories in the cities, freed from the bondage of village toil only to be subordinated to a new brutal capitalist regime; they were restlessly stirring.

When Tilak, who had been given the title of *lokmanya*, "honored by the people," was sentenced by the British to a six-year sentence in the Andaman Islands in 1908, this working class, predominantly textile workers crowded into the heart of Bombay, expressed their nationalism by going on a massive six-day strike—though Tilak himself had never been associated with workers' struggles, though his followers were reluctant to involve them in nationalist organizing. It was an event noticed by Lenin:

> In India the street is beginning to stand up for *its* writers and political leaders. . . . The proletariat has already developed to conscious political mass struggle, and that being the case, the Russian-style British regime in India is doomed! . . . There can be no doubt that the age-old plunder of India by the British and the contemporary struggle of all these "advanced" Europeans against Persian and Indian democracy, will *steel* millions, tens of millions of proletarians in Asia to wage a struggle against their oppressors which will be just as victorious as the Japanese. The class-conscious European worker now has comrades in Asia.[2]

It was not, of course, to be so simple—and not only because of the ambiguous pro-imperialist role of the European "class-conscious" worker.

Swaraj or Hindu Raj?

There was, first of all, the problem of the "class" status of the Indian intelligentsia, leaders of the national movement. They were not only English-educated professionals or "petty bourgeoisie"; they were drawn from Indian landlord and feudal bureaucratic sections, and they almost overwhelmingly opposed land reforms that would deprive landlords of their rights. Although many Congress members were to lead tenant struggles in the twentieth century, although some Congress committees (but not the full Congress) adopted resolutions for the abolition of landlordism, and although Congressmen could get fairly enthusiastic

about struggles against land revenue by peasants who were opposing the bureaucracy rather than Indian landlords, the fact remained that the main body of
Congress resisted, from beginning to end, any radical change in land tenure or
production relations. The remark of Tilak himself (a brahman whose caste provided the main landlords of the coastal districts of Maharashtra) in this respect
was revealing, "Just as the government has no right to rob the moneylender and
distribute his wealth among the poor, in the same way the government has no
right to deprive the [landlord] of his rightful income and distribute the money to
the peasant. This is a question of rights and not of humanity." [3]

Similarly, though theories of economic nationalism were formulated and the
"drain" of wealth from India was questioned, the drain from the villages upward
to the capitalist or bureaucratic elite was never confronted.

There was much more. India was not simply a land of economic divisions, of
workers, peasants, landlords, petty bourgeois. It was what Communists were to
call a "multinational" country—a subcontinent with over a dozen major languages (and, unlike Europe, with different scripts) and with the varying ethnic
identities that went along with these languages. It was an ancient land that had
seen the incursions of varying racial groups for a period of over four thousand
years of "civilization"—invasions, settlements, migrations, from both its northwestern and northeastern land routes and from the seas as well, bringing Aryans,
Dravidians, Austro-Asiatics, Sino-Tibetans, Arabs, Turks, and finally Europeans.
All of this had resulted in a precolonial tributary society advanced in its productivity and complexity, prosperous, often brilliant but diverse and inequalitarian;
and the essence of the diversity was expressed, on the one hand, in varying
religious traditions and, on the other, in the caste system.

"Caste" is a non-Indian term with a Portuguese derivation that is used to
translate two Indian words, varna and jati. Jati means the named groups that are
ranked in local hierarchies, intermarry and interdine only among themselves, and
follow a traditional occupation. Varna is the ideological classification of these
groups. Its meaning has changed from the Vedic to the post-Vedic period, but it
is now generally understood as including four hierarchically ranked groups: the
brahmans, who were not only priests and intelligentsia but also administrators
and very often landlords and bureaucrats, and who were considered at the top of
the hierarchy of purity and pollution; the kshatriyas or rulers and warriors; the
vaishyas or merchants and businessmen; and the shudras, peasant and artisan
toilers whose job was to serve all the others.

Besides these were the outcastes, untouchables, the lowest of all, who performed tasks both laborious and polluting (carrying away dead animals, keeping
the village clean, the most menial agricultural labor, and service to village dominant castes and bureaucrats); these most frequently lived in separate settlements
outside the village itself. All castes were in some sense "untouchable" to those of
higher rank, since what marked the system was the fact that people "exchanged
bread and daughters" (roti-beti-vyavahar), that is, intermarried and interdined

only within the boundaries of the caste or subcaste, while people of higher rank would take only uncooked food or water from those of lower rank. But the untouchables were the most excluded, most clearly set aside. And finally there were the "tribes," groups of forest dwellers, shifting cultivators or peasants on high lands who maintained more egalitarian traditions. Broadly speaking, by British rule the tribes constituted 7 percent (but occupied 40 percent of the land, a proportion gradually reduced throughout the decades); the "untouchables" about 17 percent; the shudras about 60 percent, and the top three varnas (brahmans, kshatriyas, and vaishyas) about 15 percent of the population classed as "Hindu."

But what was Hindu? The official definition of the rightist Vishwa Hindu Parishad (Universal Hindu Conference), which has risen to prominence in the 1980s, is that Hindu includes all who are *not* members of one of the major world religions, that is, it classifies tribals, Sikhs, sometimes Buddhists and Jains, and members of dissenting sects as Hindus. This is a definition with which most Indians and many scholars would agree; at any rate the term "Hindu" is most frequently used as describing a community posed in contrast to "Muslim" and "Christian." Yet there are problems with this use of the term.

A very large section of tribals, Buddhists, Sikhs, Jains, and members of other "sects" (e.g., the Veerasaivas of Karnataka) not only disagree today that they are Hindu, but in many cases have never known that they were being called Hindu or have been seen as opposites and enemies of Hindus. Historically also, it makes most sense to see India as a terrain of many religions, sometimes competing, sometimes uneasily coexisting; of these, Buddhism and Jainism arose earliest, while what is today known as Hinduism was only gradually consolidated out of the myriad of traditions, crystallized as a religion based on appeals to the Vedas and to the authority of brahmans. In fact, Buddhism and Jainism remained dominant in large areas of the country until the sixth to tenth centuries A.D. and were only displaced by conquest and imposition of brahmanic Hinduism as a state-supported dominant religion. Even then, vast numbers of the lower-class peasantry and toilers continued to follow indigenous deities that were only absorbed into the "Hindu pantheon" by brahmanic interpretations that they usually ignored; and while they were subordinated to the caste system and thus to brahman authority (while their more powerful members gained brahman acquiescence to their position as kings and feudatories), large numbers of these lower classes later became Muslim converts. Islam itself had a long and creative history in the subcontinent, and many of the devotional sects that arose in later times, expressing partly popular resistance to caste hierarchy, did so syncretizing Hindu and Islamic themes.

Hindu has thus been a constructed and contested identity, and a major feature of British rule was the effort of high-caste elites to reconstruct this identity, in effect to create the inclusive Hinduism that is known today, that centers around figures such as Rama and Krishna and the Bhagavad Gita, that claims the whole mythologies of the Puranic traditions as deriving ultimately from a brahmanic, Vedic, and Sanskritic core, that incorporates and yet subordinates all the various "subaltern" traditions—and that is posed in radical contrast to such "non-Indian" religions as Islam and Christianity. This was a "Hindu revivalism" that became quite a powerful trend by the end of the nineteenth century, overwhelming the earlier traditions of high-caste social reform and castigating them as pro-Western.

This Hindu revivalism gained easy acceptance by nationalist elites. The Congress included Parsis and some Muslims, but its majority were not only Hindus but high-caste Hindu males, for the most part brahmans. When they chose to appeal to the masses on the basis of "Indian traditions," they chose the symbols of this high-caste Hindu revivalism, and these were symbols that depicted Muslims as enemies and the brahmans as the natural leaders of society. Tilak again was a good example—coming from the caste of chitpavan brahmans who had been rulers in the immediate pre-British period in Maharashtra, notorious for considering all nonbrahmans as shudras and attempting to keep down the untouchables. He may have been called *lokmanya* and declared to be the "leaders of telis and tambolis" (two low castes), but both he and his followers assumed that it was only high castes who should be respected and followed as leaders: for telis and tambolis themselves to go into political office was unheard of and even laughable.

Swaraj was a fairly innocent word that even Muslims could accept (especially when it was joined with the Persian-derived slogan, *inquilab zindabad*). But it was given a Hinduistic reading. Novels depicted the fighters of "mother India" as opposing Muslim rulers; Tilak himself helped to publicize the interpretation of Shivaji—a famous seventeenth century king who had led peasants against both Hindu feudal lords and Muslim generals—as the founder not simply of *swaraj* but of *Hindu raj*, fighting Muslims. Western racism helped this process when the "Aryan theory," originated by German orientalists, was adopted by the high-caste elite. In this theory, which saw Indian civilization as derived from Indo-European Sanskrit-speaking invaders, the Vedic tribes, the "twice-born" upper castes, were seen as descended from the Aryans, the lower shudras, untouchables, and tribals from dark-skinned non-Aryans. Tilak wrote a book, *The Arctic Home of the Vedas*, which was a popular exposition of this. He backed up brahmans who were opposing letting the ruler of Kolhapur state, a descendant of Shivaji, use "Vedic" religious rituals, in effect declaring him to be a shudra; he maintained the rituals of an orthodox brahman; he opposed the social reformers as "antipatriotic" when they urged a British law to raise the age of marriage (and cohabitation) of girls.

Tilak was most nervous about the question of untouchables. When in 1916 it was clear that political reforms would bring more of the masses into politics, various "untouchability uplift" conferences were held in Bombay Presidency. Tilak, whose followers organized one of these, found it possible to argue theoretically that "in times of war" prohibitions about caste could be relaxed, and since this was a time of war against the British, even untouchability could be disregarded. But he refused to sign a petition on the issue.

Nor was Tilak exceptional in his orthodoxy. By the end of the nineteenth century, trends of social reform were on the defensive. Indian nationalism was turning into a high-caste resurgence, and it was out of this extremely ambiguous heritage that the main trend of Indian socialism took its birth.

Hind Swaraj

And what of Gandhi?

The man who really made the Indian Congress into a mass organization—turning its language of action into the vernacular, riding third-class on Indian trains, engaging in action with every kind of popular struggle, peasant, workers, low-caste—came from a high-caste vaishya family. He was educated in England but a critic of its culture; a lawyer but a person who rejected all the professions as sheer deception. Years in South Africa had helped him formulate new techniques of nonviolent struggle and become the leader of new kinds of mass movements, law-breaking and peaceful, religiously rooted and militant.

In 1909 Gandhi wrote, in his native language Gujarati, a book called *Hind Swaraj* which was a new interpretation of what Indian independence might mean. It rejected the efforts by the Indian elite to be part of the British Empire or establish self-rule in a land in which these institutions remained. For Gandhi, industrialization was a sick civilization. "The mother of Parliaments is like a sterile woman and a prostitute," he wrote; modern so-called civilization "is a Satanic civilization. Hinduism calls it the Black Age."[4] This encompassed a critique of capitalism but from a precapitalist perspective: "Formerly men worked in the open air only as much as they liked. Now thousands of workmen meet together and for the sake of maintenance work in factories or mines. Their condition is worse than that of beasts. They are obliged to work, at the risk of their lives, at most dangerous occupations, for the sake of millionaires."[5] Independence for India had to mean a rejection of this kind of society: "By using Manchester cloth we only waste our money; but by reproducing Manchester in India we shall keep our money at the price of our blood, because our very moral being will be sapped."[6]

Gandhi's rejection of industrial capitalism led him to formulate, in opposition to almost all the nationalist and left opinion of his time, the goal of Indian independence in terms of the regeneration of Indian village society, a small-scale, labor-focused society. This has led him to be seen as a kind of early "Green," a forerunner of the ecological movement, the root of an alternative socialism in India. Indeed, much of today's Indian environmentalism refers back to Gandhi and finds much substance in statements such as "God forbid that India should ever take to industrialization after the manner of the West. The economic imperialism of a single tiny island kingdom is today keeping the world in chains. If an entire nation of 300 million took to similar economic exploitation, it would strip the world like locusts."[7]

The Gandhian rejection of industrialization and critique of centralized bureaucracies as well as of production for profit does resonate with a Green outlook. Thus, for example, the left-environmentalist theorist Ramchandra Guha can praise two Gandhian socialists, the Kumarappas, for having a critique of capitalism that "closely mirrored Marxist analyses, stressing the enslavement and alienation of the working class and the disjunction between individual profit maximization and the social good" and for their model of a socialist society, termed "villageism," based on "the decentralization of political and economic organization, and local self-sufficiency."[8]

But if Gandhi was Green, it is equally true that some at least of the ecological movement today shares the mysticism and idealism found in Gandhi. The problem was that Gandhi's own critique of capitalist industrialization and articulation of an alternative was based not on themes of exploitation and human liberation defined in material terms but ultimately on the assumptions of a religious outlook, founded on Hindu *advaita*, that stressed the limitation of human needs and was in the final analysis opposed to both technology and sexuality for their linkage with the flowering of human involvement with the material world. This is quite clear in *Hind Swaraj*:

> We notice that the mind is a restless bird; the more it gets the more it wants, and still remains unsatisfied. The more we indulge our emotions, the more unbridled they become. . . . Observing all this, our ancestors dissuaded us from luxuries and pleasures. We have managed with the same kind of plough as existed thousands of years ago. We have retained the same kind of cottages that we had in former times, and our indigenous education remains the same. . . . It was not that we did not know how to invent machinery, but our forefathers knew that, if we set our hearts after such things, we would become slaves and lose our moral fibre. They, therefore, after due deliberation decided that we should only do what we could with our hands and feet. . . . They further reasoned that large cities were a snare and a useless encumbrance and that people would not be happy in them, that there would be gangs of thieves and robbers, prostitution and vice flourishing in them, and that poor men would be robbed by rich men. They were, therefore, satisfied with small villages. . . . The common people lived independently and followed their agricultural occupation. They enjoyed true Home Rule.[9]

The self-sufficient village is linked to the paternalistic rule of kings in a society regulated by intellectuals (brahmans). It is thus not inappropriate that Gandhi gave the name of "Ram-Raj" (the rule of Rama) to his ideal for a free India, nor that he wrote of his reformed religion as *My Varnasharama Dharma*, accepting the models of *varna* (the four major caste-categories) and *ashrama* (the traditional "stages of life" for a high-caste male) and incorporating all his efforts at reform of untouchability or of women's status into this framework. Nor is it surprising that B. R. Ambedkar, leader of the liberation movement of India's untouchables, could write of Gandhi in the harshest terms, describing the pre-British villages as "cesspools of inequality and backwardness" and seeing the rejection of industrialization as a turning away from life. "There is no doubt that this Gandhi age is the dark age of India. It is an age in which people instead of looking for their ideals in the future are returning to antiquity." [10]

There was thus not only a conflict between Gandhi's vision of a village-centered society and those who placed their hopes in modern technological progress, but also between those who idealized the hierarchical caste society and saw reform in simply removing the "excrescences" that had developed and those whose vision of India was ultimately based on a community defined in terms of the low-caste majority that challenged the dominance of the traditional elite. Gandhi's Hinduism led him ultimately to accept that dominance, even praise it; this was the source of the paternalism and patriarchy at the heart of the structures he set up within the movement. His vision and understanding of India was broad enough to find ways of absorbing the energies of dalits, women, and other hitherto neglected groups; his involvement with all kinds of protest in the 1920s, particularly workers' and peasants' issues, helped to make the Congress a mass movement. Out of his tradition, largely, came the term *gram raj* (village rule) which was used by militant peasant movements under nationalist and left leadership.

But the ultimate result was to incorporate the lower castes and toiling classes into a Congress structure controlled by high castes who had an intellectual-bureaucratic tradition and an orientation to a capitalist industrial development. Thus, while Gandhi offered an alternative to the basic Nehruvian model of heavy industry–based public sector–dominated development that was followed after independence, his voice was ignored on these issues, and it was inevitable that it would be.

Hindustan or Balistan?

The extreme fertility of the soil of India, its rich productions, the proverbial wealth of the people, and the other innumerable gifts which this favoured land enjoys, and which have more recently tempted the cupidity of the Western Nations, attracted the Aryans. . . . The original inhabitants with whom these earth-born gods, the brahmans, fought, were not inappropriately termed Rakshasas, that is the protectors of the land. The incredible and foolish legends regarding their form and shape are no doubt mere chimeras, the fact being that these people were of superior stature and hardy make. . . . The cruelties which the European settlers practiced on the American Indian on their first settlement in the new world had certainly their parallel in India on the advent of the Aryans and their subjugation of the aborigines. . . . This, in short, is the history of Brahman domination in India. They originally settled on the banks of the

Ganges whence they spread gradually over the whole of India. In order, however, to keep a better hold on the people they devised that weird system of mythology, the ordination of caste, and the code of cruel and inhuman laws to which we can find no parallel among other nations.[11]

So ran the English introduction to a Marathi book, *Gulamgiri* (Slavery), published in 1885, the same year as the founding of the Indian National Congress, with a dedication ("to the good people of the United States . . . for their sublime . . . devotion in the cause of Negro slavery") that itself reflected the writer's identification with oppressed peoples throughout the world. Jotirao Phule, a man of (mali or gardener) caste, took as his goal the liberation of *shudras* (the primarily peasant toiling castes) and *atishudras* (untouchables or dalits) from slavery to brahmanism, which he saw as equivalent to Negro slavery and much worse than the slavery of colonial rule. The Indian National Congress, to him, was only a propaganda organ of these same brahmans; how could India, so divided by caste and language, and with its people so enthralled in superstition, be considered a "nation"? But Phule was asking this question not as the British did, to maintain their own domination over the people, but to aid the process of creating the nation on an *alternate* basis, using the identities and symbols of the low-caste peasant and dalit masses rather than those of the brahman elite, to build up the community. In the process he developed the rudiments of a new historical materialist theory of exploitation and liberation, which became a forerunner of the new social movements of the late twentieth century and of an alternative socialism.

Phule today is taken as a founding figure not only by the dalit and anticaste movement, but also, at least in Maharashtra, by the women's movement and the farmers' movement—for his major writings dealt with the exploitation of the peasants and the enslavement of women along with that of caste. He wrote almost entirely in Marathi, and he lacked the all-India communication network the elites of his time had, yet his historical interpretation provided the themes of most of the later nonbrahman movements and dalit movements.

Phule's theory began with a liberatory reversal of the "Aryan theory": brahmans and upper castes were indeed descended from conquering Indo-Europeans, but their conquest had imposed an exploitative caste hierarchy over an indigenous population that had lived in a state of prosperity and equality. Going beyond a pure mechanical version of this as a racial theory of history, he gave a vision of history and exploitation in which aggression, violence, and conquest played a major role—perhaps matching a third world situation where Marx himself had seen the operation of primitive accumulation, the forcible extraction of the wealth of the land and the looting of the people, where "violence is the midwife of history." He took up for his symbols the myth of the avatars of Vishnu, interpreted as stages in the Aryan conquest, in which those who resisted, the "rakshasas," were heroes. One of these, King Bali (who is indeed remembered in peasant lore in Maharashtra and other parts of South India as an ideal king) was taken as the hero-king of the original, non-Aryan peasant community; other popular deities of the region were interpreted as the various administrators of Bali's kingdom; while the seventeenth-century Maratha warrior-ruler Shivaji was seen not as a founder of a "Hindu raj" but as a peasant king.

With these themes Phule founded organizations—most notably the Satyashodhak Samaj or "truth-seekers society," which dedicated itself to rationalism, to organizing life-ceremonies such as marriages without brahman priests, and to education "of both boys and girls." He also sought to found a theistic and egalitarian religious alternative to brahmanic Hinduism, which he called *sarvajanik satya dharma*, translatable either as "public religion of truth" or "true religion of the community." Along with this Phule theorized the exploitation of the peasant by the bureaucracy, wrote of the problems of agriculture and drought, and outlined plans for remodeling society beginning from a reconstructed village. Not only did his social activity include the founding of the first schools for girls (1848) and untouchables (1851), but in the last years of his life he ferociously attacked the double standard of sexual behavior applied to relations between men and women.

Phule can be viewed as a founding figure of a low-caste, peasant-based alternative tradition, much more fragmented and regionalized than that which was linked to the Congress party and organized in the Hindu revivalist theorization of Indian identity, but with a wide spread especially in South and West India and the peripheries, as well as in tribal areas, drawing upon common themes such as a "non-Aryan" identity and referring to regional or peasant heroes. This was a countertradition that culturally and socially rejected even the liberal Gandhian version of incorporation into a reformed Hindu identity, while it had an equal thrust to a decentralized antistatist development. It can be taken to encompass, to various degrees, activities and organizations connected with women like Pandita Ramabai and North Indian peasant leaders Swami Sahajanand, Baba Ramchandra, and his wife Jaggi;[12] tribal rebels such as Birsa Munda and Veer Narayan Singh; nonbrahman and dalit leaders such as Ambedkar, Periyar, Mangoo Ram of the Punjab, and many others still not widely known outside their own region. But, throughout the period up to independence, such peasant, female, and lower-caste traditions had few resources for communication and mobilization; they remained fragmented; Phule himself was unknown outside of Maharashtra. And the Communist tradition, when it developed, derived from the radical nationalism symbolized by Tilak, defined itself against the "anti-industrial peasantism" of Gandhi and ignored Phule and similar low-caste traditions.

Why Not a Worker-Peasant Raj?

In 1923 a Tamil son of a fisherman, Singaravelu, founded a new party that he called the Labour and Kisan party of Hindustan, to "achieve swaraj by nonviolent means." It distinguished itself from the government, capitalists, the Congress, and

"Bolshevik intellectuals and spies" and declared its chief aim to be "to bring economic relief to the masses." [13] Though from a shudra caste, Singaravelu's father had been well-off, a community leader who had engaged in trading along the Madras coast up to Burma. The boy had become a lawyer, then a nationalist, and then a labor activist; finally he was attracted to Marxism. He became one of India's first Communists, the first to try to organize a party, and he presided over the first Indian Communist conference at Kanpur in 1925—a conference that most Indian Communists see as representing the founding of their party.

Communists of that period from backgrounds such as Singaravelu's were rare. Here and there were people from the toiling classes, such as the Sikh peasants who came from their revolutionary-nationalist Ghadar party into communism, or minority radicals such as the Muslim *mujahirs* who had gone to Tashkent seeking to join the struggle to free the Khilafat and then had been turned into Communists by M. N. Roy, the brilliant Bengali émigré who was concentrating his efforts as Comintern representative in building up the Indian Communist movement from abroad. But the majority, the leaders and dominating theorists (described by Singaravelu's first party as "bolshevik intellectuals"), were usually brahmans, coming out of the tradition of militant nationalism symbolized by Tilak. S. D. Dange (a party leader for sixty years after this) of Bombay, editor of a journal called *Socialist* and leader of a group then becoming involved with textile workers, was typical of this category. He did not attend the founding of Singaravelu's Labour and Kisan party, and he and others were concerned that the organizers of the Kanpur conference were falling prey to the heresies of nationalism.[14]

Organizing workers and peasants, looking toward a socialist version of independence, was becoming a theme of the times; leaders of nonbrahman movements in Bombay and Tamilnadu, involved with workers and peasants, were themselves turning in this direction. But to the young communist intellectuals, Marxism had to be more than this. It was a "scientific theory." Socialism could not come simply as a *swaraj* of workers and peasants, with cooperation, common ownership, and the end of exploitation: it had to be sharply distinguished from Gandhian celebrations of a self-sufficient village society. Marxism taught that socialism could be built only on the basis of the industrial production achieved in capitalism, and that the main source of exploitation was private property; socialism meant then the abolition of private property (hence nationalization), and "labor" meant above all factory-based wage labor, not to be confused with peasant toil and production. This meant that *proletariat* or the industrial working class had to be seen as the vanguard class. Thus one should not be too hasty or romantic about socialism; the society had to go through the necessary first steps of national independence and industrialization.

Therefore, in organizational terms, the young Communists (those who accepted the discipline and "science" of the party) worked on three levels: (1) they sought to organize the underground party network, the Communist party of

India, as the leading force; (2) they organized mass platforms for the economic struggle of workers and peasants—labor unions and kisan sabhas (peasant leagues); and (3) they worked within the national movement, which to them meant taking the Congress as the anti-imperialist united front. There were, to be sure, many other parties of the time, a period when numerous sections were leaving the main body of the Congress in disgust at its inaction (the Swarajists in the 1920s and Subash Chandra Bose in the 1930s), and nonbrahmans and others were organizing competing parties. But these were all, to the Indian Communists, "petty bourgeois" efforts in one way or another; the ones seemingly closest to them, which had a peasant or working-class base, were perhaps more danger- ous because of their attraction to similar constituencies. Indian Communists thus saw the Congress itself as the proper political platform and sought to build it up as such. After 1935 they had Comintern sanction for this (the "anti-imperialist united front"), but it was a policy they had found most amenable even earlier.

In the 1920s there were, apparently, alternative proposals within their own ranks. In 1926, M. N. Roy had proposed a "people's party" parallel to the Congress, which would comprise the peasants and petty bourgeoisie along with the proletariat.[15] Later the Communists did indeed form "Worker and Peasant parties" in a number of places. But Roy's proposal was linked to his idea that the bourgeoisie was going over to the side of imperialism and was no longer ready to fight for independence; this idea was theoretically rejected. The WPPs were seen, by Roy himself and by the Indian Communists, as simply open fronts of the party, necessary because the party was secret and banned, requiring careful control. Thus they gained no mass base; the idea of a "people's party" or "revo- lutionary nationalist party" was never taken up, and the Communists continued to build up the Indian National Congress.

In 1936 Singaravelu, who was then working in the nonbrahman movement in Tamilnadu to build up a socialist group, was prevailed upon by the Communist leaders to dissolve it:

> The address of Comrade Dange at this conference laid down clearly the path of the Socialists. He welcomed the work done . . . to spread socialist ideas in Tamilnadu and bring about a Socialist Tamilnadu. At the same time he reminded the conference that not only Tamilnadu but the whole of India is under British imperialist domination, and that unless British imperialism is destroyed on an all-India scale it is impossible even to dream of socialism. . . . Only one resolution was passed, and that resolution dissolved the Self-Respect Socialist party and decided that its members will join the National Congress and the Congress Socialist party.[16]

This showed the way in which the dominant trend of Indian communism was focused both on an all-India basis, relegating to the background the issues of linguistic-nationalism being raised even then in some areas, and on the fight against imperialism as the "main contradiction," relegating the nonbrahman and dalit movements to the category of practically British agents and ignoring issues of caste dominance. Nonbrahmans, peasants, dalits, women, and the possibilities of a different kind of "development" from the dominant industrialist model were outside the framework of the Marxism that was being created in India.

Indian Communists were "traditional Marxists" in two ways. First, along with nearly all other sections of the Communist movement of the time, they neglected caste and gender and the issues raised by movements based on these. This was also true of the time of all the socialistic trends, including those gathered around Nehru; one result was that while both Gandhians and the right-wing Hindu Mahasabhaites formulated a response to the issues of the dalit movement and evolved organizations to win over dalits, the left, from the Communists to Nehru, remained totally uninvolved and saw the whole problem as a distraction from true nationalism.

At the same time, their negative attitude toward the peasantry meant that, although they joined in organizing peasant leagues, they saw this as a secondary task and did so with the aim of keeping the Kisan Sabhas controlled by the party, the peasants subordinated to the "leadership of the working class." That is, they rejected *mazdur-kisan raj* as a slogan and as a reality. Practically speaking, this also meant that the Kisan Sabhas under their control got involved in struggles against property-owning exploiters (landlords and moneylenders), but other peasant struggles of the period—against state-imposed rises in land revenue, against the bureaucratic-commercial destruction of their forests—were largely ignored, and often fell under the leadership of Gandhians or other Congressites. Similarly, the idea of a village-centered economic development could appear to them only as a kind of "peasantist" ideology that was at best "petty-bourgeois," at worst "feudal."

This also led to the Communists being "traditional" in another sense. In many ways the neglect by classical Marxists of the potentials of state-bureaucratic domination once private property was "nationalized" fit the interests of a brahman elite whose traditional material base had been in the bureaucracy and administration of precapitalist empires. There were in fact good reasons for brahmans, if not banias, to welcome the "proletarian" era of Marxism. Along with this, in ignoring the issues of community and caste-identities raised by the nonbrahman and dalit movements, the Communists accepted at the same time the identification of India as "Hindu" and the symbols that went along with this. For instance, they never questioned the Gandhian baptism of untouchables as "Harijans" or "children of god" although nearly all militant leaders rejected the terminology and sought alternatives, such as *dalit* or "downtrodden." A heroic secular stance and the protection of Muslims in communal riots went along with a rather surreptitious Hindu identification.

This was typified in a book by S. A. Dange, one of the few by any Communist leader that tried to interpret Indian history in Marxist terms. *India: From Primitive Communism to Slavery* was a mechanical application of Stalinist "stage theory" that began from the Vedic Aryans themselves, in spite of the fact that by the time of its writing the more ancient Indus Valley civilization had been discovered. Dange thus took the cultural-historical model of the brahmanic-Hindu interpretation of Indian history as his starting point, then simply sought to show that the Aryans themselves had evolved from a collective, matriarchal society to private property. Referring to the "fundamental errors of fact and reasoning that fill the book from cover to cover with endless confusion," D. D. Kosambi, the brilliant Marxist historian, attacked it with acerbity: "This painfully disappointing book . . . would not have been worth reviewing, but for the fact that to let such a performance go unchallenged would bring Marxism into disrepute." [17] But Dange's assumptions about Indian society and history continued to form the main framework of thinking of Indian Communists.

Capitalism, Caste, and Gender

Indian Marxists saw the workings of capitalism in terms of a system of commodity production and exchange in which rapid growth of the forces of production was based on exploitation of the commodity labor power by the owners of the means of production; "socialism" would come if private property were abolished and the working class took collective control of the system of production. High-caste intellectuals in India had argued from the nineteenth century onward that there was a drain of surplus from colonies like India to contribute to accumulation in the imperialist centers; Indian Marxists fit this into what they knew of "Leninism" to include the notion that this drain and the correlated fostering of precapitalist relations of production (landlordism, peasant backwardness) held back the growth of production in the third world. For both "bourgeois nationalists" and Marxists, then, while "feudalism" had to be fought, the key was to defeat imperialism by gaining control of production and the state in India and extending industrialization with a greater or lesser degree of state-supported production. Gandhi and Phule both presented a different model, but few took their economic perspective very seriously.

But the basic assumptions of this model oversimplified the historical reality. Capital accumulation within the sphere of commodity production and exchange logically implies at least two spheres outside of it. One is the production of the commodity "labor power," mainly by the domestic labor of women in the home, labor that of course does not produce surplus value but does produce surplus and hasten capital accumulation because it allows capitalists to pay workers a lower wage (this is accentuated in many parts of the third world, where domestic labor and other costs of reproducing labor power have been borne in agricultural spheres outside of direct capitalist penetration).

The other is the appropriation of natural resources, products of the earth, including oil, minerals, timber, raw materials, and consumption goods for the European population. This appropriation, at extremely low or no cost, including the highly exploited labor (of peasants, miners, plantation workers, forest dwellers, etc.) that secured it, has played a major role in capital accumulation without being part of full-scale commodity production. Marx theorized this partially as "primitive accumulation." The notion included both the original "looting" of third-world treasures, which produced capital itself, as well as the dispossession of the peasantry, which turned them into wage-laborers. In fact, it was because production by wage laborers was taken as the central aspect of capitalism that the formation of a working class was called "primitive" accumulation; that is, it was assumed that it took place only as part of the initial establishment of the capitalist system. But again, this concept does not adequately describe the reality. The accumulation of the earth's resources for the increase of capital has imposed many facets of a money economy and the logic of production for profit on regions throughout the world, but not primarily by turning the people of those regions into wage laborers. Rather, numerous forms of relations of production, including slavery, debt-bondage, and peasant petty commodity production, have organized the accumulation of resources for capital. "Traditional" social structures have not been abolished, but have been used and transformed or accentuated in the process.

India's subordination to capitalism, then, meant not simply the policy of maintaining "feudalism" or "landlordism" because these classes supported British rule or preventing capital accumulating in the hands of the native bourgeoisie. It also meant what David Washbrook, in an article on South Asia and world capitalism, has recently called the "peasantisation" of the Indian economy,[18] and what earlier left historians called "deindustrialization," turning a complexly articulated caste-feudal economy in which agricultural production was linked to local pastoral, manufacturing, and service sectors with agricultural production into a mainly peasant-based economy whose resources were channeled upward and outward through the exchange of peasant/artisan-produced goods for money and through various forms of caste-linked labor. The process did not dissolve the caste system and the hierarchy and occupational specializations imposed by it; rather, it used it as it used other "community" forms—in a way that often increased hierarchies and internal inequalities.

As a result, many of the struggles waged by the toiling masses against the system easily took caste and community forms. At the same time, the nonbrahman and dalit movements that took organizational shape in the 1920s both fought the hierarchy as such and also tried, as part of this fight, to gain entry into education and the government bureaucracies that were controlled by upper castes and were major local centers of accumulation. These movements had their basic "class struggle" aspects—peasant revolts connected with the nonbrahman movement against moneylenders and the bureaucracy, dalit efforts to gain freedom from caste-imposed labor services and the acquisition of government-held lands for cultivation, working-class organizing in which both dalit and nonbrahman leaders were involved. In contrast to these, efforts to break down the high-caste monopoly of education and administrative employment and gain entry for the lower castes are generally described as representing the interests only of the middle classes among them. But these were also a form of "class struggle" because it was through monopoly of such positions that traditional hierarchies were maintained and the lower castes were exploited.

Because they gave priority to these battles rather than to the anti-imperialist struggle, dalit and nonbrahman movements of the 1920s and 1930s were invariably characterized as pro-British. But their most famous representative, the dalit leader B. R. Ambedkar, was quite forthright: "We cannot fight all enemies at once." Ambedkar used to hold public rallies of the untouchable community at Koregaon, the village in Maharashtra where the last army of the Peshwas (the pre-British native brahman regime) had been defeated in 1818, where there was a memorial to the Indian soldiers who had died fighting for the British: these soldiers included twenty untouchables as well as shudras. His point was of course that low-caste masses joined the British armies because they had seen their future only in defeating the Peshwai, or feudalism. "We were the ones who brought the British to power; and we are the ones who can drive them out."

In aiming at the liberation of untouchables, Ambedkar added to the fight against "brahmanism" the fight against "capitalism." In the 1930s he organized struggles of peasants and workers under his Independent Labor party, sometimes in cooperation with Communists. His main political point was that "Congress is a party of the brahmans and bourgeoisie; peasants and workers must have their own independent political party." He sought to build a broader anti-Congress front by appealing constantly to nonbrahmans in Maharashtra not to join the Congress, and by seeking allies among independent nonbrahman and peasant forces such as Periyar, the nonbrahman leader of Tamilnadu, and Swami Sahajanand, the leader of the peasant movement in Bihar.

This was a period when there were several political formations resembling what Communists in the 1920s had spoken of as "worker-peasant parties." In Bengal, the Krishak Praja party was formed as a mainly Muslim party with its base in the Muslim tenant farmers, but with support also from the Namashudras, the dalits of Bengal; in Punjab the Unionist party represented the interest of Hindu, Sikh, and Muslim peasants of the jat caste (with a good deal of anti-"brahman-bania" rhetoric) and also got the support of dalit leaders such as Mangoo Ram of the Ad-Dharm movement. In Tamilnadu Periyar was trying to rebuild the Justice party, and in Bombay Presidency Dinkarrao Javalkar was proposing that its Nonbrahman party become an anti-British Peasants and Workers party. But these attempts never coalesced. One crucial reason was that all the Communists and socialists of the time continued to take Congress as the "anti-imperialist united front" and sought to work inside it and incorporate all their mass organizations of workers and peasants within it. This was the context, for instance, in which Singaravelu in 1936 was persuaded to dissolve his "socialist self-respect" organization and join the Congress. With the aid of Communists, then, by the end of the 1930s, in spite of all the mass turmoil and the efforts at autonomous organizing by nonbrahmans and dalits, the Congress had increased its hegemony over popular upsurges. And the Congress remained under the control of the upper-caste elite.

Further, not only the Congress and the leftists, but also the nonbrahman and dalit leaders, including Ambedkar, accepted the thesis that the road to economic liberation lay through industrialization, through, in Gandhi's words, "reproducing Manchester in India." This was, in a profound way, similar to the impulse that has led millions of East Europeans, in the 1990s, to try to transcend their bureaucratized "socialism" not in new, unknown directions, but by entry into the European-American "free world" of capitalism. "Development fetishism" rather than "commodity fetishism" has been the guiding framework of contemporary capitalist ideology.

Peasant Resistance and Revolt

Indian village communities were by no means homogeneous or egalitarian, and being subordinated to the accumulation processes of world capitalism only served to increase their diversity and hierarchy; it certainly did not transform their inhabitants into homogeneous proletarians. Struggles against this process, by different sections of these "peasants," were also multifaceted, occurred under a wide variety of leaderships, and involved wide sections and varying caste-groups, including dalits and women.

Early uprisings include the upsurge of the peasantry (specifically groups such as the north Indian jats and gujars) in the 1857 revolt, as well as many tribal rebellions throughout this period against the impingement of British power on traditional authority and the economic well-being of the peasants, all aiming at "independence" of some traditionally defined type. Also important were numerous antimoneylender campaigns throughout the late nineteenth century, since subordination of the peasant through indebtedness was becoming a major form of exploitation. Among these were the "Deccan riots," in which large numbers of peasants in western Maharashtra districts of Ahmednagar and Pune burned records of moneylending transactions, as well as protests in the Punjab.

The twentieth century saw numerous antilandlord struggles that took widely varying forms under different leaderships. They included, for instance, many tenants' campaigns of the left-led Kisan Sabhas; they also included revolts associated with the nonbrahman and dalit movements, such as an antilandlord campaign uniting dalit and shudra tenants in the Konkan led by Ambedkar in the 1930s, or the Satara revolt of 1920–21 of Satyashodhak Samajists in Maharashtra, in which the peasants not only refused rent payments to mainly brahman landlords, but also deliberately challenged their ritual superiority by polluting wells and mocking their status in ribald songs. Other struggles were the campaigns led by Ambedkar, which united dalit and caste Hindu tenants in the

1930s against mainly brahman landlords in the coastal area of western India.

Moneylenders and landlords could be understood as exploiters within the framework of "private property." But beyond this a whole range of revolts and resistance posed peasants against the state and its agents. Movements against paying revenue, for instance, became a crucial part of nationalist campaigning in the 1920s and early 1930s, from Bardoli and Kheda in Gujarat to the Andhra delta—even though the nationalists who took over their leadership often compromised severely on their demands. Struggles over forest issues also posed peasants against the state, in efforts to maintain their access to forests and common lands against the claims for commercial production of timber by the bureaucracy; these took place not only in the famous area of the Chipko movement in the Himalayan foothills, but in such "peasant"-caste dominated areas as Satara district, again, where deaths took place in police firing in the 1930s "forest satyagraha" in the hilly talukas. Similarly, when the prices of agricultural products crashed in the 1930s, peasant protest was expressed in the Punjab through the Unionist party. Finally, campaigns against *vethbegar* or caste-imposed labor services involved many low castes, not only against local landlords but also against the state's appropriation of their labor, for instance, in Ambedkar's decades-long campaign against the "Mahar watan" whereby the state claimed the nonwaged services of the village dalits in return only for small land allotments. Strikingly, few of these movements were led by Communists or socialists.

All of these were "peasant revolts" whose varying types reflected the varying forms of appropriation of labor under imperialism. These forms included the labor of peasants as tenants, of artisans and village servants as caste-bonded workers, of petty commodity producers whose labor was appropriated through rent, tax, and low prices for their produce. They also included labor enforced indirectly when state extraction of natural resources from forests or common lands ruined these commons and deprived the peasant communities of the goods normally extracted from them and thus forced more labor to acquire their equivalents. The extraction of labor became more complex when caste/community/nationality features helped to shape it—when, for example, tenants were Muslims or Sikhs, while moneylenders and landlords were Hindus, when peasants were tribals while bureaucrats and moneylenders were nontribals, when nonbrahman tenants confronted brahman landlords. It also involved hierarchies and inequalities among the peasantry and very often an overlapping of categories—"dominant" caste Hindu peasants exploiting semitribal laborers in Bardoli, for instance, while they continued to produce cotton at suitable prices for European manufacturing. Peasant resistance and revolt quite naturally reflected all these complexities, which could not be understood in a model that takes only wage labor and private property as the index of exploitation. Yet this is what many Marxists, both the Communists of the time and the historians of the present, have tended to do.

The greatest peasant revolt in Indian history brought together many of these aspects of resistance to oppression and united varying sections of toilers—and yet, though it was under the leadership of the Communist party, it erupted almost accidentally. This was the Telegana revolt, when between 1946 and 1950 peasants in nearly four thousand villages in the Telugu-speaking regions of the Muslim state of Hyderabad seized land, armed themselves, and established their power, which they called, popularly, *gram raj* while the party named them for Marxist circles as "soviets." Though unplanned, the revolt was led by local Communists whose organizational base had been won by combining themes of regional nationalism (championing of the Telugu language and culture, a library movement in the villages, cultural squads), issues of dalits and service castes such as opposition to caste-defined forced labor, and struggles for rights of the middle-caste tenants against landlords. There was no "Kisan Sabha" preexisting in the area; instead the main organization of Communists was the Andhra Mahasabha, a cultural and nationalist forum for Telugu-speakers of Hyderabad state. The articulation of both varying issues and varying sections of the toiling people was crucial to the success the revolt attained; but even then later left scholars have criticized it for being "rich peasant" dominated.

The revolt was made possible by the breakdown of political power; as the biggest of the many "princely states" forced to choose between India and Pakistan in 1948, Hyderabad's ruler tried to opt for independence instead. He had little real army of his own; instead the semiprivate religious Razakars effectively had armed control; they were brutal but weak. In the vacuum the Telengana peasants under communist leadership could establish their power, but once the Indian army moved in they were badly outnumbered and outarmed, and armed squads could hang on for two more years only by fleeing to the tribal-dominated forest regions.

The problem in all of this was that the Communist party, which led the revolt, could not give it a national platform as part of any overall revolutionary movement aiming at independence or a transitional regime. They also took for granted the prevailing definition of "India" and could only think of trying to take power at an all-India scale, while the Hyderabad unit of the party actually supported, for a time, the claim to independence of the Muslim-defined Hyderabad state! In the end, both repression and co-optation allowed the brahman-dominated Congress to absorb the Telugu-speaking regions along with areas of other resistance movements and revolts by peasants and toilers. And this absorption meant that India was, in the final years before independence, imprisoned in the dialectic of Hindu-Muslim conflicts.

Hindustan/Pakistan

Phule had raised serious questions about the nature and reality of an "Indian nation" and had used the term "Balistan" (land of Bali) rather than "Hindustan" (land of the Hindus) to denote his name for the country; the Tamil nonbrahman movement in later years had put forward a call for "Dravidistan," while the term

"Dalitistan" even came to be used by some of Ambedkar's followers. All these implied notions of a separate territory as a base for independent community life. Yet these concepts attained no more political hegemony than did the notion of a "worker-peasant raj," and in the end it was the question of "Indian nationalism" and "Hindu-Muslim communalism" that came to be the dominant discourse. Metaphorically speaking, India became "Hindustan," and out of this came "Pakistan."

Gyanendra Pandey's recent study on "the construction of communalism" analyzes the stages in this process. The first involved the construction of "Hindu" and "Muslim" community identities themselves, which took place throughout the late nineteenth century. "Nationalism" was subsequently conceived of in terms of the unity or coming together of these communities—Hindus plus Muslims plus Sikhs plus Christians, in which religion formed the basic identifying feature of each "community."[19] Nonbrahman and dalit claims to a separate historical-racial identity directly challenged this characterization but were resisted by nationalists and ignored by the Communists. Gandhi, who was the dominant political leader acting within this framework, identifying himself both as a "Hindu" and as the leader of "Indians," resisted untouchable demands for separate electorates because, as he saw it, this would take them outside the Hindu community as such and put them on a par with Muslims and Sikhs. While the "Hindu community," he felt, must reform itself, he never questioned its existence and priority. His unequivocal commitment to a Hindu-Muslim unity as central to creating an India of his dreams was also within this framework.

In the 1920s a new step was taken, with the formation of both the Hindu Mahasabha as a political body and the Rashtriya Swayamsevak Sangh (RSS or "National Volunteers Society") as a nonpolitical, cadre body taking as its goal the consolidation of the "Hindu nation." Both drew on the Tilak tradition but joined it with the themes of *Hindutva*, a book by an ex-revolutionary nationalist, Savarkar, that identified "Hindus" primarily as the race or nation inhabiting the land but with the assumption that the religion known as "Hinduism" was their unique creation. With this potent mixture of race, religion (defined largely in terms of brahmanic symbolism), and territory, upper-caste Hindus began to move to the idea that the nation had to be structured around their own religious community, not as a federation of communities. In turn, "progressive" Hindu opinion, as represented by people like Jawaharlal Nehru, began to define "nationalism" as against the religious community: "Indian nationalism as we know it—a nationalism that stood *above* (or *outside*) the different religious communities and took as its unit the individual Indian citizen, a 'pure' nationalism unsullied, in theory, by the 'primordial' pulls of caste, religion, community, etc.—was . . . rigorously conceptualized only in opposition to the notion of communalism."[20]

But this abstractly secular assertion of "Indian nationalism," opposed to the identities involved in "communalism," only helped to mask the control of high-caste

Hindus over its structures of domination; thus it could not counter the effects of Hindu nationalism of driving the Muslims to put forward their own need for a political structure within which their interests would be protected. This was expressed first in demands for separate political representation in the form of separate electorates; then in taking for granted that this special representation would involve their right to control Muslim-majority areas like Punjab and Bengal; and finally in the demand for a Muslim nation made up of these areas. As Pandey describes the process, "the idea of a Hindu Raj which would reflect the glories of the ancient Hindu civilization and keep Muslims in their place" was "matched in due course by the notion of a Muslim Raj which would protect the place of the Muslims. The Hindu-Muslim problem now became 'the question of all questions'." [21]

It was a question that came to override all the various anti-imperialist, peasant, and low-caste struggles and in the end produce an India split into two countries, in a process of "Partition" that involved bloody rioting and massive transfer of populations. All along the northwestern region Hindus moved east and Muslims moved west, meeting slaughter in the process. Yet, aside from Gandhi himself, nearly all the leaders of the Congress in the end accepted Partition because Muslim (and other minority) demands for special representation and autonomy had reached the point where only in a truncated state could they institute the centralized, bureaucratically articulate nation-state that they saw as the prerequisite of development.

In part, traditional Marxist discourse helped to justify this "secular nationalism" by seeing the "essential" interests of the toiling people as purely economic and uninvolved with community. Joined with this was the idea of secular nationalism as progressive, of community/religion/caste as belonging to the backward feudal period and as thus destined to be superseded. All of this, associated with a faith in industrialism and scientific progress, was embodied most strong in Nehru. "The day of even national cultures is rapidly passing," he wrote; "The real struggle today in India is not between Hindu culture and Muslim culture, but between these two and the conquering scientific culture of modern civilization." It was also associated with *statism*. As Pandey put it,

> By the 1930s and 1940s, the importance of an "enlightened" leadership was thus being stressed on all sides as the critical ingredient that was required in the bid to advance the "backward" peoples. . . . It had taken great leaders, a Chandragupta Maurya, an Ashoka, an Akbar, to actualize the dream of Indian unity in the past, and they had done so in the great states and empires that they had established. It would take great leaders like Nehru and Patel to realize the newly desired unity of India, and the state would again be their major instrument. The twentieth-century liberal . . . could do no better than to turn to statism.[22]

Thus, as India headed toward its Nehruvian "tryst with destiny" and then to the Ambedkarite "explosion," the alternative traditions represented by Phule or even by Gandhi were forgotten or set aside. The participation of women and dalits in the peasant revolts was nearly forgotten. "We were making history" was the way the women of the Telengana movement talked about their involvement in the struggle;[23] but they were the ones most stranded or thrown back into traditional families after the revolt was crushed, and it has taken the rise of feminism even to record their contribution. Peasant revolts failed to shape the structure of postindependent India even though Congress leaders themselves have spoken in their name; it is rather the heirs of Chandragupta Maurya and Akbar who have taken power.

But "Telengana" continues to be memorialized in song and left tradition as a symbol of revolt:

> They are going forward with torch in hand, the people of my village,
> Now they will conquer the darkness, the people of my village.
> Every hut asks, every field asks,
> How long will we go on being looted, O people of my village?
> Knowing that nothing here can be won without struggle
> The people of my village are fighting their battle.
> Telengana will live again in every village of this country
> Now they will become guerrillas,
> The people of my village.
> See, my friend, that morning which up to now was pale—
> The people of my village will fill it with red.

If the longed-for revolution did not come, the struggles for it remained, their memory retained in popular tradition. To re-erupt not only in the calls to armed struggle that consciously identified with the Communist-led peasant revolt, but also in unexpected guises in the themes of "alternative" socialism that are beginning to be put forward in the new social movements of the late twentieth century.

2

From Independence
to the Naxalite Revolt

"WHAT is the difference between you and us?" an old Congress freedom fighter of Kasegaon always used to ask us (the leftist or the Communist faction of the village). "You are twelve annas, we are four." He was referring to the old rupee of sixteen annas, a typical Marathi way of saying it's a matter of degree.

In fact, "four-anna socialism" was an apt way of characterizing India's postindependence path of development. The Congress party had come to power after leading one of the longest and most mass-based non-Communist third-world independence movements. This was bound to give weight to a worker-peasant ideological discourse, to promises that independence would mean a new India and the creation of something like a socialist society. Not only had socialism exercised its magical influence over the minds of young freedom fighters, but even the anti-British bourgeoisie and its committed intellectuals were impressed with the achievements shown through planning and public control in a backward society like Russia. From the big industrialists with their "Bombay plan" to the Congress to Ambedkar with his "state socialism," a broad consensus developed around what was in fact a modified version of a state-socialist model of development: a focus on heavy industrialization, planning, and a public sector "commanding the heights" of a mixed economy substantially integrated into the world capitalist economy. Even Communists agreed on the basic aspects of what came to be known as the "Nehru model," calling only for more nationalization, more thorough land reform, a more equal distribution of welfare. The argument was, as our Kasegaon freedom fighter would have it, only one of degree: four annas or eight annas or twelve annas.

There were good reasons why such seemingly antagonistic social-political forces could agree, having to do with the world ideological atmosphere in which common assumptions about "development" were shared by the bourgeois liberal model and its main alternative, the technocratic Marxism exemplified at the time in Soviet industrialization. In these assumptions, development was equivalent to "industrialization," that is, the growth of heavy large-scale industries producing steel and machinery and using primarily nonrenewable fossil fuel resources. Agriculture was considered to be fundamentally backward, and peasants, by nature of their rootage in the soil, primitive; development meant not only removing people from agriculture but extracting them from isolated far-flung villages to the "modern" collective life of the neighborhoods and factories of the cities. In both industry and agriculture, "advanced" production was thought to be the large-scale, centrally organized production in which thousands of laborers worked collectively, whether in urban factories or on mechanized farms.

Both liberals and technocratic Marxists assumed a centralized state and bureaucracy and the superiority of the cities (where masses work together) over the countryside (where people live and work in small groups). Their common model also carried with it crucial assumptions about the social groups of the developing society: the industrial working class (primarily male and drawn from more advanced national and racial groups and, in India, from the middle and higher castes) is the advanced class, growing and playing a vanguard role due to its association with the most modern forces of production. The peasantry (with both men and women as toilers and made up of a variety of middle and low castes) was a backward and dying class; women were also considered to be relatively backward due to their association with the isolated, low-technology, and non-"value-producing" domestic labor of the home.

The quarrel between bourgeois liberals and technocratic Marxists was over who should spearhead or manage this development. Liberals placed their faith in capitalist entrepreneurs and private initiative; without this, only state tyranny was said to exist. Marxists argued for an intelligentsia that dominated mass-based political parties and the state bureaucracy within a framework of "social control"; without this, capitalist exploitation would predominate. In third-world countries neo-Marxist views tended to dominate, not only because of "objective" necessities of development, but also because the leading classes/elites of the independence struggle had most often been those whose power was traditionally in the precolonial state machinery and as "intellectuals" claiming status due to their wisdom and purity (in India, brahmans). Still, almost all societies were in fact a mixture of forms of ownership, with varying degrees of private capitalism and state management and control. Thus the development debate, though put in terms of "plan" and "market," most often resolved itself into matters of degree: how much nationalism, how much regulation, how much the state was to invest and in which sector. It did not question the nature of the forces of production (the factories, mines, etc.) to be run under private or state control, nor did it question the assumption that the (centralized, intelligentsia-dominated) state should do the investing, on the basis of the surplus it continued to extract from the people. Four annas or twelve.

And of course the material basis for this development was the extraction of surplus from the peasantry and from the fields, forests, and mines that dotted the country, from the natural resources of the land. In the original European development of capitalism, "primitive accumulation" had been largely from colonies and conquered or looted third-world territories. European agriculture itself was transformed to the extent of forcing out enough of its producers to provide the labor in the new factories; after this most Marxists forgot about the issue of the peasantry, and only Rosa Luxembourg was left to argue that an "ongoing primitive accumulation," or the continued exploitation of "noncapitalist" sectors, was necessary for the very survival of capitalism. The Bolsheviks, catapulted into power in a still agriculturally based and backward society without colonies, seized consciously on their own peasantry as the source of "primitive socialist accumulation"—not only because growing factories needed the surpluses but because the "small commodity-producing" peasantry itself was (in spite of the official rhetoric of the "worker-peasant alliance") seen as the antithesis and even antagonist of the factory proletariat, needing not only "leadership" but control. The forcing of peasants into collective farms took place in a particularly brutal fashion in Stalin's Russia; in Mao's China and elsewhere the process was much less murderous, but there also first the revolution and then collectivization allowed both control over the peasantry and the extraction of agricultural surpluses.

In India, with its greater democracy and the more drawn-out, independently organized role of the peasantry in the independence struggle, there was no talk of "primitive socialist accumulation." Nevertheless, the planners and state managers saw the peasantry in the same terms as the Bolsheviks had: as backward, primitive, tradition-bound, and resistant to modern ideas and technologies. Quite naturally the peasantry was resistant to its exploitation by modern industry and the state, but it was assumed that even for development in agriculture the necessary irrigation, road-building, research, and distribution of improved seeds and fertilizers had to be done from above, by the state and modern scientists. Like the Bolsheviks, the Indian elite argued that the resistance came from rural vested interests who oppressed the rural poor, from the village "dominant castes," the "kulaks," the landlords. But the basic assumption was the same: that surplus had to be extracted from the peasantry and centralized in the hands of the bureaucracy for investment in industry and agriculture. The peasantry was a tradition-bound, caste-ridden primordial force that had to be controlled. If collective farms were not possible, then other means could be sought—the price system, state control of trade and investment.

"Gandhian-Socialist Collaboration": Sharing the Loot

Gandhi, the only major figure of India's independence struggle who offered a substantially different vision of development, was marginalized by independence. For that matter, the elements of paternalism and acceptance of hierarchy in his own worldview gave scope for acceding to statism. Francine Frankel cites without comment the characterization of Gandhi's unquestionably authoritarian ashrams as a model of socialism, and his statement that "Real socialism has been handed down to us by our ancestors who taught 'All land belongs to Gopal, where then is the boundary line?' Gopal literally means shepherd; it also means God. In modern language it means the State, i.e., the People." [1]

Behind this easy identification of "state" and "people" was the Hindu paternalism that made it quite natural to assign duties to intellectuals (brahmans) in guiding the social order, to state officials in protecting it, to businessmen in managing wealth accumulation for all. This helps to explain why Gandhians could be prominent in supporting the "four-anna socialist" state and the industrialist model that it inevitably implied. For, as Frankel has noted, not only were "the ideological preferences of the first generation of nationalists . . . an unlikely blend of the religious morality preached by Mahatma Gandhi and the materialistic philosophy advanced by Marx," but in practical terms, "During the Nehru years, the development strategy was the direct result of Gandhian-socialist collaboration." [2] *Indian US · Soviet Marxism:*

The Gandhians simply added, according to Frankel, two major modifications to the Soviet model: as much decentralization as possible, and the preservation of the village as the basic unit of social organization.[3] But "decentralization" to the Indian elite meant anything but actual autonomy for local or regional political units. "Village-oriented development" came to mean Khadi and Village Industries (KVIC) functioning essentially as agriculture extension services promoting silk cultivation or linking local crafts to a wider market, while "small-scale industries" served as ancillaries producing parts for large corporations in what was in reality a centralized production process thoroughly integrated into world capitalism.

Lloyd and Susanne Rudolph have described the class interests behind what Frankel has called the "Gandhian-socialist collaboration":

> The Nehru settlement had been based on a coalition of urban and rural interests united behind an essentially urban-oriented industrialization strategy. Its senior partners were India's proportionately small but politically powerful administrative, managerial and professional English-educated middle classes and private sector industrialists. Private-sector industrialists welcomed the freedom from foreign competition and dependency that was enabled by the second and third five-year plans' import substitution and industrial self-reliance strategies. The English-educated middle classes manned the senior services, built and managed the public-sector industries, and staffed the large firms in the modern private sector. The junior partners in the Nehru settlement were rural notabilities, mostly large landowners who survived intermediary abolition and blocked the passage or implementation of land ceilings legislation. They consented to the import substitution and industrial self-reliance strategies, middle-class control of central government, and the advantages that

accrued to urban elites and organized workers on condition that they themselves control state governments. That control enabled them to allocate resources and monitor policy implementation for the agricultural sector and rural society in ways that protected their interests.[4]

This description by the Rudolphs, as well as Frankel's analysis of development strategy, neglects an important series of identifications: the ruling elite was male; the urban interests were overwhelmingly brahman and bania by caste, while the rural elite were drawn from the very mixed upper nonbrahman castes who had provided the political elite from the feudal period onward. In backward regions—peripheral states such as Assam, heavily tribal regions such as the south Bihar area known as "Jharkhand" or the Chattisgarh part of Madhya Pradesh—government bureaucrats, merchants, and even a section of rural landowners were also outsiders representing what Marxists would call an alien "nationality."

The Rudolphs titled their most recent study of India's political economy *In Pursuit of Laxmi*, with Laxmi, the goddess of wealth, symbolizing the Indian state. State power in fact was a road to wealth; it was the cow, *kamdhenu*, that provided endless milk. State planning and government programs were not simply means of development but ways of channelizing the surplus that nurtured a whole range of intermediary looters along the way. The rural oligarchy described by the Rudolphs was undergoing a transition from feudalism to capitalism, with a decline in tenancy and traditional landlordship, a rise in chemical-based agriculture in many areas, and some overall industrialization. But if they were not quite "feudal landlords," neither were they adequately characterizable as "capitalist farmers"; at their core were the political bosses, around them a cluster of contractors, smugglers, agents, merchants, and large landowners. The concept of "rent capitalism" used by the Swedish sociologist Olle Tornquist to describe a system in which political bosses profit from charging "rent" for the use of what are legally public resources[5] seems closer to describing the reality of the Indian countryside. At a popular level, rather than the term "capitalist," the word *lutaru*, "looter," seemed better to describe the exploiters who used both private property and control of state power for accumulation.

Pradhan Prasad describes the situation for Bihar:

> After independence the rural sector in India received a fair share of public works. The contracts for these also began to flow into the rural sector. . . . In the early years such contracts were undertaken mostly by those from the rural middle classes who did not belong to the feudal aristocracy. Some middle-class contractors who gathered momentum in this period gave economic support to middle caste Hindus (who constituted the bulk of the middle peasantry) in their bid for political power. This prompted the educated unemployed from the upper caste Hindus, the main constituents of the rural rich (not necessarily the big landowners) to go in for this activity. As the economic crisis deepened

there emerged a fierce competition in this sector. . . . As time rolled on, the new rural rich enmeshed in the feudal tradition of "might is right" began to emerge as a powerful category with muscle power at their command. Public works programs, mainly related to the construction of roads, helped the growth of transport and a category of transport owners who were also drawn from the rural upper middle classes. As the going in the transport business . . . was rough, arming of musclemen became a trend. Armed bodyguards gradually took the shape of armed militias which were being increasingly used during elections for booth-capturing. This category began to forge closer social links (such as through marriage) with the landed aristocracy who were in need of their muscle power to curb the rising economic and political aspirations of the poor-middle and poor peasantry. A new rural oligarchy (consisting of the traditional feudal elites, contractors and transport owners) emerged whose economic strength increased with their increasing share in the loot of public funds.[6]

Bihar was a state of overall economic backwardness, minimal industry and urbanization, lack of a historical democratic movement of all nonbrahman castes, and sharp caste distinctions. Yet even here, as Prasad has described in the case of booth-capturing, the violence for which it is noted today was not so much "semi-feudal" but part of a new gangsterism created in the postindependence period.

In Maharashtra, with maratha-kunbis representing one-third of the total population, a "dominant caste" whose elite at least seemed securely in control of state power,[7] the industrial development of Bombay, and a history of peasant-based democratic anticaste movements, the level of violence was much lower. Yet even here the sophistication of the elite only helped to conceal the exploitation of the working masses. The majority of maratha-kunbis remained poor peasants, workers, and sometimes landless laborers. In spite of the prosperity and overall high average incomes provided by Bombay industry and an apparently efficient state administration (still heavily dominated by brahmans at the top but with nonbrahmans coming in at the bottom), Maharashtrian agriculture stagnated.

Discontent was first expressed in "regional" terms, with the backward Vidarbha/Marathwada/Konkan regions posed against the seemingly prosperous irrigated western Maharashtra. Yet even in western Maharashtra drought began to stalk the countryside, and the much heralded cooperative sugar factories were becoming a means of accumulation of power and wealth for local politicians. Education societies, rum-producing auxiliary industries, and the huts of impoverished migrant cane-cutters flourished under the factories, but by the late 1980s they were giving Maharashtrian peasants a lower average price for their cane (in spite of higher recovery rates in extracting sugar) than the privately owned capitalist factories in U.P. and Haryana. With bureaucrats and contractors present everywhere, "loot" was the name of the game in Maharashtra also, and a popular song by a Marxist peasant organizer satirized the *satbara* (7/12, the term for a land record) as the "7 bottles of whiskey and 12 chickens" needed to bribe the state official.[8]

The statistics of the "development decades" of the post-1950s tell an interesting story. There are, of course, tremendous variations within India—prosperous cash-crop-producing regions (e.g., the wheat-growing belt of northwest India in the states of Punjab, Haryana, and western U.P.) versus backward, drought-stricken regions (e.g., Orissa); areas of extremely high rural inequality, usually centered in the river deltas or coastal areas (e.g., Thanjavur district of Tamilnadu) versus more egalitarian villages, usually in the hilly regions and often, though not always, tribal (e.g., the Himalayan foothills, the central tribal belt); areas where caste polarization was sharp (e.g., Thanjavur or in a different way Punjab) compared to those where caste differences were minimal or those (e.g., Maharashtra) where there was a fair amount of overlap between caste and economic status. But these axes of variation often did not coincide, and the centers of industrial development (Bombay, Calcutta, and, in a different way, the mine-based industrial area of south Bihar) were related to very different types of rural hinterlands.

Thus one can go back to the overall statistics. These show a clear decline in tenancy (area leased-in was 35.7 percent of total land in 1950–51 and 9.25 percent in 1971–72) and a rise in agricultural laborers (from 19.7 percent of total work force in 1951 to 24.9 percent in 1981).[9] But they do *not* show a growth in landlessness: in 1953–54 the proportion of rural households cultivating no land was 10.96 percent while in 1971–2 it had risen to 27.41 percent (only 9 percent owned no land) and in 1981–82 it dropped to 23.7 percent. Land distribution statistics (see tables 2.1 and 2.2) show that up to 1985–86 the proportion of poor peasantry was maintaining itself—and that with a growing population remaining dependent on agriculture, the whole agrarian structure was in a sense "pushed down": more and more holdings and a greater portion of the area operated was in marginal categories. The Gini coefficient ratio, the main measure of inequality, seems to have declined slightly overall with regard to assets of rural households since independence.[10] In contrast to conclusions of many scholars—and simple assumptions of others—that there was been a significant rise in rural proletarian-ization, the data seem rather to indicate that rural impoverishment was pushing people into wage labor, and the lack of nonagricultural jobs meant they were thrown back on the land to constitute a destitute wage-labor force but not a true proletariat. This is the conclusion of Soviet scholars like Rastyannikov, and while survey data do show a growth in agricultural laborer households, the percentage of those without land seems to be growing only minimally (see table 2.3).

If anything, the most significant and increasing differentiation seems to have been between industry and agriculture, and between the organized and unorga-nized sectors, where "organized" is defined in the Indian statistical data to in-clude all public-sector employees and private-sector employees in establishments employing over fifteen people; "unorganized" is a residual category and includes peasant cultivation, in contrast to most studies of the "unorganized" or "infor-mal" sector today. This is shown by data on the changing shares of GNP and

Table 2.1
Estimated Operational Farm Holdings and Area Operated

	1970–71	1980–81	1985–86
Percentage of Operational Holding			
Marginal (0–1 hect)	50.6	56.4	58.1
Small (1–2 hect)	19.1	18.1	18.3
Semi-medium (2–4 hect)	15.2	14.0	13.5
Medium (4–10 hect)	11.2	9.1	8.1
Large (over 10 hect)	3.9	2.4	2.0
Percentage of Area Operated			
Marginal (0–1 hect)	9.0	12.0	13.2
Small (1–2 hect)	11.9	14.1	15.6
Semi-medium (2–4 hect)	18.5	21.2	22.3
Medium (4–10 hect)	29.7	29.6	28.7
Large (over 10 hect)	30.9	23.0	20.2

Source: Centre for Monitoring the Indian Economy, *Basic Statistics Relating to the Indian Economy, 1990,* Table 12.5-1.

employment of the different sectors (see tables 2.4 and 2.5) and on income of different categories of the workers. They show that the average landowning "cultivating" workers have lower incomes than even unorganized sector nonagricultural wage laborers.

With a highly centralized capital-intensive industrial development, clearly only a minority of those expelled from impoverished villages could get secure employment. This gave rise to the organized-unorganized gap, while the increasing ability of the high-caste-dominated middle classes to generate public employment and gain higher salaries within it intensified the gap. V. M. Dandekar, one of the few Indian economists to focus on the industry-agriculture differential, has stressed it as a major factor in poverty. For the 1970–71 to 1983–84 period, he argued, "The agricultural sector is not only bearing the burden of the residual population but, in the past eight years, has further suffered from a differential rise in prices." He went on to say,

> It will be noticed that the per capita NDP in the unorganized nonagricultural sector in 1970–71 was 1.8 times the same in the agricultural sectors and that the gap widened to 2.3 in 1980–81. In the organized sector, the per capita NDP in 1970–71 was already 4.2 times the same in the agricultural sector and the gap widened to 5.7 in 1980–81. . . . Herein lies an explanation why, while food is available and at least half the population lives on a nutritionally inadequate diet, the per capita consumption of foodgrains does not increase.[12]

Table 2.2
Distribution of Rural Households Regarding Landholding

| | Percentage of Households | | Percentage Area Operated | |
	1953–54	1970–71	1953–54	1970–71
Not operating land	28.2	27.5	—	—
Small holding (0-2.49 acres)	28.2	32.9	5.4	9.2
Medium (2.5-9.9 acres)	28.0	29.4	28.6	37.5
Large (10 acres and above)	14.6	10.4	65.9	53.2

Source: Ranjit Sau, cited in Omvedt, "The New Peasant Movement," *Bulletin of Concerned Scholars*, 1988, p. 20.

Few Marxist theorists, either academicians or party activists, dealt with Dandekar's arguments or examined the industry-agriculture gap. But in various ways, Ranjit Sau, N. Krishnaji, and Maria Mies have all stressed that "impoverishment" and "marginalization," and not "proletarianization," marked the condition of the rural poor, while Mies, one of the prominent feminist theorists of a new model of world capitalist accumulation, argued that at the very bottom of its layers of exploited laborers were the rural poor women of the third-world, with studies focused concretely on the Andhra region of India.[13]

Political Hegemony and the Opposition

Within this structure of exploitation, the hegemony of the Congress party was maintained up until 1967 by organizing the web of local bosses into a hierarchy of power around the ideology of "four-anna socialism." Developmental programs, the local institutions of "self-government" known as *panchayat raj*, and all the schemes for "scheduled castes and tribes," "small farmers," "marginal farmers," and later women became further tools of patronage, loot, and power. The Gandhians did not exactly staff this structure, but they helped to legitimate it among many sections of the masses.

There was for some time little effective opposition—except for some regional/national outbursts that petered out with the formation of linguistically based states in Andhra, Maharashtra, Gujarat, and later Punjab and Haryana. Kashmir, whose ruling Hindu prince had seceded to India with the condition that the state would be given autonomy (with only foreign policy, defense, currency, and transport and communications remaining with the center, demands later to be repeated in the Punjab movement), was kept under control even after its popular leader Sheikh Abdullah was jailed by Nehru, and the region continued to

Table 2.3
Agricultural Laborer Households as a Percentage of Rural Households

	1956–57	1964–65	1974–75	1977–78
Total	24.5	21.8	25.9	29.9
With land	12.2	9.6	12.8	14.5
Without land	12.3	12.2	13.2	15.3
Scheduled castes		40.5[a]	40.3[a]	34.3[a]
With land				
Without land		40.7[a]	41.9[a]	39.1[a]
Scheduled tribes		9.8[a]	10.4[a]	12.9[a]
With land				
Without land		9.3[a]	9.5[a]	12.2[a]

Source: Agricultural Labour Enquiry (1953–54) and Rural Labour Enquiries (1964–65, 1974–75, 1977–78).
a. Percentage of all agricultural laborer households in the category.

be run by a Hindu brahman-dominated administration. The "hill peoples" of the Northeast, the Nagas and Mizos, mounted struggles for independence but were too small to win; the areas were eventually consolidated as states with a good proportion of their ex-guerrillas bought off with patronage and local power.

Politically, the various preindependence trends solidified themselves as parties.

The socialists split off from Congress, taking with them sections of the trade union, peasants, and student wings. Two trends continued to exist among them, the Praja Socialist party (PSP), which believed in an alliance with the Congress, and the Samyukta Socialist party (SSP), which took anti-Congressism as a main plank. The samyukta socialists found a distinct ideological identity under the leadership of Ram Manohar Lohia, a Bihar kayastha who tried to theorize the problems of caste, gender, and religious minorities in the Indian context and called for an alliance of "harijans, shudras, Muslims, and women." This gave the socialists (and later peasant-based parties drawing on a Lohiaite orientation to the "backward castes") a genuine political base in northern India from which they contested the Congress party's combination of low and high castes. But for a long time it was insufficient by itself or in combination with other left or low-caste parties in winning a majority to defeat the Congress, and Lohia sought to make up for this by calling for a "grand alliance," right to left, of all anti-Congress parties. This was a political strategy that was to produce some Congress defeats but was to prove quite dangerous in helping to foster the growth of Hindu right-wing fundamentalists. The more pro-Congress praja socialists rejected this alliance with the right, but only at the cost of tending to get swallowed up by the equally socialist-sounding Congress. The socialists as a whole stressed decentralization, village autonomy, and some resistance to heavy industrialization, but

Table 2.4a
National Income by Sectors of Industrial Origin
(percentage distribution)

	1950–51	1970–71	1984–85
Agriculture and allied activities	54.04	49.19	37.91
Manufacturing, construction, and mining	17.14	20.62	22.17
Tertiary: defense and public administration	24.81	31.19	39.91

Source: Ashok Mitra, "Disproportionality and the Services Sector: A Note," *Social Scientist* 179, April 1988, p. 4.

Table 2.4b
Occupational Classification of Workers by Sector
(percentage distribution)

	1901	1951	1961	1971	1981[a]
Agriculture and allied activities	71.7	72.1	71.8	72.2	68.8
Manufacturing, mining, etc.	12.6	10.7	12.2	11.2	13.5
Tertiary: trade, commerce, transport, other services	15.7	17.2	16.0	16.7	17.7

Source: Centre for Monitoring the Indian Economy, *Basic Statistics on the Indian Economy, Volume I: All India, 1987* (Bombay, 1987), Table 9.1-B.
  a. Excludes Assam.

without enough force to distinguish themselves from the Congress, which could play almost any rhetoric that it wanted.

With their preindependence Hindu Mahasabha having proved inadequate politically, Hindu fundamentalists formed a new party after independence, the Jan Sangh. Cadres of the Hindu right-wing Rashtriya Swayamsevak Sangh played a crucial role in giving it structure from the beginning, and with the gradual promulgation of the ideology of a "Hindu nation," the party began to make slow but steady gains from a small early base.

The Communists, after the crushing of the Telengana revolt and the 1948 "uprisings" pushed by B. T. Ranadive, sought to shake themselves out of their theoretical chaos with the help of Stalin and the Soviet party. A "Draft Program" and a "Statement of Policy" published in 1951 rejected Ranadive's theory of an intertwining of two stages of revolution and his notion that the entire bourgeoisie and rich peasantry were outside the "peoples' democratic" front; the Congress was to be opposed but as "comprador," for carrying on the heritage of imperialism

Table 2.5
Income of Organized and Unorganized Sector Workers,1981

	Work force (thousands)	Income (Rs crores)	Average annual income per worker
Wage and salary earners	965	43,121	4,468
Organized sector	229	24,850	10,851
(Public)	155	16,495	10,643
(Private)	74	8,354	11,289
Unorganized sector	736	18,271	2,482
(Agricultural workers)	555	9,454	1,703
(Nonagricultural workers	181	8,817	4,871
Self-employed	1,260	24,719	3,549
Cultivators	925	27,754	3,000
Noncultivators	3535	16,971	5,066

Source: Centre for Monitoring the Indian Economy, *Basic Statistics on the Indian Economy, 1985, Volume I: All India* (Bombay, 1985), Table 10.1.

and not being truly nationalist. A statement on tactics of the same period stated that "neither only the Russian path nor the Chinese path but a path of Leninism applied to Indian conditions" was called for.[14] This was later defined by P. S. Sundarayya as "to concentrate on regions and areas with industrial working class centers and around them in vast contiguous areas, the peasant movements have to be developed in depth, firstly as political base areas, then guerrilla areas which may develop into liberation areas; the working class in these centers should take the leading role in developing such areas."[15]

The Communists went into the first general elections with the slogan of a "false independence," which was believable only to a few. Quite quickly, however, the party came to be dominated by a characterization of the Congress government as representing a "national bourgeoisie" and by the ideas of a possible peaceful transition to socialism. This was perhaps a natural outcome of the existence of "four-anna socialism" in which the Congress government appropriated large sections of the Communist program of nationalization, land reform, and planning. The two main trends in the party, the "peoples' democratic" and "national democratic," were to split in 1964 into the Communist Party of India (Marxist) or CPI(M) and Communist party of India or CPI, with the CPI(M) more oriented to militant working class and agricultural laborer struggles and containing more cadres who believed in armed struggle. But neither had any *different* program of socialism. For both trends, revolutionary development was to be "democratic," thus implying not a complete collectivization in agriculture but a more thorough land reform than the Congress carried out or promised, more nationalization, state control of trade, inclusion of the "right to work" as a constitutional right, the extension of existing industrial technology throughout the country, and a universal availability of "green revolution" technology for agricultural development.

The "democratic revolution" was in fact a "twelve-anna socialism" in Indian conditions. Both the main Communist parties came to believe it could be achieved through parliamentary means of taking state power, the CPI in alliance with the "national bourgeoisie" in the Congress, the CPI(M) on its own. But a section within the CPI(M) who continued to believe that this "democratic revolution" could only be achieved through armed struggle, erupted out of the party in the 1967 crisis. This was the Naxalite revolt, and it burst out first in West Bengal, a state that seemed to fulfill many of the conditions of the old "tactical line"—a big and mobilized industrial center and a turbulent rural hinterland. In the context of economic crisis, drought, and food shortage in 1965–66, the political defeat of Congress in many states in the elections of 1967, and the coming to power of a CPI(M)-dominated Left Front government in West Bengal itself, a wave of revolt overtook the Communist parties as well.

"A Mofussil Revolutionary"

The Naxalite revolt (named after the Naxalbari region of northern Bengal where it first broke out), bringing the "spring thunder" of Maoism to India, challenging established Communist practice and throwing a fright into the ruling class, was in some ways the first "new social movement" of India, although under fairly orthodox Marxist-Leninist clothing.[16]

On one hand, there was a clear crisis in agricultural development, when drought and rising food prices brought mass upsurges in both rural and urban areas; as a study by John Roosa of the circuits of capital and crisis puts it, "The countryside saw increased incidences of looting of warehouses, seizure of harvests, struggle over the workers' share at the threshing floor and the cities saw a rapid rise in strike activity."[17]

Accompanying this in Bengal, with its left heritage, was a greater exposure to Maoism and to the impact of the worldwide "new left" uprisings of the period. At a time when India was in economic and political crisis, when revolution was in the air and youth all over the world were stirring, in Bengal "the entire line of the ruling big bourgeoisie of India seemed to hang in balance" as Ranabir Samaddar wrote in the later post-Naxalite journal *In the Wake of Marx*: "Its fate was being challenged from all quarters—Right and Left, from masters above and masses below. . . . Everywhere the peasants were up in arms for food and land and starting revolt against a semi-feudal countryside, which was already in the way of the first phase of a change towards capitalism in Indian agriculture."[18]

Charu Mazumdar, at the time a district cadre of the CPI(M), disgusted with "the elitist way in which Calcutta baboos manipulated the local rural struggles,"[19] had been protesting the reformism of the CPI(M) and circulating his "six documents." These stressed that the Chinese path was the path of liberation for India also (none of this wishy-washy "neither the Russian path nor the Chinese path but both" talk), that workers and peasants must be organized into a secret party organization with the propagation of the politics of the agrarian revolution, that agrarian revolution had to be completed through armed struggle. In discussions with others, it was reported, Mazumdar refused to make such compromises as admitting the indispensability of mass organizations and mass movements, or the necessity of inner-party struggle inside the CPI(M).[20]

The Naxalite revolt was thus getting nourished as an extremist propeasant militarism. In the late 1960s, as Samaddar notes, anticolonial liberation movements made the peasant seem a typical folk hero, and in India "the new burst of revolutionary upsurges, mostly peasant revolts, found its true ideological expression in CM's writings." And, he added, "they show a constant harping that the present CPI(M) leadership is not comprehending the agrarian question in a revolutionary way."[21]

It was an "agrarian Marxism par excellence" in which "the peasant arrived as a political force in the arena."[22] To the CPI(M), whose leadership was symbolized by the sophisticated *bhadralok* Jyoti Basu, Charu Mazumdar may have been a "mofussil revolutionary" (in essence, a rural hick). In fact he voiced quite well much of the antithesis of "four-anna socialism"—an antibureaucratic, anti-organizational impulse, centering on the exploited peasant in which (since under capitalism the peasantry was thought to disappear) "feudalism is the main contradiction."

Naxalbari itself was a small semitribal area near the tea estates of Darjeeling district bordering on Nepal where people were getting agitated on issues of the harvest and land. Partha Mukherjee describes how the major confrontation began, following the death of two women and a police constable the previous day: "One such village meeting was scheduled to be held in Prosadujote, largely at the initiative of the womenfolk who reacted sharply to the death of two women the previous evening. At this juncture the SDO's police party was confronted by a babble of screaming women abusing them in unspeakable language. . . . The overall impression one gets is that the police insisted on going ahead and the women insisted on their returning back, fearing that otherwise their menfolk would be arrested."[22] Ten people, seven of them women, were killed in the police firing that followed, but the response was a mass upsurge in which the whole area was declared a "liberated zone" from June through August 1967. The militancy of women (by the 1980s Mukherjee's description of their shouting at their oppressors as "babble" would have been targeted as male chauvinism) thus played a significant part in the historic Indian revolt.

Whether the peasants were women and men, tribal or caste Hindu, and whether they were fighting for wages or a share of the harvest or actual land, was not very relevant to the now inflamed Communist cadres; the issue, they insisted, was one of political power. "The struggle of the Terai peasants is an armed struggle—not for land but for state power. This is a fundamental question," insisted one of its leaders, Kanu Sanyal, in a famous early article.[23] Subsequent debates after the initial crushing of the movement, mostly carried in the journal *Frontier* in 1971–73, were to pose the question of "land" versus "political power" and "mass mobilization" versus "armed struggle"; later, more reasonable Marxist-Leninists would argue that both "economic struggle and political struggle" must be intertwined, that peasants after all were fighting for land. But for the early Naxalites state power and the armed struggle had to be the center; there should be no diluting, no compromising of the fundamental question of political power.

The CPI(ML) was formed out of the vast conglomeration of militant youthful activists known as the All-India Coordinating Committee of Communist Revolutionaries, nearly by fiat of Charu Mazumdar. Officially founded at an underground meeting in Calcutta in 1969, it had its first open rally in 1970 and its first split in 1971. By 1972 the first phase of the Naxalite movement was over, crushed. As Samaddar notes, "The party CC never met again after its inaugural meet; the local units were given absolute freedom to operate; military activities overtook political activities; hit and run overshadowed even political coordination; party unit became the military unit, and the whole edifice broke down at the first strike of state violence and every one took to one's own way. In a sense, the CPI(ML) was an antiparty." [25]

The Cost of "Fire Worship"

To Samaddar and to many of the pro-Moscow analysts of Naxalbari, this "petty-bourgeois anarchism" was a characteristic of its peasant orientation; the peasantry was inevitably anarchistic, individualistic. But militarism? The same characteristics could be seen—even magnified—when the movement shifted to Calcutta. A "cultural revolution" was adopted with a five-point program of "(a) destroying schools, college examination halls, libraries, and lavatories, (b) the breaking of idols of gods and goddesses, (c) attacking clubs, recreation halls, and civilians' trains, (d) annihilating small or middle traders, businessmen, merchants, and capitalists, and (e) annihilating general cadres of the revisionist parties." [26]

This rather breathtaking program did have understandable points: the opposition to schools, for instance, could draw legitimacy from the national movement when Gandhi called on students to boycott British schools, while destroying gods and goddesses (and the students also smashed statues of such "Bengal renaissance" heroes as Vidyasagar and Tagore) had its roots in disgust with tradition. But militarism had its roots, conversely, in a tradition itself, that of terrorism and *shakti*, which was essentially upper caste and elitist. "Peasant anarchism" and "lumpen goondaism" were too stereotyped categories to characterize a movement that assimilated vast energies and brought youth all over the country—and outside of it—to forsake their education and plunge into village poverty and challenge to the state. The Naxalite revolt at this level does make more sense as part of a worldwide "new left" upsurge.

The rural orientation, the spirit of "cultural revolution," the emphasis on building local people's power rather than trying to exert pressure on a distant Delhi seat of power, the disregarding of the urban proletariat, the organizational anarchism, the total refusal to see the state sector as "socialist," the distrust of state power itself—all had not only new left characteristics but forecast some aspects of the new social movements to come. The Naxalite movement contrasted with these, however, in being enveloped both in Marxist-Leninist dogma (which also increased the sense of apocalypse, that the "Indian revolution would come by 1970") and militarism. Its "antirevisionism" led to savage infighting with CPI(M) cadres, which was quickly taken advantage of by police agents. In the process, the Communist movement that had been carried on the wave of popular uprisings in Bengal after 1965 seemed to tear itself apart, and the savage repression that followed the Congress' political victory in 1971 brought the first chapter of Naxalism and the new Indian revolt to a close.

Criticizing this militarism of the Marxist tradition, a participant in the 1960s Bengal ferment later wrote,

In our country this "fire worship" was especially costly. We already had a rich tradition of democratic and peace movements within the people. . . . But we also had an uppercaste, elite male "heroic" sacrifice tradition of "revolutionary violence." This had created a cynical culture of non-aggression as co-optation. . . . Compare the level of despotism in China in the feudal-colonial era. So our anticolonial antifeudal revolution could be much less bloody. But how did we of the Marxian tradition react? The majority tendency around Dange to Jyoti Basu did not have a program to extend the democracy of the people—particularly the toilers at the bottom—and their control over political institutions and resources. Rather they gave priority to expand the power of the "Party," even at the cost of compromising with the middle and upper classes, concentrating on the parliament. Thus they became reformist and co-opted. The other factions rightly grew angry with this reformist path. Led by B. T. Ranadive, Charu Mazumdar, Sitaramaiah, etc., till today they tried to fight cooptation with the "cleansing fire of violence." Imagining that we are in Russia of the Czarist times or China of the 1930s under a warlord state, they put emphasis on "army building" as the key task. Instead of championing and extending the democratic powers the people had, they wanted to "break down this hypocrisy." These attempts to copy Russian/Chinese paths were so pathetic, so costly. This militarized "reading" led us to give the vote boycott slogan from 1966 through 1977. . . . We helped the despotism to unleash the savage massacre of 71–76 in Bengal. Tens of thousands arrested, mass organizations beaten up all around, killer squads operating freely . . . It is good that the people did not listen to our boycott call, and defeated the Congress creating a much better democracy for themselves and saving us also from such agony of prisons and underground existence.[27]

This was the reaction of at least some of the Naxalbari generation (and subsequent generations) to the trauma of the events. The aftermath of the Naxalite volcano saw some activists in total physical or mental breakdown, while a whole section grew allergic to any kind of organization and to the very idea of "party"; they tried to maintain their social action but admitted only the idea of "friends' circles." Another trend slowly worked its way from Naxalite "extremism" to more orthodox Marxism under the name of "combining economic and political struggle" or "combining mass organization and armed struggle" and ended up with some similarity to the revisionist parties they had rejected. Some remained faithful for long years to the commitment to armed revolution; some simply dropped out and returned to jobs—even high ones—in the establishment, lending a red color (or at least a rosy glow) to certain sections of the IAS.

But for very many of the Indian circles of political activists the commitment and dedication of the Naxalites, mixed though it was with fanaticism, continued to glow in such statements as that of Nagabhushan Patnaik, for his Vizagapathan conspiracy case trial in November 1970:

> We are not fatalists nor are we dreamers. We are dialecticians, that is why we see today the luminescence and imperativeness of the Indian revolution which cannot be equated by any force on earth, however powerful. In the international context also we see as pointed out by Chairman that the present era is one during which imperialism headed by U.S. imperialism and modern revisionism headed by Soviet revisionist renegade clique are fast heading to total collapse and world revolution heading to total victory.[28]

The combination of poetry and claim to a scientific certitude that sounds strangely archaic twenty years later is typical. Later movements would found their own poetry and claim a different science, but the Naxalite revolt of the late 1960s cleared the ground for new initiatives.

Part II
Emergence of the New Movements, 1972–1985

3

The Anticaste Movement

"One Day I Cursed That Mother-Fucker God"

We do not want a little place in the Brahman Alley. We want the rule of the whole country. Change of heart, liberal education will not end our state of exploitation. When we gather a revolutionary mass, rouse the people, out of the struggle of this giant mass will come the tidal wave of revolution. . . . We will build the organization of the workers, dalits, landless, poor peasants throughout all city factories, in all villages. We will hit back against all injustice perpetrated on dalits. We will well and truly destroy the caste and varna system that thrives on people's misery, which exploits the people, and liberate the dalits. The present legal system and state have turned all our dreams into dust. To eradicate the injustice against dalits, they themselves must become rulers. This is the people's democracy. Sympathizers and members of the Dalit Panthers, be ready for the final struggle of dalits.

Dalit Panther Manifesto, 1973

THE YEAR 1972 proved to be a turning point. It was the year of formation of major and pioneer organizations of nearly all the new social movements and of regional-national organizations as well. The Jharkhand Mukti Morcha, the All-Assam Students Union, the Self-Employed Women's Association (SEWA), and such farmers' organizations as the Zamindari Union of Punjab, the Tamilnadu Agriculturalists' Association, and the Khedut Samaj of Gujarat were all founded in that year. In addition, the Anandpur Saheb Resolution (demanding autonomy for Punjab) was drafted in 1972, and India's most famous environmental movement, Chipko, began at that time. But of all the new organizations, the one that most immediately caught the imagination of youth and progressive intellectuals throughout India was that of the Dalit Panthers, the organization of ex-untouchable (or *dalit*, literally "downtrodden") youth of Maharashtra which represented the first wave of a new anticaste movement.

Drawn from young employees and slum dwellers, holding marches, demonstrations, and rallies to announce their rejection of all establishments and their readiness to fight back against atrocities, the Panthers burst into prominence in 1972 in Bombay and Pune, the major cities of Maharashtra state and the capitalist center of India. With their language of exploitation and revolution, with their spearheading of the dalit claim to be the "true proletariat," the Panthers seemed almost an urban reincarnation of the Naxalite revolt. As with the Naxalites, in fact, the question of political power represented one of their major thrusts. But rather than armed struggle against the state or "capture of power at the local level," the Panther project aimed at the symbolic heights of brahmanical Hinduism. They represented a cultural revolt premised on the full-scale rejection of the caste system, its religious ideology and cultural symbolism; at the same time they brought forward the earliest contemporary challenges to traditional Marxism in the form of the necessity for "class and caste analysis," "class and caste struggle."

Retrospectively, it is striking how much of the Panther revolt was at a symbolic level, dealing with symbolic issues, dependent on media and communications networks. The Panther founders were, almost without exception, young poets and writers; their previous meetings and discussions had centered on the homes, office cubicles, public libraries, and teahouses where prominent dalit writers and critics held audience; the name for their new organization had been planted in a discussion of "Negro literature" at a dalit literary conference earlier that year. And it was the controversy aroused by the publication of a collection of their articles and poems in a socialist magazine, *Sadhana*, that hurled them not only into prominence among Marathi progressive intellectual circles, but into the vanguard of an erupting *dalit movement*.[1]

The symbolic nature of the initial revolt by no means made it secondary. The *Sadhana* controversy had real, material forces behind it—though not of the type familiarly depicted in traditional socialist theory. The most scandalous of the articles was one by Raja Dhale, and it centered on two points: one was Dhale's bitter and profane comparison of a fifty-rupee fine for molesting a dalit woman with the three hundred rupees levied for insults to the national flag, and the other was his written reiteration of comments made earlier at a publication ceremony of the collected poems, *Golpitha*, by one of the most talented dalit writers, Namdev Dhasal. The *Golpitha* poems centered on Bombay's red-light district, and a well-known doyen of Marathi literature, Durgabai Bhagwat, had remarked at the ceremony that since prostitutes performed a "necessary function for society," they should be treated with respect. Dhale responded with a hilariously applauded attack, which he repeated in *Sadhana*, that "Bhagwatbai wants to keep prostitutes as prostitutes but give them honor. If she thinks this is the way to uplift the downtrodden, why doesn't she take up the occupation herself?"

Middle-class outrage over this led to demands for the banning of the magazine issue. A defense march, rapidly organized by the dalit youth, saw the unfolding of a red-on-black Panther flag and the spontaneous adoption—for they had wanted to get away from conventional organizational names—of a new name, Dalit Panther. Early the next year the Panthers adopted a hard-hitting, eloquent manifesto proclaiming their alliance with all the exploited and oppressed and calling for revolution.

The manifesto stressed economic and political oppression. But the themes reflected in *Golpitha* and the *Sadhana* controversy have to be understood against the background of the material life faced by these youth. Most were the first educated generation of their families, with parents who were workers or poor peasant-laborers, coming out of poverty yet with the heritage and pride of Ambedkar's movement, which gave them aspirations raised and then dashed by urban life and the co-optation and fragmentation of the dalit movement after his death. The Bombay setting was probably crucial in producing the Panthers. Seething slums existed in close proximity to the middle-class homes of liberal sympathizers, the bungalow of the chief minister on which they marched, the newspaper offices they went to for getting publicity. Behind this was the reality of rural life, where drought was producing floods of refugees to the cities and increasing violence and tension among castes and classes. Hunger and unemployment were hard realities, but caste discrimination was not simply a "social" or "cultural" issue but rather the framework for their experience of hunger and unemployment. They saw in their villages their fathers laboring for low wages, mothers and sisters forming liaisons or simply used by caste Hindu men, their whole families living on the edge of ("outside" in popular terminology) the village and forced to use separate wells. They experienced discrimination in schools, the inability to enter the houses of caste Hindu friends, the village Patil throwing a mat at them for sitting on the floor, and middle-class supervisors in their offices implying that they had only gotten jobs due to governmental favoritism.

Increasingly, violence was the imagery through which they saw this life. The burning to death of dalit laborers in villages like Kilvenmani, the tearing out of eyes of assertive men, the rape and molestation of women all expressed the horror of what was happening to their people after twenty-five years of independence. Durgabai Bhagwat's argument, in its historical and cultural context, was nothing but the reiteration of the Gandhian attitude of keeping the social structure intact but "uplifting" the downtrodden, prostitutes or untouchables. Let shudras continue to be shudras, let people follow their traditional occupations, that is, keep the caste structure intact, but give "respect" to all occupations within it. What the youth heard of this was *keep in your place*, and what they responded with, in one voice, was *no longer*.

This initial dalit revolt, like so many that were to follow it, centered around issues of women and sexuality, and later feminists were to point out the male chauvinism involved in this linkage of community honor with the "defense of women." But the Panther response was at least partly liberatory, for it involved an identification with those stigmatized, a refusal to accept the brahmanic and patriarchal dichotomy of purity and pollution. Their poems showed a full-scale attack not only on economic and political oppression but also on the symbols of brahmanic cultural/symbolic superiority:

> One day I cursed that mother-fucker God (Keshav Meshram)
> No! No! No! A triple rejection
> To your economic, social, political, mental, religious moral and cultural pollution.
> You ever-living, ever-luminous suns!
> Your very touch brings a contagious disease! (V. L.Kalekar) [2]

At the same time the Dalit Panther revolt very quickly took on political overtones. The assertion of the goal of political power, a central theme in their manifesto, had been inherited from the earlier dalit movement of Ambedkar, who had always taken the issue of power and the initiative of the state as central to the liberation of the lowest sections of society. His constant exhortation that *we must become a ruling community* was part of the collective consciousness of the Mahar neoBuddhists of Maharashtra. But Ambedkar's last effort at founding a political party capable of organizing the poor for liberation, the Republican party, had foundered in personality-based splits. Of its contending factional leaders, many joined Congress, others allied with it, reaping sufficient personal rewards in the process. By the 1970s this new generation with its heritage of
• aspiration were conscious of their powerlessness and disgusted with the leadership that had left them in it. A proposal was put to the Panther youth that they work for the unity of the existing Republican party factions and function as its youth wing; they rejected this on the grounds that the leaders, each one revolving in some sphere or another of Congress patronage, were incapable of coming together, that they had sold out completely. Then came a parliamentary by-election in the constituency of central Bombay in 1974—a constituency that had been since the early 1920s the main center of both dalit and working-class organizing in Bombay, a historical stronghold both of the Communists and of Ambedkar and his movement. In an atmosphere of growing revolt against the Congress party throughout India, the Communists put up the daughter of their oldest leader, S. D. Dange, and the Congress formed an alliance with the Shiv Sena on the one hand and the Republican party factions on the other to sponsor their candidate. They came to ask for Panther support.

The Panthers refused and instead boycotted the election, which resulted in a Communist victory. But, in rejecting Congress co-optation, what they faced in return was confrontation with the Shiv Sena—the rabid, gangster-linked organization that had been growing since 1968 on a theme of "Maharashtra for the Maharashtrians," anti-South Indian, anti-Muslim, anti-Communist. In contrast to the Panthers, the Sena chose symbols and rhetoric compatible with Hindu revivalism (it was later to take up militant Hinduism or *Hindutva* as its main ideology), though it appealed to a class very similar in economic background to the dalits and with an almost equal inclination to militancy. Poor nonbrahman or "other backward class" youth (known as OBCs in political government terminology) and dalit youth confronted each other in the form of the Sena tiger and the Panther. Massive rioting occurred in Worli, the largest working-class tenement area in central Bombay. The electoral defeat of the Congress and the rioting seemed to symbolize the potentials of revolutionary development and anarchy in the tumultuous pre-Emergency period.

"Who Is Your Father? Ambedkar or Marx?"

But there was no revolution. Instead, events in India marched through a rising crescendo of protest against Indira Gandhi's authoritarian brand of populism in a movement led by both left- and right-wing forces to an "Emergency" imposed by Gandhi herself using populist rhetoric to crush her opponents of both the right and left. The pre-Emergency period showed apparent promise: there were united demonstrations of agricultural laborers and workers under the leadership of the mainstream left parties, and there were broad middle-class protest movements such as the "Gujarat movement" and "Bihar movement" generally under socialist leadership with both right and left participation. The Bihar movement, led by the veteran socialist Jayaprakash Narayan, even had slogans of "total revolution" and people's power, and involved large sections of the rural and urban working masses.

Yet this mass movement failed, and part of the reason had to do with the kind of conflict symbolized by the Worli riots: the severe split throughout almost all of India in this period within the oppressed majority of toiling people between the dalits (ex-untouchables), on the one hand, and the other low-castes non-brahmans or "OBCs," on the other. Jotiba Phule had begun a tradition of "alternate socialism" in India with a call for revolutionary unity of the "shudras and anti-shudras" (nonbrahmans and dalits); Ambedkar had also worked for such an alliance and had worked consistently, first to bring kunbis into his Independent Labor party, then to ally with various political forces representing "shudra" interests (peasant organizations, nonbrahman-based political parties). By the end of his life he was extremely pessimistic about such an alliance, and he saw the ability of the "Hindu social order" to isolate the untouchables from the shudras as a crucial reason for its success: "It is obvious that these three classes [dalits, shudras and tribals] are naturally allies. There is every ground for them to combine for the destruction of the Hindu social order. But they have not . . . the result is that there is nobody to join the Untouchable in his struggle. He is completely isolated. Not only is he isolated he is opposed by the very classes who ought to be his natural allies." [3]

The alliance had been effectively stymied by the early 1940s, and by the 1970s it indeed seemed to be in tatters. It was sidetracked not simply by the hierarchy of traditional Hinduism and conflicts of interests between caste Hindus and dalits, peasants and agricultural laborers, but also by the "four-anna socialist" strategy of the Congress, exemplified in Indira Gandhi's authoritarian populism. After 1967 Congress had, in a sense, given up its middle-caste peasant base (especially in the north) to the opposition, with the compensation of having strong support among the "rural poor," the "weaker sections," "harijans, adivasis, Muslims, women." Even though Congress village leaders usually represented the direct exploiters of these sections, they did so in many cases with enough concessions to maintain their power. (We had the spectacle of a state Congress committee president urging the farmers of Kasegaon to pay higher wages, or "the agricultural laborers will burn down your houses"; nobody took this too seriously, but the rhetoric was not insignificant and the concessions were often highly visible, such as the building of a Buddhist community center). The dalit-OBC split was thus replicated in a Congress-Opposition political polarization in which the Congress drew its main support base from dalits and others, while the socialists and right-wing opposition sought OBC support.

The Communists—mainstream and Naxalite alike—by and large fell victim to this strategy, taking "landlords" and "rich farmers" as the main enemies of agricultural laborers and poor peasants, and the middle castes as the main enemies of dalits. In fact, as tables 3.1 and 3.2 on rural "class-caste structure" show, there was considerable overlap, with a significant proportion of dalits, though lower than that of caste Hindus ("others" in the tables), as cultivators, while agricultural laborers included a good number of other low and middle castes; if anything, data on both rural economic structure and employment (see table 3.3) show the dividing line between the upper castes and the rest to be stronger than that between all caste Hindus and dalits and tribals. Nevertheless, Communists also found themselves falling into the rhetoric of posing "caste Hindu" versus "dalit," even landholding peasant versus agricultural laborer.

By the early 1970s they found themselves in a dilemma—on the one hand with a support base and rhetoric that allowed Congress to be seen as progressive and a natural ally, on the other with their antisystem instincts that gave them an urge to be with the peasant and middle-caste, urban middle-class opposition movement that was developing under the leadership of Jayaprakash Narayan. There was no logical consistency in their theory, except to oppose both tendencies (Congress-led and Opposition-led), which the Naxalites tried to do without much success. Thus it was almost inevitable that the Communists themselves should split at the time of Emergency, with the CPI(M) going into opposition and the CPI (and some other small parties) giving support to the Emergency and to Indira Gandhi as representing a "progressive national bourgeoisie" facing "right reaction."

In this whole political process the Panthers, like the Naxalites, represented a kind of revolutionary romantic thrust outside of both, and, like the Naxalites, they were torn apart before they could even engage in organization building.

Table 3.1
Caste and Rural Class: Distribution of Caste Groups among Hindu Rural Households (late 1950s; in millions)

	Scheduled caste	Lower caste	Middle caste	Upper caste	Total
Agriculture					
Farmers	0.18	1.69	0.93	1.09	3.89
	(6.95)	(6.95)	(7.57)	(24.38)	(7.35)
Cultivators	3.19	10.20	6.52	1.96	21.87
	(27.05)	(41.79)	(53.30)	(43.91)	(41.35)
Sharecroppers	1.00	1.51	3.76	0.17	3.44
	(8.50)	(6.17)	(6.18)	(3.91)	(6.50)
Agricultural laborers	4.27	4.11	1.46	0.05	9.89
	(36.19)	(16.85)	(11.91)	(1.09)	(18.70)
Forestry, fishing, livestock	0.28	0.81	0.17	0.02	1.28
	(2.38)	(3.31)	(1.39)	(0.62)	(2.42)
Others	2.87	6.09	2.39	1.17	12.52
	(24.34)	(24.93)	(19.65)	(26.09)	(23.47)
TOTAL	11.79	24.41	12.23	4.46	52.89
	(100.0)	(100.0)	(100.0)	(100.0)	(100.0)

Source: P. C. Joshi, "Perspectives on Poverty and Social Change," *Economic and Political Weekly Annual Number*, February 1979, p. 363.

Definitions: farmers: those cultivating mainly with hired laborers; *cultivators:* mainly cultivating owned or rented land; *upper castes:* those who use sacred thread by custom; *middle castes:* those from whom Brahmans take water by tradition; *lower castes:* other castes who were not scheduled.

But, unlike the Naxalites, this was not done through direct repression, and the Panthers were not after all engaged in armed struggle. Much of the Panther élan had been built up in dialogue and clash with the brahmanic elite, its figureheads, and its symbols; now they seemed unable to move beyond this. They found themselves the center of radical attention in a way for which they were unprepared. Whereas in the past the Congress had co-opted and destroyed the Republican party founded by Ambedkar, now it seemed to many that it was the intellectuals and activists of the left who were doing in the Panthers. The first indication was the split between the organization's two best-known leaders, Raja Dhale and Namdev Dhasal. In this Dhale was taken as representing an "Ambedkarite" position and Dhasal a "Marxist" trend, but later activists charged the literary establishment (the *Maharashtra Times* and the socialist *Sadhana*) with playing up the differences between the two, while the Communists were accused of seeking to infiltrate the Panthers through the patronage of Dhasal.[4]

There was no really considered debate between "Marxism" and "Ambedkarism." Themes of "class" versus "caste," the "economic" versus the "social"

Table 3.2
Scheduled Caste and Scheduled Tribe Occupations,1981

	Scheduled caste Lakh %	Scheduled tribe Lakh %	Others Lakh %	Total Lakh %
Agricultural sector (a+ b)	289 (76.4) (19.5)	192 (87.1) (13.0)	999 (61.4) (67.5)	1,480 (66.5) (100.0)
a. Cultivators	107 (28.2) (11.6)	120 (54.4) (13.0)	698 (42.9) (75.4)	925 (41.5) (100.0)
b. Agricultural laborers	182 (48.2) (33.8)	72 (32.7) (13.0)	301 (18.5) (53.2)	555 (24.9) (100.0)
Nonagricultural sector	89 (23.6) (12.0)	8 (12.9) (3.8)	628 (38.6) (84.2)	745 (33.5) (100.0)
TOTAL (1+2)	378 (100.0) (17.0)	220 (100.0) (10.0)	1,627 (100.0) (73.0)	2,225 (100.0) (100.0)

Source: Centre for Monitoring the Indian Economy, *Basic Statistics on the Indian Economy, 1985, Volume I: All India* (Bombay 1985), Table 1.8c.

ranged through all the dalit demonstrations and discussions of the period. But generally arguments seemed to take place in a stereotypical fashion, in which dalits (and many socialists) rejected the economic interpretation of history by arguing for the centrality of cultural, social and religious factors. Superficially, the "Marxist" position was by far the most reasonable, since its spokesmen never remained at the level of traditional Marxism but spoke of "combining caste and class struggle" and "uniting all the oppressed." The Ambedkarites could have argued that Ambedkar himself had put forward the first "class-caste" line, but instead their position seemed almost casteist: *Tuza bap kon? Ambedkar kiva Marx?* was the popular challenge hurled at leftist dalit youth by anti-Communists: "Who is your father—Ambedkar or Marx?"

But it was more than simply caste attraction that helped to explain why, in the end, the "Ambedkarite" position easily won out in the Panther split. The fear of brahmanic co-optation had real grounding. The pressures held out by socialist and Communist organizations were more subtle, but no less real, than that represented by the Congress. The Dalit Panther Manifesto, for one thing, *had* been written by a young brahman Naxalite, though most dalits in subsequent years continued to express support for its broad positions. The very real fear of the Panthers was of the control by brahman leftists of supportive organizations, platforms, money for campaigns, even the media. Their deep-seated suspicion was that they were now given only hypocritical support by Communists who had always seen Ambedkar as pro-British, had always refused to recognize the reality of

Table 3.3
Representation of Caste Groups in Central Government Services

	Scheduled castes and tribes	Backward castes	Forward castes	Total
Ministries/departments				
Class I	840	303	10,564	11,707
	(7.18)	(2.59)	(90.23)	(100.0)
Class II	5,985	1,742	36,076	43,803
	(13.66)	(3.98)	(82.36)	(100.0)
Classes III				
and IV	5,518	1,500	10,811	17,829
	(30.95)	(8.41)	(60.64)	(100.0)
All classes	12,343	3,545	57,451	73,339
	(16.83)	(4.83)	(78.34)	(100.0)
Autonomous bodies, attached bodies, etc.				
Class I	5,399	4,147	71,779	81,325
	(6.64)	(5.09)	(88.27)	(100.0)
Class II	91,431	59,079	352,827	503,337
	(11.74)	(18.16)	(70.10)	(100.0)
Classes III				
and IV	67,118	67,786	188,044	322,948
	(20.78)	(20.98)	(58.24)	(100.0)
All classes	163,948	131,012	612,650	907,610
	(18.06)	(14.43)	(67.51)	(100.0)
Public sector undertakings				
Class I	3,652	3,719	73,623	80,994
	(5.68)	(4.59)	(90.90)	(100.0)
Class II	68,566	36,242	260,977	565,785
	(19.74)	(9.91)	(71.19)	(100.0)
Classes III				
and IV	45,646	22,689	75,575	143,910
	(31.72)	(15.77)	(52.51)	(100.0)
All classes	117,864	62,650	410,175	590,689
	(19.95)	(10.61)	(69.45)	(100.0)
Total				
Class I	9,891	8,169	155,966	174,026
	(5.68)	(4.69)	(89.63)	(100.0)
Class II	165,982	97,063	649,880	1,112,925
	(18.18)	(10.63)	(71.19)	(100.0)
Classes III				
and IV	118,282	91,975	274,430	484,687
	(24.40)	(18.98)	(56.62)	(100.0)
All classes	294,155	197,207	1,080,276	1,571,638
	(18.72)	(12.55)	(68.73)	(100.0)

Source: Government of India, *Report of the Backward Classes Commission (Mandal Commission)* (New Delhi, 1981) 2:92.

Percentage of population: Scheduled castes and scheduled tribes: 22.5 percent; backward castes: 52 percent; forward castes: 25.5 percent.

caste, and only took a combinatory "class-caste" position because a pure Marxist one would have gotten them nowhere.

As a thoughtful "Ambedkarite" intellectual later wrote, "From the viewpoint of using the growing power of the Panthers for their political self-interest the Communists were trying to take control of the Panthers. On their intellectual front, they tried to show the flaws of Ambedkar and give the Panthers a Marxist baptism. . . . But, since the Panthers would have rejected them if they had openly opposed Ambedkarism, there was a forceful proclaiming of the need to fight class struggle and caste struggle together."[5]

Gaikwad went on to complain that the Ambedkarites were "unable to give an Ambedkarite economic ideology that would be an alternative to the ideology put forward by the Marxist trend." But behind this long-standing failure was Ambedkar's own assumptions of both liberal and traditional socialist economic positions related to private property and nationalization.[6]

On the other hand, the Marxist left at the time was not really in a position to teach the Panthers much about economic struggle and class alliance, when their own political positions were so close to those of the Congress itself. Their notions of differentiation of agriculture under capitalism inclined them to accept the idea that middle-caste or "OBC" rich farmers were the worst enemies of dalits and to rhetorically pose the contradiction as *savarna/dalit* or "caste Hindus versus dalits"; to this they simply added the need for a working-class alliance, leadership of the working-class party, and so forth. The Naxalites with their antifeudalism tried to make their own contribution that of *militancy* (armed struggle, smash the state, we don't compromise like your own petty-bourgeois leadership)—but Maharashtrian dalits did not at the time need militancy so much as a strategy for a broad, united mass movement that could identify its real enemy. That the left, with all its articulation and dedication, did not give.

The Dalit Panther-left interaction thus began the process in which the left picked up issues raised by movements and tried to divert them to a "class struggle" of their own understanding without examining their own presuppositions. For their part, dalits, whether as "Panthers" or otherwise, gradually became confirmed in their autonomous tendencies, in their conviction that they were the "true proletariat" and that, however slowly, they were moving toward an understanding of the situation.

In the meantime, the Panther organization fell apart, then regrouped. At a conference called in Nagpur in late 1974 the Dhale group took control, rejecting the manifesto, expelling Dhasal, beating up a couple of the leftist dalits and their upper-caste Naxalite friends. The Dhasal activists did not even try to attend; they failed in building an alternate organization. Dhale's Panther faction itself lasted only about a year, until its leader declared it dissolved and announced the formation of a new organization called "Mass Movement." This was in the middle of the Emergency, and his opponents charged that he had done so out of fear of repression. In 1976 the younger section of the Dhale group, led by Arun Kamble and Ramdas Athavale, took up the cause of rebuilding. They called themselves the "Bharatiya Dalit Panther," making a claim to all-India status, on the grounds that units were getting built up all over the country.

The reconstructed Dalit Panthers also had a strong cultural focus. Their demands included a number of issues regarding the educational system, extending facilities to dalit converts to Buddhism, and a nominal demand for "nationalization of basic industries" that put them in the radical camp—but the really operative issue became the demand to rename Marathwada University in Aurangabad, where some of the greatest educational work of the dalit movement had been done, after Ambedkar. Panther units were also getting built up in city slums and small towns and even in some villages, taking up issues such as slum clearance, fighting for housing land, holding numerous cultural and political programs and rallies, but it is striking that once again a symbolic issue was dominating the movement. The leftist charge of "no economic program"—by which they meant the Panthers were not organizing the rural poor on wage issues or fighting for land—was to this extent valid.

But the Panthers were themselves a symbol. The assertion of dalits in slums and villages was a growing reality throughout India, and in Maharashtra this militancy was expressed by calling themselves "Dalit Panthers." In the beginning itself the Panthers had only an expressive link with the masses of men and women in the slums of Bombay, but this expressive link was powerful because it represented the fury, growing readiness to fight repression, and sometimes nihilism of the lower-class mass. "We didn't know what was in the manifesto," a slum activist later declared; "we knew only one thing: if someone puts his hand on your sister, cut it off!"

The militancy continued, but it was never really channeled. On one hand, "fighting atrocities" against the "caste Hindus," the "Patils" was carried on, a necessary but negative task. On the other, at the broad political level, the Panther-like earlier dalit leadership continually fell victim to Congress blandishments and Congress progressive rhetoric: both Dhasal and Dhale supported Indira Gandhi during the Emergency, and even the reorganized Panthers gradually came to be a kind of political reserve army of the Congress (Athavale ended in 1990 as a social welfare minister in a Congress government). Through this remained the stark failure not only to bring caste Hindu toilers into the organization but even to break the caste-barrier among dalits: the Panthers, like Ambedkar's earlier organizations, remained overwhelmingly a party of one dalit caste, the mahars of Maharashtra, now known as Buddhists due to their massive conversion.

But with all these limitations, the Panther explosion of the early 1970s made important contributions to Indian socialist politics and theory. The biggest achievement was to enlarge the framework of discussion for revolutionary movements. Henceforth, in some way or another, "class *and* caste," "economic *and* social" issues would have to be discussed, not simply by left parties but by all movements. Opposition to "brahmanism," targeting of the mythical brahman lawgiver Manu as a source of oppression, identification of such submerged figures as Shambuk, Ekalavya, and Ravana (the non-Aryans, dalits, tribals, demons of the epics) would become a common vocabulary for the women's movement and for most sections of the environmental and peasant movements also. Insistence on their own autonomy, suspicion of political parties, a rejection of outsiders who only spoke in the name of the oppressed would be common for all movements.

Most important to the new dalit explosion, perhaps, was the kind of self-confidence and hope expressed in poems like "Comrade" (quoted at the beginning of this book) and in the early poem of Namdev Dhasal from the *Golpitha* collection:

> Turning their backs to the sun, they journeyed through centuries.
> Now, now, we must refuse to be pilgrims of darkness.
> That one, our father, carrying, carrying the darkness is now bent;
> Now, now we must lift that burden from his back.
> Our blood was spilled for this glorious city
> And what we got was the right to eat stones.
> Now, now we must explode that building which kisses the sky!
> After a thousand years we were blessed with a sunflower-giving fakir;
> Now, now, we must, like sunflowers, turn our faces to the sun. [7]

Bihar: "The Caste War Becomes a Class War?"

One state of India where the effort to combine "caste struggle" and "class struggle" appeared to be taking shape, where the new men and women born of the dalit revolt not only "turned their face to the sun" but also picked up the gun, was Bihar—the most tumultuous, violence-pervaded state in India. Here, in fact, the class war of the Naxalites became a caste war as those who survived the first repression settled in among landless laborers and built a base in Bhojpur district in the first half of the 1970s.

Historically, before independence the dalit movements had bypassed Bihar. "Ad-Dharm" and "Adi-Hindu" movements had been launched in Punjab and western U.P. in the 1920s and 1930s in which dalits claimed to be "original" (*adi*) inhabitants, and in Bengal the biggest dalit caste organized as the "Namashudras." But in eastern U.P. and Bihar, marked much more by landlordism and within this the domination of the "twice-born" upper castes (brahmans, bhumihars, and rajputs), even the "shudra" peasant castes (kurmis, koeris, and yadavas) were cruelly subordinated, and there had been little of a broad anticaste movement. Landlord power had been challenged by an early militant peasant movement, the Kisan Sabha, which had socialist and Communist cadres and a charismatic leader, Swami Sahajanand, one of numerous indigenous peasant leaders who had used the robes of a sadhu in the goal of transforming society.

But this had a large portion of upper-caste tenants, and its left activists pursued only "class issues." At the same time the Triveni Sangh, based on the kurmis, yadavs, and koeris, fought on caste issues, but they did so from a Sanskritizing perspective (fighting for the right to wear the sacred thread, for instance) that contrasted with the antibrahmanism of the South Indian movements and divorced them more strongly from dalits. In the end it was the Congress that captured much of the dalit base in the 1930s, under Jagjivan Ram, a capitalist protégé who appealed to them as dalits to oppose Ambedkar and as agricultural laborers to oppose the Kisan Sabha.

With this history, Bihar remained a state with unreconstructed landlordism, sharecropping, patriarchy, extremely low wages, and social oppression. The Naxalite challenge developed in the central districts where some agricultural development was producing an objective base to challenge the bonds of exploitation they called "semifeudalism." Its first mass leader was Jagdish Mahto, a koeri teacher who had read Ambedkar before he discovered Marx and started a paper in the town of Arrah called "Harijanistan" (dalit land), even leading a march of dalits on this demand. This was similar to innumerable assertions throughout India at the time, but Bihar contradictions drove Mahto in a more violent direction. Beaten up after supporting the CPI in the 1967 elections, he turned to Naxalism and began to organize murders of landlords and their gangster henchmen in the area around his native village. The issues on which dalits were stirring were not only those of their abominably low wages, but also *izzat*, social honor, and especially honor defined in terms of the unrestricted and arrogant access of the upper castes to dalit women. In 1971, before he was killed, Mahto told a fellow teacher, "Brother, I know that I am going to die one of these days. But I will die partly satisfied. For one change that our movement has brought about is that landlords now do not dare to touch the women of the poor." [8]

The awakening of the dalits of Bihar was harsher than for those of Maharashtra, who had had a long and powerful social movement behind them. As described by Arun Sinha, a left-wing journalist, "This man has risen from the grave; he seems to have gone berserk and is frenziedly chopping the branches of feudalism. His desire is to see the 2,500-year old tree felled here and now. So far he has only been humiliated, whipped and slain, denied the status of a man; his wife treated as a prostitute. Then one day somebody brought him news of Naxalbari and things began to change. The Harijan died, the Koeri was burnt; the new man who rose from the flames felt that he was neither a Harijan nor a Koeri but a man." [9]

This upsurge produced what Vinod Mishra of the "Liberation" group of CPI(ML) was to call the "flaming fields" of Bihar. Massive struggles arose and faced police repression, private gangsterism, and the formation, after the Emergency, of caste-based landlord armies known as the "Bhoomi Sena" (of the kurmis), "Lorik Sena" (of the rajputs), and others. Against these the agricultural laborers fought with their "Lal Sena." Bihar became a center of the "atrocities against Harijans" that were becoming notorious throughout India and that leftists were insisting represented only "class conflict in the guise of caste." In fact, dalits were prominent among those killed, but there were also members of other low castes. The killers often included the "backward caste" kurmis and others, though most were rajputs and bhumihars.

Caste contradictions were also in part class contradictions between small peasants and laborers, since large numbers of the low-middle castes who found themselves posed against the dalit upsurge were poor and middle peasants. The Naxalites, in fact, were facing ideological dilemmas, for in spite of their attachment to class they found themselves mobilizing a caste-based upsurge with a good deal of social content, while the organizations that called themselves "peasant associations" were actually fighting on the wage issues of agricultural laborers. But whether among dalits or among the upper-caste youth and intellectuals drawn into defense of the rural poor, a scientific ideology was perhaps less important than the call to struggle. As Sinha put it, "The new man found out new gods in Lenin, Mao, and Charu Mazumdar. It was not difficult to follow the new oracles: the line of Charu Mazumdar meant killing a Havildar Singh or a Dayalu Rai, while one thing which Lenin and Mao wanted to establish was a society where all men will be equal. Bhojpur's new man need not go into the details. . . . He had grasped the quintessence of Marxism." [10]

By 1980 the Naxalites were turning to mass organizing and were stepping up efforts to unite with middle peasants and middle castes. Two main groups, the "Liberation" and "Party Unity," began to spread in the central districts of Patna, Jehanabad, and others. Party Unity formed an open front, the Mazdur Kisan Sangram Samiti (MKSS), with the help of an ex-socialist mass leader, Dr. Vinayan. The Liberation group mounted a series of demonstrations in Patna district in 1981, ranging in number from 1,000 to 35,000, climaxing with the massive demonstration of their newly formed Bihar Pradesh Kisan Sabha (BPKS—taking the name of the preindependence mass organization) on February 21. The two organizations fought the landlord gangs and sometimes each other, with mutual accusations of compromising or taking former gang leaders in underground armies. But there was no denying that they were growing.

By 1983 the Liberation group moved to its next stage of forming a mass political front, the Indian Peoples' Front (IPF), which stood for elections in 1985. The Party Unity group in turn forced the formal surrender of the kurmis' Bhoomi Sena to the MKSS, which in part was necessitated by the withdrawal of support by the kurmi poor peasants, for whom this "caste" army was becoming an unbearable burden, harassing their women, taking liquor and food. Thus one IPF sympathizer could argue that because both sides included members of different castes, "it has now become impossible to assert the naive argument of a 'caste war' in Patna district. What we see instead is the nucleus of a class-based political formation." [11]

But Bihar was providing a new challenge to the "semifeudal" theories of the Naxalites. They had won a firm base, but the thrust on social and wage issues was a long way from the projected "agrarian revolution"; "taking state power" was finding its interpretation not so much in fighting the police or military but in battling it out with the armed gangs of the rural oligarchy and in establishing the power of the marginalized to assert their rights as human beings; it was also veering to parliamentary participation. The 1970s' shape of the movement, which often posed agricultural laborers against peasants and dalits against middle castes, was a result not of Marxist-Leninist ideology but of the social structuring of the conflicts of that period, and some of the hard questions of waging a "class war," in particular what one observer called the "challenge of the *smytchka*" (the old Russian term for "worker-peasant alliance"), which in India meant agricultural laborers and peasants, dalits, and middle castes, were just beginning to be confronted in the 1980s.[12]

Summing up the Bihar achievements, Dev Nathan, an activist-theoretician of another CPI(ML) group, wrote:

In the course of the protracted antifeudal struggle, landlords have been forced, after many bitter battles, to accept and come to some kind of terms with the agricultural laborers and the dalit castes. As a result of this struggle wages have gone up to some extent (though inequalities in wages paid to men and women remain and have never even been an issue taken up by the movement); some government lands have been seized by the landless; in some instances fishing rights have been secured in village ponds; and blatant day-to-day sexual attacks on dalit and other low caste women by men of landlord families have considerably lessened.

Then, noting that the middle castes were over 50 percent of the population and contained the bulk of the peasantry and a good proportion of agricultural laborers, he went on to caution that "The class mobilized in the course of this struggle has been more or less confined to the dalit castes. The middle (backward) castes have not been drawn into the movement in large numbers; that is particularly true with regard to the middle peasantry."[13]

But in the turmoil of the 1970s, Naxalite achievements among the Bihar rural poor could capture the imagination of educated youths of all castes throughout India. Never mind that Dev Nathan could caution that support for armed resistance in social-economic struggles "is very different from support for an emancipatory war against the state"; never mind that IPF leaders themselves could admit the limitations of their Bihar movement and argue by the mid-1980s that the majority of Indian people after all were still attached to parliamentary politics.[14] Dalits were fighting a thousand-year old battle against their exploiters; as a dalit trade union activist in Maharashtra put it, justifying his excitement about the Bihar and Andhra Naxalites, "Let the party leaders worry about strategy; someone has to take revenge."

Karnataka: "Throw the Brahmans into the Gutter along with the Gita"

A quieter locale of the varied but nationwide upsurge that took place among dalits in the 1970s, but one that posed very similar issues to those posed by Maharashtra and Bihar, was Karnataka. That Karnataka should have early vigorous dalit organizing was, on the face of it, surprising, for it was one of the more prosperous and relatively quieter states of the Indian Union.

The core of the South Indian state was the former princely state of Mysore, hailed by Gandhi himself as the closest thing to "Ram-Raj" in India because of the reformist traditions of its Hindu ruler. These reforms had included various concessions, such as reservations in public service for nonbrahmans and dalits, strong support for Gandhi's village-reconstruction and "harijan work" (upper-caste reformers wandered into untouchable quarters to hold religious programs, clean up children, preach against drunkenness, and occasionally support a temple-entry effort), and a major drive for government-sponsored industrialization. It was the ideal example of a "four-anna socialism," and a relatively prosperous rural economy in which even dalits held some land to begin with helped it maintain itself.

Nevertheless, crisis began to arise even in the kingdom of Rama; metaphorically speaking, Shambuk—the mythical dalit youth killed by Rama for the "sin" of trying to gain brahmanical esoteric powers—rose in rebellion. Even the mild form of assertion promoted by Congress and Gandhian "harijan" propaganda would have an effect that was to erupt in 1973. At that time the chief minister, Devraj Urs, a reformist Congressman, was carrying out his own version of Indira Gandhi's populist programs with partial land reforms (relevant primarily in the still landlord-dominated coastal districts) complete with "land tribunals," increased reservations for middle castes, and the incorporation of increasing numbers of dalits and the smaller "backward castes" in positions of power. In spite of this progressive orientation, riots broke loose throughout the state in 1973 when the dalit minister Basavalingappa referred to upper-caste-dominated Kannada literature as *bhoosa* or "cattle-feed." Caste Hindu students attacked dalit hostels and students, and the dalits retaliated and began a poster war that proclaimed "Throw the brahmans into the gutter along with the Gita!" and "Down with the literature produced by the high castes, the lingayats, the vokkaligas, and brahmans."[15]

The result was that Urs forced Basavalingappa to resign, and dalits moved to autonomous organizing. By 1974 local organizations were established in several districts, and a final state-wide meeting at Bhadravati formed the united Dalit Sangarsh Samiti ("Dalit Committee for Struggle" or DSS).

Of all the dalit organizations in India, the DSS was perhaps the most successful in building a formal democratic organization with units in most of the districts of the state, with the ability to unite the major dalit castes (in Karnataka these were the madigas and holeyas) and differing ideological strands. These were identified as Lohiaite, Ambedkarite, and Marxist, though what these represented in practice was not always clear. "Lohiaism" was primarily the idea of the unity of dalits, backward castes, and minorities and connected the DSS with socialists and the Janata party; "Ambedkarism" involved an emotional attachment to autonomy and a militancy in self-assertion; "Marxism" meant a focus on the economic issues of agricultural wage laborers that posed them primarily against nonbrahman "rich peasants" or "landlords."

In spite of their differences, these trends coexisted in the DSS, which politically supported a broad left alliance, though Marxist dalits might complain of the emotional attachment to Ambedkar and a "whispering campaign" against Marxism.[16] Perhaps the fact that Karnataka lacked Bombay's combination of the overbearing presence of sophisticated bourgeois-brahman elite life and festering, nihilism-breeding slums helped its dalits to maintain more balance. In any case, between 1974 and 1985, the DSS took up many local village struggles on wage and land issues and on women's issues (making, for example, a heroic effort to oppose the dedication of girls to the goddess Yellamma in north Karnataka, the site of India's most famous "devadasi" cult). At the same time they held training camps and broader meetings and began to think through their relation with the middle nonbrahman castes and left groups in a series of study camps and seminars on issues ranging from the question of reservations to that of alliance with the farmers' movement. In the process, they became "the single largest left group in Karnataka with a wider following than the CPI and CPI(M)," according to a dalit Marxist activist,[17] building effective alliances with the peasants' Rayatu Sangh, with women's organizations, and with civil liberties groups.

Karnataka and the *bhoosa* controversy also fostered a militant but extremist anticaste ideological tendency, represented by the journal *Dalit Voice*, established in 1981. Its founder, Rajshekhar Shetty, was a radical journalist who had lost a job in 1979 as reporter in the *Indian Express* due to a confrontation with the high-caste managerial and editorial staff. Rajshekhar himself was from a nondalit low caste and later dropped the surname "Shetty" as being caste-indicative. He began by identifying himself ideologically with the "class-caste struggle" trend, and as late as 1984 he could write that "Marxism is nobody's monopoly; we are also Marxists." But even then "class" was dropping out of his scheme of things. In the same booklet he asserted, "Caste is the principle contradiction in India . . . an artificial division of Indian society into rich and poor, exploiter and exploited, may be made for limited purposes in cities, but India lives in its villages where people are divided on caste lines." [18]

Dalit Voice began to attack all brahmans as "Nazis" and to depict the left movement as simply "Brahmo-Communist." Eventually it moved to a racially oriented "cultural nationalism" of the non-Aryan theory that identified dalits as blacks and Dravidians, and brahmans as Aryans. Though Rajshekhar was associated with some Bangalore-based dalit organizations, these remained small and middle-class based; the journal's strength was not in its links with the Karnataka mass movement but in its militant writing and ideological fervor, which was winning it readers all over India and abroad.

With all of his limitations, Rajshekhar was making some apt criticisms of Marxist positions, attacking arguments that shudra rich peasants, or OBCs, were the main enemy, and that the solution to every problem was nationalization. "Dalits are born Marxists," he asserted, arguing that they must read and translate Mao's *On Contradictions*: "Because we have not understood the law of contradictions, we get confused and therefore come to the wrong conclusion." Rajshekhar argued that "brahmanism" was the principle contradiction: "As Dalits, we become the natural leaders of the Indian Revolution and therefore it is our responsibility not to commit any mistakes. . . . We have to convince the OBCs that fighting Brahmanism is as much their duty as freeing themselves from Shudra slavery. The enemies of OBCs are not Dalits. . . . Similarly, every Dalit organization is pointing out that Dalits are the victims of Brahmanism. . . . Hence, the contradiction between Dalits and OBCs is nonantagonistic." [19]

The question was not only of a dalit-shudra (OBC) alliance; dalits, according to Rajshekhar, must *lead* the OBCs.

But, in Maharashtra in 1978–79 mass regionwide attacks on dalits in which the middle castes were the main perpetrators seemed to bring "atrocities on Harijans" to a new level and show the ferocity that a "nonantagonistic" contradiction could produce.

"Marathwada Is Burning!"

In late July 1978, after much pressure by dalit groups, the Maharashtra state assembly passed a resolution to rename the Marathwada University after Dr. Ambedkar. The result was a wave of rioting throughout the region. Its justification was "Marathwada" (regional) pride, the claim that a regional name must be kept for the university, and it was legitimized by a Marathwada Citizens' Committee made up of leading high-caste intellectuals, many of them former freedom fighters. Protest strikes in Aurangabad against changing the name of the university were followed by what were in effect mass pogroms against dalits affecting some 1,200 of 9,000 villages in the region, rendering about 5,000 people homeless and forcing 2,000 more to flee their villages. [20] Beatings and rapes of women occurred, and one local activist, Pochiram Kamble, was burned to death. It was a shock to intellectuals throughout a state that had prided itself on a progressive image and that had depicted Marathwada itself as the "land of saints" for being the home of most of the *bhakti* saints who had expressed the medieval reform Hindu tradition.

And the main attackers were the middle castes, the maratha-kunbi peasants. In the context of "atrocities against dalits" in Bihar in which OBCs were often involved, and of the growth of the Shiv Sena in Maharashtra, it seemed one more evidence, the decisive evidence because of the mass nature of the rioting, that the "main contradiction" had changed, that a unity of shudras and *atishudras*, or dalits and nonbrahmans, was no longer possible. It was also argued that most of the rioting had taken place in the areas of greatest agricultural development, where caste tension had as its basis the rising wage demands of agricultural laborers opposing rich farmers.[21]

But the Marathwada riots were also not so simple. The history of the region showed unresolved caste tensions exacerbated by a freedom struggle that had strongly divided caste Hindus and dalits. During colonial rule Marathwada had been part of the feudalistic, unreformed Muslim state of Hyderabad, and its Congress-led independence movement was dominated ideologically by the Hindu-nationalist Arya Samaj. These considered Muslims as enemies, while on the other hand many dalits were attracted by the promises of the Muslim ruler, the Nizam, especially when he offered them government-held "waste lands" for cultivation. The critical last days of colonial rule saw dalits first exposed to Muslim armed fundamentalists who tried forcibly to convert them and then to vicious reactions from caste Hindus who turned their hatred of Muslim gangsters into attacks on dalits in the villages. Thus the independence struggle itself increased caste confrontation (in contrast to nearby Telengana where Communist leadership united dalits and the middle-caste peasantry), and this heritage of tension remained. Dalits fought in Marathwada to retain possession of lands for cultivation; caste Hindus reacted violently. Dalits getting education, reservations in jobs, building new houses in the villages provoked burning resentment from other low and middle castes in this backward and impoverished region.

This resentment was fueled by propaganda that depicted reservations for dalits as the main cause of the unemployment of the middle-caste youth, and by interpretation of Marathwada regional identity in Hinduistic terms. As one dalit activist noted, the intellectuals of the Citizens' Action Committee hailed the Hindu saints of the region and some monuments such as the fort at Devagiri (though this was always known as Daulatabad to the Muslims), but disregarded the world-famous Buddhist temples and caves at Ajanta and Ellora, the Sikh center at Nanded, and smaller Muslim monuments.[22]

In any event, dalits throughout the state reacted with fury to the attacks, and the cause of renaming the university mobilized hundreds of thousands in 1979, climaxing in a "Long March" on Aurangabad organized by very factionalized committees that included the Dalit Panthers, smaller dalit organizations, the Republican party factions, socialist individuals and groups, and the Communist parties. Men, women, and children poured into the campaign, holding marches and *satyagrahas*, going to jail, and singing new songs of struggle such as Vilas Ghogare's "Marathwada is Burning":

> One Pochiram Kamble, sweating to fill his stomach,
> He became the enemy of the village,
> "Jay Bhim" was on his lips . . .

Accosted in the fields, bound with a rope,
His hands and feet branded, then thrown in the fire,
He burned fiercely, the son of Bhim . . .
We see all this with open eyes,
Still we live our lives,
By our own hands feeding
The fire that burns the corpse.
We the people of Bombay and Pune—
How hollow is our pose!
We gossip about revolution
But lead the lives of eunuchs.
Oh, kill, smash, cut, break
Whatever comes in our way!
Marathwada is burning, Marathwada is burning!

The caste Hindu majority, on the other hand, dug in its heels on the issue, and the university is still not renamed.

The Strategies of Class-Caste Struggle

Marathwada, nevertheless, was to be the last widespread violent confrontation between dalits and middle castes in India—and there were at least two anticaste leaders of the time who reasserted with vigor, though in very different ways, the theme of a caste alliance.

One was Kanshi Ram, who was to become for a time the most powerful dalit leader in India and who deliberately stayed out of the agitation for the renaming of the university. A Punjabi chamar (the leather-working caste) who had been employed in a Pune defense laboratory, Kanshi Ram had resigned his job in 1964 following a dispute over caste issues. This incident and his discovery of Ambedkar led him to dedicate his life to the movement; but he found the Republican party, for which he worked for seven years, too co-opted and ineffectual, and the later Dalit Panthers too emotional, to suit him. He had his own ideas about how to organize.

The main theme, as with Rajshekhar, was to take brahmanism as the main contradiction and to build an alliance of dalits, minorities, and "backward castes." This meant *not* falling in with the leadership of political parties, left or right; the "alliance of the oppressed and exploited" must be independent. Kanshi Ram planned to build it by first organizing government employees to create resources for later agitational and political work, and in 1976 he formed the Backward and Minority Communities Employees Federation (BAMCEF). In 1978 a growing BAMCEF was holding its convention in Nagpur, but Kanshi Ram refused to take part in the agitation to rename Marathwada University, arguing that upper castes were using dalit emotions on the issue. "Who led the Long March?" he inquired in his journal. His answer: "The Poona Brahman" (the socialists) were using dalits to fight "the Delhi Brahman" (the Congress party). "We claim that BAMCEF should become the brain-bank of the oppressed and exploited society. In that case it must lead, not be led. In any case it must not be misled. . . . BAMCEF, therefore, must not be deterred by the momentary displeasure of our own people. This is more so today, when we are convinced that Ambedkarism is being destroyed in the name of Ambedkar, especially when our own people have taken to stooging in a big way." [23]

If this was similar to the line of Rajshekhar, Kanshi Ram was no intellectual but a hard-working and persevering organizer, touring India's villages and small towns under arduous conditions, mobilizing bicycle campaigns, and building up a solid and well-financed organization. His first major offshoot of BAMCEF was organized on September 24, 1982, as the Dalit-Shoshit Sangarsh Samiti, better known in its short form as DS-4. In the same year it put up candidates for elections in Haryana. With its most solid base among the chamars of north India, the single biggest dalit caste in the country, campaigns were carried out everywhere, and Kanshi Ram's organizations became successful in involving minorities and backward castes as well as dalits. He ignored economic questions entirely and focused on building up a caste alliance as expressed by the slogan "Brahman, bania, thakur cor; baki sad DS-4" (Brahmans, banias and thakurs are thieves, all the rest are with us). The goal? To take political power, Kanshi Ram's one-point program. "Why should we make alliances with any party? We ourselves represent 85 percent of the population, we are the majority," was the way his Delhi office secretary put it. DS-4, later transformed into the Bahujan Samaj party, went on to become the most successful of dalit-based political parties, with its strongest base in northwest India, where it came to play a major role in challenging Congress hold among the lower castes, but with some networks and support throughout the country.

Very different from Kanshi Ram was Sharad Patil of Maharashtra, maratha-kunbi by caste, and an activist of the Communist tradition who forcefully put forward the necessity of combining "class and caste struggle." In contrast to Kanshi Ram he was a vigorous participant in the movement to rename Marathwada University. But like Kanshi Ram and Rajshekhar, Patil argued that "caste struggle" required an alliance of dalits and shudras against brahmanism.

Patil had been a district organizer of the CPI(M), working in Dhule district of Maharashtra mainly among tribals. He had had disputes with the party leadership from the beginning, and in the 1970s he took time out from organizing to learn Sanskrit in Baroda, engage in a study of ancient Indian texts, and write a two-volume historical work entitled *Dāsa-Sudra Slavery*. Published in both Marathi and English, this was an interpretation of ancient Indian society that argued that caste (first varna and then jati) was the major material reality and unit of exploitation. Patil interpreted this to mean that Marxism, the theory of "class struggle," was insufficient to analyze Indian society and so must be combined with the thought of Phule and Ambedkar, who had produced a theory of "caste struggle." Since British colonialism had brought classes into existence, the current reality was a mixed "class-caste," one that therefore required a theory of "Marxism-Phule-Ambedkarism."

Patil was not the first to use such a hybrid (a Nagpur group had formed an organization in 1970 called Phule-Ambedkar-Marx or FUAMMA), but he gave it a vigorous theoretical and organizational articulation. By 1978 he had broken with the CPI(M) to form his own political party, the Satyashodhak Communist party (named after Jotiba Phule's Satyashodhak Samaj). His mass base remained that of tribals in two talukas of Dhule district, but he won a wide audience throughout Maharashtra, and his series of popular lectures in villages and towns throughout the state on characters from the India epics (Sita, Draupadi, Karna, Vidura, etc.) played a role in shaping a rural historical-materialist consciousness.

Regarding the strategy of an anticaste movement, Patil argued not only that the correlation between *jati* and occupation meant that caste remained a major material base of exploitation in the postindependence era, but also that an alliance of dalits and OBCs, especially the peasant castes, was crucial. Charging that those who thought the fundamental contradiction was now between dalits and shudra rich farmers were falling prey to the "propaganda of the Brahmanical caste-class establishment," he argued that "the way to the correct resolution of the basic conflict in Indian society" was a political economy that could link the economic exploitation of peasants, dalits, and adivasis with the caste system:

> Deficit financing and inflation have doubled in a year and the resulting precipitate and disproportionate fall in the prices of agricultural produce is already bringing vast masses of the peasant castes/classes into a national conflict with the present Indian state ... [the kernel of the struggle] is caste annihilation. The new political economy will steer the impending struggles of the restive peasant castes/classes clear of caste war with the ST/SC and towards lasting unity with the latter masses which alone is the guarantee of the destruction of this age-old order and thus pave the way for the Indian socialist revolution.[24]

Thus, by the end of the 1970s, from the vantage point of both the left (Sharad Patil) and the dalit movement (Kanshi Ram), efforts to argue for and organize an autonomous alliance of dalits and the middle caste shudra peasantry were gaining new force.

The Mandal Commission and the Reservation Issue

While dalits were mobilizing to fight their immediate oppressors and debating the possibility of taking some of them as allies in a broader anticaste struggle against "brahmanism" and for (as Sharad Patil would put it) the "democratic revolution," a major government report was submitted to parliament in 1980 that was to create some of the objective conditions for such an alliance. This was the report of the Mandal Commission, which recommended reservations (quotas) in government service for "socially and economically backward classes," more popularly known as OBCs or just BCs, that is, the vast shudra category.

What was at stake in the reservation issue was not a small matter. Reservations already existed, by constitutional right, for dalits ("Scheduled Castes" in official terminology) and tribals ("Scheduled Tribes") according to their proportion in the population, roughly 15.5 percent and 7 percent. What the Mandal Commission proposed was additional reservations for the OBCs, which it estimated at 52 percent of the total Indian population; however, only 27 percent of jobs could be reserved since total reservations, according to a Supreme Court decisions, should not exceed 50 percent.

Even so, this was a significant jump. Further, even though employment in government service could benefit only a minority of any caste and thus could not solve the basic problem of poverty, still it would substantially shatter the monopoly that upper castes continued to hold. The Mandal Commission had estimated that the 25.5 percent "forward castes" (mainly the three upper caste groups of brahman, rajputs and vaishya status or those that Kanshi Ram had called the "brahman-bania-thakur" combine, plus a few smaller upper castes, plus the estimated upper sections of religious minorities) held 69 percent of all government jobs and 90 percent of Class I positions. "Backward Castes," though comprising 52 percent of the population, were lower in all categories than the Scheduled Castes and Scheduled Tribes (see table 3.3, p. 55). Independent estimates confirmed this caste monopoly,[25] and a threat to it clearly had tremendous implications.

It is not surprising, then, that there was substantial resistance to extending reservations, and that opinion on the issue overwhelmingly followed caste lines. Reservations had been a common demand of dalits and nonbrahmans before independence and had been implemented by British regimes and some princely states in South and West India. But elite opinion, mobilized in the Congress, opposed them. At the time of independence, only a strong dalit movement and the physical presence of Ambedkar in chairing the committee writing the Indian constitution had made reservations statutory for Scheduled Castes and Scheduled Tribes. For the rest, the Indian elite tried to ignore the issue (one of the scholars of the "backward classes" notes "Nehru's extra-ordinary reticence about using the word 'caste' "[26]), and the constitutional clause under which reservations were justified for shudras did not talk of "castes" at all but of "backward *classes*," making it necessary for all subsequent commissions to justify the inclusion of various castes by data showing them to be "socially and educationally backward." The fact that the census did not take caste data after 1941, the inherent ambiguities in pinpoint specific castes, left ample ground for challenging any data on these issues.

The newly independent Indian government made no move to implement reservations for the "backward" and instead struck down some of the programs that had existed in the southern states. The first Planning Commission estimated the "backward" as only about 20 percent of the total population; a subsequent Back-

Table 3.4
Incidences of Untouchability

State	Total villages surveyed	Village wells prohibited	Temple entry prohibited	Hotel entry prohibited
Andhra Pradesh	60	17	17	14
Gujarat	141	89	130	126
Karnataka	100	100	100	100
Kerala	68	68	68	68
Maharashtra	61	29	26	4
Madhya Pradesh	199	92	95	95
Orissa	50	50	50	50
Haryana	44	7	23	—
Rajasthan	75	61	63	—
Tamilnau	148	115	136	36
Madurai district	72	72	72	—
Uttar Pradesh	170	55	78	113
Himachal Pradesh	51	—	51	51

Source: Sharad Patil, "Should 'Class' Be the Basis for Defining Backwardness?" *Economic and Political Weekly,* December 15, 1990.

ward Classes Commission estimated 32 percent as "backward classes," but was marked by strong controversy and the eventual resignation of its Gandhian brahman chairman, Kaka Kalelkar. With Kalelkar's last letter protesting the very principles of reservation, this gave the government an excuse to do nothing. Then in 1962 the Supreme Court struck down more state-level reservation programs with the order that the criteria for reserving posts should be "economic" and not in terms of caste. Renowned sociologists like M. N. Srinivas (a Karnataka brahman) joined their voices to what Galantar calls the "campaign for economic criteria," stressing the harmfulness of politically dealing with caste, and coming near to saying that it was "class" instead that was the major Indian reality (contrary to much of their sociological work). Thus in the 1960s, the avowed ideal of creating a "classless and casteless" society in India became interpreted in terms of *ignoring* caste rather than finding ways of abolishing it.

The upper castes were, in effect, doing a concerted public relations campaign on the reservation issue, and once having stalled the extension of reservations to the shudra castes, they then tried to keep these same castes in their fold with the propaganda that reservations were for dalits, that they were the source of unemployment of the caste Hindus, and that the government was unnecessarily pampering the dalits (they were "dalit brahmans," "sons-in-law" of the government, and so on). A large part of the dalit middle-caste tension in the 1970s was due to the success of this strategy, to the anger fueled in the minds of also poor, disdained low and middle castes that dalits were being favored by reservations.

But the issue of "backward caste" reservations would not go away. In 1972 two Congress state governments appointed new commissions, the Baxi Commission in Gujarat, which recommended 10 percent reservations for Backward Classes along with 14 percent for Scheduled Tribes and 7 percent for Scheduled Castes, and the Havanur Commission in Karnataka, which recommended reservations for nearly all nonbrahmans. The storm that was beginning to rise against these was stalled by the Emergency, but then the "restoration of democracy" brought to power at the center the Janata party with its substantial component of backward caste, peasant-based North Indian political formations with their Lohiaite heritage of promising reservations for shudras as well as dalits.

In 1977 this government appointed a new Backward Classes Commission at the national level, this time chaired by a "backward caste" man—B. P. Mandal, a yadav from Bihar. At about the same time in the turbulent state of Bihar the new chief minister, Karpoori Thakur, a tailor by caste, announced the extension of reservations, with 25 percent of government jobs for BCs plus the 24 percent that existed for SCs and STs. Widespread rioting followed as upper castes sought to maintain their power against the threat of the once-despised shudra castes.

Then in 1981 the Gujarat government announced the implementation of the reservations of the Baxi Commission. Massive attacks on dalits began, with agitations initiated by a medical students' strike accompanied by garlanding of Gandhi's statues and emotional propaganda about the effects of being operated on by incompetent dalit doctors. The strike turned into gangster-type attacks on dalits in the cities and dominant caste onslaughts in the villages of north Gujarat. The working class was split: dalit workers went on strike one day, and on the next caste Hindu workers struck in protest, and this was in the very heart of the labor union founded by Gandhi himself! In fact, the reservation riots were striking at the very moral heart of "Gandhian" Gujarat. It is noteworthy that of all the Gandhian social workers of the state, the only one to stand up solidly for dalits was Ela Bhatt, the socialist labor leader who had founded the Self-Employed Women's Association (SEWA). The riots were a massive refutation of Gandhian paternalism, and they were followed by the formation of the Gujarat Dalit Panthers and large-scale conversion to Buddhism. Gujarat dalits began rejecting their "harijan" identity, and Rajshekar's *Dalit Voice* "congratulated Gujarat dalits on winning the caste war."

Initially, though, it hardly appeared a victory. Progressives were depressed by the evidence of another large-scale conflagration involving caste conflict among the poor. Reservations seemed stalled. The Mandal Commission submitted its report in 1980, but by that time a Congress government was back in power, and it stalled, shelving the recommendations of the report. After attempts to launch agitations had fizzled out, Kanshi Ram's *Oppressed Indian* lamented that "Nowhere, not even in the capital, the strength, tactics and statesmanship of the leaders of the backwards could make any efforts to impress authorities or inspire the masses." [27]

Yet the issue had been raised again, and it is striking that the recommendations of the Mandal Commission justified reservations not simply for economic gain or social status, but in terms of the necessity of political power—just as the Dalit Panthers, the Bihar Naxalites, Kanshi Ram's Bahujan Samaj party had all argued, in different forms, for the centrality of power. According to the commission, "In a democratic setup every individual and community have a legitimate right and aspiration to participate in ruling this country. Any situation which results in a near-denial of this right to nearly 52 percent of the country's population needs to be urgently rectified." [28]

"India Shall Become Dalitistan"

The Gujarat riots illustrated a great irony: though the issue was the extension of reservations to backward castes, it was *dalits* who were attacked, with the backward sometimes even participating in attacks. The middle castes were, for the most part, still unconscious of the fact that their own rights were involved, whereas dalits were steadily getting more politicized and militant, aware that if the upper castes won on the issue of "backward" reservations they would try to end the ST and SC reservations as well.

They had at first few political and intellectual allies. In Gujarat as elsewhere, the overwhelming weight of "progressive" and "left" opinion was against caste-based reservations. By the 1970s no one could attack reservations for dalits and maintain a progressive image, but the "backward castes" were said to represent, after all, the rich peasants and other wealthy oppressors of dalits. Arun Sinha, the Naxalite-sympathizing journalist of Bihar, reflected this in a sarcastic description of a backward caste march said to comprise the same groups who were in the "landlords' armies" attacking dalits in the rural areas. Backward caste reservations, he charged, were a ruling class ploy for "advancing class interests in the name of caste." [29] In Bengal the Left Front government refused to co-operate with the Mandal Commission, saying that there was no issue of caste in Bengal, only "economic backwardness." In Gujarat the Gandhian scholar I. P. Desai, famous for his studies of tribals, argued for economic criteria and became the adviser of a new backward caste commission set up by the chief minister in the aftermath of the riots. Ruth Glass, writing in *Frontier* and *Monthly Review*, reflected the consensus of the left establishment that reservations had done nothing even for dalits themselves except give birth to a small, co-opted middle class: "The institution of protective discrimination has not brought the downtrodden peoples of India closer together; nor has it reduced the disparities between them. Quite the reverse. It is essentially a conservative and divisive institution." [30] Glass thus saw Gujarat as "divided and degraded" not by casteism but by the efforts to overcome caste.

Yet, in spite of the left intellectuals, reservations and the Mandal Commission report were factors that operated slowly and steadily over time to reunite dalits and the shudra castes, particularly as the poor caste Hindus got it into their heads that reservations were *their* issue. Mobilization—demonstrations, one-day satyagraha campaigns, rallies, local conferences, even "gate-meetings" in front of factories—began to be held from the late 1970s on the issue. The backward castes were slowly getting detached from the upper castes, and in spite of intellectual protests on one hand and violence on the other, reservations were inexorably getting extended.

Some of the complications of this process could be seen in a second phase of the antireservation riots in Gujarat in February–May 1985. The Rane Commission, appointed by Chief Minister Solanki after the first riots, had recommended increasing reservations for the backward castes, from the 10 percent of the Baxi Commission to 28 percent. To be sure, the Rane Commission followed the advice of its intellectual advisers in recommending that these be given on an economic, not caste, basis, but Solanki simply ignored this latter clause and proposed to implement the Rane Commission quota with the Baxi Commission list of castes! Again there was extended and vicious rioting, but this time the backward castes remained aloof and, in the end, even turned against the upper castes in the form of attacks by the police (who were heavily backward caste) on high caste urban areas and on a popular brahman-controlled newspaper.[31] This new backward-forward split was followed by what may be described as an engineered diversion of the issue into Hindu-Muslim rioting. The elite was attempting to maintain its hold over a fractured Hindu community by emphasizing religious differences.

Nevertheless, the broad trend since independence had been of the slow extension, in the face of upper caste resistance and rioting, of both the numbers of castes to get reservations and the percentage of jobs to be reserved for them. At the same time, bridges were getting built to the left, in spite of its traditional resistance to dealing with caste. Some Marxists, mostly from the ranks of the Naxalites, were beginning to defend reservations: "Struggle against casteism simply means standing by the side of the oppressed castes in their bid to end caste oppression, and this is the watershed between progress and reaction on this burning question, and this struggle must have as its demand overdoing the compensations for the accumulated age-old effects of varnashrama."[32]

Gradually the debates of a decade on "class and caste" were having an effect, and a broad anticaste unity was slowly becoming a reality. At an Inequality Eradication Conference in 1985 in Maharashtra, a socialist platform to bring together issues of dalits, tribals, women, and related concerns, Dalit Panther leader Arun Kamble could say, "We don't want Dalitistan as a separate country. We are 85 percent—we are the majority—India shall become Dalitistan!"

Conclusion

The anticaste movement had been nurtured in the nineteenth century with Jotiba Phule's Satyashodhak movement and organized with vigor after 1917, both in the form of nonbrahman parties and movements in West and South India and in dalit movements scattered throughout the country, but merging under the leadership of B. R. Ambedkar in the 1940s. In the 1970, after the failure of the independent Indian state to eradicate caste hierarchies and untouchability, or even to mitigate very much the oppressions of caste for millions throughout the country, it rose again, spearheaded by the birth of the Dalit Panthers. This time it took shape first as a *dalit movement*, in which organizations of ex-untouchables, expressing their identity as *dalit* or "downtrodden," fought their immediate village oppressors on one hand and "brahmanism" on the other, forcefully rejecting Hindu gods, myths, and values. The 1970s saw dalits posed against caste Hindus as a whole, and very often against the shudra middle and low castes out of whose ranks (except for North India) came the rich farmers and political leaders at the village and even state level. But dalit leaders themselves began to argue that their "main contradiction" was with brahmanism, which should be fought in alliance with low and middle nonbrahman castes, along with peasants and workers generally. They projected a broad *anticaste* movement. From 1980 this alliance began to take shape in processes of unity with the left and the new farmers' movement; one major form was in struggles to implement reservations in public service to "other backward castes."

The dalit and anticaste movement emerged on a firm ideology of autonomy, hostile to upper-caste leadership even when embodied in progressive political parties. (The main exception here were the dalit-based Naxalite movements in Bihar and Andhra, but these were not considered as "dalit movements" by the organizers, and dalits have also been ambivalent about accepting them as such). The dalits' symbolic rejection of compromise with Hindu society was embodied in their refusal of the "harijan" identity imposed by Gandhi, a rejection that succeeded in becoming hegemonic by the late 1980s (expressed in journalistic and state-level political decisions to use the term "dalit" rather than "harijan") in spite of the fact that most upper-caste progressives, including Communists, continued for a long time to use the Gandhian term.

Theoretically, the movement brought forward the question of a combined analysis of "caste and class." As a result of the movements, the debates, and the caste-shaped violence of the 1970s, Marxist "class analysis" would never be the same again, and the slogan "Will the green revolution turn into a red one?" was replaced by that of "Will the caste war turn into a class war?" As Marxist writers insisted that the "caste war" was already in reality a "class war" under different "forms," dalits and their theorists rejected this "form-content" approach to argue that a "caste war" *by itself* was progressive.

However, the "class-caste" debates often ended with a sterile additive analysis rather than a genuine synthesis. One problem is that while dalits claimed that their movement was against the system as such, not just for "reforms," they did not economically conceptualize the system in a different way. They did not challenge orthodox left economic theories. Thus, in spite of other aspects of economic liberalism, Ambedkar himself had argued for "state socialism," including the model of industrialization, large-scale agriculture, and public planning. Mandal's report, in turn, reiterated the need to change "exploitative relations of production," but simply characterized this in terms of land reforms without dealing with exploitation in industry or in the relation between agriculture and industry. Kanshi Ram's organizations tended to avoid economic issues altogether or else reproduced leftist analysis in changed language attacking "brahmans/banias/ksatriyas" as equivalent to bureaucracy/capitalism/feudalism. Dalit activists also raised no questions about the traditional organizational forms of party and state. One major consequence of this was the neglect of one important base of upper-caste (especially brahman) power and wealth, the state machinery itself.

Nevertheless, the movement embodied two crucial contributions. First, in focusing on the question of identity, it raised the possibility and the necessity of creating alternate symbols of community for the Indian subcontinent as a whole: not Rama but Shambuk, Ravana, and the rakshasas were heroes, not Arjun but Ekalavya. This helped in showing the way to other social movements to move toward a broad rethinking of the nature of "India" itself.

Finally, dalits and low castes set their sights on state power, rejecting "benefits" handed down paternalistically from above, insisting that the downtrodden, marginalized, and excluded must themselves become a part of the ruling class. Some put this in terms of parliamentary power, some in terms of access to the state bureaucracy, some in terms of armed struggle and "smashing the state," but the underlying drive was common—an insistence on power, on challenging the heights, on laying claim to all that the promises of "modernity" could offer, a refusal to stay any longer "outside the village," or in any way outside the best of what not only Indian but world society had to offer. Dalits, the most marginalized section of one of the poorest countries in the world, laid claim to the heritage of the ages and insisted on their right to be part of the process of carrying it forward.

4

The Women's Movement

"For a Mouthful of Water I Wander the Land"

THE YEAR 1973, a tribal village in Dhule district of northern Maharashtra. Here, activists associated with a "new Marxist" organization in the state called Magowa had been working for two years. Women's participation in struggles to win land and wages had been enthusiastic, and for the first time they decided to organize a women's *shibir* or training camp. As one activist described their experience:

> We expected 25 women—but 125 came. We sat and discussed many things. The issue of drunkenness came up. One by one the women stood up and talked about their husbands' drinking, about wife-beating. "It hurts the family, it hurts the organization. Drunken men don't organize!" Finally one woman said, "My village is only a few miles away—I know where all the liquor shops are. Why don't we go there and destroy all their liquor?" We activists were astounded. After all, it was nighttime. But the women wanted action. So we marched to the village, stormed the huts of the liquor-sellers, poured the liquor on the ground. The women were wildly enthusiastic and marched back in triumph.

Magowa means "follow after, search out critically," and the group leaders, who had written in 1971 in the first issue of their magazine that "We will examine everything, even Marxism itself, under a microscope," were ready from this experience at least to begin to think about the coming new ideas of "women's liberation." Several months later their magazine published what was the first "women's liberation special issue" in India, its cover a collage of a middle-class housewife, a beauty queen, a nightclub singer, a group of poor peasant women, and a militant demonstration, together expressing the varied facets of women's oppression in India.

The new women's movement in India had its beginnings in 1972–73, the same time as the dalit movement and pioneering organizations of other new movements. It had the same dialectic of a rural and toiling people's base and the interaction of middle-class urban intellectuals—a dialectic with new energies, new themes, new forms of struggle.

The rural base was crucial. In Maharashtra, which was to become a center of much of the new activity, these were years of drought, and poor peasant women were at the forefront of antidrought struggles everywhere; they were even, it was said, the initiators of road-blocking actions that were later to become so prominent as a form of protest in peasant movements. The experience of drought and the struggles against it were so crucial to women's consciousness that they became themes of many of the later songs of the women's movement—songs that marked the hunger of those who fed others, that described wandering through parched fields in search of work, that described the toil and thirst of the women who helped build dams:

> What shall I say of the heat's ferocity?
> Like a stonecrusher it shatters me.
> I bind my feet with rags,
> Woman, I'm building a dam—
> The sugarcane waves
> In your teeming fields,
> For a mouthful of water I wander the land.[1]

Yet the struggles of rural women did not immediately give birth to a new movement on women's oppression. There was no simple, one-way process. There were links, but there was also a strong alienation between rural toilers and the upper-middle class. The links were complex, mediated by political organizations, different experiences, prejudices, and misconceptions. Rural and toiling women's struggles occurred in many places, but they did not always yield a feminist articulation.

For example, tribal women had been at the forefront of the Naxalite revolt itself, the first to charge the police—but women's issues played no ideological role in the formulation of the "antifeudal revolution." Similarly, 1972–74 was a period that saw the emergence of the Chipko movement in the Himalayan foothills, when peasants "hugged" trees to prevent loggers from cutting them down. Women were prominent in the actions of this most famous Indian environmental movement, and Chipko itself was later to be publicized as a "women's movement," but only in the 1980s; at the time it was not thought of in this way, and no communication existed between the Himalayan peasant women and the networks of women activists that were forming in cities like Bombay or Delhi.

Communists, who had the most militant working-class organizing and were most sensitive generally to issues of exploitation, might have been ones to provide such linkages, but they did not do so. Take the example of the CPI(M). In

1968, women and children had been the main victims of the "Kilvenmani atrocity" when landlords and their henchmen burned down huts of dalit agricultural laborers in Thanjavur district of Kerala, a major crisis for a militant agricultural laborer movement in this rice-growing delta region and a symbol to all of India of increasing caste conflict and atrocities. Six years later the first state conference of the Democratic Women's Association was held in Kilvenmani itself. Yet no specifically women's issue was taken up. It was a period when, throughout West Bengal, Andhra, and Tamilnadu, CPI(M) women were leading their "Democratic Women's Association" through conferences, demonstrations, and hunger strikes that rallied large numbers of women to oppose rising prices. In Bombay, socialist and Communist women united in a new Women's Anti-Price-Rise Front with the *latna* or rolling pin as its symbol and held *thali* (empty plate) marches in which women beat their steel plates eerily and rhythmically.[2] Again, these women's anti-price-rise movements involved little mention of other women's issues; the Democratic Women's Association stressed only the demand for work and for equal wages, and in its 1974 West Bengal conference, the resolution on the International Women's Year clarified that "women's emancipation could be fully established only under socialism and the struggle for equality must be linked to the struggle for a new socialist order."[3]

Marxist preconceptions made CPI(M) activists wary of "bourgeois feminism" and led them to focus on "work" issues, narrowly interpreted as wage work, along with an insistence that women must "join the broader struggle" for socialism. Socialist women also tended to accept this line, although their organizational heritage from the freedom movement period had more of an element of personal-life radicalism in it and even antifamily strains coming out here and there in old Gandhians. The Self-Employed Women's Association (SEWA), an Ahmedabad working women's organization linked to the Gandhian-led trade union in Gujarat, was itself founded in 1972 and was at the forefront of organizing women petty venders of all types. But it did not give birth to organizing on other issues of women's oppression. Working women themselves were very often strongly feminist, even "antimen"; they suffered under a multitude of oppressions, but the "nonclass" issues of their lives were not automatically articulated by their left organizers.

At the same time, there were reasons why the new women's movement would remain dependent on the traditional left, even while it emerged with a challenge to it. This dependence had a material and structural base.

All the new social movements were, like the women's movement, organized around a dialectic of a mainly rural poor peasant or working-class base and middle-class intellectuals who provided articulation and leadership. But there were differences. Poor toiling women were not, like dalits or members of oppressed nationalities, a separate community that could simply affirm its existence; they were caught up themselves in different castes, classes, and communities. This meant that their exploitation was, in the words of later feminists, both "specific" and "simultaneous."[4] That is, they were exploited both as women and as dalits, tribals, peasants, and workers. At the same time, the women—middle-class, upper-caste, urban—who articulated the exploitation of women and the need for liberation were much further removed from the actual lives of the rural poor than was the case with dalit or peasant movement intellectuals. The poets, writers, and young employees who founded the Dalit Panthers and led similar organizations throughout the country were not themselves workers or poor peasants, but they were normally the first educated generation. Their parents had been poor, and even if they themselves were caught up in alienating processes and institutions, they were close enough to the edge of poverty to know they were being alienated. This was not true in the women's movement. Not only were rural poor peasant women often voiceless themselves, but the educated or half-educated "cadre" springing directly from their ranks was missing. Women's education was, to begin with, less than that of men (see table 4.2, p. 90); it was the boy from the dalit or poor peasant family who was likely to get educated, more rarely his sister. If she did get educated, she was quickly married off, and once married was buried in her in-laws' home just as effectively as her uneducated sister. Young unmarried girls and new daughters-in-law simply did not wander the village as boys of their age did; they were unable to go out of the home for meetings.

The reason, of course, had to do with the sexual terrorism faced by women:

> I am a girl studying in ninth standard in the rural areas. I have to travel by bus every day to go to school. Some loud-mouthed boys always make bad remarks seeing me alone at the bus stand. The conductor deliberately touches me when giving the ticket. A man as old as my father nudges me and touches my foot when I sit. The driver stares at me through the mirror. When I get out of the bus the rickshaw drivers honk their horns. The older boys in my class whistle. The teacher is good but I don't even dare to look at him. My father is an agricultural laborer. If I told him this he would make me leave school; he wouldn't even keep me at home, he would get me married. I want to study so much. I want to grow up. But from reading what comes in the papers every day I feel so afraid. You please do something so that girls can get protection.[5]

This was a letter from a fourteen-year-old girl in a developed part of rural India, but it told the story of how a conventional patriarchal society put pressures on women everywhere. The result was that it was women activists of an older generation or of a much higher socioeconomic status who ended up articulating the issues of "women's liberation." They themselves were of course oppressed; they had from the beginning a strong identification with the problems of working women, but nevertheless there was a gap, and it had its consequences in the limitations of their perceptions and programs.

It was a gap that could be seen even in the new women's liberation songs. They often sang of "going to the women of this country," much in the way the high-caste Nehru had written of his "discovery of India"—of coming to the women from outside; they exhorted women to "join the struggles of the toilers" as if they were talking to nontoiling women. Many of the songs written by male organizers had much more of a "bottom" perspective. Whether it was a socialist organizer writing in the national movement days ("we are working women, we are peasant women . . . the world of looters will fall at our feet"), a Marxist orphan-poet describing peasant women's life ("my field in the hills, how long do I go on weeding it?"), or one of the new dalit writers like Daya Pawar writing of water and building dams, these poets wrote more instinctively of the hard life of rural women, of the burning sun and barren soil, and their songs more quickly became "ours" to the women. The fact was that the women's movement remained dependent on the left or on mass movements and on their male organizers because they were usually closer to the lives of rural and urban working women. The traditional left, at least, was for a long time resistant to the challenge of feminism. Nevertheless, feminist themes were beginning to come through.

"This Is the Challenge of Women's Liberation"

With the women's liberation movement growing in the West and with new ideas spreading, the narrowly defined "work" focus of traditional Marxist organizing was coming under challenge, both from within and from without. CPI(M) senior women leaders like Godutai Parulekar could write major articles on women but were likely to get challenged for dogmatism by the equally senior Durga Bhagwat, drawing themes from feminism.[6] In groups like Magowa, with its openness to much of "new left" thinking, male activists might continue to maintain the traditional insistence that only "working-class women" were exploited, but women in the group now had arguments to challenge them with. In Naxalite circles, this process was aided by the Maoist language of "contradictions" and by a sensitivity to cultural or "superstructural" issues.

In Hyderabad, this resulted in girls connected with the Naxalite movement organizing themselves into the Progressive Organization of Women, or POW. The resemblance to NOW and the militancy of the English acronym was probably not accidental. POW activists became involved both in working with slum women on anti-price-rise issues and in organizing Hyderabad college girls against harassment. Their manifesto, published in 1974, began with a kind of traditional juxtaposition: "To people who talk of Sita and Savriti we talk of harsh, depressing reality," but their analysis of this reality included not only poverty but "feudal culture" and "male supremacy" and gave equal weight to "the ideology of oppression," "economic dependence," and "household drudgery" as pillars of the oppression of women. While it treated cultural and family factors as "superstructural," it also argued that all women, not only working women, were oppressed.[7] Its representative could claim in a Bombay meeting, while stressing the fight for socialism in Marxist-Leninist terms, that a separate organization for women was necessary because "we have to accept that there is a contradiction between men and women."

This was a new note. It drew from the turmoil of the times, when the liberation themes of the Western women's movement could intermingle with the image, drawn from Asian and African national liberation struggles, of "women with guns," women leaving their homes and domestic responsibilities to fight for their people, an image that gave courage to young women to defy conventional family restrictions and brave the dangers of the gangsters outside the home. But it also drew sustenance from the rawer lives of working-class and rural women: there is a story that once, when CPI(M) women organizers were talking to a crowd of Delhi working-class women, in beginning with the familiar "some people say that women's liberation means fighting men but," they were interrupted with a round of applause before they were able to follow with their disclaimer that "we are not against men." It is clear that lower-class women, while inclined to side with their men in the end, were also quite ready, at times, to fight them and to express their "nonantagonistic contradictions" in quite strong language. In homes and on the roads, men were quite often experienced and dealt with by these women as immediate oppressors from whom they wanted some relief. In the early 1970s this sense of a need for "liberation" and of a "patriarchal" power to be fought was beginning to be articulated on the left.

Finally, important national-level legitimacy was provided when the official Status of Women Commission, headed by Veena Mazumdar, issued its report in 1974. *Towards Equality* was in many ways a remarkable document. It was dryly written; there was little mention of the "atrocities"—dowry deaths, rapes, violence—that were to become a central preoccupation of the new movement, and women's work was treated mainly in terms of wage labor, neglecting along with the Marxist left the question of unpaid domestic work or subsistence agricultural work. But its elaborate and official documentation of women's low and even declining status was to provide powerful legitimacy to women's organizing, and there was even a debate, in the section of political representation, on whether reservations should be recommended for women in parliamentary bodies (this was rejected by the majority, but 30 percent reservation was strongly recommended by a few—the very proportion that would be implemented fifteen years later).[8]

It was on this background that the organizing of 1975, International Women's Year, took place, dominated by traditional left assumptions about women's work and the relation of the women's movement to the broader movement for socialism, but fueled by the energies of a rising assertion of rural and urban toiling women, and with the dissenting and subordinate themes of a new feminism finding a place.

The United Women's Liberation Struggle Conference, organized by a coalition in Pune in October, brought seven hundred women agricultural laborers, *hamals* or porters, tribals, teachers, students, bank employees, and professors together for two days to pass resolutions on issues ranging from clean drinking water and latrine facilities to Devadasis, dowry, housework, and a common civil code. It stressed the organizing of agricultural laborers and demanding employment for women: "Every woman should be able to participate in social production." And it featured the first songs of the new women's liberation movement, songs with a feminist touch but written by a young male activist, Madhav Chavan: "This is the call of women's liberation that reaches the skies! Reactionaries, exploiters, take heed that times are changing."

In Trivandrum, the CPI(M)-dominated School of Social Sciences organized a conference on women in December. In discussion groups, activists and academicians saw resolutions pushed through the groups and passed in final plenaries. Its focus was also on work: "Emancipation depends on participation in social production; therefore, the right to work should be incorporated in the Constitution and guaranteed for all citizens." (The "right to work" would be a common theme of the left for all movements throughout this period; for women it had the unrecognized difficulty of implying that their unpaid work was not *really* work and that subsistence production was not "social.") Its conclusion was that "Crucial to the emancipation of women and of all oppressed mankind is the struggle to liquidate landlordism, monopoly capitalism and all other forms of exploitation and their replacement by a democratic society leading to socialism." [9]

For both conferences, the focus on rural women was defracted through particular interpretations. For the Pune conference it meant organizing agricultural laborers; for the Trivandrum conference, abolishing landlordism. This reflected the rural "class analysis" of the dominating organizers. Neither gave consideration to the fact that demands for work and wages were (even in Marxist terms) within the framework of capitalism, nor that peasant women had no claim to land, nor that agricultural laborers had no rights even to the huts they lived in—that is, ownership of the means of production (property rights for women) and political power were issues beyond their frame of reference. Similarly, neither reflected issues such as drunkenness, which had so concerned the tribal women in Shahada; when some women at Trivandrum argued for an antialcohol movement, party activists rejected it on the grounds that it would "split the working class."

Nevertheless, there were some new critical notes. The Pune conference, for instance, had a resolution that "men should help with housework," reflecting a feminist thrust rather than the traditional left idea of "socializing housework." This resulted in some mocking items in the press. [10] When women objected, the journalists (none of whom were women) replied with the complaint that their reporters were not allowed in the meeting hall. This turning over of the entire meeting to women was a new step.

The Trivandrum conference's heavy-handed control and Marxist dogmatism also could not escape criticism from young, feminist-minded journalists. Criticizing a statement that "focus on women alone is a diversionary tactic" and the insistence that "women's problems cannot be seen in isolation from the problems of the entire exploited class," Olga Tellis wrote, "all this sounds like an industrialized version of the biblical creation of Eve from Adam's rib, where Eve had no identity except as part of Adam." Other reports were headlined "Marxist dogmas," and even the left *Economic and Political Weekly* reported the meeting as "Marxist cobwebs," with a call for a broader approach.[11]

Internally, five left dissidents submitted a statement that urged greater attention to the "family system" and the "relation of production to reproduction," stressed the need for women to organize separately as women, argued that "women's struggle against their own oppression in the home, community and workplace *is itself a struggle* for revolutionary transformation of society," and critiqued indirectly the subordination of women's organizations to the party.[12]

While ferment was developing in left circles, a thrust from anticaste movements was providing militancy and a strong cultural focus. *Janwedena* (Peoples' sufferings), a dalit-edited monthly from the district town of Nanded in Maharashtra, had a special issue leading off with "women hold up half the sky" and editorialized that it "is essential to change today's oppressive marriage system from the roots." In Aurangabad, another dalit movement center, young women formed a Mahila Samta Sainik Dal (League of Women Soldiers for Equality), named after an early Ambedkarite organization, with a polemical manifesto that rejected *pativrata*, condemned as "phony" the male attack on feminism of saying "freedom does not mean free sex," called Buddha the "first to free women from slavery," and concluded with a salute to Angela Davis and the vow that "we are battling for equality with men in the liberation war for human liberation called for by Dr. Ambedkar.[13] Both the Mahila Samta Sainik Dal and *Janwedena* were short-lived, and the dalit movement did not show any special imagination in helping their women to organize independently—but the undeniable similarity of the critiques of caste and the family and the dalit challenge to brahmanic culture were helping women sharpen their challenge to patriarchy in India.

The new women's movement developing after 1975 did so in a new atmosphere of cultural radicalism that had been absent for most of the preindependence movement women leaders, who had tended to insist on their own "Hindu" roots and to idealize the Vedic period. Instead, for the new movement, Rama, favorite god of Hindu orthodoxy, would symbolize the patriarchal male ready to cast his wife into the flames rather than accept a "dishonor" to his name. Instead of idealizing Sita's loyalty to her husband, as generations of middle- and upper-class women activists had done, a broad section ranging over both "feminist" and leftist circles was coming to question both Rama and religion itself.

"Let Us Examine the Whole Question":
Autonomous Women's Groups, 1977–80

"Today we no longer say—Give us more jobs, more rights, consider us your 'equals' or even 'allow us to compete with you better.' But rather—let us examine the whole question, all the questions. Let us take nothing for granted. Let us not only redefine ourselves, our role, our image—but also the kind of society we want to live in" (Manushi Editorial Collective, January 1979). This conclusion to the opening editorial of the new feminist magazine *Manushi* summed up the spirit of the late 1970s. The "internal critique" became a full-fledged one as small groups of Marxist women separated themselves and began to analyze women's oppression on their own. The period 1977–80 was the one in which the "autonomous women's movement" was born, and it produced the most vital theoretical initiatives of this section of the new women's movement.

During discussions after the Pune and Trivandrum conferences, three differing concepts of strategies for organizing women were put forward. Some stressed the force of rural women; others felt a beginning made among women students could produce "cadres" for later mass organizing. The more "traditionally Marxist"-influenced talked of the revolutionary centrality of factory workers, of proletarian women. These were to become most influential among the "autonomous feminist" circles. The groups that sprang up at the time were also varied in thrust, some of it shown in their names. The Purogami Stri Sanghatana (Progressive Women's Organization), formed in 1976 in Pune, remained a kind of coalition effort; the Stri Mukti Sanghatana (Women's Liberation Organization) in Bombay included women connected mainly with the Magowa group and the Lal Nishan party of Maharashtra; the Socialist Women's Group, also sometimes called the Feminist Network, formed in 1978 in Bombay, was at once more "autonomous" and more Trotskyist in its orientation and was made up of mainly non-Marathi speakers; the Stri Sangharsh (Women Struggle) (1979) was a short-lived feminist group in Delhi; the Stri Shakti Sanghatana (Women Power Organization), formed in 1978 in Hyderabad, was a much longer-lived organization that included some old members of the POW (which had dissolved during Emergency repression) and some new women. These organizations kept some relation and work with the urban working class, with textile workers and young chemical factory workers in Bombay, and with the strongly unionized dalit municipal workers in Pune, but the rural connection came to be lost as their contradictions with the left parties intensified.

Like earlier party women leaders, the older generation they argued against and defined themselves in opposition to, these young feminists were from middle-class or even upper-class and upper-caste background. In the expansive lawn-flanked bungalows of South Delhi, in the high-rises of Bombay ("tenth floor Marxism" was how some activists taunted the intellectual Marxists of that period), they met and debated. Some maintained their membership of left groups, some left, but all began to find new meaning in women's collectives. All continued to see society through traditional Marxist spectacles even when they began to add the "women question"—they saw "proletarian" women as the most revolutionary, they had a somewhat unreal picture of rural areas that saw nothing but marauding landlords persecuting landless laborers, they developed a romanticization of dalits and tribals that substituted for any real analysis of the caste system. Within this framework, they rebelled, asserting *patriarchy* as an additional fact of society, and began to focus on the problem of *violence*, to reexamine the nature of *work*, and to assert *autonomy* and *collectivity* as organizing principles against the party bureaucracies.

It was the Bombay middle-class feminists who, for at least a short time, played a leading theoretical role in the new women's movement.

Work

The issue of "housework" had been a subject for amusement in the comment on the Pune conference resolutions, and men's help with housework became as much an issue in urban left circles in India as in the West. On this background, feminists began to challenge the traditional notion ("traditional" not only to left activists but to the masses of women themselves) that "work" meant wage labor only. Long theoretical manuscripts began to be circulated in Bombay dealing with the role of "reproduction," questioning whether housework generated surplus value, questioning the idea that women had to "participate in social production" to become a part of a revolutionary movement. The Bombay-Delhi groups included women with Western connections, part of an international left, and some of the theoretical level was fairly high.

Two trends developed. The more Trotskyist Socialist Women's Group put forward a fairly conventional picture of women's labor under capitalism, one that ignored the continuing existence of the peasantry, reproducing the analysis of domestic labor current in Western Marxist circles as if only the bourgeoisie and proletarians existed: "In capitalist society, the family is totally atomized. It has the *appearance* of being a private sphere separate from social production. As a result, the functions of reproduction and the rearing of children, the maintenance of labor power in general, cooking, cleaning, etc., are relegated exclusively to the 'private' sphere of the family."[14]

The other trend drew on ideas of "subsistence production" being put forward by a group of German feminists. One of these, Maria Mies, had herself lived and worked in India, and Chhaya Datar—an ex-Magowa activist and a leading organizer of the 1975 Pune conference—spent a period in Holland at the Institute for International Studies where Mies was heading up a women's studies program. After returning, Datar began to develop these ideas for India, arguing that domestic labor was not simply "reproduction" but as *subsistence production* was the fundamental basis of all forms of capital accumulation. This theme, which stressed the "marginalization" of rural women and the "housewificization" of the middle class rather than "proletarianization" as the main form of exploitation, fit the Indian reality much better and had a wide appeal: a Hindi songbook published at the time illustrated the theme with a picture of a woman cooking at the base, on her back the factory worker, on his back the capitalist. The peasant was still missing in the imagery, but there were other women and men, outside the initial groups of feminists, ready to take up the theme.

Violence

From the "dowry deaths" that had sprung into consciousness in 1975 to the emergence of the rape issue in 1980 to the ongoing realities of wife-beating and harassment that were coming out in group discussions and public exposures, violence against women became a focus in India as much as elsewhere. In the "socialist/radical/liberal feminist" division that they took for granted, most Indian women activists identified themselves from the beginning with the "socialist feminist" trend, which gave impetus for a "work" focus. But there was always a lurking sympathy for Western radical feminists precisely because of the problem of violence. "The element of truth in this extreme form lies . . . in the protest against the sexual subjugation of women by rape and many other more subtle forms of violence which are at the root of other forms of women's oppression and explain why even economically independent women . . . not only keep and support their husbands but also bow to the traditional role and sexual division of labor in the house." So wrote Gabriele Dietrich in summing up a theoretical workshop in 1978. She added, "When we tried to define the overriding characteristic of women's oppression, our attention was more drawn to the aspect of physical subjugation and coercion than we had been aware of before." [15]

But few women were ready to go so far as to see violence "at the root" of patriarchal subjugation. The fact was that with no formal Marxist categories like "reproduction" available to handle violence, the practical preoccupation with it did not lead to a new theorization of violence in the same way that a theorization of "subsistence production" was beginning. Instead, while Marxist categories reigned at the mental level, in practice many urban women activists became preoccupied with violence in the family, with a tendency in practice to think of men as the enemy. "All men are potential rapists" was a sentiment that also began to be heard in Bombay in the early 1980s, and the practical definitions of patriarchy and women's exploitation used in the urban-based groups began to be used in the sense of the exploitation of women by men. [16]

Party

Trivandrum dissidents had raised the question of the parties' control over mass organizations and their habit of treating them simply as fronts to create party presence and party membership. In subsequent years it was on this question of "autonomy" that feminists of all kinds insisted most strongly. Against bureaucracy and hierarchy they began to proclaim nonstructured, democratically functioning small-group collectives as the ideal form of organization. They argued that the problem of the relationship of family/society and domestic labor/wage labor found its organizational parallel in the relationship between political struggle and social relations:

> Revolution is not *mere* seizure of state power, though it is also that. Revolution is the process of changing the social relations in society, revolutionizing them, abolishing the hierarchical structures and ideas between classes, sexes, groups, individuals. Thus revolutionary politics is not confined to the questions of the party, the state. Revolutionary politics *also* relates to questions of the relations in society, their direction of change, and a struggle to change these.[17]

These formulations were cautious, with "also" allowing a retention of much traditional left organizational ideas. But many women began to go farther. Chhaya Datar, for instance, came to critique heavily the assumption that the "women's movement must be part of the mainstream," that is, come under left party leadership in order to be "revolutionary," and to assert the meaning of "autonomy" as "autonomy from the state, autonomy from the party, and autonomy from the class." She wrote: "Feminism is contributing to revolutionize Marxism, and thus aspires to be another Copernican revolution, which will change not only androcentrism in the present theory but also change the entire theoretical perspective about human relationships and also about the relationship of human beings with the universe, with nature."[18]

With all the limitations of the debates of these years—the ignoring of caste, the tendency to reject all religion and traditional culture rather than look for alternatives, the ignoring of political power, the ignoring of the issue of sexuality, the tendency instead to see simply the oppression of women by men—the theoretical creativity was undeniable. A new feminist challenge was taking its place in the framework of Indian political and social life.

Expansion and Stagnation: 1980–85

In 1980 first the "Mathura rape case," then the "Maya Tyagi rape case," then the "Rameeza Bee" case in Hyderabad grabbed headlines everywhere. Mathura: a fifteen-year-old tribal girl raped by policemen after being called to the station at night; the police let off by a district court, convicted by the Bombay court, then let off again by the Supreme Court on the grounds that with no wounds on her body the girl must not have resisted: a typical case of the victimization of women and police atrocities—brought out years after the event by four progressive lawyers, it led to demonstrations all over the country demanding "justice for Mathura." Maya: an upper-caste Hindu raped and shamed by police in a northern India town; the resulting furor saw demonstrations and walkouts in the Indian

Table 4.1
Sex Ratio (Females per 1,000 males)

All India		By State	
Year	Sex Ratio	State	Sex Ratio
1901	972	Haryana	874
1911	964	Uttar Pradesh	882
1921	955	Punjab	888
1931	950	Bihar	912
1941	945	Rajasthan	913
1951	946	West Bengal	917
1961	941	Jammu-Kashmir	923
1971	930	Assam	925
1981	934	Madhya Pradesh	932
1991	929	Gujarat	936
		Maharashtra	936
		Karnataka	960
		Andhra	972
		Orissa	972
		Tamilnadu	972
		Himachal Pradesh	996
		Kerala	1,040

Source: Census of India, 1991, as reported in K. Nagaraj, "The 'Missing' Women," *Frontline*, May 25–June 7, 1991.

parliament. Rameeza: a Muslim woman raped by Hyderabad police, her husband killed: the result was rioting throughout the city and burning of police stations. Only a few years before "rape" had seemed too extreme to talk about; now it was a national-level issue.

The rape issue, the rising consciousness of "atrocities against women" in this period, led to an expansion of organization as well. Feminists, while doubtful of the way rape was often taken as an issue of community honor, organized themselves in Bombay as the Forum Against Rape, later to become the Forum Against Atrocities on Women (FAOW), and held a national conference in December, the first of a series in which "autonomous feminist" groups played a major role. Organizations were formed, one after another, in many other major cities. Two important new women's centers were established to provide help and genuine feminist counseling to women in distress—the Women's Center in Bombay and Saheli in Delhi.

Even more than the feminists, perhaps, party women expanded their activities. The CPI(M) finally decided to go national with an All-India Democratic Women's Association. Up to this time their Delhi work had gone on under the name of the "Working Women's Coordinating Committee," while some states had the "Toiling Women's Association" and others had "Democratic" women's groups. The official change represented a party-debated shift from the position that "only working class women are oppressed." The CPI, of course, already had its national women's organization, the National Federation of Indian Women (NFIW), as did the socialists. One of the Naxalite groups formed an official women's front with the Nari Mukti Santha (Women's Liberation Organization) of Assam, also in 1981. All of these expanded their activities geographically.

United fronts also began to be formed. In Maharashtra, a coordinating committee had been discussed after the Pune conference, with a good deal of debate about whether it should be called a "coordinating" or simply a "communications" committee. It was finally formed as the latter, the Stri Mukti Andolan Sampark Samiti, after a second state conference of many organizations in 1979. In Delhi, various party wings came together with feminist groups in the Dahej Virodhi Chetna Manch, or Anti-Dowry Consciousness-Raising Forum. In both platforms the "national organizations," that is, the big party-linked women's organizations, tended to dominate, often trying to exclude the feminists. In Maharashtra, the feminists and smaller rural-based groups fought this and won an "executive" that included representation from every women's organization and not just the "big" party-linked ones; the Sampark Samiti survived as a platform of troubled unity. In Delhi, though, this could not be done, and in the politically overheated atmosphere of the capital, without links to small town and rural organizations, a much wider gap developed between "feminists" and "party" women.

Women involved in nonparty mass organizations were also beginning to organize. In 1980 in the tribal area of Dhule district, women of the Shramik Sanghatana formed their own Shramik Stri Mukti Sanghatana (Toiling Women's Liberation Organization) quite spontaneously after a Muslim woman of the town came to them for help over a harassment case. This ended a long debate in which the male activists of the organization, connected with the "new left" Magowa group, had been continuously arguing that there was no need for a separate women's organization because "the Shramik Sanghatana itself takes up women's issues" and "you don't really want to have rich farmer women in the organization—only working women are really oppressed." In their rally, the adivasi women themselves proclaimed that "all women are exploited and should organize as women" and "even if a rich farmer's wife comes to us we'll help her!" These women had been exposed to "feminist" debates and to Bombay-Pune women since 1975, but there were no middle-class feminists to coach them at this time; it was on their own initiative that they began to form small teams of activists, going from village to village to take up cases of beatings and harassments, often confronting the tribal men themselves.

This was heartening; so was the formation, also in 1980, of a tribal and working-class women's organization, the Chattisgarh Mahila Mukti Morcha, associated with a radical mineworkers' and regional-nationalist organization in Madhya Pradesh. Women from this group attended the Bombay-organized "national conference" at the end of the year, though they were the only working-

Table 4.2
Literacy by Gender, Caste, and Rural/Urban

		Total	Male	Female
Scheduled caste	Total	21.38	31.12	10.93
	Rural	18.48	27.91	8.45
	Urban	36.60	47.54	24.34
Scheduled tribe	Total	16.36	24.52	8.04
	Rural	14.92	22.94	6.81
	Urban	37.93	47.60	27.32
All	Total	36.23	46.89	24.82
	Rural	29.65	40.79	17.96
	Urban	57.40	65.83	47.82

Source: Census of India, 1981, cited in Centre for Monitoring the Indian Economy, *Basic Statistics Relating to the Indian Economy, Volume I: All India* (Bombay: 1990), Table 1.6-B.

class women present. Another important step was the formation of independent organizations of slum women in the major cities of the South. Spearheading these were Penurimai Iyakkam, the Movement for Women's Rights, founded in 1979 in Madras and in 1984 in Madurai, and Women's Voice, working among Bangalore slum women in association with a mainly dalit organization from the same period.

But with all this organizational expansion, problems were also emerging. Many of the mass-based independent organizations proved to have only a sporadic existence. At the same time the creativity of the early years of feminism seemed to be damming up. A 1981 National Women's Studies Conference, also held in Bombay, saw an impressive turnout and a largely attended debate on "Marxism and feminism"—yet this seemed to be a last mutual exchange. Positions were hardening, and party women and "autonomous feminists" stopped talking *to* each other, and only went on talking *about* each other, with accusations of "bourgeois feminism," on one hand, and "bureaucracy" and "neglect of women's issues," on the other. As the party women began to organize and publish, they crystallized themselves ideologically around traditional positions such as Engels's interpretation of private property and the family, and some began to accuse the feminists not only of being "bourgeois" but of even having links with international conspiracies to alienate people from the left parties. The feminists, in turn, not only proclaimed their own "autonomy," but also began to think of themselves as apart from the left; a way developed of posing the issue itself—"our relations with the left"—that suggested their alienation.

But while "Marxists" and "feminists" were clarifying themselves as different ideological trends in the women's movement, in the field of action it was often hard to discern such differences. Both focused on the same issues—atrocities, rape cases—and both organized mainly in reaction to these, defensively. For all their proclamation of "working-class leadership," the parties did not formulate a policy and program that could lead the women's movement (for instance, they never effectively led a movement for equal wages, and issues of property and political power continued to be ignored). In practice, "working-class leadership" simply seemed to mean increasing the party base among women. In turn, the autonomous feminist groups could not link their concern for democracy and antihierarchy with a true mass orientation; they began to critique party women "for only making speeches" as if they did nothing else, and with the argument that speech-making itself was simply imposing ideas upon the masses, while group discussions were inherently democratic. This obviously involved unrealistic ideas about organizing and group processes. And in spite of the concerns for democracy, many seemed unconsciously to assume that they were a theoretical vanguard.

Indeed, a trend was developing in which the independent feminists developed university and academic links—and considerably more sophistication than party women activists, often leading more comfortable lives—and with the inpouring of foreign funding and the rise of "NGOs" began to have their main links with the masses through such funding. The availability of money both for "rural developmental" work by "voluntary agencies" and for organizing conferences and seminars on feminist issues was a powerful temptation. It provided resources for organizing and exchange of ideas, but in a way that institutionalized a different kind of hierarchy between those at the top of such organizations and the people. Such funding could produce impressive looking activities but normally failed totally to mobilize mass activities. The alternative of working with the mass organizations of the established left parties or building up mass organizations of their own seemed impossible to most feminists, and there were at the time few independent mass organizations. A deep alienation from "politics" was developing as quarrels began to mark many of the common meetings. As a Delhi feminist later wrote,

> Working with the entrenched and hierarchical organizations of the orthodox left, and finding their own voices increasingly drowned by the cacophony of competing center and right parties, Indian feminists discovered the ironic process whereby an agitation gained numerical strength by being joined by political blocs, but at the same time found itself constrained intellectually, morally and strategically by them.[19]

But this sense of helplessness felt by many feminists—their feeling that their ideas were ignored—came at least partly because they could not explain them in language convincing to common women, and they could not prove the power of their ideas by bringing in sufficient women to mass programs. From the point of view of party women, there was no reason they should turn over "our women" to

Table 4.3
Women's Customary Access to Land

A. Norms of Land Inheritance

Region	Communal Ownership	Patrilineal	Matrilineal	Bilateral	Total Number Communities Examined
Northern	—	53	—	—	53
(percent)		(100)			(100)
Central	—	16	—	—	16
(percent)		(100)			(100)
Eastern	—	14	—	—	14
(percent)		(100)			(100)
Northeastern	2	14	3	—	19
(percent)	(10)	(74)	(16)		(100)
Southern	1	34	7	1	43
(percent)	(2)	(79)	(16)	(2)	(100)
TOTAL	3	131	10	1	145
(percent)	(2)	(79)	(16)	(2)	(100)

B. Mention of Actual Possession under Patriliny

Region	As Daughters in Sonless Families	As Widows	Usufructory Rights Only
Northern	1	4	—
Central	2	2	—
Eastern	—	—	1
Northeastern	—	—	—
Southern	2	2	—
TOTAL	5	8	1

Source: Bina Agrawal, "Rural Women, Poverty, and Natural Resources, *"Economic and Political Weekly,* October 28, 1989, p. WS–50.

the whims of a few upper middle-class intellectuals; from the point of view of the feminists, a numbers game was being played.

Not all feminists felt so "constrained." Chhaya Datar, for instance, had suffered through an attack by party women after some of her statements about sexual freedom during a Stri Mukti Yatra (women's liberation campaign tour) were blown up by a right-wing reporter in a local paper, but she later remarked, "Why do we worry so much about our relations with the left parties? There's a whole world outside of them!" And the flamboyant Madhu Kishwar, editor of *Manushi* along with Ruth Vanita, had started out the journal's career with a quarrel with both "Marxists" and "feminists"—first over the issue of who would control the journal, then in a determination to orient its writing to simple, concrete descriptions of women's lives and the need for organizing, rather than theoretical abstractions. In turn, the feminists expressed a feeling of betrayal. At their 1985 second national conference, again in Bombay, its discussion on the media evaluated *Manushi* as "autocratically run":

> Today most feminists feel ambivalent towards *Manushi*. While we are glad of its success, we are unhappy about its editorial policy, which is incompatible with feminist principles. Internationally considered the voice of the Indian women's movement, *Manushi* is not closely associated with women's groups . . . it often uses its editorial power to attack other feminist activists.[20]

In turn, Madhu began to proclaim that she was "not a feminist," that the term was a needless imposition of Western categories, and that *Manushi's* success was precisely because it was *not* based on "feminist" principles.

In the year of the Nairobi world women's conference, this was an unfortunate symbol of the situation of the Indian women's movement: as vigorous and assertive as it was, it had not been able to produce an effective national organization or even a united alliance, but was caught in its own processes of sectarianism.

"Let Us Go into Politics, Let Us Take the Lead in Struggle"

Yet there were ongoing sources of creativity, often from the same rural and toiling women who had provided a motor force for the original upsurge in 1973–75, acting again outside the establishment of either the party women's wings or the urban feminist groups.

Political power, for instance, was ignored by both trends, by the feminists because they felt alienated from the whole world of politics, by the party women because they considered it to be the province of the party and not of the mass organizations. Yet the idea of women campaigning to reverse their millennia-long exclusion from power never really went away. In 1974 it was expressed by some on the Status of Women Commission; in 1975 a leading woman politician of Maharashtra had organized a meeting to demand 50 percent reservation for women.[21] In 1978, village women in Ahmednagar who had been to the Pune women's conference three years earlier got the idea of organizing a woman's panel to fight *gram panchayat* or village council elections; they eventually joined with a dissident youth group of the village to assert themselves.[22] In 1982–83 V. M. Dandekar, the prominent and often eccentric economist of Pune, began to hold a series of seminars for rural women in his Indian School of Political Economy at Lonavala—a kind of vacation spot in the western mountain range where the village women could enjoy unexpected luxury ("tea five times a day!") for several days of discussion. Dandekar had the idea that village governance should be simply turned over to women, and his *shibirs* were managed by two young feminists who quite enthusiastically promoted this.

Then in 1985 Ushatai Nikam, a peasant woman activist of Indoli Village in

Table 4.4
Women in Elected Bodies

A. Women in Parliament

Year	Number of Women Candidates	Number of Women Elected	Total Seats	Percentage of Women MPs
1952	51	23	489	4.7
1957	70	27	494	5.5
1962	68	35	494	7.1
1967	64	31	520	6.0
1971	80	22	521	4.2
1977	70	19	542	3.5
1980	142	28	530	5.3
1984	164	44	543	8.1
1989	198	27	517 (525)	5.2 (5.1)

B. Women in State Assemblies

Year	Number of Women Candidates	Number of Women Elected	Total Seats	Percentage of Women MLAs
1952	216	98	3,641	2.7
1957	490	197	3,284	6.0
1962	233	175	3,387	5.7
1967	230	134	3,709	3.6
1972	381	146	3,679	3.9

Source: P. Manikyanba, "The Participatory Predicament: Women in Indian Politics," in *The Changing Division of Labour in South Asia,* ed. James Werner Bjorkman (Delhi: Manohar, 1987), p. 115 and Subhash Kashyap, "It Takes All Types to Constitute a Lok Sabha," *Times of India,* March 17, 1990.

Satara district, decided to organize an "all-woman panel" to fight her village council election. Usha had been exposed to both feminist and Marxist ideas for several years, but the idea of women fighting the election was hers alone. The Indoli election was noteworthy for the savage reaction of the Congress local bosses, who took a woman's panel not only as a political threat but as an insult to their manhood. "What, your wife is running for election? Why don't you put on bangles," they told the husbands of the candidates, using a common (and male chauvinist) Marathi insult. The panel lost, but a precedent had been set, and the women remained enthusiastic, if still politically unrepresented.

The issue of property rights also began to be taken up on the initiative of rural and urban toiling women (see table 4.3, p. 92). In the late 1970s the Chhatra Yuva Sangarsh Vahini (Student-Youth Struggle League), a youth organization founded by the socialist leader Jayaprakash Narayan, began to work among the poor in Bihar.

They were socialists, they were Gandhians; they wanted "total revolution" but through nonviolent means. Their group included many young women, and with new ideas of "women's liberation" floating around they made various attempts to give them scope; in shibirs, for instance, it was the men who did the cooking and other work, women were totally excused.

Work among dalit landless laborers focused on the demand that those laboring on the lands of a huge religious estate or *math* should be given lands. Demonstrations and campaigns were organized. Women took part also, though highly repressed even among this most "proletarianized" Bihari section. They also organized for demonstrations on wider cases of atrocities, such as protesting the Maya Tyagi case. Going out of the home began to radicalize the women also, and when in 1983 a meeting was held to discuss what to do with land now likely to be won, and when as usual the formula of giving it to "landless laborers" first was decided on, the women protested. Giving land to "landless laborers," they objected, meant giving it to families (only "landless widows" were classified as a separate group to get land)—and this meant giving it to the family *heads*, who were invariably men. Women would continue to be left out; not only that, "If you give our men land, they'll become more egotistic and beat us more!"

"Give us land!" began to be a discernible cry. And, in a momentous decision, the activists and landless laborers of Sangarsh Vahini voted to give the first land won in the names of women only. Even though there was foot dragging among cadres and open opposition from some landless laborers, and even though officials often refused to turn over land to women on the grounds that they would have no incentive to stay with their husbands, the decision was a historic one whose effects began to reverberate through the women's movement. Property rights were an issue, and it was possible to win them.

About the same time, Sharad Patil of Maharashtra's Satyashodhak Communist party, added the goal of "ending women's slavery" to his program of ending caste as central to the democratic revolution. This was due not only to the influence of outside women's liberationists—Patil saw almost all feminists as "brahmanic" in any case—but also to pressure from the tribal women in his organization who were raising the main issue that concerned them, that of land. Nazubai Gavit, a tribal woman leader, reported that during a discussion of land distribution (the organization, its base mainly in two tribal talukas of Dhule, was then engaged in a struggle of occupying government "forest" lands and then seeking to legalize this) she had passed a note saying that women who were part of the fight should also be part of the list to be included in the distribution of its benefits. With this the Satyashodhak Communist party and its women's front decided to take up the fight for land as the main point of their movement. But Patil did so in his own way, with the slogan, "Apply the Hindu code bill to tribal women." This had its difficulties—it ignored the fact that "Hindu" women to whom the law already applied in fact could not get it implemented; tribal women often did not like to be identified as "Hindu"; and in the end the feminist lawyer with whom Patil worked filed the petition saying that the Indian Inheritance Act of 1925 (a law for non-Hindus) should be applied to the women.[23] For the tribal women themselves, there was only a vague understanding of the technicalities of the slogan, and they most frequently spoke only of "getting rights to land." Nevertheless, the slogan (and debate over it) of "apply the Hindu code bill to tribal women" got into women's forums throughout the state and at least succeeded in stirring up more thinking on property rights.

About the same time that rural women were raising the question of land rights, urban toiling women began to raise that of housing, as they became dominant forces in a gathering series of struggles against eviction of slum dwellers in the 1980s. The Madurai women's organization, Pennurimai Iyakkam, organized women's committees in a struggle for house-sites that began in 1981, resulting in finally winning these in the names of women themselves.[24]

Sexuality was another issue that was, outside of small group discussions, avoided by feminist activists. It was one of the most sensitive in terms of ideological challenges to Indian patriarchal society, and dalits in their own way were bringing up the issue. (One of the first Marathi books on extramarital relations was edited by a dalit writer—himself "dalit" not because of being born in one of the ex-untouchable castes, but for being the product of such an "illegitimate" relation.) Yet it could not, in the long run, be avoided because it was affecting rural women involved in organizing as much, if not more, than their urban middle-class sisters. The latter were very often choosing new relationships—but in the relative anonymity of city life they could have some freedom to do so. Rural women activists, including those from agricultural laborer or poor peasant families, had a "public" gaze fixed on them everywhere; scandal often dogged their public life. Jealous husbands then tried to limit their involvement in the movement. Behind this working of the "scandal factor" was a remorseless social logic: women who went out of the home, who became organizers, were exposed not simply to dangers but also to temptation. They were likely to form companionships, new relations with men and women they worked with, and these were again often much more attractive than those with men they may have been handed over to before they could even understand what sex and companionship meant. Husbands were jealous; they had reason to be. The issues of "man-woman relations" were complex, in spite of the continuing tendency of urban feminists to see them simply in terms of male violence against women.

For example, when one of the Naxalite organizations working in Bihar split in the early 1980s, the fact that the marriage of a leading couple had broken up and both were forming new relations was a subject of political controversy. Why did it happen? "We grew apart naturally, we were working apart." "I've been away from home for years on end and my wife has always remained loyal," growled the patriarchal old Bihari leader of the group, and this time he got the reply, "You've treated her like a feudal baron, that's why!" But this defiance was possible not only because of "feminist" ideas but because the activists were ready for a split, and in the whole process it was the woman who was slandered from top to bottom of the activist circles.

In another case, Shramik Sanghatana, the most powerful tribal organization in Maharashtra, experienced two major internal cases in the 1980–85 period. One was that of the molestation of a tribal woman by an unmarried nontribal activist, the other that of an affair between two tribal activists, the man already having a wife. Two wives did not go against tribal norms, but they did challenge the combination of bourgeois and women's liberationist values held by the activists ("we're against polygamy; what about the injustice to the first wife?"), while the fact that the two staunchly denied that anything was going on for nearly two years heightened tension considerably. Neither case was handled well, the first reverberating throughout the state. The notion of "personal is political" was making it necessary for activists to take a stand on such issues, but not necessarily giving the basis for a satisfactory resolution of them.

The years from 1980 to 1985 also saw a new growth of rural *mahila mandals* or village women's organizations. In their original phase, as part of village development programs in the 1960s, they had involved mainly rich peasant and upper-caste housewives meeting for ceremonious occasions or for religious singing, sometimes using a sewing machine or other gentile developmental work. The mahila mandals of the 1980s were different. Now there were various new government welfare schemes being offered, and masses of poor women, often abandoned by their husbands, desperately searching for work or some kind of social and economic support. These provided a constituency for an emerging spontaneous rural leadership, energetic and entrepreneurial women, sometimes from richer families but in many cases also from poorer and low-caste families.

Conclusion

Yet, with all of this, the mid-1980s saw a troubling impasse. In spite of all the furor over rape cases and dowry deaths, the cases of "atrocities against women" continued to rise, and the demonstrations and court fights by women's groups most often proved futile—it was almost impossible to get convictions. The economic ravages of uneven development continued to push more and more women into the unorganized sector: mines in Dhanbad announced the retrenchment of 10,000 women workers due to modernization (promising in compensation jobs to one more educated *son* of every family) while SAIL, the huge public-sector steel conglomerate, announced on the eve of the Indian delegation's departure for the Nairobi women's conference that 13,000 women would lose their jobs. Women's wages as agricultural laborers continued to be one-half to two-thirds those of men, regardless of the slogan "equal pay for equal work" shouted at almost every rural demonstration. Amniocentisis, that most modern and "scientific" attack on women through female feticide, was appearing not only in cities but in district towns throughout the country. India, with its caste-linked patriarchal, patrilocal kinship system, was one of the most patriarchal countries in the world, and as the tables in the appendix show, there seemed to be little change in women's access to education, property, power, and income relative to men over the decades.

The growing forces of religious fundamentalism in the 1980s also threatened women's interests. In 1984–85 a huge debate broke out on the issue of Muslim women's rights, taking a form that practically drowned the voice of feminists and Marxists alike. Muslims, fearing the imposition of Hindu domination, rallied around their own religious traditionalists over the demand for maintaining separate personal laws that allowed daughters only half the share of men in inheritance and made it possible for men to divorce their wives legally by simply saying "talak" three times. Hindu fundamentalist organizations, on the other hand, trumpeted the demand for a "common civil code," using a major slogan of the women's movement as a propaganda point to show the backwardness and cruelty of Muslims. Those concerned with secularism or simply the issue of justice for women (and laws or no laws, Hindu men also were abandoning their wives without even bothering to say anything) seemed to be able to mobilize very little in contrast to the huge demonstrations of the fundamentalists. Then, in November 1984, came the assassination of Indira Gandhi and the election of her son Rajiv following massive pogroms against Sikhs in Delhi and some other North Indian cities—riots involving the most brutal murders of men and rapes of women. For all of its creativity and new thinking, for all the rising assertion of women at the grass roots level, the new women's movement seemed unable to build a mass power to confront the forces of patriarchy and exploitation.

Though still limited in its social power, however, the 1975–85 "international decade of women" had seen the growth of a new women's liberation movement and the emergence of a self-defined "feminist" trend that had made many important theoretical and practical challenges to traditional Marxism.

The concept of *patriarchy* had been brought to the fore. For many this was left undefined and simply viewed as an oppressive and exploitative structure alongside that of class; this trend verged into the ultimately unsatisfactory "additive" approach of "class and caste," "caste and gender/patriarchy." But some went beyond this to reject the definition that made "class" the economic factor and "patriarchy" simply a cultural part of the "superstructure." Women like Chhaya Datar, for instance, drawing on a broader European theoretical trend that itself had roots in Indian experiences, made attempts to "redefine exploitation." The knotty issue of housework or domestic labor in fact was forcing some new thinking on the whole issue of work. Party theoreticians found themselves in the uncomfortable position of having to refute ideas that not only continued to emerge from "bourgeois feminists" but also proved to have a wide appeal. When Suhas Paranjpe, a young theorist of the Magowa group, wrote a Marathi rendition of *Capital*, it became a major left publishing event in Maharashtra—but party leaders who attended the book's publishing ceremony were horrified at an appendix on housework and surplus value, urging its withdrawal.

But the demon would not go back into the bottle. In rethinking the issue of work and its relation to capitalism and exploitation, the women's movement was going beyond the dalit movement in its theoretical challenge to Marxism. At the same time, the concept of patriarchy helped in a critique of the major religious traditions. Finally, while the early organizations of the new women's movement, in contrast to the anticaste movement, tended to avoid the issues of political power (and thus the strategies of building a mass movement), the issues raised regarding political organization, democratic functioning, and the nature of revolution itself were to become important for all the new movements. In fact, because of the particular position of women in being a part of all oppressed sections, the women's movement was only in part a separate movement; in part also it was acting as a force for renewal of all the varied movements.

5

The Farmers' Movement

"We Don't Want Alms But the Payment for Our Sweat"

IN 1972, with four years of intensive agricultural labor agitation in Thanjavur district coming to an end, smallholders elsewhere in the state unleashed one of the most militant agitations seen for some time in India. In protest against high electricity rates and forcible collection of loan arrears from peasants, and demanding higher prices for their produce, they blocked roads, organized processions of peasant women, and mobilized a forty-eight-hour blockade of government offices with 30,000 bullock carts in the district town of Coimbatore. In the statewide agitation that followed this on June 30, fourteen people were killed in seven separate incidences of police firing.[1] The agitations were organized by the Tamilaga Vyavasayigal Sangham (Tamilnadu Agriculturalists' Association), which had existed in Coimbatore from 1966 as an independent, nonparty farmers' organization but became formally statewide only after the 1972 agitation.

In the same year Gujarati peasants marched in a newly formed Khedut Samaj to the state capital to protest land ceilings and agitated the following year against crop levy. Meanwhile, in the heart of "green revolution" Punjab, militant struggles took place between 1972 and 1974 under the newly formed Zimindara Union on issues of cotton prices, cuts in power supply, and electricity rates. The agitations included militant clashes with police who tried to collect bills and a month-long *dharna* or sit-in at the electricity board center.[2]

These events heralded a new era of peasant movements in India, one that harked back to and used slogans of the old pre-independence dream of a "peasant revolution" sung of by socialist and Communist organizers alike: *aataa petwu saare raan, aataa petwu ladhaa mahaan* ('now let us ignite the fields, now let us ignite a great battle'). However, these were not sharecroppers or poor peasants fighting landlords; they were "independent commodity producers," peasants caught up in the throes of market production, dependent on the state and capital for their inputs of fertilizer, pesticide, seeds, electricity, and water and for the purchase of their products. So different was the situation from the traditional understanding of the peasantry that most scholars and left commentators have refused to call it a "peasant" movement at all, but instead have described it as a "farmers' " movement, though there is no terminology for the distinction (presumably that between subsistence peasants and commercially oriented farmers) in any Indian language. With this in mind, there is no harm in using the terms interchangeably.

The 1972 events also gave birth to new organizations of struggle—the nonparty, "all-peasant" organizations that emerged during the 1970s and by the 1980s were the bearers of one of the most powerful social movements of the decade. Like the anticaste movement, the women's movement, and the environmental movement, the new peasant or farmers' movement raised crucial issues of exploitation and the direction of revolutionary change, and with a capability of mobilizing in the hundreds of thousands it was one of the few to have a direct influence on political events. Yet none of the new movements has had a more difficult relationship with Marxism; none has been more ignored by the theorists of "new social movements" and "alternatives" in India.

"Simmering Discontent"

What lay behind this upsurge was a seething discontent among the very "middle and rich" peasantry that was supposed to be a beneficiary of the green revolution. Punjab, considered the richest part of India, can be taken as an example. In spite of increased production, 1974–75 statistics showed that of landholding households, 31 percent of those with under one hectare, 24 percent of those with between one to two hectares, 19 percent of those with two to three hectares, and 11 percent of those with three to five hectares were below the poverty line. Although the study insisted that there was "no situation of destitution and misery; for essential food items, e.g., cereals, salt and spices, pulses, vegetables and fruit, they are not much behind higher classes of farmers," [3] it was clear that this was relative prosperity only by Indian standards where *real* poverty, in the backward and often tribal areas, meant not only no meat and milk but also no vegetables and insufficient calories. Punjabi poor peasants and agricultural laborers had their vegetables, but not much else. They were equally involved in the market economy, spending nearly as much per acre on fertilizers, manures, and biochemical inputs, getting a slightly higher percentage of their income from nonfarm activities than did the larger farmers.[4] Another study showed that for all classes of landholding (even those above twenty-five acres), the value of family labor outweighed that of hired labor in 1968–70.[5]

Thus, the issues that moved the "big farmers"—the prices of crops, zonal restrictions that kept prices down, debt, access to electricity and fertilizers, and the bureaucratic procedures that lay behind all of these—were also issues for the small peasants. What this meant in concrete terms was described in an anonymous 1981 article in *Frontier*:

> There was not a single village where the murmuring of simmering discontent, frustration, anger and often utter resignation was not observed among the once robust Punjabi farmers. Everywhere and each time the discussion with a peasant would bring out inevitable stories of corruption among colluding officials, police, politicians, big landlords, rich men, bank managers, private traders, all those brokers of the degenerating social structure.[6]

These were the same peasants who were in conflict with their dalit agricultural laborers, who used migrants brought in from Bihar and eastern U.P. working cheaply and often in semibonded conditions; they were also the peasants whose fathers had fought British colonial rule (often in armed organizations such as the Ghadar party) and who had struggled earlier against merchants and moneylenders. Now they found themselves in new relations of exploitation and conflict:

> We were also told how the FCI inspector made immense amounts of money in one cropping season by rejecting the grains on some plea of quality and then in the dark hours accepting the same grains or even worse at the usual market price, only after the farmers had made the inspector "happy" by bribing him at some fixed rate per quintal.... "Why don't you protest?" we asked. With a sarcastic smile the farmer replied, "We made lots of protest. We have even beaten some of these corrupt officials. But what happened? Some of us got arrested and there were long-drawn court cases. The whole problem is that even the higher-ups in the whole chain of officials are involved in this racket.... Look at the level of contradictions. We farmers produce the basic needs of the country. We also supply cheap labor to urban industry. We only give, but we do not get anything.[7]

This description was pointing to a new *economic* nexus: exploitative relations between government officials and the peasantry, and a process of extraction of surplus from the peasantry. Naxalites would also identify "bureaucratic capitalism" as an enemy, and the later "ecological" analysis of Vandana Shiva's Punjab book, *The Violence of the Green Revolution*, would see the conflict between the peasantry and the state—involving indebtedness, the provision of high-priced high-technology inputs, the licensing and regulation of production and of the movement of produce—as a part of the total web of exploitation and ecological destruction following from the new "scientific" agriculture.[8] But in the 1970s the peasant-state relation did not fit into the framework of Marxist class analysis, and when in 1974–75 the J.P. movement pinpointed "corruption" as a major enemy, it was taken as a "nonclass" issue.

But to the peasantry, the situation was very material, and in the 1970s peasants began to organize against it. In doing so they gave birth to new forms of struggle. They initiated on a wide scale the road blocking and railway blocking that later came to be known as *rasta roko*. They took the *gherao*, which workers (or women demonstrating against price-rise) had used as a technique by which a few dozen or few hundred could surround managers, owners, or officials, and turned it into a mass siege of government buildings with tractors and bullock carts. They took up the *bandh* or civic strike that political parties had always used, but whereas union-backed bandhs normally relied for their effectiveness on the degree to which transport workers joined and right-wing organizations relied on a combination of influence and terrorism of shopkeepers, the peasants shut down public transportation by the sheer force of their numbers, being practically the only mass movement that could threaten a *chakka jam* ("not a single wheel should turn"). They initiated *gavbandi*, the closing off of villages to officials or politicians, on the one hand, and brought peasants in their masses into the cities for indefinite occupations of public places on the other hand. The latter came to be called *kisan panchayat* (thus ranging from "delinking" to a new version of the "cities surround the countryside"). Throughout the 1970s and early 1980s the movement had hundreds killed—not in clashes with landlords or their armed mercenaries, not in faked "encounters" staged by police hunting down militants at night, but in police firing on open, mass and unarmed demonstrators.

All of this indicated an underlying socioeconomic process in which an unequal, caste-bound, but still cultivating peasantry with some community traditions was not being "differentiated" into agricultural laborers and capitalist farmers engaged in class struggle against each other, but rather was pulled (with all their hierarchy and inequalities) into a new kind of capitalist enslavement to the market and the state. The focus on officials, on the state, on the cities itself pointed to a new location of the "main enemy"; the forms of struggle—sporadic efforts at "delinking" interspersed with assaults on the power centers—pointed to the "social relations of production" that existed between the peasantry and the cities and states, or between agriculture and industry. Peasants were resisting their exploitation and getting precious little appreciation for this from Marxist intellectuals.

"A Big Show of Tractors and Trolleys"

Although the peasant movement itself borrowed terms of struggle from the left, proclaimed itself as against exploitation, called for a "kisan raj" and "worker-peasant unity," it was in turn stamped as reactionary, described as a "rich farmers' " or even "landlords' " movement.

This was true from the very beginning, when a study of agrarian radicalism could ignore the movement apparently on the grounds that only a landless, labor-based movement on wage issues could be "radical"; [9] when the one study that did describe the beginnings of the Tamilnadu organization admitted that the vast majority of the peasants involved were poor but that the movement itself, however militant, was conservative and a "deceleration in the process of social change" because the small cultivator was "conservative in ideology"; [10] when the only article that took note of the Punjab movement described it as aimed at "protecting the economic interests of the emerging rural bourgeoisie" and (again while admitting broad poor peasant support) argued that a "big show of tractors and trolleys" at a demonstration was "indicative of the class character of the agitation." [11] All of these left and progressive analyses shared the assumption of the first report in an international journal that talked of "the coming of age of the *kulak* class as a formidable political force." [12] From this time through the late 1980s, when Naxalite publications were still using the Russian term *kulak* and the English term *farmer* to describe a movement they refused to baptize with the word "peasant," where American scholars coined such terms as "bullock capitalists," the gap between the way the peasant movement saw itself and the way it was seen by the left intellectuals seemed absolute.

The fact is that while a traditional Marxist framework could to some extent handle the other movements by using concepts of "nationality" or even "caste" and "gender" alongside of or supplementary to a "class analysis," the peasant movement directly challenged the class framework itself. It based itself on and theorized the exploitation of the "peasantry" as a whole, but a Marxist framework that took "private property" in the means of production as the only factor for getting to the heart of exploitation and contradiction was simply incapable of seeing the "peasantry as a whole"—though it had no such difficulty with the working class, which is arguably equally hierarchized and fragmented in terms of income, place in the production process, nationality, community, and gender. Peasants under feudalism could be conceived of as a group, in spite of differences of size and landholding, because the primary property holders were the landlords (or so it could be argued), and all categories of peasants were dependent tenants. But under capitalism, the Marxist framework nearly forced its proponents to view the rural community through ideological spectacles that identified the main divisions as "agricultural laborers," "poor, middle, and rich peasants," and "landlords" or "capitalist farmers." "Class analysis" was then the exercise of identifying the numbers in each category and their mutual relation, and "class struggle" meant organizing the rural poor against landlords or capitalist farmers on issues of land or wages. The relationship of peasants as a group with supravillage exploiters (the state, the buyers of their produce, those who taxed them) and the struggles they organized against this—however militant and involving however many deaths—fell outside the scope of "class analysis" and "class struggle" as it was understood.

Similarly, an organization including all sizes of peasants was, inevitably, a "multiclass organization," and since such an organization had to have a leadership of one or another class, if it was not that of the "proletariat" (which by another logical leap was exerted through a Communist party), then it was inevitably that of "landlords" or "rich farmers." This followed from the same law that defined the necessity of the differentiation of agriculture under capitalism—the "peasantry" as a whole did not exist, and the "middle peasantry" was a vanishing, politically impotent class incapable of leading anything, even itself.

Added to this remorseless logic was the special character of the Indian situation, marked by "four-anna socialism." Since the middle 1960s, the Congress party itself, and the bureaucrats and intelligentsia associated with it, had been quite articulate in distinguishing the "rural poor" and "weaker sections" from their village exploiters, in trying to mark the latter as the main enemy. They not only fostered the political strategy of building an electoral bloc made up of the lowest and highest castes; they also headed an intellectual offensive that charged "middle and rich peasants" with being the main beneficiaries of the green revolution. Seeing "rich peasants" as part of a *ruling* bloc and "middle peasants" or "family farmers" as on the exploiting side of the lines of class struggle was a major shift from classical Marxism itself. But in spite of the sanctity of the notion of the "worker-peasant alliance" within the Communist movement, in spite of Marx's own writings on the peasantry against capitalism, this thesis of a fundamental polarization was taken up by Marxist intellectuals for reasons that have to be attributed to their own class/caste background. As salary-paid urban employees they found it easy to see petty-commodity producers as exploiters of agricultural laborers, and as upper castes they found it easy to see nonbrahman "dominant caste" peasants as the main perpetrators of "atrocities on dalits." One indication of this in-built bias is the fact that while the demand for higher crop prices has provoked innumerable studies on the effects of "higher terms of trade" for agriculture on living standards in the unorganized sector, there has been almost no research on the overall economic effects of the constant increases in pay of professors and government employees.

This double standard was not to go unnoticed by intellectuals of the farmers' movement: when in the late 1980s professors' strikes were occurring all over India, an article in the Shetkari Sanghatana-connected weekly *Gyanba* attacked the suggestion (by a college professor) that peasants should take up profitable auxiliary occupations like raising rabbits rather than try to get higher prices: "Why tell this to us? Let the professors raise rabbits in their backyards instead of shouting themselves hoarse for higher pay!"

If, from the point of view of the traditional left and especially the intellectuals of "traditional socialism," the new peasant movement was doomed before it took off, this did not prevent it from taking off. Its audience was a different one, the millions of rural poor scattered throughout the villages of India. And if the left refused to recognize the movement as one of "class struggle," the movement reciprocated by denying the concept of "class" altogether.

The 1970s: A Decade of Transition

Overall, the decade of the 1970s can be seen as one in which most activists of the Marxist left threw themselves into the effort to organize agricultural laborer and poor peasant struggles and—while these struggles and their organizations stagnated or even fizzled out—a very differently focused "agrarian revolution" was gathering strength.

Thus Marshall Bouton's study of agrarian radicalism in Tamilnadu, noted above, showed the subsiding of its "second wave" by 1972, with mild tenancy reform and some wage gains, but little way to go ahead.[13] Nationwide "land grab" movements led by the CPI and CPI(M) in 1970–71 also had little overall impact—some land was occupied, another wave of land ceiling legislation resulted, but after this the struggles ceased. Similarly, while both Communist parties gave some attention to agricultural laborer unions—the CPI's was organized nationally in 1968, that of the CPI(M) somewhat later—these also did not emerge as a *movement*, though they continued to exert pressure for higher wages. Demonstrations at taluka offices and at district offices and then marches on state government centers to present a charter of demands constituted the "struggles" organized by the mainstream left. This was done with agricultural labor unions on such demands as a "national minimum wage law" for agriculture, and with the party-led Kisan Sabhas on the same issues on which the new peasant organizations agitated. But charters of demands and demonstrations did not make a movement, and both the Kisan Sabhas and the agricultural laborer unions connected with the parties proved comparatively ineffectual bodies.

This stagnation of agricultural laborer-focused organizing could be seen in Maharashtra, a highly industrialized state with a strong bureaucracy and relative "capitalist development" in agriculture, but without the overall prosperity that existed in northwest India. In the 1971–72 period the Lal Nishan Party, a state-based Communist party with roots in the rural nonbrahman masses, began attempts to organize the rural poor. Its strategy was based on a proposal to use unions of village workers—*kotwals* (general village servants, once a hereditary caste profession, now secularized and unionized) and road and construction workers—as entry cadres to form general agricultural laborer associations among the low castes from which they were drawn. They also seized the opportunity of the drought-based upsurge in the rural areas in the early 1970s. Laborers on government relief works were mobilized in massive numbers, holding in 1971 a major statewide conference of agricultural laborers and poor peasants, and undertaking agitations culminating in a million-and-a-half-strong strike in 1973. These efforts led to the formation of an agricultural laborer union, the Maharashtra Shetmajur Parishad, in 1975. But with all its promising start, this did not grow. Nor did organizing attempts of the CPI, the CPI(M), or the socialists develop into a movement.

A similar fate came to the most promising "pocket-based" organization, the Shramik Sanghatana. In contrast to the LNP's strategy of a statewide spread, the Magowa group, in helping to build the Shramik Sanghatana, concentrated middle-class cadres in an area thought to be promising and attempted an all-around, struggle-oriented organization. Originally formed in 1972 out of a spontaneous adivasi-based upsurge in Shahada, the most proletarianized region of Dhule district, the Shramik Sanghatana organized militant struggles to regain land lost by the tribals to big farmers. Then wage issues were taken up, and not only higher wages but even arrears were won—significant sums in back pay for the years when the legally declared minimum wages were not implemented. In addition the Sanghatana not only mobilized on women's issues, but also participated in anticaste agitations and took some initiative in bringing together other tribal-based organizations in the Dhule-Thana district tribal belt to fight to win control of forest lands for cultivation. Yet even this, the apparently most vigorous of new organizations, stagnated after 1980, caught up in political splits, disputes about scandal cases involving activists, and some unresolved problems: the question of "adivasi identity" versus "agricultural laborer/class identity" of its members, and the question of how the movement was to go ahead once the tribals had won a minimum of decent treatment from the caste Hindu rich farmers and some gains in wages.

Naxalite organizing efforts in the state, aside from those in tribal border regions of Andhra Pradesh, also petered out. An organization in Nanded district never got beyond a few villages, while a sister unit in Nasik district allied itself with the farmers' movement briefly in 1980 and then went into opposition, charging that the Shetkari Sanghatana and its leaders were "landlords." Another group tried, in Ahmednagar district, an "annihilation campaign" that involved helping the mass of peasants to organize an attack that resulted in the murder of a particularly hated village boss. But this, once again, failed to be the "spark that set off the prairie fire": it was, in a way, smothered by the left itself as the various Communist parties joined to provide legal aid for the peasants and, in the process, prove that the system was not really against them.

In all of India, it is striking that one area where agricultural laborer organizing really took off in the late 1970s and 1980s was Bihar, where Naxalites built a strong movement based on dalit laborers and organized around issues of wages and *izzat*. But, as has been seen, this was not conceived of as an agricultural laborer organization, and the Naxalites continued to view the land struggle as central, even when they could not do much on it. A CPI(ML)-"Liberation" admission in a 1988 document that "our persistent effort to direct every struggle against the landlords and towards land-seizure often turned into a futile search for big landlords and large-scale concentration of land"[14] was typical of many Marxist self-critiques of the period over the failure to lead land struggles. Was this simply out of fear of challenging the rural power structure, or were there more objective reasons behind this failure in the lack of "excess land" of big holders on a sufficient scale to satisfy the land-hunger of the rural poor? Some have suggested the latter,[15] but the issue was never confronted. In any event, the main gains in "land for the landless" campaigns continued to be won by encroaching on, and then fighting to maintain and legalize, "waste lands" and "forest lands."

Thus, the 1970s saw a gradual decline in the viability of a poor peasant/

agricultural laborer-based movement, concurrent with the rise of militant agitations based on the issues of market-dependent, bureaucratically oppressed peasantry —and a decline in mobilization of "antiprice rise" movements concurrent with the rise in the agitations for higher crop prices, on the one hand, and continuing wage struggles by workers, on the other.

Peasants, Laborers, and Dalits

At the same time, the period saw a gradual maturation of the farmers' movement. In the beginning, the various accusations of leftists about the antidalit, antiagricultural laborer nature of the peasant organizations had a solid base. Peasants (as well as the industrial working class) were after all of "mixed" character—the caste Hindus among them were ready to assert their superiority to dalits and resent lower-caste assertion; those of "dominant peasant" caste were inclined to adopt the "village ruler" model; hirers of wage labor (even small peasants) had objective interests in contradictions with the sellers of it, and so on. In the face of considerable objective contradictions pervading the villages, the peasants involved in the new movements *were*, as Marxists charged, trying to assert their hegemony over the village. The questions remained: how "antagonistic" were these contradictions? Was there an objective basis for unity? Was it desirable and possible? And could a "socialistic" hegemony be asserted?

"Nonparty" peasant organizations focusing struggles against the state were a new phenomenon, but this did not immediately become clear. There were a large number of self-defined "peasant" organizations in the field. As Alexander's studies of South India show, these were of at least three different types: the new nonparty ones; those that arose as defensive organizations of landowners against agricultural laborers (primarily the "mirasdar's associations" of Thanjavur district, which was highly inegalitarian in its social structure and saw the strongest agricultural laborer organizing); and party-linked organizations, including not only those of the left but also peasant organizations floated by right-wing parties such as Swatantra and the Jan Sangh/BJP.[16]

Not so surprisingly, many organizations had antilabor clauses, and even local units connected with the left party Kisan Sabhas might fight agricultural laborers. Youth of big farmer families might attack dalits or put on the badges of farmers' organizations. But the trend during the decade was for the independent nonparty organizations to move toward a pro-agricultural laborer position, to assert the need for "peasant-worker unity" and to develop an ideology that asserted broad populist values and the image of a society that, whether or not it used the term "socialist," claimed to be one of egalitarianism and welfare equivalent to the Marxist version of socialism.

The complex character of the 1970s movements can be seen in the Kanjhawala agitation of 1979. In this, mainly jat peasants from the jat belt of northwest India (Haryana, U.P., Rajasthan) were mobilized on a massive scale with a broad platform of demands, with rallies of up to 200,000 and 70,000 offering satyagraha at one point in Delhi. But the focal issue was opposition to government efforts to give 120 acres of common land of Kanjhawala village near Delhi to dalits for cultivation. This agitation clearly reflected the tension between jat peasants and chamar (the main dalit caste) agricultural laborers throughout the whole of the Northwest. It was also clear that calling for the commons to remain under "village control" meant, practically, under the control of the dominant jats. Yet, while most left critiques simply condemned the agitation as representing the self-interest of a kulak elite (and it has to be added that jat relations with the Delhi upper castes were equally hostile), one commentator did notice that as mobilization was growing to include large sections of the peasantry cutting across caste and religion, its focus was shifting to an attack on the capitalists who owned vast tracts of land, profited from the low prices of agricultural produce, and got overwhelming concessions from the state: "The top twenty big houses were held responsible for the misery of poor peasants. It appears that the Kanjhawala agitation which was triggered by anti-Harijan and antiland reform feelings has a potential of becoming a broad-based peasant front against industrial capital."[17]

The issue of the village commons—of government-held "waste lands" or "forest lands" generally—was not itself a simple one. The environmental movement later was to become a big voice for keeping the commons as a commons, rather than allowing it to be split into plots for individual peasants, on the grounds that in fact it was the village poor who got most out of the commons, while giving it in individual plots invariably left other sections of the rural poor still landless.[18] The contradiction here was not simply one of caste Hindu "big farmers" against landless dalits, but one of alternative socioeconomic organization at the village level, of collective versus individual control. It was the mixture of the two issues that made for the complications.

The official policy of the independent farmers' organizations regarding agricultural laborers showed a clear change. Under the initiative of Maharashtra's Shetkari Sanghatana and its leader Sharad Joshi, in the 1980s nearly all organizations began to include demands for higher minimum wages for laborers. This was linked to the argument that this higher wage cost be made a part of the calculation of the cost of production by the Agricultural Price Commission; this gave a clear linkage of wages with crop prices, and a material basis for agricultural laborer-peasant unity.

At the same time there was some development of positive assessments of the peasant movement by both Marxist and dalit organizations. In contrast to institutionally based Marxist intellectuals, party activists and theorists had a tendency to support it, as shown in the 1979 reports of the Kisan Sabhas of both the CPI and CPI(M). In 1982 the CPI's Andhra peasant organization held a seminar on capitalism in agriculture in Hyderabad, with most papers giving a positive assessment, arguing that in fact small farmers (with holdings less than ten acres) controlled the largest share of the marketed surplus and were the ones to benefit most from enhanced support prices since they were forced to enter the market more immediately after harvest. Agricultural laborers were also said to benefit "indirectly via the rise in wage rates and wage bill and through higher investment in farm business." [19] And the theoretical leader of the Kisan Sabha, Indradeep Sinha, concluded firmly that

> the whole agrarian economy is in the grip of a deep structural crisis, the crisis of small peasant farming, which is being crushed under the juggernaut of the crisis-ridden capitalist path in India. Hence, the small peasantry is fighting to preserve its existence. . . . This is exemplified by the countrywide peasant upsurge, unprecedented in tempo and sweep in the postindependence period. The big industrial and commercial bourgeoisie headed by the monopolists and the multinationals are seeking to disrupt, divide and crush this peasant upsurge. Radical-minded intellectuals have to choose as to whether they will side with the peasantry or with the monopolies. There is no middle course. [20]

Similarly, dalits who were originally very suspicious of the movement were also rethinking their policy of alliances, just as they were moving to build a broad anticaste front with the "OBCs." Karnataka's Dalit Sangarsh Samiti held a seminar on the issue of the farmers' movement, and in November 1983 its journal *Panchama* published a special issue. Articles took varying positions, but the editorial expressed a hope of alliance, though rather cautiously:

> From the point of view of the dalits, the editorial said, it is the castes which exploit them which are united under the Ryotu Sangh. It suggested that once the farmers' movement transcended their economism and act genuinely for a social and cultural transition of the country, and for the eradication of casteism, the two progressive movements—the Farmers and the Dalits—would come together to achieve common aims. [21]

While these renewed hopes for a reconstructed "peasant-worker alliance" were being put forward, a leading Naxalite spokesman, Vinod Mishra of the "Liberation" group, assessed the rising farmers' movement more positively as representing a "new type of crisis caused by the saturation of the strategy of green revolution and 'overproduction,' " though he still saw the issue as one of competition between movements and ways of organizing. Mishra forecast

> . . . a battle for supremacy between the East and West winds within the peasant movement, blowing sharply from Bihar and Maharashtra. In sharp contrast to the farmers' movement in Maharashtra, the peasant struggle in Bihar has in its forefront the agrarian laborers. . . . But even as the latter lays the highest stress on thoroughgoing land reforms, it does also strive to incorporate the issues arising out of the crisis of the green revolution, issues that affect large segments of the middle and upper-middle peasants. The outcome of this battle between the two winds has not yet been decided. [22]

"The Peasants' Armies Go Forth"

The armies of the peasants will go forth,
The shackles will fall from their wrists.
With unity we will sing the new song of freedom—
Now let us ignite the fields,
Now let us ignite a great battle.
We dedicate our lives to the liberation of the peasants.

Song of the independence struggle

The Emergency, with its pro-agricultural laborer rhetoric and antipeasant bias, called a halt to the first round of peasant struggles. The end of Emergency, with a government that in places drew its electoral support from the middle and low-caste peasantry, released a new wave of agitations. In Tamilnadu in particular, the TAA went on the warpath in 1977–78, again on issues of writing off loans and reduction of electricity rates. Roads were blocked, bridges destroyed, goods of farmers confiscated by cooperative societies taken back; the chief minister labeled it a "naxalite pattern of agitation," and there were at least six killed in police firing.[23] Agitations in various parts of north India were reported by the CPI's Kisan Sabha, including struggles of potato growers in U.P.[24] And in December 1978 the "peasant spokesman" inside the Janata party, Charan Singh, made an attempt to ride the waves of the movement by organizing a two-million-strong rally in Delhi on his birthday, described by an observer as the occasion in which the "peasant is standing up as a class."[25]

It was in 1980, however, that the peasantry really exploded, as new movements arose in Maharashtra and Karnataka. In July there was a militant agitation of peasants in the Malaprabha irrigation project area of North Karnataka against the imposition of a "betterment levy," exorbitant water taxes and irrigation cesses. This coincided partly with antiprice rise movements in towns, and there was heavy police repression resulting in five deaths. The agitation was led by a local coordination committee including left party leaders, but by August nonparty "Rayatu Sanghs" were active in many districts, including Belgaum, Bijapur and Billary, and Shimoga. When the Malaprabha committee met with the latter groups to draft a common set of demands, it was described as the end of leftist domination and a shift to "an ideology of ruralism" in which there was clear enunciation of principles for determining agricultural prices.[26] In fact, neither this nor the original farmers' committee had included a mention of agricultural laborers, and the main difference in demands was the dropping of the emphasis on ending private marketing through state takeover of trade and monopoly purchase schemes. But clearly a new trend was making itself felt.

In November the farmers' movement hit Maharashtra. It began with a stir on onions in which the leadership was taken up by a retired UN official (from the Universal Postal Union) who had taken up farming with twenty-four acres of dry land about thirty miles from Pune—Sharad Joshi. In 1980 the movement burst into nearby Nasik district, the main center of onion production in India as a whole (with 30 percent of the total crop produced there), with weeks of agitation that included *rasta roko*, *rail roko*, satyagrahas, and two killed in police firing. Maharashtra, a state that had had little rural militancy, was electrified. In Vidarbha there were clashes between police and cotton producers; in Mehsana district of Gujarat, cotton-growing peasants formed a new organization; and in Tamilnadu a bandh at the end of December left eight dead. In the process Sharad Joshi began putting forward his theory that the primary contradiction in the country was between "Bharat" (primarily the villages but also including the unorganized urban sector, "refugees from Bharat in the cities") and "India" (the Westernized industrial-bureaucratic elite, inheritors of colonial exploitation). The issue was one of exploitation, in which surplus was being extracted from the peasantry via the market mechanism and unequal exchange. The key to fighting this exploitation was the demand for higher prices for their crops, that is, "remunerative prices." As he told journalist Olga Tellis in a 1980 interview,

> Before independence it was the British government which took their raw materials for a song, processed the raw materials in London and Manchester, and then sold the finished product at enormous profit. Today, Pune, Calcutta and Bombay are the London and Manchester. And our current rulers have replaced the British in grabbing the wealth of the country. I do not believe in sophisticated terms like "class struggle." You may call this whatever you like. But I call this the struggle between Bharat and India, the fight for liberation by Bharat from India.[27]

The left and opposition parties, though partly caught by surprise, attempted to respond to the new movement by drawing up "charters of demands" that included the price issue along with efforts to inject a "proletarian leadership" by the injection of demands for nationalization of trade in foodgrains, some emphasis on agricultural laborers, and attempts to "sideline the rich peasants" by various ways (e.g., demanding forgiveness of debts for small peasants only). They organized marches to state capitals such as Nagpur and Bangalore that were planned to climax with the opening of legislative assembly sessions in December and that united the Communists, Janata party socialists, and Congress dissidents. A nationwide meeting of opposition party leaders planned a similar "long march" to Delhi that was scheduled to converge on the capital on March 15, 1981.[28]

But, these "left and opposition" party marches did not draw much spontaneous response from the peasantry, although party cadres were mobilized and held many discussions about "class and caste" issues on the way, and although workers in the cities provided food and in some cases joined the final demonstrations. Politicians also more or less ignored them and did their serious negotiating with the independent peasant organizations. There was a growing recognition that a new force was coming into existence beyond the claims of the parties. As Raj

Krishna of the Planning Commission said, "I think the Assam movement and the farmers' agitation in Nasik are going to set the trend for the future. As days go by, politicians will be thrown into the dustbin by the people."[29]

But Indira Gandhi and many of the state-level governments took a hard line, describing these as "rich farmer" movements and attempting to appeal to a rural poor/dalit base against them. Tamilnadu chief minister M.G.R. accused Narayanswami Naidu of trying "to bring back the golden days of feudalism," while Gandhi chose a meeting of police officials to make hard-hitting charges of "obstructionism" against the movement.[30] Negotiations between Sharad Joshi and agricultural minister Rao Birendra Singh got nowhere, and 1981 saw a resurgence of struggle. There was a March meeting of H. S. Rudrappa of Karnataka, Joshi, and Naidu at Hassan in Karnataka; following this, another statewide agitation was held in April that resulted in police firing, leaving three dead in Hassan district. In Maharashtra a stir on milk and rice prices sponsored by the Shetkari Sanghatana on November 10 saw clashes in Nasik, Ahmednagar, Dhule, Jalgaon, and Aurangabad districts, leaving four dead.[31]

In early 1982 the Shetkari Sanghatana held its first official conference in a small taluka town in Nasik, with 18,000 delegates representing half the districts in Maharashtra and a concluding rally of one lakh. (The "one lakh" or 100,000 figure was to become the "defining level" for major farmers' agitation rallies). Many of the leaders, with a focus on elections, argued for caution, but Joshi took a militant line, asserting that the structure of the Sanghatana should be kept amorphous on the grounds of a need for flexibility and secrecy: "We shall use guerrilla tactics and ensure that all our agitations can be launched at forty-eight-hour notice." The conference closed with the warning, "Let the rulers of India be warned: The age of the peasant has arrived."[32]

The Geography of "Bharat"

The farmers' movement, or new peasant movement, was a product of the commercialization of agriculture, but it did not arise in the most inequalitarian regions of capitalist agriculture. Coastal Andhra and Kerala saw little of the movement, and in Tamilnadu it was not the extremely hierarchical delta region of Thanjavur but the upland, commercialized Coimbatore that was the heart of the movement. In Maharashtra it began in Nasik, a poorer and drier part of western Maharashtra, and gained its main base in the eastern cotton-growing region of Vidarbha and in dry, relatively backward Marathwada: the western sugarcane belt, focus of political-economic power of rural Maharashtra, always evaded the hold of Shetkari Sanghatana. Northeastern India—backward and "semifeudal"—was left outside its purview, while it swept the northwest (Punjab, Haryana, then western U.P.). But the northwest, though a center of green revolution "development," was not highly inegalitarian by Indian standards: although the gap between peasants and agricultural laborers was strong and nearly coincided with the caste gap between primarily caste Hindu jats and primarily dalit chamars, among peasants as a whole there was relatively less inequality.

This was, then, a movement of peasant smallholders, of those peasants who worked on their own land, though some also hired labor and some hired themselves out as laborers. It was a "new social movement," given birth to by the realities of uneven statist-directed capitalist development in India, and with an ideology and thrust that pointed to a different kind of "liberation." It was defined by several characteristics:

Regional Variations and Nationality/Community Identities

Although there were efforts from the beginning at coordination and all-India organization building, the new farmers' organizations were formed independently within the different "linguistic states" or "nationalities" of India, and they bore the stamp of different regional-national traditions and self-consciously defined themselves in relation to these. All the new social movements in some sense had both an all-India and a regional-national thrust, but this operated in different ways. The women's movement was slower to define itself in relation to "vernacular" traditions, and the dalit movement and anticaste movements arose in ways that were determined by local traditions but still saw themselves as an all-India movement. In contrast, the farmers' movement had an all-India thrust and took the country as a whole as the most meaningful frame of action, but it was very consciously organized in terms of regional-national peasant "communities." Their innovative "discourse," to use a popular academic term, was not only at the all-India and English-language level in posing the new contradiction of "Bharat versus India," but also functioned at the vernacular level in relating to regional traditions.

These traditions could be constraining as well as democratic. For example, the Bharatiya Kisan Union (BKU) in western U.P., and indeed the whole jat-based upsurge in the northwest, were organized through the *khap panchayats* (clan councils) of the jat peasants. These allowed strong mobilization and a powerful projection of a peasant community—but they also helped to maintain the anti-dalit and patriarchal character of the caste panchayats. The BKU was able to expand beyond a single caste in drawing Muslims, gujar caste peasants, and to some extent the artisan castes into its movement, but it found it difficult to cross the dalit-caste Hindu barrier.[33] In contrast, in Maharashtra where caste panchayats were irrelevant to the broad Maratha-Kunbi caste cluster and where there was a greater overlap of caste and economic categories, the Shetkari Sanghatana developed with a more purely "scientific" rhetoric of surplus and exploitation, on the one hand, and a strong appeal to the democratic traditions of the Marathi peasantry, on the other, above all invoking the images of Shivaji and Phule. Shivaji was depicted as a "peasant king"—in self-conscious opposition to the fundamentalists' projection of him as the founder of a "Hindu raj"—with frequent reiteration of the rhetoric of guerrilla warfare-based militarism popular among the Maharashtrian peasantry. Phule was appealed to for his analysis of peasant exploitation, and the Shetkari Sanghatana adopted his mythical invocation of "Bali Raja" as the symbol of a primordial egalitarian peasant-warrior Marathi identity.

An analysis of these regionally based identities of the farmers' organizations on "peasant communities" should note that although their names incorporated the regional words for "peasant" (kisan, shetkari, rayatu), they often defined themselves in a much broader form. Thus, for example, Nandjundaswamy of Karnataka argued that the Rayatu Sangh was a "village movement" and not simply a "peasant movement," while Joshi's projection of "Bharat" sought to encompass the urban unorganized sector and exclude the rural oligarchy, and even *shetkari* was defined in Sanghatana terminology to include artisans and agricultural laborers, indeed all those dependent economically on agriculture, as well as cultivators. Conversely, some of the "nationality" movements arising in peripheral or "internally colonized" regions of India like Jharkhand (the south Bihar mainly tribal belt) very clearly had a peasant base and expressed some of the "peasant community" opposition to external state-bureaucratic exploitation that was expressed in the farmers' movement on a broader scale. The opposition of Jharkhandi/daku, for instance, in the south Bihar region had some similarities to the "Bharat-India" distinction in its theses of exploitation. In other words, while within the spectrum of "nationality" movements (Punjab, Assam, Jharkhand, Kashmir, etc.) there was a gradation of demands ranging from full independence to regional autonomy, so there was also a very thin line between these and the farmers' movements, which were also based on a peasantry perceived as a community, theorized a process of surplus extraction to an outside or urban center, organized for autonomy, and politically supported a decentralized state structure. (Some Naxalite groups theorized this similarity by seeing the farmers' organizations as representing the "national bourgeoisies" of their states).

Mass Base

The mass base of the new peasant organizations also reflected the structure of local peasant communities. By and large it has been broad, centered on the shudra middle castes, including many of the groups classed as OBCs, not but tending to exclude dalits. In Maharashtra, the Shetkari Sanghatana draws only on the "dominant" maratha-kunbis, but also includes the very broad range of "other backward castes," artisans, herding castes like dhangars, and so on. Dalits are also members, but in low proportion. Gujarat's Khedut Samaj and Kisan Sangh are centered on the patidar community, though its leadership includes some of the brahman and bania upper castes, while many koli (OBC) cultivators are included. The Tamilnadu organization was described as drawing its members from the "gounders, naidus, reddiyar, tewar, vanniyars, and nadar," while "Muslims, chettiyars, pillais, brahmans, and mudaliars" who don't usually do agriculture were said not to be in it, and harijans were also underrepresented.[34] In Karnataka, the Rayatu Sangh is said to be based mainly on lingayats and vokkaligas, with its internal politics often reflecting the competition of these two dominant caste-clusters, though it made alliances with dalits. In BKU the base was clearly the jat peasantry, but with an inclusion of other broad categories of caste Hindu and Muslim peasants and artisans. In all cases, it must be noted, the organizations take pride in overcoming religious divisions, and their claim to include Hindus and Muslims, or Hindus and Sikhs in the case of Punjab, is not unfounded.[35]

Autonomous Character

The autonomous character of the new peasant movement was expressed with each organization's firm assertion of their independent, "nonparty" character. Members of political parties might be part of these organizations (those who were usually from the Congress, the BJP or the Janata Party/Janata Dal, or from regional parties, since Communists usually associated themselves with their own party-linked peasant organizations), but their leaders were firm in rejecting a direct political link. As with other new movements, this was in part a result of a growing and general distrust of politicians and a disillusionment with established politics; parties, whether of the "left" or "right," were seen more and more as simply trying to "use" the movements; they were characterized variously as all being brahmanic/upper caste, patriarchal, or representatives of "India" exploiting "Bharat." But there was also the failure of both left and right parties to evolve as political formations that could articulate the themes of the movements. In the case of the peasant movement, neither the "four-anna socialism" of the Congress nor the "twelve-anna socialism" ("democratic revolution") of the Communist parties nor the Hindu nation ideology of the right suited its needs. The socialists and their political formations (Janata Dal, Janata party) came closest with their invocation of political decentralization, Gandhism, and village-focused development, but this was not linked to an analysis of exploitation and it was simply— given the reformist, even statist and authoritarian practice of these parties—not taken seriously.

Forms of Struggle

The forms of struggle were also distinct from both the "armed struggle" orientation of the Naxalite left (and of the guerrilla-based or "national liberation fronts" of various types in the peripheral regions/nationalities of India) and from the reformist practice of the mainstream left parties. Techniques such as satyagrahas, rasta rokos, mass rallies, and fasting might become generalized enough to be used in a variety of movements, but where the mainstream political parties generally oriented these to trying to affect parliamentary decisions, the farmers' organizations were more often oriented to direct action that expressed independence rather than "making demands of the state." Thus, for example, Nanjundaswamy might say, "Another political right we have been asserting, not demanding, is concerning the relationship between the people as sovereign and the so-called burra sahibs, the bureaucrats and salaried servants. . . . We now make them take the permission of the villagers, before entering the village." [36] Or, while the government talked of "debt-relief" (*karz-mafi*) programs, implying a "forgiveness" of something owed by the peasant to the state, Sharad Joshi was to use the term *karz-mukti*, "liberation" from debt, claiming that peasants were "declaring themselves liberated" from their debts and were simply not going to pay back the loans. This was militancy of a particular type, embodied in language as well as in the actions of the movement, which included both efforts at pressuring the state and a rather different practice of locally based, sometimes spontaneous self-assertion by villagers. Struggles (in particular the mass occupation of public spaces in the cities that began to occur after 1984) also involved an important demonstration effect that was important in overcoming traditional and imposed social divisions. For instance as Dipankar Gupta has written of a 1988 campaign of the U.P. BKU, "Less than a year before the BKU chose Meerut as its site of agitation, the city had been engulfed by one of the worst communal carnages in recent memory. . . . The brutality of the carnage left a pall of gloom over the city and the atmosphere was surcharged with mutual suspicion and hostility. . . . The peasants of the BKU changed all this: they opened Meerut up to its residents again by publicly avowing in their thousands to uphold communal harmony." [37] Indeed, the mass intermixing of people in the huge rallies, city occupations, and long-distance "nonticket" train travel was a crucial experience for all participants.

Vision of Social Transformation

Finally, the farmers' movement involved a new vision of social transformation. Peasants, like all exploited sections, had dual tendencies in their actions and thinking: they struggled for survival and then for what they understood as a better life within the framework of the system; and they rejected it and made efforts to formulate an alternative system. More specifically, their attitude toward "green revolution" agricultural technology was ambivalent: they sought more inputs, more technology, and were part of the thrust toward consumerism in growing in Indian society, but at the same time they recognized the destructive effects of the new seeds and inputs and looked for alternatives—a dualism embodied in the Punjab BKU's demand for the implementation of the Pepsi Cola multinational project because it promised diversification of agriculture, and in the campaign of the Karnataka Rayatu Sangh to uproot large-scale plantations of eucalyptus. But while the first tendency led to integration into the world capitalist system, the second gave impetus for an alternative that was clearly different in direction from the traditional Marxist developmental path. Sunil Sahasrabudhey calls this Gandhian anti-developmentalism:

> An important feature of the peasant movement is that none of its demands are for development in the rural areas. They have neither asked for easier terms of credit nor for opening of hospitals and schools. In fact, the movement presents an entirely new concept of development. . . . When the peasant gets the extra money, which is his due, he will invest it in the manner which he deems fit. It will be up to him to decide whether to build roads and canals, establish schools and hospitals, develop research laboratories, carry out research on the farm or do whatever else he may think necessary and useful. Let not anyone else try to determine what he should do with his money. His money has always been spent by someone else and the result is there for everyone to see. Eradication of the poverty of the rural people, not through development, but by giving them fair returns for their produce is the strongest and most radical argument for decentralization. Let not the professional social scientist worry about the effects of such decentralization on the nation-state. The peasant movement is thus committed to eradicate the poverty of the rural people by undoing "development" in theory and in practice. This may give some idea of what one means when one says that the peasant movement today exhibits signs of transcending modernity in continuity with the Gandhian ideology.[38]

In opposing state-controlled capitalist development as basically exploitative, movement ideologists were putting forward a vision of transformation that was also radically different from that presented by Marxists in India (with the partial exception of Naxalite arguments for "people's power at the local level"). When Marxists appealed to poor peasants and agricultural laborers with the argument that the village would be transformed into a socialist utopia through "land to the tiller" followed by collectivization, they assumed the same type of industrialized agriculture (based on chemical inputs and where possible mechanization) characteristic of modern capitalism. The role of the state in controlling trade and marketing and of the bureaucracy that would manage collective institutions continued to be taken for granted. It was also taken for granted that ultimately the rural "citizen" of tomorrow would be something like a wage-paid factory worker.

In contrast, peasant movement leaders not only challenged collectivization and were ready to argue that it involved atrocities against peasants, but also argued against "proletarianization" itself. Thus, when Nanjundaswamy stated that "every day a cultivator is becoming a landless laborer. It is exactly this phenomenon we want eliminated—cultivators becoming landless,"[39] or when Joshi stated that "we say everybody should become a property holder" and expressed support for the landless getting control of government lands on the grounds that "then they'll become part of our movement," what was implied was

that all should become petty commodity producers (or partial subsistence producers) rather than the universal wage laborers of "actually existing socialism."
In other words, the generalization of property rather than the abolition of property was the issue. This was not always clearly formulated, and at other points
there were arguments for keeping aspects of "common property" of the village,
but the resistance to any kind of state control or "ownership" was clear. It was
not without reason that exponents of a traditional left point of view saw in this an
"ideology of ruralism" that was quite alien to what they understood of "proletarian principles."

"A Marxist Has to Recognize Reality"

But was this ideology of the peasant movement basically Gandhian? Its most
articulate exponent said no. Argued Sharad Joshi,

> I make it a point to say that this is an independent system of thought,
> comparable only with the Marxist system of thought. We share with Marxism
> the materialist approach, find out errors in Marx where he was not materialist,
> we also accept the importance of capital accumulation as a generating force,
> we find his analysis of surplus value incorrect, and therefore we find ourselves
> in a position to explain Marxism's failure, i.e. why the revolution did not take
> place in the industrialized countries, why workers have never acted as a class
> as such. The two reactions to the industrial revolution up to now are the
> communist and the Gandhian; both are intellectually inadequate. We are defi-
> nitely making up for the errors in their logic.[40]

If audacious, this was part of the style of the man who emerged as one of the
major charismatic leaders of the period, making the transition from Geneva to
the dry land of Maharashtrian farms, claiming his knowledge of agriculture out
of having his own feet in the dirt, putting time and energy into long and arduous
rural campaigns, able to talk of Preobrazhinsky and Rosa Luxembourg in one
breath and in another to evoke the image of the peasant woman driven by
poverty and drought to give birth to her child while breaking stones on a government relief project. It was consistent with Joshi's style that he would occasionally identify himself with Marxism, but in the provocative form of "sometimes I
think I'm the only Marxist in India," charging that others refused to recognize a
material reality that had made notions like the labor theory of value and the
leadership of the working class simply outmoded. It was a style that infuriated a
good section of political activists in India and made him a hero to a major part of
the Indian masses.

Sharad Joshi's ideological contribution is associated mainly with his "Bharat-
India" division and with the price issue as a "one-point program" for the peasant
movement. But "one-point program" is misleading in the sense that a large number of other issues were taken up by Shetkari Sanghatana. In fact, the insistence on a

"one-point program" had a dual polemical and ideological purpose: on one hand, against the left and other movements, it made the claim that giving fair prices for agricultural produce was the main way to remove poverty; but on the other hand, within the movement itself, it posed itself against the tendency to argue for more and cheaper inputs, more fertilizer subsidies, higher investment in agriculture, and so forth, and insisted instead that the issue was exploitation and that peasants did not need anything from the government, that they only sought justice and a fair return for their labor. The central slogan of Shetkari Sanghatana is exactly this: *bhiknako, have gamala dam*, that is, "we don't want alms but recompense for our sweat." "We're not asking for anything, only that you stop exploiting us." As Joshi distinguished himself from Devi Lal (and all the politicians who attempted to use the peasant movement), "Devi Lal also attaches a lot of importance to the proportion of budgetary allocation for the rural areas and the agricultural sector. In our opinion that is not an important issue at all. Agriculture is the source of all wealth. So what is ploughed back into agriculture couldn't be that important. What is ploughed *away* is far more important." [41]

Capital accumulation and exploitation were thus central in Shetkari Sanghatana theory and rhetoric. But with Sharad Joshi distinguished himself from conventional historical materialism on several counts. One was in stressing that capital accumulation had taken place primarily from agriculture, by extracting both the surplus labor of the peasant and the produce of the land; this centrality continued, he argued, even into the modern era with provision of cheap raw materials and cheap food for factory production and urban populations. The second was his argument that the basis of such accumulation was not so much property ownership as force and violence. The first point led to a fascination with Rosa Luxembourg's notion of "primitive capitalist accumulation" and its ramifications; the second to a characterization of the main exploiters as looters (the Marathi terms *lutaru, lut* are basically the same) or as bullies and gangsters (dadas and *goondas*) rather than as "capitalists" or the "wealthy." Joshi's theory argued, in effect, that the main capital accumulation took place *outside* the realm of commodity production and exchange in which surplus value reigned and labor-power-selling workers engaged in class struggle with property-owning capitalists; it rather involved a wider "looting system" in which accumulation was from the surplus of the peasantry and the wealth of the land and organized mainly by force and violence. This "looting system," according to Joshi in a somewhat casual borrowing from Marxist "stage" theory, had gone through various stages in the course of history, from pure robbery to slavery, the extraction of surplus by feudal lords, and now the state-backed looting of the market economy.

Since "class" continued to be defined in the conventional sense as based on private property, the farmers' movement was not a "class struggle" (and here the inequality of the village community was admitted), but it was an "economistic" struggle. Its aim was to stop this to stop the looting form of capital accumulation that resulted in uneven development, with the centralization of capital in industrialized metropolises, on the one hand, and mass rural poverty, on the other. Rather than ask for concessions, cheaper inputs, more investment in agriculture, the entire course of development should be reversed. But while this involved a projection of a possible nonexploitative ("nonlooting") accumulation of capital that would be balanced and decentralized, with a village-centered agro-industrial economy, Joshi also strongly distinguished himself from the Gandhians. His claim was to have a scientific and materialistic analysis of peasant exploitation as well as a substantial appreciation of modern technology; the Gandhians in contrast were seen as romantic, antitechnology, idealistic, and reformist.

In stressing "nonviolence" as part of the movement, he claimed an appreciation for "Gandhian methods of struggle," but insisted that his attachment to nonviolence was on the basis of its practicality, not on "principle." In fact, a hard-headed approach to movement strategy, which took seriously the realities of conflict with the state, was also one of his points of pride, and it is striking that this nonviolent movement was full of militaristic language, from *ran-niti* ("rules of the battlefield") to *senapati* ("general") to *fauz* ("army") and similar terms. Gandhism in any case had taken a different incarnation in Maharashtra (where a peasant leader of the 1942 "Quit India" movement would insist that sabotage, robbing trains, and physical punishment of traitors were all part of "Gandhian nonviolence"), but the nonviolence of the farmers' movement was also compatible with Mahendra Singh Tikait, the later jat leader, having with him a constant armed guard. Clearly, new forms of struggle were being generated.

"Bharat Declares War on India"

By the mid-1980s, Punjab on the one hand and the farmers' movement on the other were at the center of a developing confrontation over prices and the provision of foodgrain that came to a head in 1984 and, according to Marxist theorist John Roosa, "marks a critical turning point in the cycles of post-World War II class struggles in India."[42] But it was the kind of "class struggle" not admitted as such by the vast majority of Indian Marxists or even by movement leaders like Sharad Joshi who was rejecting such notions as "class" and substituting instead "economistic struggle."

From 1981 onward two major all-India trends, the farmers' movement, as a main representative of the new social movements, and rising religious fundamentalism seemed both to be centering in Punjab. In this premier state of the "green revolution," the late 1970s saw an upsurge of protest but also a religious interpretation given to it by Bhindranwale and other Sikh fundamentalists; the Akali Dal tried to take hold of this with a *dharm yudh* or "holy war" agitation that actually embodied more economic (farmers' movement) demands than religious ones. It was the central government, Roosa has argued, that played up the more fundamentalist leaders outside the Akali Dal's main force in an effort to stamp all Punjabi farmers as "Khalistanis" and "terrorists." Nevertheless, the Akali Dal was getting some precedence over the pure farmers' organization, the BKU—an indication of the continuing problem the movement would have with politics and religious/community identities.

At the same time, the farmers' movement itself, born on a regional-linguistic basis, was making serious attempts to establish an all-India center and coordination. Narayanswami Naidu of Tamilnadu had taken the initiative to organize an "All-India Kisan Sammelan" at Hyderabad on December 12, 1980. This was attended by representatives of many states, in particular the Zimindari Union of Punjab, the Rayatu Sangh of Karnataka, the Kisan Sangarsh Samiti of Haryana, and Naidu's own organization. Shetkari Sanghatana, then involved in struggle, had no representation. This meeting resulted in the formation of an all-India body called the Bharatiya Kisan Union (BKU); the Punjab organization changed its name to BKU, the others kept their names, interpreting them as the equivalent in regional languages. The BKU adopted a flag, with green border and white center and a peasant holding a plough.

This first effort quickly came to grief. In May 1982 Naidu organized a political party, the Peasants and Toilers party, without consulting others in the organization. In a May 29 BKU meeting at Khanna, Punjab, he was expelled by the northern majority. But this resulted in two BKUs—the BKU(N) and BKU(M) after Bhupinder Singh Mann of the Punjab. At this point Sharad Joshi intervened, arguing for a federal structure rather than a unitary one, with membership open to state units which would retain their autonomy; they should be "nonpolitical" (independent of political parties) and accept nonviolence as the form of protest. This was accepted at a meeting of all groups in Wardha, Maharashtra, in October 1982, when the Interstate Coordinating Committee was set up.

The movement now set its sights for an assault on Delhi. An initial agitation, planned for the Asiad games in 1983, could not be organized due to the lack of a base around Delhi at the time. Then Chandigarh was selected for an agitation in 1984 with a planned foodgrain embargo. This quite fit Joshi's orientation to battlefield strategy: an embargo here had every prospect of really hurting the Indian ruling class, with Punjab at the time contributing 60 percent of foodgrains brought to market—the main source of food for the cities.

In February 1984 the Shetkari Sanghatana held its second conference at Parbhani, in the dry region of Marathwada—the locale marking a significant jump east from its original western Maharashtra base. This was concluded with the usual huge rally and a continuing tone of militancy. Declaring 1984 as the "year of independence of the peasantry," Joshi announced an all-around program designed to "delink" Bharat from India: peasants would simply withdraw from the market. They would grow grain only for themselves; convert foodgrain land to vegetables, fruit, and trees; revert to the practice of keeping part of their lands fallow; and for at least one year would not purchase tractors, power tillers, diesel engines, or synthetic cloth. As Joshi argued in an interview, "The list of goods to be boycotted has been very carefully composed. We have singled out highly capital-intensive industries which derive a large part of their revenues from the farmers. Thus we intend to use the enormous power of the farmer both as a producer and a consumer and also in this election year as a voter."[43]

The business magazine that published the account of this "Bharat-India war" commented that the strategy was "a much stiffer challenge than that posed by Bhindranwale's reactionary zealots."[44]

The Punjab agitation was planned, with as its first step a gherao of the state capital at Chandigarh. Peasants from Maharashtra and elsewhere joined their Punjabi brothers (there were not too many women on this occasion) to make it a massive event, nearly 40,000 peasants with tractors and bullock carts occupying Chandigarh. An account of the event illustrated its spirit of unity and tolerance as a main sign that "there is still hope" in spite of growing religious fundamentalism and violence in the state:

> It is in Chandigarh where the ultimate proof that Punjab is still not burning manifests itself. It is in the form of a massive 40,000-strong farmers' rally under the banner of the Bharatiya Kisan Union. A rally which has created a city within a city, with numbered and well-ordered kothis, a daily supply of fresh vegetables, eggs and milk from the villages. There is *akhand path* and a *langar* on the golf course, and all entrances to the Punjab Raj Bhavan have been blocked. The farmers, mainly Sikhs of course, but with batches of Hindu supporters from Haryana, are exemplary in their nonviolent conduct, but utterly determined to stay on in the state capital until the government negotiates on their demands.[45]

This Chandigarh gherao was followed by a weeklong boycott of rural market towns in May that "was a complete success" and was joined by the wings of the Communist parties and the Akali Dal. The BKU also announced a banning of officials trying to recover loans from the villages, which was described as a situation "tantamount to a parallel government being run by the union in the villages."[46] Then, in an effort to grab the initiative, the Akali Dal announced that its volunteers would block the movement of all grain out of the Punjab with effect from June 3.

The day after this announcement, the Central Reserve Police force took up, for the first time, positions in buildings surrounding the Golden Temple—the central holy place of Sikhs, where fundamentalists had been holed up for some time. Firing started on June 1. On June 3 the army began firing again, and the actual invasion took place on June 4. According to government figures, 493 civilians and "terrorists" were killed, a low estimate by most counts. Gurudwaras (Sikh temples) in the countryside were also besieged, and some 6,500 Sikh men, women, and even children were thrown into jail. This massive reign of terror which included the promulgation of various draconian ordinances led, after an ominous lull, to the murder of Indira Gandhi in November by two Sikh body-guards—one a dalit Sikh—and from there to massive pogroms against Sikhs in Delhi and other north Indian cities. It accomplished what the entire period of earlier Khalistani propaganda and agitation for the Anandpur Saheb resolution had never done, the beginnings of a real alienation between Hindus and Sikhs in the Punjab and the permanent communalization of the situation. The "hope" felt by journalist Baljit Malik in April and embodied in the farmers' movement was buried.

And the peasants were decisively defeated. As Roosa notes,

> The reason for the Indian government's state terrorism, with all its atten-dant mendacity and hypocrisy, is the crushing of the Punjabi farmers' move-ment.... The Punjabi farmers have been soundly defeated. Without any organizational power and without any increase in procurement prices they have been forced to make ends meet by concentrating on increasing their production. Thus, despite all the commotion about communalism and terror-ism, both 1985 and 1986 yielded record-breaking harvests.... Before 1985 the government was having problems procuring enough wheat and rice from Punjab's farmers, after 1985 the government was procuring more than it could handle.[47]

Through all the subsequent years of Khalistani guerrilla activities, the Indian state continued to procure grain from the Punjab. But while it remained an important state for grain procurement, gradually the neighboring states of Hary-ana and western U.P. became major producers in wheat, with the farmers' move-ment in the region so weakened and divided that it could do little to use its blockading power in this area. Not simply Punjab, but the farmers' movement of India had suffered a defeat in this major "cycle of class struggle" and their first big confrontation with the state.

Conclusion

In the years between 1972 and 1985 the new peasant movement emerged with one of the strongest challenges to the Indian state. In the process, it also posed new questions to the traditional Marxist theory of social change.

It challenged Marxist economic analysis in two ways. First, in asserting the unity of the peasantry and the role of the exploitation of peasant labor in capital accumulation, it directly challenged the notion of "class." (This was in contrast to the dalit and women's movements, which had generally simply posed "caste" and "patriarchy" as additive to "class"). Marxism has generally used the term/concept of class in two ways, one (which we might call the "general con-cept of class") defined in terms of *exploitation*, those who produce the surplus as against those who appropriate it; and the "specific concept of class" as defined in terms of *property*, or owners versus nonowners of the means of production.

What the challenge of the peasant movement (in practice, and as formulated often aggressively by Sharad Joshi) laid bare was the fact that the two definitions did not identify coinciding groups, that is, that some "owners of the means of production" could be exploited, while some nonowners could be appropriators of surplus. (In different ways, the questions raised by statist societies were similar.) Marxists were faced with the dilemma of either changing and vastly broadening their concept of class, or admitting that class as defined in terms of private property did not explain all cases of exploitation and often not even the most important cases. The fact that most Marxists ignored the issue and did neither did not change the gravity of the challenge.

The attack on the notions of "class" and "surplus value" was put forward most clearly by Maharashtra's Shetkari Sanghatana leader Sharad Joshi and was linked with a general argument that the primary basis of capital accumulation was the exploitation of peasant production (including peasant labor and natural resources) outside the realm of capitalist production and commodity exchange and mediated mainly by force, not the ownership of property. Because of this "externality" to the realm of property-defined classes, the struggle of the peasantry against exploitation was seen as an "economistic" one but not as a "class struggle."

Second, and more indirectly, the antistate and decentralist thrust of the movement, the aim of retaining the accumulated surplus at the village level, challenged the traditional Marxist notion of industrialization and large-scale urban-based "collective" production as progressive. In this it coincided with the critique of the environmental/green movement; though it did not articulate the need for an "alternative development" as clearly as the environmental movement was to do, it did stress much more the role of exploitation of human labor in the current destructive development.

Ideologies of the farmers' movement thus provided a clear challenge to a Marxism that limited its analysis only to capital-labor struggles as defined within a realm of commodity exchange; they looked to a wider arena of capital accumulation and economic exploitation taking into account factors other than class defined in the narrow sense, and in many ways their thrust coincided with that of the developing environmental movements. At the same time, there was an incompleteness in the theories put forward; for instance, the nature of the wider "looting system" was not linked to an analysis of the development of capitalism as such; nor were projected visions of a new village-oriented industrialization linked to analyses of the development of the forces of production. These were linked to a failure in the end to really deal with the role of local inequalities (e.g., inequalities within the village, between laborers and peasants, between castes) in relation to the wider system, and a failure to make a theoretical articulation with the environmentalist critique of industrialization. Finally, although the movement was very strongly oriented to developing as a mass movement putting pressure on the state as well as reconstructing and promoting the autonomy of village society, though it was apparently one of the most successful in doing so, with its huge mobilizations and the resultant expressed fears of the Indian elite that the "rich farmers' lobby" was becoming a dominant political force, in the end the political sphere remained as much of a problem for it as for the other new movements.

6

The Environmental Movement

O brothers and sisters, run and seek shelter
A dust-storm draws near,
A storm fills the earth, a mist overhangs the sky,
Our land drifts away.
Afterwards you will not find the pathway.
Our land was filled with darkness.

—Song of the Birsa Munda revolt[1]

Jharkhand: The First Red-Green Movement

IN THE TUMULTUOUS 1972–75 period a united movement of mine workers, tribals, and low-caste peasants arose in the hilly districts of South Bihar and adjoining districts. This area was the center of India's coal and iron mines and much of its steel industry, but more than almost anywhere else in the country this industrialization was visibly a parasitical enclave, grabbing the land of the local population, and destroying much of the rest through deforestation, and pollution, sucking the life of the native communities to turn their men into unskilled workers and their women into prostitutes sent all over India. This "Jharkhand" or "forest area" was thus quite visibly a symbol of the way in which the realm of capitalist production and accumulation was extracting resources and exploiting labor drawn from outside the realm of commodity exchange, destroying natural resources and dominating and marginalizing whole communities in the process.

It showed, in particular, the community aspect of this process of accumulation and destruction. Nirmal Sengupta, arguing for the continuity of "tribe" and "peasant," has noted that "Jharkhand . . . presents essentially the same dichotomy—but in a more vivid form—between industry and agriculture common to every part of the country."[2] Here, though, the "India-Bharat" contradiction protested by the new peasant movement was accentuated by the fact that the industrialists, managers, merchants, moneylenders, contractors, and even skilled workers in mines and factories were outsiders—north Biharis, Bengalis, Maharashtrians, Punjabis—and these viewed the locals as backward "adivasis." The local people included several communities classified as "tribes" (the biggest of these were the huge million-strong agricultural communities of the Mundas, Hos, and Santhals, speaking a language distantly related to those of Southeast Asia) as well as dalits, artisans, and caste Hindu peasants. But, as Sengupta has argued, the "tribal/nontribal" distinction was in many ways artificial; the "nontribals" were also groups that had become drawn into the caste Hindu fold only a few centuries before and in that sense had been "detribalized." In the nineteenth and twentieth centuries, major communities like the mahatos went through varying processes of self-identification as "tribal" or as "peasant/ksatriya" communities linked to the kurmi-kunbi groups elsewhere; as for the Munda-speaking group, their earliest "modern" organization, the Adivasi Mahasabha, evolved into a political platform, the Jharkhand party, which included both "tribals" and "nontribals." The source of unity was regional-national: those clearly classed as "tribal," those ambiguously "tribal," and those (dalits and others) not considered "tribal" at all were now coming together again as Jharkhandis, inhabitants of the forest region of Jharkhand.

Their new upsurge began with the formation of the Jharkhand Mukti Morcha (Jharkhand Liberation Front) in 1972, almost a direct result of events following the nationalization of coal mines in 1971 when—due to the prospect of a rise in wages and benefits for government workers—nearly 50,000 local miners lost their jobs and were replaced by North Biharis.[3] The tribals were joined by a militant organization of mine workers under A. K. Roy and by mahato community leader Benod Bihari Mahto. Their long-standing demand for a separate Jharkhand state began to take on socialist overtones, proclaiming a Jharkhand without exploitation. By 1974, on "Jharkhand day," the struggle could field a huge demonstration of workers and peasants with red and green flags flying and slogans of Jharkhand-Lalkhand, "the forest land shall become a red land."

This was worker-peasant unity enough to gladden the hearts of any Marxist, particularly the Naxalite trends who thrilled to the fact that the tribals nearly always brought their bows and arrows to demonstrations. Articles in *Frontier* hailed the "fusion of the fight against national exploitation with that against class exploitation" and urged that "the vast working class in the Jharkhand region be integrated with the movement."[4]

But things were not so simple. For one, the majority of the working class, being outsiders to the region, speaking a different language, considering themselves of higher caste and with a life-style at least superficially higher than that of the local peasantry, remained aloof from the movement. As Sengupta admitted, "The Jharkhand struggle . . . is also directed against another oppressed class. . . . The most numerous section of the peasantry not merely grudges the organized working class, but actually holds that class responsible for its own wretched existence."[5]

To A. K. Roy, the miners' leader, this was because the organized working class did in fact share in the exploitation of the Jharkhandi peasantry. Roy—himself a Bengali brahman who had founded his mine workers' union on the "one-point program" of physically fighting back against the gangster mafia who held the entire mines area in thrall—took up the notion of "internal colonialism" for this reason. Roy argued that there were three geosocial regions in India: the egalitarian and nonstate hill regions, the river valleys, which were the centers of the feudal-agrarian regimes, and the capitalist and colonial coastal enclaves. Inequality began from the feudal period and was structured by caste: "The first ingredient of internal colonialism is the caste system which . . . broadly determined the division of labor within the country" and was now "reinforced by capitalism and turned into racism." [6] This perspective combined the theoretical thrusts of the anticaste and peasant movements, though Roy placed "propertied peasants" along with "organized employees and gentlefolk" on the other side of the "internal colonial" divide. He also excoriated left organizations for being dominated by middle-class intellectuals ("Tell me, how many tribals, low castes, minority communities or women . . . are in any key position in the Communist parties?" [7]) and took up the language of the anticaste movement to call for a *new dalit revolution*.

The Jharkhand movement in practice was bringing forward many of the new movement issues, from the peasant-worker alliance to the problems of caste and gender and even those of environmentalism. For instance, a kind of people's development attempt arose in the early 1970s, when the most popular of the new tribal leaders, Shibu Soren, took up the task of organizing an all-around movement in the rural areas of Dhanbad district. Beginning with the forcible harvesting of crops in a land-grab movement focused against outsider money-lender-landlords, it moved to get involved in issues of self-initiated development. As a report described the vision of the Jharkhand Mukti Morcha for "dynamizing the rural economy,"

> The local water resources would be tapped to provide irrigation. . . . Tribal peasants would take to high-yielding variety seeds and chemical fertilizers. Local resources would also be tapped to provide increasing quantity of organic manure. . . . Each village would have a grain-bank. . . . Village disputes would be settled in the village itself to avoid litigious expenses and to foster horizontal solidarity. . . . Each village would run a night-school. . . . The status of women would be elevated through ban on child marriage, polygamy, wife-beating and indiscriminate divorce. They would be imparted special skills in sewing and knitting. . . . The movement would ultimately aim at the creation of an autonomous state of Jharkhand comprising parts of Bihar, Madhya Pradesh, Orissa, and West Bengal. . . . [The Jharkhandi] would be a producer irrespective of caste, tribe or religion. [8]

What kind of mixture was this? Feminists would be quick to see the problems involved in trying to force the "petty-bourgeois morality" of the nuclear family and turn the toiling adivasi women, with their historical agricultural and forestry skills, into seamstresses, and they queried, "will feminist standards survive in Jharkhand?"[9] But throughout the 1970s there was little appreciation of the effort at alternative development, and no critiques of introducing fertilizers and HYVs through the help of nontribal "agricultural experts."

In any case, this popular developmental effort faded away, with its leader Shibu Soren temporarily won over by Indira Gandhi during the Emergency and drawn into direct government-sponsored developmental programs. It was replaced by a more direct clash of adivasi peasants with the Indian form of developmentalism. This was the militant resistance to two large dams in the area, both part of the Subarnarekha "multipurpose project"—Koel Karo, in the Ranchi area, where tribals mobilized to prevent trucks or any construction machinery from reaching the site, and the Icha dam in Singhbhum district, where there was near guerrilla warfare, leading to police combing operations in which at least twenty died in 1978–79.[10]

In Singhbhum a militant struggle also began to be organized against the Forest Corporation, which after being set up in 1975 had undertaken a program of commercial forestry involving the planting of teak, sometimes chopping down mixed local forests to do so. Teak is a tree native to western India, but in the Jharkhand region it was a commercial interloper, particularly in contrast to the native *sal*, the all-around tree so important to tribal economic and ritual life. Tribals undertook a campaign of uprooting teak, particularly destroying nurseries, which again led to clashes and loss of life.

During the same period one of the Naxalite groups, the Santosh Rana-led CPI(ML), was organizing the rural poor in one of the eastern parts of the district where there were nontribal landowners. "While the CPI(ML) is trying to organize laborers and poor peasants on the wage issue as part of the general agrarian program of the party," noted a PUCL report, "the Jharkhand Mukti Morcha is fighting for a separate Jharkhand state. The CPI(ML) supports the demand." The Naxalites considered wages and occupation of land the "main issue" and did not, according to the report, give much importance to the struggle of *sal* versus *sag*. To the adivasis this symbolized both their identity and their mode of life ("sal is ours; teak belongs to the exploiters"), but to Rana, the CPI(ML) leader, "an economy dependent on forests and sal trees was a primitive one from which the adivasis had to be uplifted."[11]

Had the Marxists looked deeper, they might have seen the dilemmas of development and the broader meaning of "agrarian revolution"; they might also have seen internal contradictions in the current developmental/antidevelopmental thrust, in which the uprooting of teak was named as *jungle kato*, "cut the forest," as tribals took land for cultivation. But while Marxist youth were involved in the Jharkhand movement from the beginning, as radical students, workers, trade union activists, and hard-working activist supporters, what Jharkhand meant to them was simply the "class and nation" debate. Here, local journals like

Shalapatra and *Jharkhand Varta*, as well as a major book on the "Jharkhand and the National Question" by Sitaram Sastri, helped forward the debate on the "nationality question," on one hand, and combated the notion of tribals as "primitive," on the other. But other issues, which could not be so easily theorized in traditional Marxist language, were neglected. A. K. Roy made an alternative attempt at conceptualization, but no one took him and his Marxist Coordination Committee very seriously at the intellectual level. In turn, Roy attacked the Marxists:

> The paradox of the situation in India is here the revolutionary philosophy is in the hands of the reactionary class while the reactionary philosophy has kept the revolutionary class submerged. All the unproductive people are the champion of revolutionary thesis and moving in the country with "fool proof" blueprints of revolution in their pockets but with nobody to read and hence perhaps no revolution; while the productive downtrodden, the Harijans and Adivasis meekly tail behind the ruling class.[12]

There was in the end little merger of Marxism with the "Jharkhandi nationality movement." Most of the nonparty Marxist intellectual-activists left; the Naxalite organizing stagnated. The Jharkhandis rejected the "red-green" combination for "green only," and their own politics evolved through splits and compromises with the ruling Congress party; for a time in the early 1980s the militancy of the movement died away. But they also moved to foster their own "organic intellectuals"—in 1980, the same year as a brutal police firing at Gua in Singhbhum district killed dozens in a major atrocity case, the Department of Tribal and Regional Languages at Ranchi University was formed, bringing together the U.S.-trained Ram Dayal Munda, the middle-caste B. P. Keshari, a woman tribal professor, Rose Kerketta, and others who collectively built a center for a Jharkhandi cultural revival.

Chipko: "What do the Forests Bear? Soil, Water, and Clean Air"

A peasants' movement, a women's movement, an ecology movement: the Chipko movement of the Himalayan foothill regions of Tehri Garwhal in Uttar Pradesh was all of these, as well as the most famous of India's "new social movements" in recent times. What was it "really"? In fact it contained in itself varying trends and facets, and the academic-intellectual debates about its significance in part reflected these internal ideological streams.

The area, as its historian Ramchandra Guha (himself a participant in the Chipko debates) has noted, had a history of peasant resistance to British-imposed commercialization; while these were not theorized at the time as "ecological," they did represent the peasantry's subsistence-oriented attitudes to the forests and opposition to the devastations that commercial forestry wrought on their lives, and they did reflect the relative egalitarianism (both in terms of caste and gender) of Himalayan peasant communities.[13] Independence came but did not change the mode of development, and pressure on the Himalayan forests intensified with increased felling of trees, road-building, and planting of pine for commercial wood. One of the European women disciples of Gandhi, Mira Behn, described how the relationship between "development" and destruction had led her to settle in the area:

> I became very realistically aware of the terrible floods which pour down from the Ganga catchment area, and I had taken care to have all the buildings constructed above the flood high-mark. Within a year or two I witnessed a shocking flood: as the swirling waters increased, there came first bushes and boughs and great logs of wood, then in the turmoil of more and more water came whole trees, cattle of all sizes and from time to time a human being clinging to the remnants of his hut. . . . The sight of these disastrous floods led me each summer to investigate the area north of Pashulok whence they came. Merciless deforestation as well as cultivation of profitable pines in pace of broad-leaf trees was clearly the cause. This in turn led me to hand over charge of Pashulok to the government staff and to undertake a community project in the valley of the Bhilangana. Here I build a little centre.[14]

By 1960s environmental pressures of the type pinpointed by Mira Behn were building up, and it was a disastrous 1970 flood of the Alaknanda River that woke people to take action on the problems.

The whole region was dominated by the Gandhian trend in the national movement, and Gandhian workers in the area had built up a series of Gram Swarajya Sanghs ('Village Self-Rule Leagues') that sought to develop alternative technology to use forest products to provide local employment. It was one of these, Chandi Prasad Bhatt's Dashaoli Gram Swarajya Sangh, that became the main organizing base of the early Chipko movement. The struggle developed when the forest department refused permission to fell ash trees to be converted into agricultural implements in the village of Mandal and then turned around and alloted the same patch to a sports manufacturer. In protest, the people turned to "tree-hugging," placing their bodies before the trees to prevent their felling. From this it got the name "Chipko" and the struggle became generalized in the region, with women being often more deeply involved than the men (who had less immediate interests in a forest economy because they were the migrant laborers to the plains) and even taking the major role in some cases, notably in the village of Reni in 1974.[15]

Then Sunderlal Bahuguna, working in the Bhagirathi Valley, took the initiative, and with his prophetic style, padyatras, and theorizing in radical Gandhian fashion on the relationship between humans and forests, projected the issue on a national and even an international level as an ecological one. As he later wrote,

> During the period of six years, Chipko movement has developed into a powerful, mass-based ecological movement for permanent economy against

the traditional short-sighted and destructive economy. The main contention of this movement is that the main gift of the Himalayas to the nation is water and its function is to produce, maintain and improve soil structure. Hence felling of green trees for commercial purposes should be stopped forthwith for at least ten to fifteen years, until green coverage of at least 60 percent area is restored as professed in the National Forest Policy of 1952.[16]

Bahuguna was an ecological radical who on the one hand was often voicing women's concerns (his wife Bimla Behn had been in the ashram of Sarla Behn, another of the Gandhian forerunners in the area, and he himself was inspired by Mira Behn to settle in the villages), and on the other came to almost reject an agricultural economy altogether on the grounds that it took more land to feed people with grain than with tree products. He also rejected Bhatt's alternative technology orientation, which focused on using resources for local development projects: "Today I see clearly that establishing sawmills in the hills is to join the project to destroy Mother Earth."[17]

These trends in the movement gave rise to ideological-academic debates that are still going on. One has related to how much Chipko was in fact a "women's movement." Vandana Shiva has projected it powerfully as such; Ramchandra Guha has denied it. Part of the issue here certainly rests on the definition of what a women's movement actually is; certainly studies have outlined differing "gender interests" in the forest economy, have shown the developing conflicts between male-dominated gram panchayats that were interested in commercial development of the forests and the women's *mahila mandals*, which were more concerned about provision of food and fodder and very naturally came to voice a subsistence and ecological orientation. They also experienced and protested the effects of commercialism on men and the family: "The men will sell the fruits and purchase liquor or tobacco."[18] It is also clear that there was a Gandhian heritage in the organization of women in the area, provided by the ashrams established by the various women pioneers.[19]

The debate over the "feminist" character of the movement has converged with another one, over the differing ideological trends within it. It is not accidental that Shiva was associated with Bahuguna, and in an article traced the development of the struggle from its early days to the focus on providing supplies of water, fodder, and other products not only for the local inhabitants but for the Gangetic plains as a whole as one from an "economic" to an "ecological" perspective. Guha considers this unfair to Bhatt, and in a reply to Shiva and Bandhopadyaya entitled "Will the Real Chipko Please Stand Up?" tends to favor a third tendency, represented by the Uttarkhand Sangarsh Vahini working in the Kumaon area on issues that included an anti-alcohol campaign and a demand for a separate state of "Uttarkhand." "Influenced as much by Marxism as by Gandhism, it believes that the human-nature relationship must not be viewed in isolation from existing relationships within humans. Subscribing neither to the 'appropriate technology' vision of Bhatt nor to the 'deep ecology' of Bahuguna, the USV sees social and economic redistribution as logically *prior* to ecological harmony."[20]

The USV was obviously trying to find ways of combining class struggle with ecological concerns. But Guha provides little other information on its overall theory or practice. The organization became a part of the Indian People's Front when it was organized in 1984, and there is little evidence that it succeeded (if it tried) in projecting any serious ecological orientation into the overall politics of the IPF. The controlling party behind the IPF, the "Liberation" group, wrote only in its later "political-organizational report" that "In the recent past the area has witnessed powerful movements by democratic forces on the questions of development of the area, against liquor lobby, for ecological balance etc. These movements have only gone to consolidate the demand for Uttarkhand. We should support the demand for a separate state. . . . However, the primary duty should be developing class organizations and the mass political front [i.e., the IPF]."[21]

What did "class organizations" mean? Later Marxist studies of the Chipko movement have continued to see the development of an "ecological" perspective as a kind of imposition over the "class" movement of a peasantry said to be oriented to issues of survival; ecology is placed in opposition to "the economic." Marxism was almost coming to mean a negation of ecological issues.

However, there is sufficient evidence that at least some sections of the peasantry were evolving an ecological ideology as one of a broad, popular, and ultimately political struggle. Shiva describes the confrontation in 1977 in the village of Adwani, with Bahuguna fasting, women gathering together, ax-men coming and going. "We have come to teach you forestry," the women told the officials of the department. "You foolish women, how can you know the value of the forest? They produce profit and resin and timber." And the women sang back to them the song of the movement,

> What do the forests bear? Soil, water and pure air.
> Soil, water and pure air sustain the earth and all she bears.[22]

Kerala Fishworkers' Struggle:
Harvesting the Sea, Reaping Destruction

At the other end of the subcontinent, in the southwestern coastal state of Kerala, now Communist-governed, with a heritage of both "class" and "caste" struggle against one of the most hierarchical societies of traditional India, a movement arose based on traditional fishing communities caught in the throes of destructive development, a movement that was to bring "liberation theology" Christians and Marxists into confrontation and dialogue as it developed almost beyond the visions of both into a popular ecology struggle.

As their climactic 1984 agitation was described in the leading newspaper of South India, *The Hindu*,

The current agitation, in its organization, style and discipline, has all the trappings of a mass movement usually organized by communist parties. Campaign marches by priests and nuns through the fishermen's villages, corner meetings, street plays, rallies, sit-ins and rail and road blocks were organized so systematically that the tempo of the agitation always remained at a very high level of placard-holding attention. But, more than that, the response it evoked made the authorities sit up. The rally leaders—whether men or women—had rehearsed their roles to perfection. They would read out slogans from a piece of paper for the other participants to repeat. They knew how to block traffic on the road or on the rail track, come rain or sun. Unlike the demonstrations commonly seen in the state capital, the rally participants were not brought in trucks and unloaded at vantage points. Neither were there hirelings. . . . Such a response could not have been build overnight. It spoke of a systematic tutoring over a pretty long period. That the agitation has a political orientation is beyond doubt judging by the tenor of the statements being made by the leaders, particularly some of the priests and nuns who visualize a "socialist society free from oppression." [23]

Who were these priests and nuns? How did a struggle of fishworkers (the movement adopted this terminology quite early to avoid the male chauvinism of "fishermen") fit into "class struggle" as the Marxists of Kerala conceived it? What kind of socialism did they want? The fact was that the movement was upsetting not only to the establishment (including the church establishment in Kerala) but also to the dominant Communists, for its new themes and the assertion of autonomy. As an article in one of the liberation theology journals asserted, "It is of considerable significance that a people's movement had arisen which does not owe its origins to any political party, and that too in a state like Kerala where there is little free 'political space.' " [24]

The struggle, which was said to involve 800,000 fishworkers and 120,000 households over the "entire continental shelf of Kerala," actually grew out of a 1953 development project for the "transfer of technology" from that progressive European state of Norway. The technology to be transfered was that of trawling—sweeping the bottom of the sea with mechanized boats—which promised both to increase the fish catch and to transform a traditional artisan sector into a "modern" industry. But restrictions had been imposed on trawling in Norway itself after fishworkers' protests (which, of course, those who were absorbed into the "transferred technology" did not learn about until later), and the same technology was leading to widespread upheavals in other countries also, notably in Indonesia in the 1970s, to the point where even the military dictatorship was forced to undertake a phased ban there in 1980. [25]

In Kerala, as fishworkers' leaders later protested, the huge increase in mechanized boats and indiscriminate fishing during the spawning season with trawls that destroyed young fish also caused "considerable damage even to the acquatic ecosystem." In fact, Kerala marine fish production was declining from 4 lakh tons in 1973 to 2.68 in 1980–81. [26]

The movement against this arose among fishing communities that were, by many counts, conservative and traditional, whether Hindu or Christian. But from the 1960s, priests, nuns, and some lay Christians began to go to work among the poor communities. Tom Kocherry, later to become a leader of the movement, began simply with working among a particularly low-status (barber caste) fishing community, getting involved with efforts to form cooperatives. Women also were active, often working with local "prayer groups" but getting involved in organizing quite early; the women themselves handled the marketing of the fish in the communities' traditional division of labor and became mobilized early in discussions and agitations. (A women's organization was to develop out of this process after 1985.)

Struggles of fishworkers were spontaneously breaking out in many places: one took place in Goa in 1973, and in Tamilnadu in 1976 nineteen fishermen were killed in a clash over the issue of mechanized trawlers. Kocherry got into his first struggle also after the Emergency with a fast over a local issue of boats seized for debt, but gradually the fishworkers were organizing—a network of cooperatives, welfare organizations, and marketing networks, on the one hand, and a trade union, on the other. The Communist parties were not much interested in their cause; as a woman activist, Nalini Nayak, reported, the reaction in the CPI(M) study circles she participated in was that "artisan fisheries are a backward and dying sector." Instead, the fishworkers organized autonomously as the Kerala Swatantra Matsya Thozilali Federation and then helped form an all-India union, the National Fishworkers' Federation, formed in 1978.

The agitation of the fishing communities against mechanized trawling in Kerala fought both Congress-controlled and CPI(M)-dominated state governments; it arose in the late 1970s, resulted in a law banning mechanized trawlers in 1980, and then fought numerous impingements of this. Throughout there was both confrontation and cooperation with the left. "Critical collaboration" was the term used by one of the fasting nuns in 1984, and, as Kocherry put it, "We are certainly not Marxist. We may follow the leftist ideology, but that does not make us Marxist." For one thing, the movement was itself struggling with organizational issues (relations of unions with the cooperatives, centralized versus decentralized structures) and putting forward a different notion of politics, which liberation theologist Kappen called *politics from below*: "Whereas traditional politics aims at gaining power over the people and control over the state apparatus, here it is the people who seek to exercise, though within limits, power over the parties and the government." [27]

Also, the movement was being pushed—from the involvement of women (both the fishing community market women themselves and the young nuns and activists) in its struggles, and from the very real confrontation of the community with ecological devastation—into gender and ecological issues that did not fit very well into the Marxist perspective existing in Kerala. For that matter, even the current perspectives of "liberation theology" did not appear to help them very much. As noted by Gabriele Dietrich, a feminist with a long association with the movement,

> There remains the predicament that liberation theology as it developed in Latin America, has itself been closely linked up with Marxist ideology and thus with a fairly exclusive focus on economistic perspectives and class, while a feminist perspective, environmental awareness and critique of science and technology has not really been integrated. The Leftist perspective on "progress" has been deeply akin to the capitalist faith in unlimited growth.[28]

It appears then, that the feminism, democratizing impulse, and ecological perspective that were to become prominent in the Kerala fishworkers movement came from the people themselves. And they were part of a diffuse but widespread development of a mass-based Indian environmentalism that was rising out of popular experience with drought, deforestation, and ecological devastation in the 1970s and 1980s.

Drought, Deforestation, Desertification

What was producing this growing ecological perspective was not the theorizing of middle-class environmentalists, but the experience of ordinary working people. Kerala fishing communities, for instance, had traditionally mythologized the sea as a goddess and had woven a whole set of ritual restrictions (especially regarding the chastity of women) around this notion. Now, however, their perceptions of the sea were changing from, as Dietrich puts it, "as an infinitely powerful and resourceful force of nature to an understanding that the sea can be raped and can be destroyed by technological intervention and forces of the market."[29]

This was happening in a context where the growing environmental devastation of modern development was having an impact all around them:

> Sardines and prawns were once the food of the poor, it was possible for a hardy peasant to feast occasionally on a stew of tender cashew. There was an abundance of seasonal fruit: mango and jackfruit and pineapple and varieties of plums and berries. In our unique spreading out of homesteads, where even the very poor had a little plot of land around their huts, there was at one time hardly anyone who did not grow something or other. Root tubers needed no tending, and pomengranate and guava and custard-apple grew wild along the hedges. We could fish with our upper cloth in streams and within yards of home. . . . I am not becoming sentimental and mushy, but only trying to communicate through certain tangibles the tragedy of a people who have let their sumptuous life-endowments be irreparably damaged. The prawns and sardines and cashews are exported. . . . Two, three generations forgot the taste of "export quality" prawns; prawns do sell in the home market, but these are the sick brothers of the ones shipped out, often infected with salmonella and less than edible. And yet the prices are astronomical.[30]

This was O. V. Vijayan, writing in this case of the linkage of gulf money with degradation in Kerala, but similar descriptions could be made of the degenerating resources throughout India.

The environmental movements thus first developed in India as a movement of the rural poor. They were fishworkers toiling on the waves of a sea that itself was getting transformed before their eyes. They were herders, forced to roam farther and farther so that their sheep or cattle could scratch out fodder from withering grass and shrinking forests, often coming into conflict with local peasants or tribals in the process. They were artisans, who could no longer find the fibers to make their baskets or mats. They were women who had to climb miles up and down hills to get water for their cooking, who had to roam through the forests to get fuel. And they were peasants struggling to survive drought, trying to scratch out a living on lands whose topsoil was getting blown away or that were being degraded by waterlogging and an overload of fertilizers or being threatened with total disappearance by irrigation projects trumpeted as providing water to flood the fields of others.

Environmental movements were "peasant movements" as much as the new farmers' movement, but with a different focus—immediate survival in the face of a threat to their traditional way of life. Whereas the farmers' movements arose as those of peasants in the "green revolution" areas, the supposed beneficiaries of development who found themselves facing new forms of oppression and exploitation, the environmental movements were those of peasants (and other "artisanal" groups—herdsmen, craftsmen, traditional fishworkers) who were in immediate terms more clearly the victims of development. Originally with the NIMBY ("not in my back yard") focus, aimed simply at demanding new land to replace that to be flooded by a development project or at halting, in their own area, the encroachments of "progress," they came to have an ecological perspective that challenged the very notion of modernization and formulated, in the Indian context, an "alternative development" or "people's development." In contrast to the farmers' movement, this environmentally oriented peasant movement became the darling of a section of the middle class that itself was being repulsed by the visible degradation of life even in the cities, and which theorized the movement in its own way (for instance, accepting the dichotomy between "tribals" and "peasants" that Nirmal Sengupta had criticized, and then depicting "tribals" as the main victims of development and caste Hindu "peasants" as very often the cash-crop-hungry perpetrators of the onslaught). But while the interaction of the rural poor and middle-class environmentalists was to have its problematic features, it remained true that the new ecology/environmental movements that arose in India did so as on a localized basis, but very much as mass movements.

There are reasons, it might be added, why environmentalism and generally a "green" perspective more naturally has a peasant than a "proletarian" base (and why, therefore, the debate about whether Chipko was a "peasant" or an "environmental" *or* a "women's" movement was in a sense irrelevant). The industrial working class and urban unorganized workers are also affected by environmental degradation, pollution, health hazards on the job, accidents, and so on, and they were also through this period organizing in various ways to fight this. But the main effect of these circumstances on their lives is at the level of *consumption*; immediate economic and survival interests impel them to maintain their jobs even when these are destructive to life itself. Similarly, for the salaried middle classes, the growing degradation of life is felt mainly at the level of consumption. In contrast, environmental destruction destroys the *conditions of production* of peasants, fishworkers, hunters, and gatherers; it affects their production process itself, not merely the "quality" of their daily lives.

In the long run, of course, both sections of toilers and middle-class employees are faced with the need to change and develop both production processes and life-styles if there is to be a sustainable development; nevertheless, the immediate incidence of environmental devastation does affect them in different ways. They also, of course, affect peasant communities in ways mediated by "class," "caste," and "gender": that is, economically better-off peasants, males, and specific castes objectively have better chances of surviving and apparently improving their condition in the production processes and competition of a commercialized economy, and thus more of an interest in developing such an economy. Nevertheless, while many Marxists (and intellectuals in the environmental movement) were pointing to "cash-crop-growing rich peasants" as a major force interested in promoting destructive capitalist development, the fact remains that even commercial farmers are affected by environmental degradation more directly than the wage-paid working class.

By the early 1980s this diffuse but pervasive environmental destruction began to have a wide impact throughout India, and the hitherto silent struggles of the rural poor against drought, and being evicted for irrigation and development projects began to get a new hearing from the press, media, and other sections of intellectuals. The localized struggles began to take on a "national" scope as part of a movement: environmentalism.

Antidam movements began to gather force. The earlier protests over the Subarnarekha dams in the Jharkhand area were not seen as "environmental" movements, but other cases were becoming too numerous to be ignored. The demands of "evictees," those who were about to be flooded out of lands and livelihoods by the dams, were being linked, on one hand, to the realization that the victims of past projects were among the most wretched of the displaced of India, that they had never really gotten justice, that the welfare of some was built on the misery of others—and on the other to a growing consciousness that the projects were not really providing "welfare" at all, but were part of a process of simply plundering forests and natural resources.

A turning point was the protest over Silent Valley, a proposed medium-sized dam in Kerala that would have flooded an irreplaceable "natural forest." This emerged as mainly a middle-class environmental movement, gaining wide publicity and coming into conflict not only with the central government but with the Communist-led state government still concerned about "development." In central India, however, opposition developed to the Bhogalpatinam and Inchampalli irrigation projects, which had a different character: on one hand, it was expressed by an old Gandhian leader of the area, leprosy worker Baba Amte, who began to align himself with Bahuguna as an opponent to all dam projects and who sought to win his way first through letters to Indira Gandhi; on the other hand, the tribals in the area were being organized under Naxalite leadership, with the threat of a more violent oppositional movement arising. Both cases managed to produce victories: the Silent Valley project was finally given up, and the Central India dams were stalled.

Then two important antiproject movements arose in the hitherto quiet northeastern state of Orissa. One of these, in the partly tribal Gandharmadhan hills, rose in opposition to the devastation of the hills by the roads and mine construction of an aluminium mining project for the public-sector BALCO company. The other, which was just emerging by 1985, developed in a relatively rich, cash-crop coastal area, Baliapal, which the Indian government wanted to take over for the development of a missile testing range. Here local peasants, agricultural laborers, fishermen, and others barricaded the roads, formed committees, and made it clear that the missile range would be built only over their dead bodies. Both movements developed on the basis of local all-party committees, including Naxalite-inclined activists and local leaders connected with the established political parties, very often the opposition socialists.

The year 1982 was also the year that the government brought a new forest bill for parliamentary approval. In essence, this continued the century-long process begun by the colonial state of taking over more and more forest and land control and depriving the local communities (including peasants, but especially tribals) of any rights. This time, however, a broad national opposition arose to the bill.

Finally, it was probably the pervading drought of the early 1980s—affecting practically all of India outside the Gangetic plains—that brought home the reality of environmental degradation to so many. By the mid-1980s, recurrent drought was producing localized peasant struggles in many areas, and some of these began to develop broader perspectives of going beyond "drought relief" to "drought eradication." New voices of experts were emerging to articulate the growing devastation of the land itself and its linkage with deforestation and the technologies of Green Revolution development. As one of these, B. B. Vohra, a former government expert, wrote in 1984,

> Out of a total land area of 266 million hectares, as many as 175 million hectares suffered from degradation, caused for the most part by soil erosion, but also by waterlogging and excessive salinity. This means that, on the average, at least two out of every three acres of land in India is today in poor

health. . . . at least half the sick lands, i.e., one-third of the total, are almost completely unproductive. . . . It should be obvious even to a superficial observer that there is no earthly chance of eradicating poverty, or even surviving as a self-respecting nation, so long as such a state of affairs persists.

Describing the "most serious threat as posed by deforestation," Vohra went on to call for a massive government expenditure in response, linked to a cut in defense expenditure.[31] In fact, this illustrated the typical planners' faith in the possibility of remedying through governmental machinery what this machinery had itself been responsible for inducing. Nevertheless, it was becoming clear that a new kind of crisis and contradiction was enveloping India and its people.

"The Consumption of the Rich"

The decisive rise of middle-class environmentalism began at the end of the 1970s.

The first organizational expression it took was in the people's science movements. These did not give central importance to environmental issues in the beginning and were definitely not "green," yet the impulse was clear. The forerunner and inspirer for many was the Kerala Shastriya Sahitya Parishad (Kerala Science Literature Conference, or KSSP), working since 1964 as a strong, mass-based organization of science teachers and professionals carrying on village campaigns and producing a wide variety of popular science literature. It had been the KSSP that had given the strongest opposition to the Silent Valley project in Kerala, even though the KSSP was losely linked to the CPI(M), which was supporting the project. The organization held a well-attended Trivandrum conference in 1979, and in October of the same year many of the Maharashtrians who had participated joined with Gandhians, other scientists, and mass organization activists in a meeting at Anandwan—the center of Baba Amte in eastern Maharashtra—to debate the formation of a similar group.

Activists at the Anandwan meeting debated how much the organization should be oriented toward workers and peasants (and hence mass movement-focused); how much to middle-class issues; how much it should deal with "social science" (and hence an analysis of the exploitative structures of society) or simply with "natural science" (presumably more neutral, in the minds of all those present). Then a February 1980 solar eclipse saw a jump in popularity of the idea of "people's science" as activists hastily distributed cellophane spectacles through which to view the eclipse, and in April the mainly CPI(M) activists who were controlling the work of Shramik Sanghatana in Dhule district held a successful "science fair" in one of the predominantly tribal villages. The Lok Vidnyan Sanghatana (LVS) was founded on June 15 of that year, with the KSSP as its model, and primarily a natural science focus, a dominance of CPI(M)-oriented activists, and a major thrust against popular superstition.

A quite different trend emerged out of science-minded activists working in Kanpur, U.P. on the one hand and Madras on the other. A mixture of Naxalite-influenced young intellectuals and old Gandhians founded a "Patriotic People's Science and Technology" (PPST) group at a meeting in June 1980. In the first issue of their bulletin, which came out in December, the Kanpur group summarized their debate as centering around the issue of the relation of science and technology to imperialism—a rather different focus of concern from that in Maharashtra. There was a broad agreement, they noted, that modern science and technology is an instrument of exploitation, but there were still differences as to whether "freed of imperialist stranglehold modern S and T can be harnessed to serve the interests of the people" (this was broadly the position taken for granted by the LVS and KSSP), or whether "modern S and T cannot, even in the absence of an imperialist stranglehold, be a genuine means of social development as it owes its existence solely to the needs of imperialism." [32] The group concluded that there was a need to evolve a people-oriented science and technology through the study and repudiation of colonial science and technology.

The rather "conventional Marxist" position of the LVS, that modern science was inherently beneficial and only needed to be freed from the monopoly power of exploiters, was summed up in its most popular song, "Wake Up, Man":

> The sun of knowledge has been eclipsed, all is in darkness. . . .
> in today's atomic age, have they no shame to keep a monopoly of knowledge?
> . . .
> Let the light of science shine in every house
> and light the torch of consciousness—
> the eclipse is over, the eclipse is over!

An October 1982 "Vidnyan Yatra" organized as a massive campaign to bring "science to the people" with programs in every district of the state featured antisuperstition campaigns (dramatic performances in which activists first disguised themselves as godmen and miracle workers, then exposed the miracles, and concluded with a fire-walking ceremony in which local youth were invited to take part), a number of slide shows, and propaganda against the nuclear bomb with a feature on Hiroshima.

In both cases agriculture, drought, and development-related issues began to be expressed. The Maharashtra Vidnyan Yatra also included programs dealing with issues of irrigation and drought, while the Madras PPST group, in its study of "colonial S and T," was led to look at traditional (pre-British) technology, particularly as it related to agriculture and the preservation of environmental resources. In Sangli district of Maharashtra, encounters and confrontation with the local peasantry, just getting mobilized on antidrought issues, began to force at least some LVS activists to transcend their original assumptions that a beneficial store of knowledge called "science" existed, which they only had to make available to a backward and superstition-ridden people. When a local Vidyan Yatra was organized in 1984, not only did a debate develop among outside activists and the peasants (the outsiders insisted the area was always drought-prone; old peasants of the area claimed that it used to be full of trees and one couldn't get across the river during the rainy season), but the science activists found that they had little actually to tell the peasants about the ways of removing drought.

While these encounters and debates were going on, it was the *Citizens' Reports on the Indian Environment* that were to provide a major intellectual articulation of environmental concerns, with impressive coverage and wide popularity. The moving spirit behind these was Anil Agrawal, who had attended the 1972 Stockholm conference on environmental issues (the same one at which Indira Gandhi had voiced third world suspicions about the antidevelopmental thrust of environmentalism with the often-quoted statement "poverty is the biggest polluter") and returned to India to found the Center for Science and Environment (CSE) in Delhi. The first *Citizens' Report*, in 1979, was produced with impressive input of material from groups and individuals working all over the country, and with sections ranging from land to dams to industry. With subsidized cheap editions and a Hindi translation, it had a major impact. The second was even more thorough, and it included a final section on "Politics of Environment" in which Agrawal and others took up broader issues of analysis. Their main thrust was a critique of industrialization, a condemnation of imperialism, and a focus on "consumerism" as the main enemy. According to Agrawal,

> One lesson is, therefore, clear: the main cause of environmental destruction in the world is the demand for natural resources generated by the consumption of the rich (whether they are rich nations or rich individuals and groups within nations) and ... it is their wastes that mainly contribute to the global pollution load. ... These trends raise serious doubts about the sustainability of the Western industrialization model based on global management of resources for the consumption of a few. The growth of science and technology has indeed been humankind's most magnificent achievement, but definitely not the ends to which this knowledge has been used.

He went on to draw an eloquent picture of the environmentally destructive aspects of the "consumption of the rich" in India:

> A resident of Delhi who uses shirts made of cotton which has been produced in a field in Maharashtra heavily sprayed with pesticides leading to multiple resistance in mosquitos; electricity from a dam in the Himalayas that has destroyed forests and blocked migration of fish; paper produced in Madhya Pradesh by a factory that has polluted the local river and logged forests in an ever-widening circle, disrupting the life of tribals; cereals from Punjab where food is produced using a technology that drains soil fertility.[33]

This helped to pinpoint the "main enemy" in the way modernization was destroying the environment, reducing diversity, rendering "nature" and natural resources subject to urban/industrial needs and a cash nexus. But it had its problems: it did not really take a position on the issue of "science and technology," it had a tendency to adopt the traditional Marxist avoidance of the peasantry and define the groups most affected by environmental destruction only as "artisans, nomads, tribals, fisherfolk, and women from almost all landless, marginal, and small farm households"[34] (why not men from "small farm households?), and it neglected the role of exploitation and production as determinant factors. It also tended to look to state action to remedy the problems that it accused state policy of causing. Nevertheless, in spite of the "consumerist" ideology, Indian environmentalism was clearly developing with a critique of imperialism and with a strong base in popular movements of the toiling people.

People's Science, Patriotic Science, and Seeking Truth

The different trends in the people's science movement and their implications for the overall development of the ecology movement in India became clear with a debate that emerged over the 1981 publication of a "Statement on Scientific Temper" from the intellectuals of the prestigious Nehru Centre in Delhi.

The statement itself reflected the "four-anna socialism" of the Nehru model, secular, oriented to "development" and the relief of social-economic inequalities in India, but with the assumption both that the elite in charge of planning was capable of doing so, and that the technology itself was inherently beneficial: "We have all the technology, available right now within the country to give water, food, shelter, and basic health care to our millions. And yet we are not. Something has gone wrong. The logic of planning and the logic of our socioeconomic structure are at variance."[35]

Sharing the same assumption of the beneficence of technology, the "traditional Marxist" critique of this—put forward by Rajendra Prasad in the CPI(M)-dominated journal *Social Scientist*, attacked it only for the lack of a "class perspective," arguing that "if the toiling masses themselves had access to the science and technology which the ruling classes controlled, all would be well."[36]

The emerging environmentalist, alternate-development trend, however, took a different tack. The neo-Gandhian Ashish Nandy, linked to the largely NGO-based intellectuals associated with Lokayan in Delhi, published an article entitled "Humanistic Temper" in which he characterized modern science and technology itself as colonial, destructive, and evading any responsibility to the masses. But it was the Madras group of PPST that took the harshest line, linking the issue both to imperialism and to the growing popular movements: "Can it be just coincidence that such a profound defence is being trotted out precisely at a time when the entire Western-inspired, city-centered, high-technology developmental path is increasingly coming under the fire of farmers' agitations, environmental movements, tribal movements, etc.?" It went on to criticize the statement as "a repulsive exercise in cynicism and hypocrisy" since those defending the institutions of modern science and technology were the people managing them. Attacking the claim that "science and its temper" were responsible for the material advances of the West, while India's backwardness was due to the lack of these, the PPST group asserted that instead, "From the very moment of its forced entry into the third world, modern Western science has been far from being a liberating and revolutionary force as far as the people of the third world are concerned. It has since then been playing an increasingly greater role in the plunder and destruction of the third world economies and cultures." [37] This was not to claim that all was flawless in tradition, or that Indians should not learn from people the world over, the group went on to say, but the major task should be to take what was most effective from local/national traditions. As a survey of environmental trends by Ramchandra Guha noted, in contrast to the conventional Marxist-style critiques, "these scholars are challenging not merely political-economic structures such as capitalism, but the very foundations of modern civilization." [38]

But Guha's attempt to find a middle way between the more conventional critique and what he described as the "civilizational" approach floundered on some of his own traditional Marxist assumptions. Casting the PPST group and the Ashish Nandy-Alvares-Lokayan group into one category allowed him to criticize the whole trend by accusing it of believing in hierarchy, and his major critique of the PPST tendency simply took over the pervading notion that a large section of the peasantry was becoming an enemy class. Thus Guha argued that while the "alternative science" advocates used concepts of "oppression," "power," and "exploitation" derived from Marxism, they were selective in doing so and ignored the division of India into castes and classes, citing as the main example of their "ambivalence to socialism" the fact that they extended support "to the farmers' movement around remunerative agricultural prices." [39]

It was not the elite neo-Gandhians of the Ashish Nandy type, but the activists associated with the PPST tendency in Kanpur who gave this support. It was expressed by people like Sunil Sahasrabudhe and by others grouped around the early 1980s Hindu journal *Mazdur-Kisan Niti*, who tried to link an environmental critique with the peasant movement and theorized the split described by Sharad Joshi as between "Bharat" and "India" as one between *paschimkrut* or "Westernized" and *bahishkrut* or "boycotted" India. The PPST tendency did idealize the society of "traditional" India; however, in arguing that the main barrier to a genuine scientific and sustainable development was not the "traditional" values of the village but rather imperialistically determined "modern science and technology," it was focusing its challenge against imperialism.

A third trend in the developing people's science movement was less articulated at the national, English-language level, but had strong roots in the anticaste tradition of Maharashtra. In Bombay from 1979–80, a group of young activists and workers calling themselves the Krantiba Phule Sanskritic Manch, drawing inspiration from the tradition of Jotiba Phule, began to perform street plays and

hold celebrations attacking the brahmanic values of neo-Hindu festivals, exposing modern "godmen" who used the name of science itself to rally crowds, and
calling for a movement for alternative culture. It was they who argued, against
the dominant tendency of the Lok Vidnyan Sanghatana in the state, that a science
movement should include the "social sciences" as well as natural sciences, and it
was they who associated themselves with the peasants of drought-stricken southern Maharashtra in seeking a solution to the ongoing onslaughts of drought. This
satyashodhak or "truth-seeking" tendency thus brought Marxist and anticaste
tendencies together with an environmentalist perspective to challenge traditional
notions of organizing the rural poor by seeing the struggle against drought and
deforestation as part of their "class struggle."

Conclusion: Peasants, Marxists, and Gandhians in the Environmental Movement

The environmental movement arose because the people of India, in both the
cities and the villages, of all castes and classes and genders, were affected by the
ecological destruction of world capitalism. But they were affected in different
ways, and their responses were different. The first expression of Indian environmentalism was as diverse localized movements, of peasants (tribal and
nontribal) and other sections of the rural poor fighting the specificities of their
own situation.

In fact, the environmental movement and the farmers' movement could be
seen as two major wings of a broad peasant movement in India that arose against
the exploitation and destruction resulting from the incorporation of the peasantry
into the world capitalist system. Generally left intellectuals have argued that the
farmers' movement has been based on cash-cropping "rich and middle peasants," belonging to upper and middle castes, representing a specific exploiting
class category; in contrast, they have seen the environmental movement as based
on subsistence-oriented poor peasants, usually tribals and dalits. But this was a
misrepresentation of both movements. The farmers' movement involved a wide
range of castes and economic categories and expressed not simply a desire to be
incorporated on better terms in the market economy but also a protest against it
that included various types of "delinking" activities. The environmental movement, in turn, was based not simply on tribal subsistence peasants; in Baliapal,
for instance, there was a wide range of caste Hindu peasants, laborers, and
fishworkers fighting the takeover of their land in a productive market economy;
in the Chipko region itself, the peasants actually involved in the movement were
upper-caste Hindus (brahmans and rajputs), while the low castes in the area, the
traditionally landless service castes, frequently became dependent on the services
of Green Revolution government technocrats when they did get land. A similar
movement in Karnataka, the Appiko movement, was based on cultivating brahman
castes. Both movements had their "economistic" aspects (fighting for survival or for

better terms within the system), and both had a thrust to challenging the system as inherently destructive and posing an alternative model of development.

If we are to understand the difference, we can look at two factors. There was some geographical differentiation that was reflected in the social base of the movements. If one considers India as divided into three basic types of agro-ecological zones—the highly inegalitarian but productive coastal deltas and river valleys; the relatively more egalitarian plateaus and grasslands, and the most egalitarian hilly and mountainous areas—the farmers' movement arose *primarily* (not entirely) in the second region, while the environmental movement arose *primarily* (not entirely) in the third region. This did give it frequently more of a "tribal" component and a more egalitarian community base to movements, but this was only a relative difference. Similarly, farmers' movements were less likely to arise in more polarized regions, and when they did (e.g., in south Gujarat), they were both relatively weaker and more based on rural upper castes.

A second important difference was while they were more localized in terms of their mass base (those adversely affected by developmental projects), developing peasant-based environmental struggles in India flowed into a stream of growing ecological consciousness that was rising around the world and having a major impact on sensitized sections of the urban upper middle classes. Peasants, nomads, and fishworkers struggling locally, then, were joined with significant numbers of these middle-class intellectual activists. The environmental movement was thus articulated as a "movement" on a national scale, not through the "federation" or united actions of local or regional mass organizations, but through the ideological and networking activities of these intellectuals.

The first articulation of the local movements as a single movement challenging the modern "industrial system" itself was by Gandhians. They were prominent as activists in many of the localized movements, and they drew on Gandhi to formulate an Indian version of "deep ecology." But along with Gandhi, they idealized pre-British caste-feudal "Hindu" society and values, and they tended to neglect the aspects of exploitation and surplus extraction in the process of development. In theorizing "consumerism" as the main aspect of environmental destruction, they had a tendency to idealize subsistence-oriented "tribals" in contrast to the "cash-crop oriented" caste Hindu peasants, presenting only the former as the victims of development, the latter as almost its progenitors. They also had a leaning to reformism, appealing to political leaders like Indira Gandhi or to the bureaucracy at various levels.

In contrast, Marxists came into the environmental movement with a strong ideological orientation to the exploited masses and to liberation through struggle. But at the same time, their tendency to see subsistence production or petty-commodity production as nonproletarian and to ignore the issues raised about the nature of technology (the forces of production) meant that environmental movements, as such, were seen as "nonclass" and thus "nonpolitical" movements. To Marxists, an opposition to large-scale industrial development was anti-working class, and they often argued that those raising issues of alternative development were opposing progress from a traditionalist perspective and aimed at "going back to the Stone Age." They took up ecological struggles or local struggles of resistance to developmental projects only as a means of gaining mass support and with the intention of giving them a political thrust against the capitalist state.

For example, an important 1990 review article in *Frontier* on "Naxalism in the Nineties" urged that such problems as environmental issues and remunerative prices could only be solved by "breaking with the imperialist system". It asserted that: "the questions of ecology, deforestation, big dams, trawler fishing and so on . . . are seen by the people involved in them as basically ways of protecting their means of livelihood from the depradations of imperialism and comprador capitalists . . . only in a system where exchange value and profit do not dominate and determine accumulation [can environmental destruction be prevented]."[40] This urged an "unequivocal stand against the project," but it identified that stand with a struggle for socialism under leadership of the party. But environmental activists could no longer see struggle against private property as sufficient. The argument that "exchange value and profit" were the sole factors behind ecologically destructive production simply ignored the issues raised by the critique of industrialism and was increasingly sounding simply invalid as the ecological problems and overall crisis of the state-socialist societies were more and more revealed.

Marxists, then, became involved in environmental struggles and in debates with the movement activists, but they remained in a sense external to the development of the movements. The "mainstream" Marxists associated mainly with the CPI(M) got involved in "people's science" organizations in a big way, came to sponsor nationwide science marches, but continued to insist that the problem was primarily to bring scientific knowledge and a scientific outlook to the masses; to them, large-scale irrigation and power projects and even defense testing sites were necessary for the development of a powerful, modern India. Even the Naxalites, more oriented to struggle against the state and to seeing public sector as "comprador," could not conceptualize an entirely different developmental path and simply sought to establish their unique politics in terms of militancy.

Through most of the 1980s, the Marxist tendency could not offer any convincing alternative to the Gandhians in the environmental movement. As a consequence, the slogans of "alternative development" that were formulated lacked a serious linkage to the organization of politically effective mass struggles to achieve such a development. The environmental movement developed as one that raised very serious questions about the destructiveness of the existing system; it also questioned proposed Marxist alternatives of working-class control and, like the farmers' movement, challenged some of the economic "fundamentals." But it failed to develop a conscious and organized challenge at the level of political organizing, and even at the cultural and community level, the tendency to idealize pre-British society failed to deal with the problems of exploitation and inequality in Hindu caste society.

At the same time, more than the other social movements—and more concretely even than Marxists themselves, in spite of slogans—the environmental movement was raising the question of imperialism. At an international level, in spite of the localism involved in much environmental ideology, and in spite of the fact that movements in advanced capitalist countries often had a very myopic, not to say chauvinistic, vision, environmental activists were coming into conflict with bodies such as the World Bank and concerning themselves with GATT and the trade issues involved. In India also the rise of environmentalism meant increased attention to problems of the international economy, particularly when it was so obvious that the energy use and consumption patterns of the "North" were a threat to ecological balance much more than the steady encroachment on forests and land by impoverished peasants.

Environmentalists began to target imperialism, and strikingly, the 1975–85 decade ended with the December 1984 the release of poisonous gases in an explosion at a Union Carbide fertilizer plant at Bhopal that killed thousands and left many times that number crippled and incapacitated for life. It inaugurated an era of struggle, repression, and betrayal—factionalized struggle by the victims organized by one after another group of nonparty activists, and repression and betrayal by Union Carbide and by the Indian state and its governing party, attacking and jailing organizers as "CIA agents," telling them lies about the extent of damage, forcing on them the most meager settlements. Bhopal was the major disaster that revealed for the whole world the murderous nature of the multinational companies and of the capitalist "development" that was the major ideological base of postindependence third world regimes.

"The final class war has not yet come . . ." Red flag song sung by tribal women, 1971.

Tribal-forest Conference, 1986.

Tribal-forest Conference, 1986. Waharu Sonavane announces drum contest winners.

"Take up the red-green flag." Tribal women in Chattisgarh, 1985.

Bali Raja Memorial Dam (peasant-built small dam). Gail Omvedt, Tatya with baby Surya, Indutai Patankar, 1990.

Women activists of Stri Mukti Sangarsh.

Activists in front of Bali Raja Dam, 1991.

Ganesh festival exhibit showing woman beating government official.

Anti-drought demonstration in Bombay.

Activist Bharat Patankar and radical engineer K.R. Datye discuss problems of "alternative technological horizons."

Delegates' session, 1989 conference.

How they travel; women come by truck and train to the conference, 1989.

On stage during the conference, 1989: Madhu Kishwar, Sharad Joshi, Chetna Gala.

Crowd at public meeting, 1989 conference.

Activists at village with all-women gram panchayat. Standing: village head, Maya Wankhade. Seated women include: Aleyamma and Mercy of Kerala fishworkers' organization.

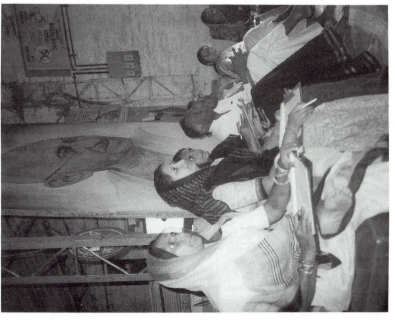

Women activists at study camp on "Sita sheti" or natural farming. Second from left, Indirabai Patel, who initiated campaign to give land to women.

Part III
Responses, System and Antisystem, 1975–1985

7

The Marxist Vision
and the Working Class

WHAT was the working class doing during this period? In one sense, the answer is easy: it was stepping up its fight against capital through the medium of what I have been describing as the "new social movements."

Capitalist development in India, the subordination and organization of India's production in the worldwide capitalist system, had been taking place through the process described as "four-anna socialism," a state-controlled and planned industrialization. On the one hand this had meant a reconstitution of the ruling class—the brahmans, banias, and political overlords of the traditional society becoming bureaucrats, managers, industrialists, and political bosses, controlling the countryside as sugar barons, contractors, heads of "cooperatives" and local political institutions. On the other hand the dalit and shudra toilers were reconstituted as workers, peasants, and agricultural laborers in new hierarchies and divisions, ranging from the nationalized mines, public sector factories, and multinational industries to the transformed (by drought, deforestation, or the new "green revolution trinity" of hybrid seeds, fertilizers, and pesticides) fields on which they worked as toiling peasants caught in a cash economy, daily or semibonded laborers, unorganized sector wage workers roaming the countryside and towns, and unpaid toiling women hauling water and fuel and doing the heavy tasks of housework.

Traditional Marxist theory did not comprehend the new forms of exploitation; the traditional left parties were unable to organize their struggle. They struggled anyway—in the form of new movements that asserted the need to destroy brahmanism as an ideology, to fight the caste bonds that limited them to living and working in specific ways, and to displace the brahmans and other high castes from their control of the bureaucracy. They also struggled for the recognition of their unpaid "domestic" labor, against the "atrocities" that had the effect of binding them to the home or to narrow spheres of work, against sexual repression. They struggled against their exploitation as peasant producers, for higher prices for their products, for freedom from debt, for access to inputs for agricultural production, and against the ongoing corruption of and harassment by the bureaucracy. They also struggled against the depradation of nature that was destroying their very basis of life and production, beginning the fight against development itself (in its experienced form), and articulating the need for an alternative development.

Whether they identified themselves and were identified as "dalits," "OBCs," "adivasis," "women," and "peasants," they were in all these cases fighting the way in which capital was subordinating their labor and their lives; they were also fighting as sections of the Indian working class. But, though India's Marxists did have available to them terminology—*kashtakari, shramik*—that named all these sections as "laborers" of one kind or another, they were not ready to see the "working class" in such a broad sense. Dalits asserted that they were the "true proletariat," women that their labor was the foundation of all exploitation, peasants that all they wanted was the "return for their sweat"—but to the Indian Marxists, wage workers continued to be the real proletariat, and factory workers the vanguard.

Still, Marxists as intellectuals and as Communist party members responded to the new movements in somewhat different ways.

Marxism of the Intelligentsia

Peter Waterman—a former Communist organizer and "new labor internationalist" theorist-activist, one of the many Europeans intermittently associated with India—had commented in one of his articles about

> . . . two phenomena that puzzled me considerably in India. The first was the extent to which openly-avowed Marxists were to be found employed, in senior positions, within organizations which would not grant them even low ones— and which usually they would not even desire to enter—in other capitalist countries. Alongside what one Indian friend entitles "the Indian Administrative Service (Marxist-Leninist)" there appears to exist a parallel phenomenon in other state agencies—and even in capitalist companies. The second feature was that a large part of political discourse takes place within a Marxist universe of discourse.[1]

This was, in fact, an aspect of "four-anna socialism." But this considerable implantation of Marxism among the Indian intelligentsia had as its consequence not simply a "leftward" shift of discourse, but also a hegemony, at the theoretical level, of a brahman, male, bureaucratically based elite *over* Marxism in India.

An article in 1974 by an influential (and largely pro-Congress) Marxist academic argued that a major aspect of the failure of Marxism in India up to that time was at the theoretical level, in the failure adequately to politicize the masses. Writing in the period of the pre-Emergency upsurge, Bipin Chandra argued that

> ... the Marxists are not even in a position to make a bid for power. They stand paralyzed now that the bird of revolution stares them in the face. They suddenly find themselves facing two choices: they can either, ignoring the semi-fascist threat, cheer, usually from the sidelines, the spontaneous right-wing-led petty bourgeois populist movements, or rely on the Congress, the main party of the bourgeoisie, to save the day for democracy, even if it does so by becoming more and more authoritarian.[2]

By "petty-bourgeois populist movements" Chandra meant, of course, the first upsurge of the new movements and the student and middle-class-linked movements of Bihar and Gujarat; and by "right-wing leadership" he meant the opposition combine. The "two choices" he mentioned were in a sense to be followed by the two main wings of the Communist movement, the CPI(M), which was to ally with the forces opposed to Congress, and the CPI, which was finally to give its support to the Emergency as the inevitable action of a progressive "national bourgeoisie" fighting right reaction.

Chandra's point that "the basic failure of Indian Marxists lies in their inability to emerge as the standard-bearers of an alternative social system, an alternative political leadership, however small"[3] made one important assumption: it accepted the model of the vanguard party that already possessed the "alternative." Throughout his article it was taken for granted that Indian Marxists possessed the correct theory, that their main failure was to educate the masses, to politicize them, to teach them Marxism. Though he spoke in terms of "making them their own leaders," this remained in the framework of the belief that the theory to guide them was, in its fundamentals, complete. Marxism was a completed theory of revolution; the intellectuals of India were its bearers—their need was to make connection with the masses. This was the fundamental viewpoint of the teacher, reflected in so much of the thinking of the Indian Communist movement and even its songs:

> The lamp of class struggle,
> the view of Leninism
> telling the secret of poverty
> and of its abolition—
> the working class shall be the leader,
> now it will gain class-consciousness
> wandering we hold high
> the red flag, the red flag. [4]

Chandra also made the other pervasive assumption of the Marxist intellectuals of his time: the "basic classes" to whom they were to go were consistently identified as "the urban worker, the agricultural laborer, the poor peasant." In a footnote he went even further, criticizing the reformism of the Communist parties on the basis that "the reforms they fight for benefit not the basic exploited rural classes and the vast mass of the unorganized urban proletariat but the middle and rich peasants and the strata of organized white collar and factory workers."[5] Criticizing "organized workers" was not a theme that could be easily maintained even for academic Marxists, but in the new era of capitalist development in India, in an almost axiomatic way, "middle and rich peasants" became the new villains of the intellectual left.

The famous "mode of production in agriculture" debate that raged through the 1970s filled innumerable pages in the major left weeklies and party journals and won international laurels had the crystallization of this notion as one of its major effects. It was not simply, as Waterman referred to it sarcastically, "how many modes of production can dance on the head of a social formation." The debate had its very real roots in the Naxalite upsurge of the late 1960s, in the expressed fear (or hope) that "the Green Revolution will turn into a red one," and in an intellectual effort to comprehend and hegemonize the process. There were two striking features of the debate. One is that both sides assumed that "capitalism in agriculture" meant the differentiation of the peasantry into agricultural laborers and poor peasants, on the one hand, and rich peasants/capitalist farmers on the other; the implication for action was in defining where the main contradiction was, where mass movements should be directed, who was the enemy, who was the main enemy, who were potential allies, and so forth. For the proponents of "semifeudalism," the main enemy continued to be the landlord (and the state) and the middle-rich peasants were allies; for the proponents of "capitalism," rich peasants and capitalist farmers, now to be known as "kulaks," were the main enemy and middle peasants an untrustworthy and vanishing ally. In spite of some interventions on the role of international capital or on the "colonial mode of production," the possibility that "capitalism" meant not just a transformation of the village but a new relation between the village and the state, a new relation to the world system, and that it could include nonwage workers was ignored by most of the Marxists who took part in the debate.[6]

The second striking fact about the debate is that while almost everyone conceded that the proponents of "capitalism" had won in theory, in practice the two decades following it saw an upsurge of rural movements led first by the semifeudal "losers" of the debate (i.e. Naxalite movements in Bihar and Andhra) and second by forces articulating forms of peasant subordination to capital that had been totally ignored (i.e., the environmental and farmers' movements).

Nevertheless, Indian Marxist intellectuals (and a good many party activists) held firmly to their theoretical foundations and continued to ignore the issues raised by these movements or to declare them inadmissible, as movements of nonexploited and even exploiting rural sections.

There were some breakthrough attempts, aside from the theorists arising from the movements themselves. In March–April 1981 a month-long workshop was held in Delhi on "Trade Unions and the Labouring Poor," organized by Peter Waterman and an Indian colleague who had himself come out of the Naxalite movement, Arvind Das. This was to be part of a longer research project focusing on people's movements in the Dhanbad (Jharkhand) region. Their approach, which they described as a "workers' autonomy" tendency, built in part on the theoretical perspective that had been put forward by Harry Cleaver in one of the "Mode of Production" debate articles. Cleaver had argued for analyzing the agrarian structure in terms of an increasingly internationalized struggle of capital and labor, in which "labor" meant not only wage labor but also the unwaged, in which the waged/unwaged division and the imposition of various forms of unwaged work was seen as a part of the actions of capital:

> From the peasant's point of view, the structure of work may not be changed—its form may still be feudal, tribal or what not—when capital comes in. But the structure of exploitation has changed. The peasant is now exploited by capital just as capital is exploiting the village. . . . Moreover, as the flow of goods and information grows through the market, the link between the peasant and the rest of the working class grows too—not only by the degree of exploitation but through the peasant's awareness of the mass of wealth capital is accumulating at the expense of workers everywhere. As Marx emphasized so often, the accumulation of wealth is the accumulation of the working class, of its poverty and of its struggle. The various parts of this struggle have to be linked consciously, as well as economically and politically.[7]

Citing this, Waterman, Das, and their colleague Fernando Rojas went on to argue for an approach that could integrate the industrial proletariat with the housewife, the rural poor, tribals and dalits, and students and intellectuals, dealing with gender, caste, urban/rural, and manual/mental labor contradictions:

> The new approach begins with a new understanding of work. "Work" is labor for capital, the source of profit, and the means of capitalist control. Work is not only waged labor, it is also the unwaged labor of the "unemployed", who have to reproduce themselves, of the housewife, laboring to reproduce the labor power of her husband and that of the next generation of laborers, of the peasant laboring for the capitalist market, of scholars and students, qualifying themselves for the labor market.[8]

But although the workshop involved a wide number of movement-involved activist intellectuals, this perspective made little dent on the dominant Marxist framework. Even its main Indian exponent, Arvind Das, went on to emphasize the process of the working class "creating itself" only within the dominant framework, in which the "poor peasant" or "agricultural laborer" could be admitted to the fold but certainly not the "middle and rich peasant"; in which rural struggles could be admissible (or revolutionary) only if rural actors defined themselves as "workers" and not as "peasants," in which the middle "backward castes" continued to be seen as enemies of dalits.

With the mode of production debate behind them, having firmly established the generally capitalist character of Indian society, the dominant Marxist intellectual analysis saw this society as ruled by a "power bloc" including the various sections of the bourgeoisie, the bureaucracy, landlords, and "rich peasants"; "exploited classes" were said to include workers, artisans, poor peasants, and agricultural laborers; while "middle peasants" were thrown in with white-collar employees and various sections of the urban petty bourgeoisie as "intermediate classes."[9] The "urban intelligentsia" could thus be seen (as an "intermediate class") as playing a generally progressive role—but the peasant movement, far from being a struggle of one section of laboring people against a new form of capitalist subordination, was classed instead, due to its presumed rich peasant leadership, among *struggles within the ruling class*, as a conflict between its industrial and agrarian sections. This notion of the "agrarian bourgeoisie" (often estimated as including peasants with holdings over ten acres) as a part of the ruling bloc enabled its proponents to bring together the farmers' movement itself with the regional forces and parties (Akali Dal, the DMK, and the BKD group in the north) and the broader nationality-based movements, as part of the conflict of the "rural bourgeoisie" with the centralized and centralizing industrial bourgeoisie. Along with this the dalit movement (OBCs were not mentioned) represented a "class struggle" in caste form of the agricultural laborers against their rural rich peasant exploiters, while the women's movement and environmental movements (where the latter was not interpreted as a tribal-based poor peasant struggle) were effectively ignored.

This interpretation, crystallized by the early 1970s, continued practically unfazed by any challenges up through the 1980s. And, it may be added, it left the Marxist intelligentsia in a mood of unrelieved pessimism as they saw the increasing predominance of what was, according to their analysis, the "intra-ruling class struggles" of rich farmers versus the industrial bourgeoisie, of "rich backward castes" against the upper castes, and of "nonclass" environmental movements.

The pessimism of the intellectuals would not have been of much consequence but for the fact that even more than the parties, it fashioned the thinking of the Marxist activists who debated with the activists of the new movements. For the Communist parties—which, as Bipin Chandra had lamented, had never been movers of events in India—were becoming even less so, throughout the decades after 1967.

The Mainstream Communists

The CPI(M) had developed as the more militant and radical of the two mainstream parties. But the Naxalite revolt had sucked away some of its more militant cadres, especially in the rural areas, and the 1972 Congress electoral victory in West Bengal resulted in a regime that wreaked repression and havoc upon both CPI(M) and the Naxals. The party slowly moderated its activities, swinging to a policy of what some sardonically called "Stalinism in words and social democracy in deeds." In 1975 P. Sundarayya, a veteran of the Andhra Telengana uprising, resigned from his position as general secretary, protesting against the party's alliance with Hindu rightists to oppose the Congress, against "not taking the agrarian revolution" seriously by building up the unity of agricultural laborers and middle peasants for a strong movement, and for not taking seriously preparing for a revolutionary-insurrectional struggle of workers and peasants by developing the party base in the rural geographical areas outlying the big industrial centers. "The tactical line," he wrote, "has been put in cold storage for all practical purposes."[10] Sundarayya also criticized the policy of building "all-India" unions under the leadership of the party in every field regardless of the actual strength of the party, and indirectly protested the dominance of the West Bengal and Kerala units (where the party had its electoral base).

Sundarayya's criticism had no impact. Following the Emergency, the party regained electoral control of West Bengal in the 1977 election and then, after the Jallandhar (1978) party congress, accepted the proposal of Kerala's Nambudiripad to build up its strength in the "Hindi belt," which surrounded not the industrial centers but the political capital, Delhi. The party central office was shifted to Delhi, and the policy was adopted of building up not only separate trade unions but mass organizations of every type under party leadership—rather than working (where the party was a minority or there were many competing political groups) within one broad mass organization. This meant, in effect, building the party as one that could have a strong impact on a parliamentary democratic system—where numbers and mobilizing ability counted: a machine with one to three states and vast numbers of people mobilized in front organizations under its control.

In the party congresses following this (Vijayawada in 1982, Calcutta in 1984, Trivandrum in 1988) there was no debate on the "tactical line" of revolution; rather, discussion and disputes primarily concerned evaluation of the existing political parties (Congress, right-wing, regional, the Janata) and the degree to which the party should make adjustments even with the BJP to oppose the Congress. (The West Bengal unit consistently tended to favor some adjustment with the BJP; the Kerala leadership opposed it.) In other words, "politics" came to mean in effect party fronts and parliamentary politics, control or share in control of the government.

This meant a significant difference from the new social movements, all of which had an inherent suspicion of parties and formulated their relationship to politics in a different way. The women's movement and much of the environmental movement tended to avoid politics, to stress "social" change from the base, but the farmers' movement also, which operated as a strategically concerned mass movement, saw its role as primarily a pressure group, and in regard to parliamentary politics, shared the Naxalite critique that no matter who got elected, it would make little difference. Thus Sharad Joshi saw direct involvement in politics as a way of leading the movement into disaster and argued for a political strategy of acting to maintain "a balance of power" among the existing big parties; this normally meant supporting the anti-Congress opposition. The dalit movement had the longest tradition of direct political action, but even here the new organizations tended to see themselves more as pressure groups or as extraparliamentary revolutionary organizations, with even Kanshi Ram ready to say, "We want balance of power to ensure that neither the Congress nor the National Front gets an absolute majority. . . . There must be a coalition government at the centre and we must ensure for ourselves a balancing act." [11]

The fact was that the movements were involved in struggles in very different ways from the parties. Issues such as remunerative prices, renaming Marathwada University, getting the Mandal Commission implemented, stopping Silent Valley or the Narmada dams were taken up in determined seriousness as long-term uncompromising projects of the movements, to be pushed whatever government was in power. While these had all the problems of "single-issue politics," they meant greater agitational seriousness. In contrast, while the Communist parties had their central slogans (especially "land to the tiller" and "right to work") with which they sought to embody the democratic revolution, these did not provide the basis around which to organize long-term struggle. Instead, the parties held demonstrations, marches, and rallies and presented petitions and "charters of demands," but they did all this with a view to influencing legislators or political coalitions and electoral activity. Slogans of "land" or "work" may have appeared again and again in the demonstrations and demands, but the idea was less to get them implemented than to make them a part of the "political consciousness" of the masses who would presumably join, follow, and elect a Communist party to work toward a socialist system within which alone such goals could be achieved. The movements in contrast worried less about the nature of the system than about the achievement of the goals.

At the same time, the parties were much more open to the themes of the new social movements than were the Marxist intellectuals. This was especially true with regard to the farmers' movement, where strategic concerns for "worker-peasant unity" might actually take precedence over abstract evaluations of the growth of capitalism in agriculture. The CPI with fair enthusiasm, and the CPI(M) with more debate, backed the Mandal Commission and popular science campaigns and endorsed demands for remunerative prices and debt relief. Women's issues were taken up enthusiastically, and the party went far ahead of the conscious feminist groups in mobilizing working class women to fight atrocities, in the process gaining some new cadres. Marxist intellectuals might complain about joining in with "petty-bourgeois populist movements"; movement activists might complain that the parties came only to increase their political base among the movement, or that they came only as leaders without mobilizing (in the inimitable words of Sharad Joshi, as "generals without tanks"), but at least they were there, they were part of a broad front.

But while the parties accepted the broad issues of the movements, they did so only partially, adding, for example, that debt relief should only be for poor peasants or that "economic criteria" should be added to or substituted for caste-based reservations. They did so with strong attacks on the leadership of the movements. The primary sin of the new social movements, in the eyes of the parties, was that they had non-Communist leadership. The immediate goal of the parties, in working on the issues of the movements, then, was to build up their front organizations and eventually their parties. In the 1982 Vijayawada Congress, the CPI(M) adopted a resolution on mass fronts which critized their previous "sectarianism," but sectarianism here was defined as having a narrow conceptualization of the base of the mass fronts (for instance, the women's organization should be defined as "democratic," including middle-class women, rather than just as a "working women's coordination"); there was no questioning that the main effort should be to bring a significant section of the mass under direct party leadership.[12]

Thus, qualified support for movement issues was invariably linked with a strong attacks on their leadership. Dalit leadership was "petty bourgeois"; the farmers' movement leadership was "landlord" or "kulak"; but the most notorious attack in the mid-1980s was unleashed against the women's movement and the Christian radicals involved in tribal and environmental organizations, in an extension of the parties' tendency to see the imperialist "invisible hand" in all agitations. This came in the form of an article by one of the CPI(M)'s young, Delhi-bred cadres, Prakash Karat, which criticized new "action groups" working among the masses as CIA-inspired and part of a new strategy of imperialism. The article named the Lokayan group and new Christian radicals, stressing their dependence on foreign funding, and identified the "autonomy" demanded by the new feminists as well as organizations like the Jharkhand Mukti Morcha and Chattisgarh Mukti Morcha as being antiparty. Describing the new feminism as "imported," it focused on Chhaya Datar as the bearer of an international feminist conspiracy: Datar, it noted, is "a product of the Institute for Social Studies, The Hague, which is a key intellectual center for the action groups' philosophy and bourgeois feminism." (Datar had indeed studied at the ISS, whose women's studies heads, Maria Mies of West Germany and Kumari Jayawardene of Sri Lanka, were indeed trying to build up an international feminism.) "It should be apparent," the article went on, "that this feminism can conveniently serve the interests of the imperialist agencies and even the advanced sections of the bourgeoisie in India." Even worse, the new trends were attempting autonomous theorizing: "For these new revolutionary theorists . . . [have made] a startling new discovery, that it is possible to develop a new revolutionary ideology and movement, renouncing the working class ideology and organization, which can be a credible alternative to the ruling class ideology and structure."[13]

The very heavy-handedness of this attack might have fully discredited it were it not for the fact that it was pointing to a real problem, that sections of the new movements were in fact falling into dependence on funding. It is striking, though, that the article directly attacked those sections of the new movements (Christian radicals and middle class feminists) who were, at the time, the most amenable to party influence. Activists in the dalit and farmers' movements, who were much less immersed in broad left circles, took little notice of the controversy.

The discussion of "action groups" (the small funded organizations working among various sections of the rural poor or providing services for such work) overlooked one fact. This was that the theoretical tendency of the middle-class intellectuals who worked in these movements was that of Marxist intellectuals, not of the parties: that is, it invariably identified "capitalism" as the main factor in the agrarian sector, and "middle and rich peasants" (in class terms) and "backward castes" (in caste terms) as the enemies of the rural poor they were attempting to organizing. Activists who took over the framework of Marxism and began to criticize the parties for "revisionism," whether they were the Christian radicals running the Indian Social Institute in Bangalore, or well-heeled activist groups such as the Young India Project in Andhra, or Bombay middle-class youth working among tribals in the Thana belt in Maharashtra, invariably took this line. Within such groups, the tendency was to combine work with the "rural poor" or "unorganized sector" with bureaucratic links and access to middle-class influence, media contacts, and funding.

The Naxalites

Organizations and parties coming out of the Naxalite rebellion had a different relation to the new social movements. By the mid-1980s, two groups were clearly dominant. One was the Peoples' War Group (PWG), functioning in the backward and forested regions of Andhra, holding fast to an armed struggle line, and organizing dalits, low castes, and tribals on issues such as opposing bonded labor, making gains in wages and small land occupations, and fighting the dominance of the rural oligarchy. They maintained a general Marxist-Leninist orthodoxy on issues of women's rights. Although Hyderabad had been the home of one early near-feminist organization, the POW, and although the Stree Shakti Sanghatana worked there through much of the 1980s as one of the significant urban feminist organizations, the PWG seems to have taken little note of feminism as a trend. Issues of environment were also ignored in Andhra, as were caste issues for a long time. Kancha Ilaiah, an activist of a related group, had to fight his own democratic rights organization to take up the issue in the late 1980s. The farmers' movement was definitely taken note of; but while the PWG's own publication, the *Vanguard*, argued for a broad structure of petty-commodity production in the agrarian sector, its best-known associated intellectual, K. Balagopal, attacked the movement strongly.

These "farmers" have two faces, one a democratic face that holds up traffic demonstrating *en masse* for remunerative prices or the Agricultural Costs Commission, and the other the ugly face of "atrocities on harijans" as our caste-struck Press calls them. A reality that has not yet percolated the consciousness of observers is that the "farmers" who rode their tractors behind Sharad Joshi into Chandigarh are merely the other face of the Bhoomi Sena landlords of Bihar. They are part of the same class-for-itself that is taking shape across the land.[14]

Balagopal made a careful distinction between "middle and rich peasants" and this "rural oligarchy" (which Marxist-Leninist orthodoxy required, since "peasants" were allies in the antifeudal struggle), but then saw the latter as pulling along the former in a process of class creation in which the "farmers' movement" was playing a major role. In any case, there were no stable farmers' organization in Andhra, a state with a higher than average inegalitarian rural class structure, though there were agitations. The second major group with a claim to national impact was the Vinod Mishra-led "Liberation" group of CPI(ML), named after its major organ. The biggest organization working in Bihar, and still claiming to be the true organizational heirs of Charu Mazumdar, this party changed its line significantly over the years. In 1981 it formed an open peasant front, the Bihar Pradesh Kisan Sabha, and in 1983 it made another bold initiative in establishing the Indian People's Front as a "mass political organization." Members of different Marxist-Leninist groups, nonmainstream Marxists, and some social movement organizations were invited, and many attended. Most of these later dropped away, and IPF did not emerge as a real "united front," but it did begin to function effectively as a mass front of the party. It had the problems of such a mass front—for instance that its conferences, held after underground party conferences, invariably duplicated (though in a diluted form) party resolutions and positions, while the party conferences talked of the IPF but the IPF conferences never mentioned the party.[15]

The IPF was an impressive effort in many ways, and its effort to pose itself as a "national political alternative" embodied a positive assessment of the new movements that was in contrast to the CPI(M)'s tendency to denounce any "alternative" as a threat to Marxism itself. Indeed, its 1988 "Political-Organisational Report" gave a very positive view:

> Then there is a whole range of old as well as new social movements and also sectional struggles—some of which are rooted in the specific Indian history while some are global in character—which are not easily amenable to the Left-Right classification. . . . The longstanding inability of the dominant Indian Left to grasp the significance of such movements has pushed the latter under the influence and leadership of various reformist and rightist forces. The dalit movement, the farmers' movement, the women's movement, the health movement, the science and environment campaign, the professionals' struggles are some major examples. The alternative that India needs must draw its forces

from all these popular assertions, it must provide an alternative not only to the dominant economic and political structure but to the entire process of development and to the cultural ethos.

This was very strongly put, and the report even went on to note that "while the old parties are beginning to disintegrate, a whole new range of political formations are forcefully asserting themselves," stating *"we ourselves belong to this category of newcomers."* [16]

From the point of view of the new movements, this was promising. But there appears to have been two trends working in the CPI(ML)-Liberation/IPF, one more oriented to the "new social movements" and alternative politics, the other to traditional working class party politics. It is quite possible that this involved a conflict between the party and the mass organization; there was a similar contradiction developing at the time in the Party Unity/Mazdur Kisan Sangram Samiti group, also based in Bihar. The dilemmas were reflected in the 1988 convention of IPF, which adopted a postscript to its earlier manifesto. This is worth quoting at length. The postscript began with a recognition of the new contradictions that were ravaging Indian society.

> The net result of such a distorted and lopsided process of development has been a duplication of the global North-South in India. In other words we have two Indias—an elitist India all set to step into the 21st century and a commoners' India lagging way behind, pockets of plenty and advance amid an ocean of poverty and backwardness. . . . Theories of "India vs. Bharat" or "internal colonialism" may be based on somewhat simplistic generalisation, but the great imbalance between industry and agriculture, between urban India and the countryside, between the Centre and the States, between advanced and backward regions, between the majority religious and linguistic community and minorities, between a group of big and developed nationalities and their small and neglected counterparts is there for everybody to see.[17]

But, the original version of the postscript, as presented at the conference, had gone beyond this to give a definition of the sought-for alternative itself in terms of the new movements:

> Such an alternative is already in the making, its roots going deeper in the multifarious struggles and creative efforts of our people. . . . With each passing day the battle for alternative is certainly spreading wider and gaining in strength. It gains in strength with every victory scored by the toiling peasantry and agricultural laborers in their struggle for land and wages, for tenancy rights and agricultural inputs. Or for that matter with every mobilization of the farmers for remunerative prices and for a harmonious balance between industry and agriculture. It gains in strength with every major industrial action by the workers and employees . . . Similarly when students struggle for academic freedom and the youth against unemployment; when women get organized against male domination and dalits against caste oppression; when civil libertarians protest

against state encroachment on human rights; when cultural activists join hands to resist decadence and degeneration; and scientists start spreading scientific knowledge and environmental awareness, they all advance the cause of the alternative.

Of course this still was carrying implicit distinctions between "toiling peasants" fighting for land and "farmers" for remunerative prices; it referred to caste *oppression* and not "exploitation"; to male *domination* and not "patriarchy." Still, it was eloquently written and powerful in its appeal, and it went on to talk of "alternative development" itself in a new way:

> This concept of alternative stands in sharp contrast to the slogan of "political alternative" advanced from time to time by various opposition parties and their endless exercises in alignment and realignment to provide the same.

Instead, a new developmental model must be put forward and from this, "the enforcement of a pro-people developmental model therefore calls for the establishment of people's political power" which would end by "dealing a final blow" to the Congress political current that had been dominating Indian society.[18]

Remarkably, this whole section was dropped in the final version, which instead stated that "manifold popular strivings for an alternative path of development and an alternative social order are yet to crystallize into a nationwide mass political movement." It laid stress on seeking a political alternative: "The point is to pursue the long-drawn quest for an alternative system through the immediate political agenda" and to move from this to a broad anti-Congress front.[19] This was a major shift of emphasis.

In revising the postscript, IPF moved from a powerfully written attempt to root the "alternative" in the upsurge of the new social movements (formulating at the same time the notion that an alternate developmental model would be the main counter to Congress politics) to a stress on the need to work in the conventional political sphere. The IPF's forceful assertion of itself in the 1989–90 parliamentary and assembly elections was justified by the traditional left rhetoric of identifying "right" and "left" errors (in this case IPF attacked the "antipolitical" attitude of many of the new movement activists, and the superpolitical extremism of those who rejected everything but the politics of the gun). By the time of the elections, this "politicization" of IPF was carried through when its pamphlet left out even the mention of "alternative" and instead stressed "Strengthen the Independent Assertion of the Indian Left." An earlier English-language organ, *Voice of Alternative*, was replaced by *People's Front*. IPF was being projected, in other words, not as a political platform of a new alternative or as one of many new political formations, but as the reemerged vanguard of the Indian left. For the Naxalites as well, the shift from their "wilder" militancy and ruralism to the working class and the political arena seemed inevitably to go along with a downgrading of concern for a real alternative politics and a closing off of interest in the new movements.

The Industrial Working Class

In June 1987 a small collection of Communist activists in Maharashtra (including two Naxalite organizations and the "posttraditional Communist" Shramik Mukti Dal) held three days of discussion with Sharad Joshi, later to be known as the "NTM" or "nontraditional Marxist" discussions. Joshi had proposed three points for focusing the debate: (1) the working class has been increasingly caught in economism and is not a vanguard of a broad revolutionary movement; (2) all history is *not* the history of "class struggles" (here both sides shared the conventional definition of "class"; Joshi did not deny class action so much as argue that this did not count across community/national barriers; rather than class struggles there were fights between "systems"—tribes, castes, regions, nations, patriarchal versus matriarchal societies, etc.); and (3) "parochial movements" (by which he meant caste/communal/linguistic divisions, referring in particular to the growing religious fundamentalism worrying almost everyone on the left) were overwhelming "economistic" movements (the term he used to refer to struggles against exploitation). The Marxists in addition proposed a session on the economic theories of the farmers' movement itself, leading into a wide debate on surplus value and the meaning of "capital" (which Joshi was insisting included not only embodied labor but in addition what he called "the R in the heart of C," resources, the produce of the land).

The concern about "economism" was in fact worrying Communist party activists of all types during this period, and privately if not publicly complaints about the indifference of industrial workers, particularly the highly paid employees of multinationals and public-sector industries, were quite common. In the NTM debates themselves, few of the activists present were actually ready to defend industrial workers as the vanguard of revolution, and many seemed to share the notion that the most highly paid workers were a "labor aristocracy" that was basically not even ready to fight decisively. Yet even defined in the narrowest sense of industrial worker, the "working class" during this period was waging some important battles, and if not ready to act as a "vanguard," it was at least showing important signs of unity with other sections of laborers and with the social movements themselves. But this was at times in spite of their Marxist leadership.

Joshi had opened the debate on economism by outlining the series of popular working-class leaders in the history of Bombay industry: S. A. Dange (the original Communist leader), George Fernandes (the fiery socialist who rose to prominence in the 1960s), R. G. Mehta (a "professional" unionist), and Datta Samant. "What does this mean?" he asked. In fact the sequence illustrated the problematics of working class politics, rather than a simple trend toward incorporation into the system.

If R. G. Mehta representing a profesionalization of working-class struggles, Samant represented something quite different, an antipolitical militancy. He had risen to prominence in the post-Emergency period as the leader of a new wave of militancy among Bombay workers; in fact he had been jailed during the Emergency itself for strike action, in spite of being a Congress member at the time. He was conventionally political to begin with, unconcerned with socialism or broader issues, but known for his militancy, his refusal to compromise or to concede anything to companies on arguments of ability to pay (capitalist balance sheets, he charged, were simply "lies"). Political parties were rejected as having destroyed workers' struggles by using them for narrow electoral purposes.

With an original base in the big engineering (heavy industry) firms, Samant was in 1982 pulled into the volatile textile industry—the historic center of the Bombay working class, the original base of the bourgeoisie, milked for profits, still impoverished but undergrowing the throes of "modernization" with trends to retrenchment of workers and adoption of sophisticated machinery going on all over India. In the 1980s, with nearly 250,000 workers earning half or less of what other factory workers were making, the industry was still functioning as a refuge for the flood of migrants from drought-prone areas of western Maharashtra. The majority of workers still lived in crowded slums or as bachelors in communal rooms with their families surviving in the villages; and a very large section, maybe one-fourth, were nonformalized or *badli* workers. The latter may have worked every day, but, they had none of the benefits of permanent employees. Instead they had to appear every day at the factory gates, like a casual laborer petitioning for work.

Workers in this industry, the most politically conscious of any section of Bombay workers, turned to the militantly nonpolitical Samant for good reason. Their grievances against the tyrannous work organization, low pay, and their continual subordination through legal repression to a Congress party-controlled union had been growing for a long time, and the "red flag" unions by the early 1980s, as a result indeed of their political links, had shown themselves incapable of dealing with these. Samant, at first reluctant himself to get involved in this seething industry, was dragged into leadership of the strike. In the process, he was to some extent radicalized, changing his own flag from the Congress green-white-and-saffron to a new red-bordered flag with a black smokestack from which a worker's fist arose.

The strike dragged on for eighteen months, a major event at least in the working-class life of Maharashtra. It included ongoing actions (marches, *jail bharos*, demonstrations) in Bombay, and attempts at worker-peasant unity as the largest section of workers returned to their village homes to survive. Workers themselves showed great solidarity across caste and religious lines, as well as rejecting political sectarianism. To "nontraditional Marxist" activist Bharat Patankar, it meant a new breakthrough in struggle methods:

> The term "strike" historically has meant *bandhs*, marches, picketing, etc., in the cities and idleness for the majority of workers who have gone back to their

villages. In a country like India where almost all sections of workers are still maintaining relations with the agrarian sector . . . the traditional method of struggle could not take workers beyond the limitations of trade union conflicts. . . . In recent years, however, struggles of mine workers in Dhanbad and Chattisgarh have broken new ground by working to build ongoing relations with the concerns of poor tribal peasants. By creating a conscious struggle in the countryside, the textile strike in Bombay definitely meant a historic breakthrough in the Indian working class movement. . . . Throughout the period of the strike the textile workers were a shining example of non-sectarian practice, and this in an atmosphere of extreme sectarianism exhibited by almost all Communist parties and groups. By allowing each and every group ready to help in furthering the struggle to participate in the movement, they denied the establishment of a monopoly over the workers and their movement by a single leadership.[20]

But in the end the turning point represented by the textile strike was one of a failure of an alternative politics in which the industrial working class was to have a major role in building a united movement. This was not simply because the strike was defeated,[21] for although the workers were in the end forced back into the factories and into the hold of the Congress-led union, they were unshaken in their loyalty to Samant, electing him to the Lok Sabha in a period of a Congress sweep, and pushing the formation of a new party, the Kamgar Aghadi (Workers' Front). Proposals were made at the time that the textile workers and the Aghadi take the lead in formulating a new national textile policy and organizing a movement around it. This could have been a base for a unified worker-peasant thrust: cotton-growing peasants in Maharashtra under Sharad Joshi were already opposing synthetics in a campaign in which wearing natural fibers was a sign of identity of a member of Shetkari Sanghatana, while those in Karnataka were organizing under the Rayatu Sangh to uproot the tree plantations used to supply the state's biggest synthetic textile factory.

But this opportunity was lost. Part of the problem was Samant's own economism: though he had formed the Kamgar Aghadi, and though it remained after this a part of the left-democratic opposition, he still saw its function in mainly economistic terms, arguing, "I learned from the strike and from my experience as a trade unionist that the Indian working class must get involved in politics . . . because only in that way can they pressurize their demands."[22]

This in a sense was the same kind of single-issue ("one-point program") politics shown by all social movements. A different kind of failure lay with the left, which failed to articulate any real worker-peasant unity or unity of working-class demands with other social issues. The major Communist- and socialist-led unions gave only lukewarm support to the strike, distrusting Samant's leadership and hoping up to the end that workers would realize their mistake and come back to the "red flag" unions. There were practically no solidarity actions by other sections of the unionized workers or in the bastion of Left Front strength, West Bengal. The only relatively large party that did throw its forces into the strike was Maharashtra's Lal Nishan party, but LNP's attempts to organize rural actions and worker-rural poor unity were marked by their own analysis of "class differentiation" in the countryside, which saw "rich farmers" as the main enemy and the Shetkari Sanghatana as a force to be opposed, not to unite with; in fact it was LNP that convinced Samant not to attend the first conference of Shetkari Sanghatana in early 1982. LNP could thus give no program for building ongoing worker-peasant unity. The one worker-linked peasant organization that emerged from the strike—Mukti Sangarsh in Sangli district, which Patankar and local left peasant activists had helped to form—stressed antidrought activity, which none of the other left forces involved considered an aspect of "class struggle" at the time. In the end, then, the strike did represent a failure of "vanguardship," whether of the workers themselves in relation to other forces or of the Marxist organizations claiming to be the structured vanguard. Samant and his Kamgar Aghadi became immersed in electoral politics, and no organizing on issues, whether of the national textile policy or anything else, emerged.

Yet in spite of demoralization, workers' enthusiasm for united action and their nonsectarianism remained. In early 1987, when Shetkari Sanghatana was organizing its forces for a gherao of the chief minister's Bombay residence on the issue of cotton prices, some days after 30,000 had been arrested and eleven people killed in firings on the widespread rural agitations, Samant and Joshi appeared together in a rally that workers of the Kamgar Aghadi in the Currey Road office, in the heart of the textile area, celebrated with posters hailing "worker-peasant unity." And when an LNP cadre arrived in the office, he was violently harangued: "What are you people doing saying that Datta Samant is running after Sharad Joshi? If you want to say this, don't say it behind our backs, come to Shivaji Park [the site of mass rallies] and say it openly, if you dare! And stop this 'rich peasant-poor peasant' talk and say just one thing: are they fighting the state or not?"

Thus the failure to build a broad unity occurred in the face of the workers' urge for it: Samant's economism led to his ignoring the problems of synthetics- and cotton-growing peasants and failure to move toward an overall textile policy; Joshi's reluctance to go beyond his "one-point program" meant no real concern for taking initiatives regarding alliance with workers' struggles; traditional Marxist tendency to see all exploitation in terms of wage-labor meant neglecting the "new movement" issues of environment and petty-commodity producers and inability to provide a theoretical and political articulation of unity. Movements remained oriented to single-issue struggles, and after the defeat of the textile strike no working-class movement could catch the imagination of politically conscious activists throughout the country.

"Post–Traditional Communists"

In basic ways, all the Communist trends—whether CPI or CPI(M) or the various CPI(ML) formations—shared basic assumptions about the revolution and about the party that would lead it. But in the post-Emergency period, a change began to develop from within the wide circles of Communist-identified activists themselves. In eastern India, many of the youth associated with the Naxalite upsurge continued working, in Calcutta, among the tribals of south Bihar, and elsewhere, but as unorganized clusters, so repelled by the murderous infighting of the Naxalite upsurge period that they rejected all "party" organization as domineering; in spite of a total lack of a women's liberation trend in Bengal at the time, many of these activists became drawn to the concepts of feminism. In Kanpur, U.P., a group known as the Nagarik Adhikar Morcha (Citizen's Rights Front) emerged, first promoting workers' committees and then turning to support of the farmers' movement and a broad association with the neo-Gandhian critique of development. Their Hindi publications covered many of the debates of the period.

In Maharashtra, the Shramik Mukti Dal (Workers' Liberation League) was formed in 1980 out of some ex-Magowa activists, some collections of Bombay workers who had been involved in cultural activities and scattered Marxist activists. In contrast to the old Magowa group, they had much more of a working class base and carried on their discussions and writings from the beginning in Marathi itself. They also had a viewpoint that clearly identified issues such as caste and patriarchy as crucial contradictions that could not wait until "after the revolution," and as they worked first in the Bombay textile strike and in rural organizing for this, and then began to develop a base from 1983 among drought-affected peasants in southern Maharashtra, they also developed an ecological perspective. In contrast to the Kanpur group, their identification of Indian society as dominated by capitalism led them to characterize the Shetkari Sanghatana as serving the interests of "capitalist farmers," but their assessment of the other new social movements was positive:

> These movements are not considering the productive forces and means of production as abstract, ahistorical, nonclass and nongender things given by the bourgeois society which can simply be separated from their private property form and used by the proletariat and other toiling masses. Instead they take them as historically specific forms in which the system is internalized. That is why these movements are challenging the validity of the existence of some of the means of production, and the relation of these to nature and the industrial science and technology which takes nature as an enemy to be overpowered.[23]

So wrote SMD activist Bharat Patankar, in an article arguing that just as Marx had redefined "politics" after experiencing the Paris Commune so that revolution could no longer mean just taking over state power but creating a new kind of state, so also the left today had to redefine politics. In a subsequent article he specified this: "Now, revolution means . . . the beginning of a struggle to implement a new strategy regarding the relationship between men and women and between people of different castes and nationalities. It means alternative ways of organizing and managing the production processes, alternate concepts of agriculture and of agriculture/industry/ecology, and alternative health care."[24]

The Bengali "post–traditional Communists" were to remain unorganized; the Kanpur Nagarik Adhikar Morcha group was to wither away; SMD survived (partly because its structure was nondemocratic centralist and thus flexible enough to allow for contending views), but as a small formation with some base in peasants and laborers in southern Maharashtra, tribals in Dhule district, peasants and workers in Belgaum, and workers in Bombay—hardly enough, it seemed at the time, to voice a competing politics to the big Communist parties. Perhaps theirs were the voices of the future. But it was clear that on the whole, the Indian left was not able to take any initiative in building a broad revolutionary or democratic alliance of the exploited people struggling, often quite militantly and resolutely, in the single-issue focused new movements. Though these movements were, by the mid-1980s, giving broad challenges to the Indian state, they in turn were unable to transcend their frameworks to give a real shape to overall political developments. It was on this background that in the period from 1967 to 1985, the ongoing crisis of India's Congress-dominated political system was seen to be coming under the onslaught, not of a broad revolutionary movement, but rather of the politics of ethnicity, nationality, and religious fundamentalism.

8

The Crisis of Traditional Politics

Almost everywhere where killings took place, there was first a mob attack with iron rods rendering the victims unconscious after which kerosene, petrol and other combustible fuels were used to burn the bodies. In case of trucks the attempt was to set them ablaze through piercing the fuel tanks, burning both the truck and the driver. In the case of shops and buildings, there was a greater use of charred rags and combustible chemicals in powder form. Taking Delhi and Bhopal together ... the extent to which "chemical warfare" has been waged on one's own people is terribly frightening.

All this called for a massive supply of fuel of all kinds in large parts of the city. There is clear evidence that this was planned and coordinated. So was identifying the location of colonies, households, shops and establishments; this too was systematically carried out. There was evidence of men on scooters locating the places followed by mobs who carried out the killings and the arson, in many areas supervised by higher-ups moving in Ambassador cars from one place to another.... The brutal killings were much more in the poorer colonies where women were on the whole spared but were forced to witness in full the torturous methods—pulling out of limbs and eyes, tearing off hair, beards being set on fire, piercing of bowels and kidneys with sharp weapons—through which their menfolk were put to death.... It is quite clear that all this could not have been accomplished ... but for there being a large measure of advance planning.[1]

SO POLITICAL scientist and intellectual-activist Rajni Kothari has described the Delhi riots on November 1–3, 1983, when following the assassination of Indira Gandhi thousands of Sikh men were murdered, usually burned to death, uncounted women raped, millions of rupees worth of property destroyed. The rampage was prepared for by the persistent propagandizing that depicted Sikhs as antinational and terrorists; it was carried out by mobs under the active direction of Congress politicians, and it was given sanction by the new prime minister, Indira Gandhi's son Rajiv, with the notorious remark, "When a big tree falls the ground shakes."

The police stood by and let it happen. And even after the holocaust, the political role of the police was stark. As Kothari notes, while Indira Gandhi's body was guarded in state, to be shown on television in an elaborate cremation ceremony, the police disappeared from the colonies and neighborhoods of the Sikhs: "The contrast was so shameful, so abominal. On the one side lay one body, deliberated uncremated for three days, only to be accorded a royal cremation with Vedic mantras, *chandan*, and *ghee*. On the other side there was no one even to lift the bodies—of several hundreds—for two and at places, three days.[2]

The Delhi riots represented the zenith of the Congress system in India. The "ground that was shaking" was in reality more than that under the feet of masses of innocent citizens being tortured, raped, murdered, and humiliated. It was the very moral and political basis of the party that had ruled India for so long. Not now in the far-flung villages or tribal hills, but in the capital of India itself was written the record of atrocities that could not be denied.

It is also striking that after the Delhi riots—just as in response to the Bhopal explosion—the traditional opposition political parties also remained inactive and deadened. Socialists and Communists did little by way of rehabilitation work, in spite of their tradition of activity in religious riots; nor did Hindu organizations feel concerned to demonstrate in action the validity of their assertions that "Sikhism is really a part of Hinduism," though their cadres were active in collections and relief work after floods and similar "natural" disasters. The only effective help was that organized by voluntary groups—civil liberties organizations, women's movement activists, health activists, and ordinary citizens. The initiative of the small Manushi group in holding a meeting in their middle-class Delhi neighborhood and bringing in Sant Longowal from the Punjab to meet the family of a Hindu who had lost his life protecting his Sikh neighbors was one of many such efforts. But they seemed, altogether, only small straws in the winds of turmoil sweeping over India. The old order was cracking at the base, but no clear alternative was emerging to replace it.

Disintegration of the Congress

"India is Indira and Indira is India," proclaimed Congress president D. K. Barooah during the traumatic Emergency period. Though dramatically overstated, it nevertheless expressed the way politics for a long period came to have a personalized focus. For the ruling elite, this centralization around a personality cult and power from the top was an effort to replace a system of patronage rule that was breaking down; for the opposition parties attacking it came to be a substitute for the posing of a genuine political alternative.

The breakdown of the old Congress system can be dated to the elections of 1967, "the first election," according to P. B. Mayer, "in which the political sophistication of the Indian masses made itself felt in a decisive way."[3] People, that is, could no longer be manipulated as simple vote banks of local patrons; it was even becoming harder and harder to coerce local dalits and laborers into voting as the village bosses wanted them to vote; even women, in spite of beliefs that they simply followed their husbands' directions, were showing a distinctly different voting pattern from men. The people of India were thinking; they were voting in groups, communities, and castes, but often with a collective strategy, of maximizing a temporary gain (a road, a promise of an oil pressing machine, whatever) or even preventing a "main enemy" from getting elected. Votes could still be bought, but this had to be done with more sophistication, and increasingly this meant modern techniques of impressing the electorate, so that elections came by the 1980s to be gaudy, blaring festivals of bright posters, electrically lit boards, huge cutouts of election symbols, noisy vans with audio and then video cassettes blaring out propaganda, advertising agencies, and pollsters. Economic crisis and increasing insecurity of their lives was throwing ordinary citizens into bewilderment, but they were not facing the future with a simple clinging to traditional solutions: "What has seemed evident to me ever since my initial fieldwork in the late 1960s is that these changes in the economic structure were directly reflected in an extraordinary growth of political consciousness and the emergence of a 'class-like' politics." [4]

Indira Gandhi's strategy of rule was to maintain, even heighten, the traditional Congress rhetoric—glorification of a strong, centralized nation combined with semisocialistic appeals to the poor and marginalized—but to substitute a party machine based on personal loyalty for the structure of elite patronage that was beginning to crumble. This allowed her to force some reforms and some co-optation of representatives of low-caste groups on local oligarchs who no longer had a secure base to resist power from above. It also meant the predominance of personal cliques and factionalism in the party and Delhi-made decisions about state and even local politics (from who would get party tickets to who would be chief minister). Thus, growing political consciousness among the masses went along with a growing personalized power in Delhi—to the point where the sophisticated Asian businessman's journal, *Far Eastern Economic Review*, increasingly featured articles about India titled "Empress of India," "Where Do You Go from Here, Mrs. Gandhi?" and "Will Mrs. Gandhi Become a Dictator?" [5]—and a new fluidity among the local oligarchy and an increasing breakdown of the old norms of political competition:

> The intervening years (since 1973–74) have witnessed a marked erosion of restraint, mounting disorientation and incomprehension, and increasingly aggressive, short-sighted and often brutish behavior among politicians at all levels within the "soft" parties in the broad centre of the right-left spectrum. Norms, values and constraints . . . have been increasingly abandoned, and—except in a few cases—new structures and reformulated norms have not been developed to take their place. [6]

Normlessness, repression, efforts at co-optation, political and economic crisis all intensified in the 1972 to 1975 period in spite of the impressive Congress electoral victories in the preceding elections. The opposition tried to find a way to crystallize popular discontent. The left hoped that "class-like" politics would become a true class politics—that a broad worker-peasant front under proper party leadership would emerge out of the tradition-bound and caste-defined society of rural India to move toward a revolutionary democratic/socialist transformation. This did not happen. But in the pre-Emergency years it did seem, for a time, as if there were an emerging class politics of the traditional type. Agricultural laborers, peasants, workers, frustrated middle classes were all on the move. True, they were acting in unexpected ways, and even in the 1972–75 period, the emergence of the new social movements could be seen: dalits fighting caste oppression, women fighting patriarchy, peasants fighting the state or environmental destruction. But as yet such movements were not recognized as a new social-political force, and they made no impression on the national political scene or on the thinking of the left. Peasants, women, dalits had as yet built no networks or organs of communication of their own.

As a result, the political parties continued to dominate the opposition. Thus, while Communists and socialists were active in protest demonstrations or strikes like the massive railway strike of 1974, the spectrum-spanning coalition of the Hinduist right, the socialists, and the peasant-based political parties came forward with mass protest movements in the states of Bihar and Gujarat.

Jayaprakash Naryan, who was figurehead of this coalition and emerged as the leader of the mass upsurge of 1973–74, was a product of Gandhian socialism, an old freedom fighter who had turned away from politics but now returned to try to build a political alternative to the Congress, increasingly seen in the garb of dictatorship. His slogans were radical—"total revolution," "people's power"—and they voiced the idea of a village-oriented decentralized development opposed to both capitalism and statism. But there was little content or compelling program for the people's committees that were supposed to be set up. In spite of "nonparty" slogans, party politics was very much there.

In June 1975, faced with rising mass movements that combined rural discontent with militant student and middle-class movements that had forced the dissolution of the Bihar and Gujarat assemblies, and then with a court decision convicting her of two (among many) charges of electoral corruption, Indira Gandhi shocked the nation by imposing an internal Emergency, arresting tens of thousands of political opponents throughout the country and announcing a renewed "twenty-point program" of rural-oriented social reform. Justifying her action, she referred to the "deep-seated and widespread conspiracy which has been brewing ever since I began to introduce certain progressive measures of benefit to the common man and women in India" and described the "forces of disintegration" and "communal passions ... threatening our unity" and "new programs challenging law and order throughout the country."[7] The twenty points promised such things as higher agricultural wages for the rural poor and raised the exemption limit for income tax.

The imposition of Emergency, while coming as a shock, nevertheless confirmed the feeling among radicals throughout the country that they were living in an era of repression and revolution, that fascism could indeed be seen as a prelude to revolution, that now the terrible face of the ruling class was exposed, all blinkers were off, and they could get down to battle. "Indian democracy—long dead, now buried" was how Ranjit Guha referred to it.[8] But for the Indian masses, little in fact was really exposed: the continuation of Congress progressive rhetoric, small reform measures imposed in the rural areas, and the fact that the most visible repression was against some notorious black marketeers and smugglers meant that confusion continued regarding the nature of the enemy. It continued for the Communists too, sections of whom were even supporting the Emergency, seeing the political opposition as genuinely more right wing. Probably an even greater shock for the radicals came when the Emergency was just as suddenly ended. Guha had ended his article noting "explosive and countrywide expressions of discontent" and hoping that "the corpse, however, might revive, rise from its grave and walk our parched plains and dusty streets again"[9]—but there was no explosion, only a declaration of elections and a sudden disintegration of the Congress political machinery. A surprised opposition, with masses of cadres freed from jails, met to take stock and hastily cobbled together a political party representing the coalition that had led the movement against Indira Gandhi. They called it the Janata party, and the new "wave" of electorally expressed discontent brought it to Delhi as the ruling party.

Frustration of "Class Politics," 1977–1985

The Emergency was not a qualitative change nor a turning point; the Janata party regime that succeeded it proved to be only another episode in the ongoing crisis of the ruling elite. By conventional terms the "grand opposition" it embodied was anyway too incompatible to survive, and anticaste-oriented socialists and brahman-dominated Jan Sangh sections of the party clashed in many areas. But Janata included a wide variety of cranky leaders vieing to hold center stage, from the flamboyant socialist George Fernandes to the "Young Turk" Chandrasekhar to the man who actually became prime minister, Morarji Desai, a faddist vegetarian who attained some notoriety for his urine therapy but was otherwise a typical right-wing Gandhian with connections with many large industrial houses. Charan Singh, a western U.P. jat political veteran, and Jagjivan Ram of Bihar "represented" peasants and dalits respectively in the coalition, but neither had come out of the movements. Ram was the Congress-capitalist protégé who had led the "harijan" movement in opposition to Ambedkar from the 1930s onward; Charan Singh had been a builder of the "backward caste"-based Lok Dal in the north with a strong peasant rhetoric, but aside from holding a two-million-strong rally on his birthday to celebrate "*kisan* power" in Delhi, he did little to relate to the actual movement. (As Sharad Joshi put it, in a press discussion, "I told him I would make him the leader of India's peasants, but he preferred to be prime minister.") He did in fact become prime minister for two short months that only heralded the final breakup of the Janata experiment.

The Janata party government could not last; it had no real center to hold it together in a way that the authoritarianism/populism combination of Indira Gandhi could hold at least some sections of the Congress together. It provided no real political alternative—aside from banning Coca-Cola and throwing out IBM, and appointing the Mandal Commission to push forward the question of reservations for "backward castes," its policies remained little different in fact from those of the Congress. "Political decentralization" meant simply more state-financed programs for backward regions, more of a stress on public investment in agriculture. "Four-anna socialism" went its way relatively unscathed.

Political turmoil continued, but the long-awaited class politics still failed to emerge. Instead, it was Indira Gandhi who made a political comeback, seeking to focus mass discontent by roundly attacking atrocities on dalits committed by the "landlords and rich peasants" fostered by Janata, dramatizing her sympathy by riding an elephant to the scene of one village massacre in Bihar. By the end of 1978 many were seeing her return as inevitable. Politically she took a hard line, letting discontented regional bosses go out of the party and reconstructing it around herself this time with the unashamed name of "Congress (Indira)." Some of the popular discontent did in fact focus around her; it had no other political outlet.

At the same time, Indira Gandhi was shifting away from the secular socialist rhetoric of Congress. First, 1980 (and a huge IMF loan in 1981) marked the beginning of liberalization and a prolonged, halting, but definite shift away from a state-directed economy. Second, as violent unrest was mounting in the peripheral regions of India, with ethnic-national movements growing in both the Northwest (Punjab) and Northeast (Assam), Gandhi began to lay even more stress than before on "national integration," on "keeping the nation strong" and on attacking movements as imperialist-inspired, locating the "foreign hand" behind all opposition. With the Hindu rightists regrouping themselves, once the Janata had split, as the Bharatiya Janata party, she sought to meet their challenge by herself taking over some of the Hindu rhetoric—with an increasing use of Hindu symbols and a growing association, at the personal level, with numerous of the "godmen" floating around the Indian scene.

The elections held at the beginning of 1980 resulted in a massive Congress victory. But they also saw a successful boycott by the growing Assam movement, and an increasing challenge from fundamentalists (whom Congress had fostered to begin with) in the Punjab. The year 1980 marked the beginning of a new era of "identity politics" in India.

Internationally the period was one in which new fundamentalist and ethnic forces were rising on a world scale, in which the forces of liberation were taking a disturbing garb. Three important events in 1979–80 symbolized these developments.

In Latin America a revolution occurred after two decades of unrelieved dictatorial control in the small country of Nicaragua, but hopes for a wave sweeping Central America were belied when reactionary forces consolidated themselves, with considerable U.S. help, in the neighboring countries and headed off a guerrilla victory in El Salvador at the cost of 50,000 killed in massacres and "disappearances" and nearly 400,000 forced to flee the country. In Iran, the Shah was overthrown, ending a dictatorial regime that claimed a history of millennia, not decades, but what replaced it was not the leftist guerrillas who had fought and been tortured in the Shah's jails nor the peasants and workers who established short-lived popular councils, but a fanatic fundamentalistic preacher named Ayatolla Khomeini. In Poland, a working-class movement arose to challenge a supposedly workers' state, with leftists involved and calling for new forms of socialist democracy, but with the unsettling influence of the Catholic church dominant and headed by a pro-American worker named Lech Walesa. Iran marked the rise of Islamic fundamentalism; Nicaragua-El Salvador marked the success of the United States in holding back the challenge to imperialism in its "backyard" of Central America; and Poland marked the beginning of the crisis in the Communist world and the worldwide discrediting of Communist parties.

In this context, Marxist intellectuals have tended to view the development of Indian politics with stark pessimism, as a process dominated by intra-ruling class conflicts and the growth of fundamentalism. Javeed Alam's articulation of this is striking:

> The decade of the 1980s in Indian politics has so far been one of violent sectarian upheavals which have, relatively speaking, pushed the growth of democratic forces into the background. Never after 1947 have so many people died or been allowed to be killed in the name of religion, caste and community. The inherited "social identities" of our society have been the source of passions and frenzy that have gripped the minds of our people. The very definition of what constitutes a danger to national unity has got tied up with these identities. . . . In this sense, the 1980s stand in contrast to the 1970s. The 1970s too were years of struggle, turbulence and crises. . . . But . . . Whether in Gujarat or Bihar or later in the all-India JP movement, they were essentially secular and wholly social in nature. The "agitators" then were the same men and women who are ready to kill each other now, but then they were showing their discontent and exasperation with the performance of the economy, the management of the polity and the corroding influence of corruption in society. . . . In spite of the fact that bourgeois formations provided the leadership, the movements had an all-people's character . . . inherited structures or ideologies, whether of caste or community, did not divide the people.[10]

Alam saw a decline from the 1960s (an era of left-led class movements) to the 1970s (when the movements were led by bourgeois forces) to the 1980s (when they were replaced by communal struggles). But his pessimism was in part due to classifying all movements—including the anticaste movement over issues such as reservations, the farmers' movement, and ethnic-based struggles for autonomy—as equally regressive. This was a serious misreading of the situation. But it is necessary to examine exactly what was going on with the ethnic-nationality movements.

"Internal Colonialism?"

As the center increasingly concentrated power and resources and increasingly defined itself as "Hindu," turmoil in the peripheral states and regions of India increasingly resulted in demands for autonomy or even independence from a situation getting defined as "colonial," and frequently took on strong anti-Hindu overtones as well. In the Northeast, the decade-long independence movements of the Nagas and Mizos had been stalled with a combination of repression and co-optation that poured huge amounts of central funds into the tribal-based "hill states" even as their considerable natural resources were channeled Delhi-ward. But in the 1970s dissatisfaction began to arise in Assam itself, the river valley-centered area. As a peripheral region brought into the caste Hindu society only relatively late, with a less dense population practicing a less-intensive agriculture in the rich soil of the Brahmaputra, the Assamese had experienced cultural and economic domination by Bengalis since the nineteenth century. Population pressure among the much more numerous and more "feudalized" Bengali peasants had brought waves of migration, a gradual spread and encroachment into what seemed to be "unused" lands in the Assamese valleys. After independence this continued with migration from impoverished Bangladesh, and a growing fear and resentment against these "foreigners" developed among the Assamese. This was fueled by the cultural domination of Bengalis and by the feeling that their state was subjected to internal colonialism by Delhi itself, with oil refineries located outside the state or controlled by non-Assamese within Assam. Assamese also spoke of the way in which "mainstream" Indians ignored them or treated them as semi-Mongolian aliens.

> Though very much a part of India the Assamese have always been treated as second class citizens and this narrow corridor ... has served only to carry away raw materials to feed industries in the rest of the country, while Assam's own requirements of those industrial products have to be bought back at exorbitant rates: the Assamese have watched helplessly and without protest while this colonial exploitation started by the British imperialist continued today.[11]

Thus when a student organization, the All-Assam Students Union (AASU), founded in 1972 primarily on a language issue, came forward to lead the broad Assamese unrest, it talked also of unemployment and oil refineries. But the drive that gained it most popularity was that for the removal of the Bengali-speaking "foreigners," turning into a massive agitation in 1979–80 preceding the expected elections. This could focus the discontent of peasants and educated middle class alike. At the same time, while the "Assam movement" itself was initially presented as simply a desire to maintain the integrity of the Indian borders against infiltration, there was a strong ideological trend arguing for a separate identity for the entire Northeast region that had, it was said, "never been conquered by either Hindus or Muslims." This trend had its roots in some of the tribal organizing of the 1930s and was later to emerge, in "armed struggle" form, with the United Liberation Front of Assam (ULFA). In the late 1970s and early 1980s, however, the Assam movement proclaimed its acceptance of the Indian state and took the form of mass satyagrahas punctuated by violent clashes with Bengali peasants.

The Indian state countered the movement with repression and with an effort to build its political base among the Bengali minority. The BJP gave it enthusiastic support as it saw the chance of diverting Assam-nationalist emotion to a defence of Hindus against Muslims, since the Bengali migrants were primarily Muslims. The left was ambivalent. The CPI, CPI(M), and most of the Naxalite groups opposed the movement, partly because they had their base primarily among the same Bengali poor peasants, and partly because they could see little "class base" to the movement, not even a full-fledged "nationality" question, only a petty-bourgeois chauvinism. "What is the character of the movement?" queried the major Bengali left academic expert on Assam. "Though it has the appearance of an Assamiya national movement, its content is undemocratic and rabidly antileft. Its methods are double-faced and proto-fascist." [12] While this reflected the CPI(M) position, debates in the Naxalite-oriented *Frontier* had no clear outcome.

As a result of this failure to recognize any validity of the economic grievances of the Assamese and to give an alternative direction to them, the student leadership of AASU took center stage—the first in a series of "nonparty" student formations (later Sikh students and Jharkhandi students sought to play a similar role) spearheading militant "nationality" issues. The basic problem seems not to have been the characterization of the leadership (after all, Communists had dealt in united fronts with "petty-bourgeois leadership" on any number of issues), but of the peasant base of the movement: Utsa Patnaik, even while recognizing the validity of rural and "peripheral" area grievances, nevertheless saw the movement in terms of as "intellectuals articulating the predominantly agrarian and petty-producer consciousness that represents a typical right-wing radicalism." [13] The attitude of the main Communist parties and progressive intellectuals toward the Assam question seems compounded by their negative characterizations both of the peasantry and of challenges to the Indian centralizing state. The result was that the "Assam movement" did come under the hegemony of the upper-caste petty-bourgeois students of the AASU, who proved able to do little else than manage an inept corruption when they did come to power in the 1984 elections and found themselves in facing as a result not only a reincarnation of their movement in the form of the armed ULFA demands for independence but also, at the opposite end, radical demands for further partitioning of Assam by equally mobilized "plains tribal" groups.

But if Assam was a mess, developments in Punjab were even worse. Here was a state that was India's breadbasket, a main provider of surplus foodgrains, located in the strategic Northwest close to Delhi and sharing a border with India's closest enemy, Pakistan. Traumas unleashed by the green revolution had given birth, as has been seen, to one of the first organizational expressions of the farmers' movement—but the same year, 1972, also saw the drafting of a resolution that was to become, at least for a time, a kind of theoretical and symbolic basis of a religiously linked Punjabi movement for autonomy. This was the Anandpur Saheb resolution of the Akali Dal, which, along with religious demands, made its major thrust in a call for political autonomy: let only defense, foreign affairs, currency, and communications remain with the central government, but otherwise give all powers to the states. Such demands were not unprecedented (e.g., Kashmir had agreed to join the Indian Union with its proponents putting forward such a concept of autonomy as a precondition), and they were only the most radical expression of an increasing demand for decentralization and the need to give more power to the states that was to be taken up in the coming decade by "left and democratic" parties.

But the resistance to "internal colonialism" developing in Punjab also did not get expressed in the form of a broad, left mass upsurge. It took a religious-separatist form. Punjabi peasants were primarily Jat Sikhs; urban merchants were largely Hindu; state bureaucrats were normally Hindu or Sikhs inclined to Hindu syncretist sects like the Nirankaris (one of the reasons for the murderous infighting and tensions that broke out in the late 1970s between the Nirankaris and the lower-class fundamentalist Nihang Sikhs). Sikhism itself had arisen largely among Hindus as a protest movement against brahmanism, and it retained the language of opposition to "brahman-bania domination" and a strong assertion of equalitarianism. For a long time there had continued a fluidity of identity in which "Hindu/Sikh" represented a choice for many Punjabi families. But increasingly Sikhism was asserted as a separatist force that required an independent, religiously defined state: Khalistan.

The Khalistan demand was brought forward by a lower-class itinerant preacher, Sant Jarnail Bhindranwale, who initially won popularity in the rural areas and especially among women and children for his puritanical moralism that won men away from the drink and commercialism that was rising on the backs of green revolution cash inflow, turning them into solid, well-earning family heads.[14] But Bhindranwale was also helped by the Congress in the late 1970s as a counter to their political opponents in the Akali Dal, and turned instead into an Indian version of Khomeini, a popular and dangerous religious fanatic, whose martyrdom in the Golden Temple only solidified his appeal.

An April 1986 resolution of the Damdani Taksal, the organization created by Bhindranwale, illustrated the complex trends in the Punjabi movement:

> If the hard-earned income of the people, or the natural resources of any nation or region are forcibly plundered; the goods produced by them are paid at arbitrarily determined prices while the goods bought by them are sold at high prices and in order to carry this process of economic exploitation to a logical conclusion, the human rights of the people or of a nation are crushed, then those are the indices of slavery of that nation or region or people. Today, the Sikhs are shackled by the chains of slavery. This type of slavery is thrust upon the states and 80 percent of India's population of poor people and minorities. To smash these chains of slavery, Sikhs, on a large scale, by resorting to reasoning and by using force and by carrying along with them these 80 percent people of India have to defeat the communal Brahman-Bania combine that controls the Delhi durbar. This is the only way of establishing the hegemony of Sikh politics in this country. In this way, under the hegemony of Sikh worldview and politics, a militant organisation of the workers, the poor, the backward people and the minorities (Muslims, Christians, Buddhists, and Dalits, etc.) has to be established." [15]

The mass movements represented by the Akali Dal's satyagrahas or *dharam yudh morcha* campaigns and the "economistic" organizing of the farmers' movement both gave way, after Operation Bluestar, to a cycle of terrorism in which guerrilla strikes and murders by underground Khalistani groups were matched by police repression and torture by the state. In the process, the left in Punjab also became identified not with the people, but with the state. As in the case of Assam, support for India's "national integrity" took precedence. Rather strikingly, this was happening even at a time when the CPI(M) was tending to support demands for more powers to the states and to try to make alliances with regional parties. These policy-based expressions of support seemed to be untranslated into any movements. Instead, the main activity of the two major Communist parties was to oppose Punjabi demands. And where the Assam movement had been seen as "petty bourgeois" not only for its student leadership but for the peasantry at its base, the class basis of the Punjabi upsurge—whether that of the Khalistanis, the BKU, or the Akali Dal—could be, because Punjab was an agriculturally developed state, characterized as "capitalist farmer." Thus Utsa Patnaik's description of the movement as based on "a section of the powerful capitalist landlords of Punjab, whose thirst for primitive accumulation remains unsatiated and who wish to manipulate directly the levers of state power for their own enrichment" [16] was even harsher than for Assam.

As a result of this negative outlook and putting the unity of India so much at the center, party cadres of the CPI and CPI(M) as well as Naxalites were among those who died heroically in the Punjab, but, tragically, they died as victims of Punjabi terrorists rather than as activists standing with the people against the state. Civil liberties organizations, the farmers' movement, dalit journals like

Dalit Voice, many women activists, and some of the Naxalite organizations protested against state repression in the Punjab, but the major Communist organizations kept their silence.

Yet the issues raised by the Punjab and Assam movements—the increasing centralization of power and wealth, the extraction of surplus that they characterized as "internal colonialism," the domination of the "brahman-bania combine"—were similar to those of the new movements. In neither case (and this was true also of Kashmir, where by the end of the 1980s demands for *azadi* or freedom were to become overwhelming) did movements originate with demands for independence or the building of a separate nation-state. Rather, they began with issues involving autonomy and resistance to extraction of economic surpluses, and only when these failed to win gains did the movements verge into demands for independence that increasingly in the 1980s came to be hegemonized by religious fundamentalists. The common denominator among Punjab, Assam, and Kashmir—and the assertions of autonomy in Jharkhand, Gorkhaland, the growth of regional forces in Andhra and elsewhere—was not simply "identity politics" but the drive by the inhabitants of a geographically delimited area to control its economic and political life in a situation where they were increasingly coming under the domination and exploitation of a centralized state-industrial machine of capital accumulation. And it was in the context of a growing world vacuum of antisystemic movements—when the traditional left was failing to offer a real leadership—that forces of religious fundamentalism grew to fill the gap.

"The Hindu Juggernaut"

The rise of Hindu fundamentalism in the 1980s has to be distinguished not only from the new social movements, but even from other fundamentalist trends growing among Sikhs, Muslims, and smaller minorities—if only for the basic reason that while minority fundamentalisms generally were identified with local/regional resistance to the centralized state, Hindu fundamentalism was irrevocably linked with the high-caste "brahman-bania combine" controlling Delhi itself. Hindu and minority fundamentalisms fattened and fed on each other in an intertwined development, but they had different social bases.

Much of the basic theme of Hindu fundamentalism had been laid down in the pre-independence formulations of the RSS, the Hindu Mahasabha, and their progenitors: the identification of Indian history and culture with Hindu history and culture; the assertion of the core of that Hindu culture as being the brahmanic, Vedic Aryan traditions; the characterization of Islam as the main enemy and of the Christian Europeans as a secondary enemy; the interpretation of Hinduism in masculine, aggressive, militaristic, and statist terms. While efforts at "Hindu nation-building" included attempts to define Buddhism, Sikhism, and all dissenting sects as part of "Hinduism" and to "forget caste" (significantly it was terms such as this, rather than "abolishing caste," that were used) to incorporate the low castes, dalits and tribals, the "mainstream" in which they were to be incorporated continued to be dominated by the traditional brahman Hindu priests, the high castes, and the feudal aristocrats.

Rama, who became the main symbol of this aggressive reformulated Hinduism, was a god with a North Indian, high-caste, and even feudalistic social base: the epic built around him, the Ramayana, expressed traditional patriarchal and hierarchical values in the relations of Rama and Lakshman, Rama and Sita, Rama and Hanuman. Still there were counterpoints, and India itself contained many varying traditions of Ramayana stories—emphasizing, for instance, Sita's defiance and rejection of Rama or the heroism of Ravana—and these themes were often picked up by the new social movements or by earlier anticaste movements; but the new fundamentalists ignored these countertraditions or even the more pacific interpretations of Rama-worship and instead emphasized an armed, muscular Rama, killing the infidel.

The main organizational promoter of the new fundamentalism was the Vishwa Hindu Parishad—an organization that had been in existence since 1964, but took off in the 1980s. The sparking event was the conversion of 200 dalit families in the small Tamil village of Meenakshipuram to Islam in 1981. Their motives were quite clear: ongoing conflict with caste Hindu thevars nearby and a sense that they could get protection in Islam—not so different, after all, from the millennia of history of conversions in India. But the VHP spearheaded a wave of hysteria on the issue, centering around the slogans of "Gulf money." It initiated a reconversion campaign and started a series of *jan-jagran* or "popular awakening" *yatras*—massive processions through cities and villages. The *yatra* idea had been used in the past by popular movements and the left parties, but the VHP (and later the BJP) made it a powerful weapon of mobilization that aroused Hindu fanaticism and left a trail of Hindu-Muslim rioting—rioting in which Muslims were primarily victims.

The VHP followed this up by beginning the *Ramjanmabhoomi* campaign declared for the liberation of the "birthplace of Rama" at Ayodhya (a town in U.P., also with the Muslim name of Faizabad): here a mosque, named after the Muslim conqueror Babar (the Babri-masjid), had been built over what was by tradition a temple of Rama. The VHP demanded the demolition of the mosque and the rebuilding of the temple; they proposed to carry out the task themselves whether or not the state and the law approved. The claim for the temple site was justified as the restoration of justice to Hindus whose temples had supposedly been systematically demolished through the centuries of Muslim rule, and it was projected as only the first: claims were also made to temples of Krishna (at Mathura) and Shiva (at Banaras), both also on sites of mosques, and indeed India, at thousands of mosque sites, fanaticized members of the VHP or other Hindu organizations laid claims to territory, among which, for example, was the thesis that the Taj Mahal was a Hindu temple. What was going on was a systematic campaign to wipe out the centuries of Muslim visible presence in India.

Hindu organizations proliferated. On one hand, the VHP in 1984 formed the Dharma Sansad, a presumed "religious parliament," composed of the various swamis, sadhus, and priestly orders. At the other extreme, unemployed and lower class youth became foot soldiers in militaristic organizations such as the Bajrang Dal, Shiv Senas, Arya Vir Dal, and others, often armed with *trishals* or tridents, the traditional symbol of Shiva, not to mention sticks and knives. Also in 1984, seeing the blowing of the wind, the Shiv Sena of Maharashtrian, which had started as a "sons of the soil" party claiming priority in jobs for Marathi-speakers, swung to the Hindu cause with a call for a "Hindu united front"; later, after it was able to capture the Bombay municipal corporation and so gain tremendously increased access to funding, it openly identified *Hindutva* as its ideology and with this and its newly acquired power began to spread throughout Maharashtrian towns and villages. There were few non-Marathi targets in villages, but there were non-Hindu ones, notably dalits and Muslims, and organizations like the Shive Sena needed such targets.

Such organizations joined their Hindu rightist ideology with linkage to gangsterism and big capital. At the same time, upper-caste intellectuals led an ideological onslaught of the new Hinduism, with increased emphasis on the media, hammering home the themes that secularism—or "pseudo-secularism"—was only a policy of people alienated from their own society and at variance with reality, that true "secularism" could only be based on a rootage in Hinduism, and that Hinduism itself was uniquely pluralistic, tolerant, and capable of providing the value-base for a modern society.

"Hindu nationalists" were also not ready to tie themselves to only one political party, in spite of the close relations between the BJP and the RSS, the godfather of the new Hinduism. The role of the liberal Vajpayee and the adoption of "Gandhian socialism" as an official ideology of the BJP after 1980 enraged many, and the increasing Hindu rhetoric of Indira Gandhi, her association with "godmen" and swamis, her consultation of astrologers, was much more in tune with the trend of Hindu revivalism. In the 1984 elections even the RSS surreptitiously supported the Congress and Indira's son Rajiv.

By the late 1980s the trend was clear. As an *India Today* article put it,

> The Hindu juggernaut has arrived. . . . The majority appears to have developed a minority complex. And within the confines of this mass psyche, it is embarked upon a religious unification—a zeal marked by religious purgation, Harijan and tribal uplift aimed at persuading lower caste Hindus who have strayed into Christianity or Islam to re-enter Hinduhood, xenophobia, the formation of multifarious Shiv Senas with *trishul*-wielding acolytes banded into self-defence groups, public works and educational projects, and militant demands for ending what are seen as the special privileges enjoyed by the religious minorities.[17]

But what was the social base of all of this? The most common Marxist analysis (shared in fact with liberal "modernization theory") has been to see precapitalist traditions, most normally embodied in the peasantry or artisan groups, as the source of backward, "semifeudal" religious fundamentalism. In the terms of Javeed Alam, communal and caste movements are thus linked with traditional structures in a "retarded capitalist development." [18] Characterization of the "rich peasantry" as a rising member of the ruling bloc has also led many Marxists to see this section as the base of fundamentalism, or at least to argue, with Achin Vanaik, that the new feature of the situation is the adoption of a Hindu identity by "intermediate castes" representing in class terms the "agrarian bourgeoisie and the rural and urban petty-bourgeoisie." [19]

Reality shows a contrary picture. Rather than being a product of a traditional peasant community, contemporary fundamentalism has been linked with urban elites and the processes of "modernization," the insecurities and dilemmas resulting from incorporation into the world economy; it has spread from the cities to the countryside and from upper to lower castes—and not only to "rich peasants" and "other backward castes," but to all sections vulnerable to its warped offering of a new security and new identity, including the very poorest sections and dalits and adivasis. Its twin has been rampant consumerism fascinated by Western models, its "indigenous" gods have often been only the other face of Rambo, and its preferred means have been video cassettes and motorcycles. Not "semifeudalism" or "retarded capitalism" but the specific and unexpected (to traditional Marxists) contradictions of a state-sponsored developing capitalism have been at the root of its growth.

The Economics of Consumerism and Fundamentalism

There was an increasing polarization in Indian society. By 1975, as Francine Frankel had written, "the clear outlines of an enclave pattern were emerging that threatened to harden into a permanent separation between a small high-productivity sector, both in industry and agriculture, and a vast agricultural hinterland in which the majority of the work force struggled with primitive techniques to meet their subsistence requirements." [20]

By the late 1980s, even CPI(M) theorists were admitting an industry-agriculture contradiction, with Prabhat Patnaik arguing that "The critical turning point perhaps was the decision of the government in its desperation to control the 1974 inflationary upsurge to keep [crop] procurement prices pegged in that year. The need to reverse the decision never arose. . . . This strategy therefore began as a happenstance: nevertheless it has now acquired a status where to *describe* it as a strategy of squeezing the agricultural work-force in order to sustain capitalist industrialization without severe inflationary pressures would not be an overstatement." [21] Thus, the reality of the role of the extraction of surplus from agriculture via the price mechanism as a part of economic development in India was admitted, while analyzing it as a policy matter, not a result of capitalist processes in and of themselves.

The "enclave economy" was by the mid-1980s producing a rising upper-middle class—largely urban, largely uppercaste—with its base in growingly prosperous public-sector employment and monopoly industry, a vigorous black market, and a rising entrepreneurial sector linked with these and building its connection with money pouring in from the gulf and from relatives in the United States. It was joining the world's yuppies, and by the later 1980s the term was coming into use even in India.

Color televisions; computers; Bajaj scooters and Hondas and Lunas for the women of the family; refrigerators, pressure cookers and mixers to ease the work of the housewife; videos to film the weddings of the children; designer jeans and the new "ethnic look" fashioned in expensive boutique versions of traditional bright peasant and nomad dresses; cities transformed by new hotels and expensive vegetarian restaurants and even fast-food places along with gaudy new temples, large ones vying for heights with mosques and small ones crowding even the hawkers off the walking spaces of city streets; and above all the Maruti car, the once-despised project of Indira Gandhi's youngest son Sanjay, mocked at for foreign dependence and failure to be completed during the Emergency but now turned into the prized status symbol of the rising upper-middle class. Refrigerator production rose from 150,000 in 1975 to a projected 900,000 in 1990; motor scooters and motorbikes from 172,000 to two million; television sets from 100,000 to four million; and automobiles from 46,000 in 1985 to 500,000 in 1990.[22]

The other side of the picture was unprecedented drought sweeping thrugh such states as Gujarat, Maharashtra, Karnataka, Tamilnadu, and many others. The poor lined up for hours in cities with empty pots waiting for water; nomads driven out of ravaged Saurashtra wandered into Dhule eating up the remnants of the forests in the Satpuda foothills and getting into fights with local tribals; farmers left their parched lands to break stones on government work projects; refugees from an impoverished agriculture crowded city slums. In more "advanced" states such as Maharashtra the government—grown sophisticated in its response since the drought of 1972–73—provided villages with water tankers and peasants and laborers with work; but in the backward tribal districts such as Kalahandi in Orissa, people migrated thousands of miles or simply starved and sold their daughters to survive. Floods ravaged the north and east, and salination affected irrigated lands. Dam and irrigation projects displaced more and more people with little place for them to go.

The "rich getting richer and the poor getting poorer" was a longstanding theme of left ideology. But while there was certainly a growing polarization related to the unbalanced and destructive development of the capitalist world economy, it did not give birth to the hoped-for class politics for the simple reason that it did not have the expected usual class form. The expected differentiation in agriculture, with poor peasants and agricultural laborers forming a growing opposition to kulak power, did not take place. Neither did the proletariat come forth as an exploited but banner-bearing political vanguard. In the rural areas there was clearly a rural power elite, but these were rarely "feudal barons" or cruelly accumulating "kulaks." Most were landholders, but the bulk of their power and wealth was drawn from their positions as cooperative society chairmen, contractors, holders of agencies for pesticides or fertilizers, dispensers of political benefits, merchants, with sons pushed into law, medicine, or government service or any choice in preference to land management. Against these, "poor peasants" may have sunk into poverty, but they stubbornly maintained their small plots, continued to seek the irrigation and fertilizer inputs that promised higher production, and rallied around the peasant leaders who demanded such inputs and promised higher prices for their products. Poorer and landless peasants were forced into work relationships, but more and more these were not simply for the big farmers locally, but for the small factory owners, bureaucrats managing relief work projects, contractors, road-builders, forest officials; hiring relationships and the conflicts they involved were becoming diffused and extended.

The cities also did not show a scene of capital confronting an increasingly impoverished and solidified industrial proletariat, with the petty bourgeoisie dividing and disintegrating; rather it almost seemed as if the proletariat was differentiating. The accumulation process seemed to be absorbing white-collar employees, and drawing into itself a portion of the industrial work force, skilled workers and technicians in the big companies who were now drawing thousands of rupees a month and buying televisions, scooters, and ownership flats. Strikes of government employees, professors, and "junior doctors," and ongoing organization of school teachers at all levels marked the decade. The political clout of these "organized sector" employees was much larger than the much-slandered "farm lobby" demanding higher prices for crops—and, by all statistics, a good deal more successful. Salaries of school teachers quadrupled during the first ten years of rule of the Left Front government in West Bengal, and overall, the government slashed personal income tax rates from a maximum of 97 percent to no more than 50 percent, kept the exemption limit above the average organized-sector income, and sharply reduced excise and customs duties on two-wheelers, cars, refrigerators, televisions, and consumer electronics goods.[23]

Those who insisted that "Bharat" was itself highly divided had a point—hierarchies obviously continued to operate, and class-caste antagonisms pervaded the countryside; those who pointed to the burning poverty of the unorganized sector in the cities also had a point; those who talked of "internal colonization" and argued that whole regions were more impoverished, more exploited, also had a point. But more and more it began to seem accurate that the *main contradiction*, to borrow a classic Marxist/Maoist term, was taking on the organized/unorganized sector coloring that the terminology of "India-Bharat" captured in ways immediately recognizable to millions across the country.

For its part, the growing "yuppie" middle class had its traumas. They were buying into a brash new consumer culture, but at the same time they were upper-caste heirs of empire, children of Manu made nervous by challenges from the low castes and caught in doubts about their own cultural claims. Along with the electronic marvels and bright plastics of a Western-centered capitalism, they wanted an Eastern identification; they seized on Indian/Hindu symbolisms. Nor did "consumerism" and "identity politics" have a clear class delimitation: just as no section of society was truly outside the impact of modern capitalism, so none escaped the lures of its baubles and the insecurities of the money economy. If organized workers aimed at ownership flats, two wheelers, and televisions, middle peasants aspired to "a radio, fan, chairs, and a wide variety of other consumer durables,"[24] while even landless laborers, where they could, bought baubles for their children and dreamed of planting cash crops, and tribals enthusiastically flocked to the Hindi cinema. All sections of society, it seemed, were both attracted and repelled by aspects of the new society. The difference of course, was that the rich had easier opportunities to succeed; but this did not prevent the poor from aspiring and seeking devious routes to achievement.

Thus, while the bourgeoisie provided financing and the middle class provided the cadres of the new fundamentalism organizations, it was the unemployed, semieducated youth who were its foot-troops. "Identity politics" was taking hold in the countryside as well as the cities, but not more among the well-off peasantry or the middle castes than among others; organizations like the BJP and the RSS built their wings among tribals and dalits; Maharashtra's rabid Shiv Sena made its major rural appeal to the lower shudra castes and even some sections among the dalits (for the simple reason that the maratha-kunbis were perceived as having dominance in the Congress party while the Republican party was seen as dominated by one dalit caste, the neo-Buddhists); Sikh fundamentalism could appeal to even the "untouchable" Sikhs. Only sheer romanticism could imagine any social group as being anchored securely in values of tradition and sustainable, nonconsumerist life. The hunger for progress and the hunger for community in a world in which both were being denied were affecting people everywhere, and so were their warped forms of consumerism and fundamentalism. It was the ripping apart of these hopes by the dominant political-economic system, and the failure to articulate them into a genuine alternative by revolutionary or democratic forces, that made the 1980s a decade of seemingly unrelieved political crisis.

NGOs and the Politics of "Grass Roots Action"

> There are clear tendencies towards centralization and authoritarianism . . .
> an erosion of intermediate institutions. . . . the emergence of violence as the
> principle instrument of the State to settle disputes . . . society in fractions . . .
> caste and class tensions . . . the resurgence of fundamentalist values and passions

... dehumanization ... the loss of a national culture. ... The State has lost its elan. The bulk of the people are caught in the grim battle for survival. The elite has given up its leadership role and the counter-elite is nowhere in the picture. The many protests and struggles in sight are compelled to be limited to micro-spaces—and often turned against each other. In this scenario, how does one build a feasible overall strategy for change?

So, in 1985, the Sixth Year Report of Lokayan ("Dialogue of the People") described the background to its formation and work, a dismal picture of social and political disintegration. Yet there was hope: "a far-reaching process of mass awakening, challenging age-old hegemonies and asserting the democratic rights of hitherto underprivileged people; a cognate process of social and political consciousness among some sections of the educated classes who were willing to join forces with the underprivileged against the vested interests." It was in this process—intervening in the development of growing sociopolitical conscious-ness among the educated classes, attempting to provide links, create categories of understanding, "altering the terms of political discourse" and thereby channeling the mass awakening, that Lokayan hoped to insert itself. And it was not modest about its role: "Lokayan represents a specific methodology of engaging in both the search and the intervention, of learning through linking issues and constitu-encies and actively participating in such linkage. It is a nonvanguard, nonterrito-rial, nonparty political process." [25]

But what were "nonparty political processes," what were the grass roots groups limited to "micro-spaces," and what was Lokayan? And was there a real alternative being offered?

It was not only terms like "yuppies," it was not only growing "communalism" that impressed itself on the public consciousness in the 1980s as descriptive of the new world they were finding themselves in. "Voluntary action," "action groups," "voluntary organizations," "grass roots groups," and "NGOs" were terms that became increasingly relevant—and controversial—in the same period. The growth of this conceptualization (including the tendency to conceptualize social movements in these terms) itself arose out of a material process and had an institutional and social base.

The tradition of educated middle classes working with the poor—through political parties and mass fronts, through Gandhian organizations, through more traditional social welfare institutions—was an old one in India, and "social worker" was a recognized and respected status. This work always had linkages to wider institutions and social structures and thus (directly or indirectly) to the political sphere. Political parties built a base for themselves and supported their activists by placing them in social institutions: Gandhian organizations widened support for the Congress or for the socialists; religiously backed social work increased identity with a religious community and often with the party that stood behind the institutions; traditional social work tended to link people to the sys-tem as such and to the ruling regime in particular. There were ample precedents in the use of foreign funds by radical activists to finance activity that was too controversial at home—from the nineteenth century feminist radical Pandita Ramabai financing her ashram for child widows from funds in England and the United States to nationalists and Communists raising money abroad for their "subversive" activities. In this sense, nothing was new about the "voluntary agencies" of the 1980s and the controversy generated around them.

Yet there were new aspects reflecting the 1980s processes of class formation and crisis. On one hand there was more disillusionment in the consciousness of the youth seeking new ways of relating to the masses: young people coming out of experience in "developmental" organizations with a feeling for more direct action and struggle began with a much greater cynicism and frustration with the established parties and political models. On the other hand, reformist trends in the world of funding agencies were emerging to make financing available for more radical activities in ways that bypassed some of the local rigidities of discredited bureaucratic elites. This made the rise of "action groups" possible through the transformation of "developmental" efforts into "action for change."

The "action groups" or "voluntary organizations" were hardly the "CIA conspiracy" that they were depicted as by some of the left and some governmental propagandists. Their effect also should not be exaggerated: the progressive or radical organizations were only a small fraction of all the "foreign-funded" developmental or social action agencies, though they were frequently the most visible to left parties because they appealed to much of the same constituency. On the other hand, the social movements went their own way with their own logic; the two movements with the greatest mass mobilizing power, the anticaste movement and the farmers' movement, had less access to funding than the traditional left did.

Yet overall the effects of funding were not simply ambivalent, but in complex ways they did serve needs of the elite and its international backers. The availability of funding—relatively small-scale and on liberal terms—did provide for a flexibility of action and a freedom from dependence on local elites. It made it possible for relatively quite educated activists to establish themselves and work in distant and poor villages. At the same time, however, it encouraged various kinds of local "entrepreneurship," frequently linked to hierarchy and personality-centered networks, sometimes even with an amount of corruption. In spite of action group ideologies of democracy and participation, hierarchy was an inevitable consequence of funding which provided employment to some and assigned authority for the completion of tasks and programs that were cleared with those above. Further, the effect of an organization being funded—whatever the good will of its activists—was to make it more, not less difficult to act effectively at a mass movement level: the funding process (which identified an organization as such and resulted in people relating to it as such, and included having full-time activists who were in fact employees, having no visible reliance on local support) tended to link local groups to a far-off institutionalized elite rather than to local classes, castes, and communities: it made political alliances more difficult by making them unnecessary. Funding proved effective in building up communication and documentation centers and various kinds of service activities—not in building mass movements.

It had another indirect effect. In the late 1970s and early 1980s groups that began as funded developmental organizations were moving into struggle on various issues—often wage or land struggles of the rural poor against local elites, sometimes on environmental issues. These became known as the "action groups." What the funding process did was not only to finance such activities but also to finance the formation and stabilization of intermediate, elite-managed institutions which through seminars, "documentations," training programs, "research," articles, and booklets established the ideology of "grass-roots-ism." There was an inevitable pressure for activists in local developmental organizations or action groups to "become political" and they did so in various ways—some by going into reform wings of the establishment, basically as Congress NGOS, some into their own versions of "traditional Marxism" (e.g., a broader network of "southern action groups" organized by YIP, the Young India Project in Andhra), some into alternative forms of struggle. This was a broader process. But the effects of the "intermediate NGOs"—which linked the grass roots groups to a wider national and world arena and which formulated the ideology of "grass-roots-ism"—was most often to connect the groups to a broad socialist opposition that came to be embodied first in the Janata party and then in the Janata Dal. In effect, they served as a reconstruction of the earlier Gandhian process that had linked the village poor, through "gram raj" and "constructive work" and the like, to India's elite-dominated development. The process can be seen with the most famous of the "elite NGOs," Lokayan.

Lokayan had begun in 1979 as a West German-funded research-action project of the Centre for the Developing Societies in Delhi. In its first three years of operation, it held numerous "Dialogues"—in Bihar, Gujarat, Karnataka, Goa, Maharashtra, Tamil Nadu, Uttar Pradesh, Andhra Pradesh, Rajasthan—with issues ranging from communalism and caste conflict to environment, science and technology, health, women, dalits, and tribals. Apparently the whole range of the "new social movements" was covered, and the Lokayan "nonvanguard, nonterritorial, nonparty political process" was drawing into its network wider and wider sections of action groups and emerging movement activists. Its associated intellectuals—Rajni Kothari, D. L. Sheth, Harsh Sethi—wrote a great deal during this period, making the overall Lokayan perspective almost hegemonic in the wider circles of those who were attracted to the new movements and the issues they raised. Lokayan's bold position on civil rights and communal issues also gave the organization prestige, even when it was attacked by the Congress(I) regime or by the left parties as part of the "imperialist conspiracy."

But Lokayan was not so much a search for an alternative oppositional perspective as a project of *reconstructing* a worldview and a thrust for political action from what was ultimately a broad Gandhian-socialist perspective. Lokayan theory involved both an analysis of the crisis and of the agents who might overcome it, and it was very much part of a growing conceptualization on a world level in the 1980s of the new movements that posed them as part of a world upsurge of "grass roots movements," spontaneous local efforts of "voluntary action" with a thrust and a vision far removed from conventional left parties. This conceptualization—which also got reflected in such theorizations of the new social movements" as that by Frank and Fuentes—captured some of the drive for empowerment and against destructive development that they embodied. At the same time it tended systematically to overlook the way in which movements and activities had a broader scope and organization and an antisystemic thrust. The effect of the whole "grass roots" conceptualization was to confuse the social movements with the very different phenomenon of the increasing activity of funded (and foreign-funded) local organizations in third world societies. In its very sophisticated way Lokayan performed this service for India.

The strongest influence on Lokayan was that of Rajni Kothari, a man who had been India's most well-known political scientist before he went into opposition during the Emergency. His was a perspective that saw the state (particularly the state that had been created or taken over by third world elites after independence) as potentially "liberatory"; that viewed traditional Indian society as relatively healthy and integrated; and that located present trends to violence, disintegration, ecological destruction, and increased communal or intergroup conflict in the processes of "homogenization," secularism, and domination involved in the modern state and modern science and technology. There was relatively little reference to economic exploitation or surplus extraction or processes of capital accumulation, though Kothari and other Lokayan intellectuals did talk of "capitalism."

Thus, the Lokayan *Bulletin* provided a useful platform for debates on science and technology, on the women's movement, environment, and so on, but there was no grappling with issues of class structure, of the nature of "capitalism" or the state, or of the modes of political organization necessary for changing the state. The Lokayan tendency to "anti-Communism" was evidenced not in direct attacks but in ignoring the major issues of concern for Communist activists. Its main popular conceptualization was that of "nonparty political formations," which amalgamated mass organizations like the Jharkhand Mukti Morcha or Shramik Sanghatana with the funded, "grass roots" NGOs. It also generally ignored the farmers' movement and treated the anticaste movement solely as a *dalit* movement (refusing to see the OBCs); thus, for example, a 1990 article by Kothari on "The Rise of People's Movements" would simply list the "landless, dalits, bonded laborers, and the fisherfolk" and then mention "a whole range of *new* movements of later vintage: the ecology movement, the women's movement, the alternate health movement, the dalit movement and of late, simmering movements among the religious and ethnic minorities."[26]

By the mid-1980s Lokayan had given up its dependence on funding (a result of much internal and external criticism) and was attempting to function autonomously; this deprived it of scope for intervention. At the same time a controversy erupted among all the NGOs as the Congress government moved to control and co-opt their activity by proposing changes in December 1984 in the Foreign Contribution Regulation Act and by a section in the Seventh Plan in 1986 on the role of "voluntary agencies" that meant both a legitimization of their activities and an attempt to supervise them. A "Council of Voluntary Agencies" to formulate and implement a "code of conduct" for the NGOs (which involved, among other things, possible limits on salaries) turned into a bitter debate in which some NGO activists, like Bunker Roy, attacked the "elite, urban" NGOs for not wanting any supervision of their activities, and Jai Sen of Calcutta and the Lokayan group helped to coordinate an opposition that accused Roy and others of being establishment pro-Congressites.[27]

By 1990, Kishore Saint, an activist working in the Aravali hills in southern Rajasthan, could write of the danger of voluntary initiatives being co-opted by state-based reformism: "This inviting openness [of the state] has often tempted the voluntary individuals and organizations to link energies and efforts with the corrective measures planned or launched by the command systems, giving them strength and legitimacy and, at the same time, depriving the grass roots, community and social counter-movements of intellectual calibre and coherence." This, he charged, was due to the social background of most activists, who were not inclined to work for real alternatives and "do not recognize any instruments other than state and corporate politics for transformation on such a large scale." Saint concluded that, "This is a crisis of politics itself. It has to be understood in the same manner as the crisis of politics in the nineteenth century when the Marxist idiom began to be articulated, when the socialist ideal began to be argued. Today ecological concerns and issues are waiting for an idiom and modes of organization and action for which potential lies in nonparty social movements."[28]

All the efforts of Lokayan, all the debates of the 1980s, had clearly not provided such an "idiom"; all the search for alternatives had not shown "modes of organization and action" capable of "transformation on a large scale." Lokayan and the ideology of "grass-roots-ism" had been at best a diversion.

The "Tidal Wave" of Restoration

The crisis that Saint was describing was clearly building up by 1985, not simply as a crisis in the theory of alternative politics but in the system itself; only the "crisis of Marxism" and correspondingly the crisis of an overall theory and practice of antisystem movements in the end let the system reconstruct itself.

With growing discontent throughout India, with regional-national sentiment ripening not only in Punjab and Assam but in many southern states also, with the powerful farmers' movement gathering force and with religious fundamentalism beginning to take on steam, Congress was heading for at least an electoral defeat. As V. T. Rajshekhar of *Dalit Voice* queried after Indira Gandhi's assassination, "What will be the verdict of history on Mrs. Gandhi?"

> If we go by her actions, not words, we can say that during her seventeen-year rule the country slipped from bad to worse on all fronts. But at the same time the Ruling Class, 10 percent of India's 800 million population, became fatter. The tiger turned into a maneater. Brahmanical imperialism became more bloodthirsty. Mrs. Gandhi and the Hindu Nazi party became two sides of the same coin. And at the time of her death she was trying to transform her spineless Congress into a Hindu party, thus totally antagonizing the Muslims (15 percent) Christians (2 percent), Sikhs (2 percent)—all the religious minorities. So also the conscious sections of Dalits and Tribes. The Hindu backward classes (40 percent) have cursed her for throwing the Mandal Commission report to the wastepaper basket. Had there been an election now, there was no chance of her party getting elected.[29]

But the assassination gave the ruling party the legitimacy it needed, not only to slaughter Sikhs in Delhi but to intensify its armed control of the Punjab, Kashmir, and Assam. And with the electorate dazzled by television depictions of her cremation, with election posters blazing her martyrdom and her son already taking on the image of "Mr. Clean," elections held in the end of the year were almost a foregone conclusion. "Unity" and "power" were Rajiv Gandhi's central themes for India, and now he used the word *akhandata* (unbrokenness); it was associated with the Hindu nationalist image of an unbroken emire stretching across the entire continent (khand) of South Asia. Rajiv not only appealed to his mother's martyrdom, he "played the Hindu card" in the elections, and with a disorganized and demoralized opposition, with the RSS instructing its cadres in many places to work for the Congress itself rather than the BJP, the Congress won an unprecedented victory 401 of 508 seats in the Lok Sabha. It was, in the words of *Times of India* editor Girilal Jain, "a tidal wave few could see."[30]

Writing later in the *Times*, Gopal Krishna editorialized that the massive mandate meant "a new nationalism that rises above the social cleavages of contemporary India" was now possible because Rajiv could "impart a new vision to Indian politics . . . the vision of a strong India, an India capable of coping with the challenges of the twenty-first century. This theme is characteristically Nehruvian and obviously holds great appeal for Mr. Gandhi's generation of Indians."[31]

Just as obviously, the spokesmen of the ruling class were breathing a sigh of relief. With a young man rather than an aged, discredited autocratic grandmother at the helm, India could indeed head for the "twenty-first century" complete with computer whiz kids, World Bank-trained economists and planners, and a new international image fitting into the worldview of the new right. The yuppies had arrived. The old left, and the new social movements, had endured a major defeat.

Part IV
Toward a New Vision, 1985–1991

9

Women, Peasants, Tribals, Environment

IN *Staying Alive*, a book published in 1988 by India's Kali for Women Press (its name, from the goddess Kali, itself proclaiming a tradition of women's power), Vandana Shiva wrote of the feminine principle and the world-preserving power of rural third world women:

> Indian women have been in the forefront of ecological struggles to conserve forests, land and water. They have challenged the western concept of nature as an object of exploitation and protected her as Prakriti, the living force that supports life. . . . Their ecological struggle in India is aimed simultaneously at liberating nature from ceaseless exploitation and themselves from limitless marginalisation. They are creating a feminist ideology that transcends gender and a political practice that is humanly inclusive; they are challenging patriarchy's ideological claim to universalism not with another universalizing tendency, but with diversity; and they are challenging the dominant concept of power as violence with the alternative concept of nonviolence as power.[1]

Here was a conception of the women's movement quite different from either the calls to "join the mainstream" of the party women's wings or the proclamation of "autonomy" of the urban feminists. But how valid was it? Shiva's claim that Chipko was a woman's movement has been attacked as "romanticism" by other environmentalists; her condemnation of "Western science and technology" as "masculinist" has been criticized as at best overstated; her praise of the ecologically sustaining and feminist character of pre-British Indian peasant production has been refuted as overlooking feudal and patriarchal aspects of Indian tradition involving both internal hierarchies and a history of attacks by agricultural kingdoms on forest-dwelling tribal societies.[2] "She's a poet" was an often-expressed judgment.

The depiction of women, particularly poor rural women, as powerful agents of change and not simply victims of exploitation contrasted with the language of nearly all movement spokespeople of the time. Both traditional party leaderships, and the circles of urban feminists found it difficult to recognize, let alone tap, the force of women for change. These were likely to see poor women not as a force for change, but as symbols of an exploitative capitalist society, victims of patriarchal repression, recruits for their party, objects for action.

Yet the claim that rural women are at the center of peasant, tribal, and environmental movements, that the "feminine principle" could represent a powerful transforming thrust for all movements, hit a reality that was often overlooked. Especially after 1985, the emergence of new women's organizations linked to mass organizations of the new social movements unleashed a new dynamic. These in many ways remained subordinated to the mass organization and its leadership, yet they gave scope not only for privileged middle-class women but for poor toiling women to act autonomously. New issues began to be raised, new theoretical formulations made, new campaigns begun that involved not only women but the deepening of the other social movements as well. The women's movement had in many ways been the "weakest" of the new social movements in terms of mobilizing force. Yet after 1985 the recovery of the movements was associated with women's participation and the issues raised by women.

The year 1985 had seen a "defeat" of the new social movements and a setback to the democratic movement in general. The anticaste movement was lacking in program, and its one national-level campaign, on the Mandal Commission recommendation for reservations, was ignored by the Congress government; the women's movement was in the doldrums; the farmers' movement had received a serious setback in its then strongest center of Punjab; the environmental movement had hardly begun to develop as a mass movement. Yet the latter part of the decade saw new initiatives, more dialogue between the movements, a renewed upsurge against power centers, and the posing of concrete alternatives for social and economic development. At the base of much of this was new activity among rural women.

It was the Chandwad women's conference of the Shetkari Sanghatana that signaled the opening of the new period.

Maharashtra, 1986: "A Decade of Rural Women"

Chandwad, November 10, 1986: a small town in western Maharashtra, with a minor claim to fame as the home of a queen famous in regional history, one of the *viranganas* or "heroic women" who had carried on the fight of her kingdom after the death of her husband. Now the flags of the farmers' movement rather than the bannners of feudal armies waved in the air, and Maharashtra had never seen an army such as this: nearly 200,000 peasant women and men, massed in the afternoon heat, rising to take a new vow that they would "throw away the fear in their minds," treat daughters equally with sons, claim their own rights to property and life, and live as human beings.

The themes of Chandwad were heralded in the posters plastered throughout the state, showing a woman laborer carrying her tools and her baby on her back, with the words of a famous Marathi independence-era song, "how long must I go on dying?" at the top and at the bottom the new slogan of the conference: *stri shakticya jagranat stri-purush mukti*—"the liberation of women and men through the awakening of women's power."

The event attracted the attention of the press and all other women's organizations in Maharashtra, for Shetkari Sanghatana and its charismatic leader Sharad Joshi had by this time become major figures in regional politics, and no other such mass organization was moving into the women's movement with such boldness. What women activists and reporters coming to the conference saw, both in the "representatives' meeting" of thousands on November 9 and the following day's mass rally, were poor peasant and rural middle-class women who had never before in their life spoken out on "women's issues," who had never in most cases spoken at a public meeting at all, who were more familiar with arguments for remunerative prices than discussions of patriarchy, now coming forward to talk of the bondage of women. From drought, women's work, and education to imprisonment in the home and propertilessness, women poured forth their grievances. They talked of the new energy coming from their participation in the movement, with praise of Sharad Joshi in terms that made feminist activists squirm; but in the same breath they talked of their own desires for liberation. "Sharad Joshi *zindabad*" and "We want our *hissa*," our share—of property rights, of the fruits of labor—were constantly heard themes.

Joshi, for his part, was proclaiming a new message of women's power. "Peasants cannot be a national political force," he told the gathering, "but women can be!" And along with resolutions on property rights, remuneration for work, and drought, the conference came out with an almost breathtaking innovation: a call for women's organizations to come together to sponsor "all women panels" for the local district council elections which were supposed to be forthcoming in the state. It also proposed a massive march of peasant women to Delhi to protest the state's complicity in the mass rape of women that had accompanied the massacre of Sikhs following the assassination of Indira Gandhi. The resolutions were far-reaching, and for the first time the male leadership of one of India's strongest mass organizations was returning the challenge given by the women's movement to take women's issues seriously—by charging that the women's movement itself, by focusing activities on fighting atrocities and lobbying for legal reforms, was getting stuck in defensive and nonfundamental activities.

Along with the resolutions were equally extravagant theoretical claims. Calling on women activists to leave the "sinking ship of Marxism," which could not handle such fundamentals as domestic labor, praising feminism for its daring but claiming that its "antimale" approach had no place in an Indian women's movement,

Sharad Joshi's conference booklet *Shidori* put foward the "Shetkari Sanghatana theory." This differentiated itself from both "feminism" and "Marxism": from feminism in claiming that "women's slavery" was not a patriarchal conspiracy but was determined by the process of capital accumulation and dated from the origins of surplus in agriculture, and from Marxism in seeing violence, rather than private property, as the primary means of accumulation. As its English summary put it,

> The surplus value in our epoch arose from agriculture and the savings of the land have been expropriated almost since their emergence. The modus operandi of the expropriation has been changing over time: plunder by bandits, plunderers-become-monarchs, imposing taxes, slavery, bonded labour, inadequate wages, money-lending, landlords, religious and caste systems, and finally inadequate prices. The history of human societies is the history of the evolution of the instruments of expropriation of agricultural surplus. No sooner had man settled down to organized agriculture in the expectation of an assured bounty, than started a bloody epoch replete with loot, plunder, attacks, colonialism, each with its quota of maimings, murders, rapes, burnings, et al. Men were butchered and women taken away along with the loot to help maintain the rate of reproduction. The proportion of men in all the societies, victors as well as vanquished, remained depleted. Thus sprang communities in which male offspring were a prized possession and martial arts the highest accomplishment. Whole villages and individual houses were designed like fortresses. The boys were brought up to be able to face the attackers both physically and psychologically. Girls were taught to be faceless reproducers of progeny and docile boosters of the testosterone levels of their menfolk and future protectors by a hundred arts, words and privileges. As a consequence, whoever the winner, the women on either side were invariably the losers.[3]

The final "Declaration" added one important part to this: that women were the creators of agriculture. These themes, stated so forcefully, actually drew much from the flow of thinking in the feminist movement. While the stress on violence in the process of accumulation and on women's role as producers of surplus was a break from the traditional Marxist notions, still being put forward by left-party women and taken for granted by most Indian feminists, it in fact had much in common with theories put forward by such German feminists as Maria Mies. But if Joshi had the usual disinclination of leaders to acknowledge any theoretical indebtedness, the major positive point of the conference, by any feminist standards, was its clear statement that women's oppression was a separate issue, requiring a separate and autonomous organization: even the winning of remunerative prices would not guarantee the liberation of women; "women of Bharat" and "women of India" (that is, the urban middle classes as well as rural and toiling women) were together oppressed and together should organize themselves in the Mahila Aghadi, or "women's front" set up at Chandwad. No left party had been willing to say as much, and neither left parties nor the new "autonomous" women's groups were seeing the "power of women" in quite the way Joshi was, at least as he declared in a subsequent interview: "Now I find this (Mahila Aghadi) movement has the capacity to be the mainstream of the mass movement. The women's movement is always taken as the auxiliary or 'the other.' But I see the possibility of the men's movement being that."[4]

The mass turnout and enthusiasm at the Chandwad conference was invigorating, and, for all the limitations of leadership dependence, the readiness of this peasants' organization at least to discuss such basic issues of patriarchal oppression as property rights, political power, and payment for women's domestic labor was a new and inspiring development. Yet the immediate reaction of most feminist and left activists was negative and defensive, and relations were to remain troubled. Feminists saw the whole event as male-dominated. As far as the left was concerned, Joshi was attacking it where it hurt, in terms of its ability to mobilize the masses around its ideology. His tendency to refer to left leaders as "tankless generals" illustrated his usual harshness of expression, but it was only applying to the left its own criterion of mobilizing power (feminist had always been scorned by left women leaders as "small groups" without a mass base and of no consequence in the world of power) and asking it to confront the question of why, in the 1980s, it was failing in some way to mobilize the most exploited social forces. Both left women and feminists tended to argue that Sharad Joshi was simply "using women" opportunistically, as a publicity stunt, "a front for his own political purposes," and some depicted the women of Shetkari Sanghatana as simply ready to be used, as "sheep" herded into a pen.

The idea of "all-women panels" for district council elections was ignored or rejected. For most, unable to take seriously the idea of women as women making a challenge for local political power, it was also seen simply as a way the male peasants could use women as a "front" to get control. More strikingly, one of the few left leaders who did not see it this way, who had seen women's power as a historical reality—though as a destructive reality—was disturbed by the idea. Sharad Patil, who had come with a thousand tribal women from his area to the rally, saw it in more apocalyptic terms: "It's a dream of restoring matriarchy," he said as he walked away from the rally.

The charge that Joshi was "using women" left some basic questions unanswered: if this was opportunism, then what was the force Joshi was trying to take advantage of? How was it that such an apparently "pragmatic" leader with a reputation for sensitivity to strategy could see women as a force at all? Why couldn't other organizations be equally "opportunistic" as to mobilize their women in mass and talk about issues of domestic labor, violence, political power, and property? And were women simply sheep to be herded around, a source of passive energy be evoked at will and then stuffed back in a cage—or was Shetkari Sanghatana unleashing a new dynamic in calling women out of the home on their own issues?

These were questions few asked at the time. Clearly, Chandwad represented a major event in the women's movement; clearly, the themes expressed in the conference, of violence and insecurity subordinating women, of the power of women, awoke a deep response from the hundreds of thousands of women involved in Shetkari Sanghatana activities. It was also to become clear that there was a kind of dialectic within the Sanghatana, that the women did represent a kind of mass base of loyalty that Sharad Joshi could appeal to for support for many of his programs, sometimes over the heads of the intermediary leadership. What was not so clear at the time was the way in which the gradual "awakening of women's power" was to be a part of the deepening and transformation of the Shetkari Sanghatana itself, linked to an increasingly strong stand against religious fundamentalism, and later to a turn toward policies of alternative and ecologically sustainable agriculture.

The nature of some of the obstacles faced by women coming out into a life of struggle were also not so clear or so openly admitted. Two stories perhaps symbolized the kind of personal level experiences women connected with Shetkari Sanghatana were going through. One district organizer told of a newly active village woman: the daughter of a prostitute, up to that point paralyzed in her community life by the shame of her origins, who had written a letter describing how a "new life had opened up for me" through her activity in the women's front. One year later she was hospitalized, after having been badly beaten by her husband out of suspicion of what this activity meant. The underlying and troubling drives of sexuality were to parallel the processes of women coming out; sexual scandal dogged their entry into public life.

The other story was that of Suman, a low-caste woman abandoned by her husband (an increasingy common fate in India at this time), making her living as a tailor and as a singer of religious *bhajans* or songs until she became a Sanghatana activist. One day she had come to Sharad Joshi, with the announcement that she was going to get married, followed up by, "You won't be so happy when you find out to whom!" It turned out that her husband-to-be, by whom she was already pregnant, was a brahman boy nine years younger than herself, and there was ferocious opposition from his family. "We're going to run away." "Don't do that, they'll simply send the police after you; we'll have a Sanghatana wedding." And so it happened: the two were married in a meeting of three hundred activists, with Sharad Joshi playing the role of father of the bride and a Pune feminist standing in for her mother. The irony of the situation only fully came out when Suman, who had the reputation as something of a feminist in Shetkari Sanghatana circles, began to interact with feminist networks and dissasociate herself from "urban feminists who don't understand that rural women's problems are economic!"

Stories of personal life breakthroughs, and failed attempts at breakthrough, were also part of the dynamics unleashed in the masss movement revealing itself at Chandwad. It was a new beginning, for both the women's movement and farmer's movement, going toward taking up fundamental material issues of women's oppression and formulating an alternative development for all. Chandwad heralded the birth of a new international women's decade, a decade of rural women.

Kerala, 1986–89: "The Rape of the Sea"

It was not only in Maharashtra that new feminist trends were coming forward. The formation of women's organizations linked to independent mass organizations or new movements was happening in many places—with the Jharkhand Nari Mukti Samiti, tribal women linked to the Jharkhand movement asserting their autonomy; with the formation in March 1987 of a women's front of the Bharatiya Republican party, the dalit-based political party; with the organization of Stri Mukti Sangarsh Calval, connected with antidrought movements of peasants in Sangli district of Maharashtra, with the independent organizing of women linked to the Kerala fishworkers' movement.

The latter showed, in a way different from but parallel to that of the peasant women, how women's organizing brought forward new issues. There was no dramatic single mass conference like Chandwad, but rather a slow process of formation, in which some leaders supported while the majority of the patriarchal Catholic community resisted the independent organization of women.

Women in Kerala had been heavily involved in activities sustaining the fishworkers' struggle from the beginning. But for a long time they were not organized on women's issues. Their first meetings started from the religious forms available to them in community life, as they began to meet from 1971–72 in a "pious association" whose contemporary interpretations of religious texts helped them deal with the problems of their lives. But women had in fact preceded men into agitation, first on local issues of schools and neighborhood cleanliness and then in a demonstration in 1979–80 over their right to use buses to go to the market. This experience helped to put them in the forefront of the movement against trawling in the early 1980s, though it took another struggle to turn their official membership of the union into a reality.

From the late 1970s, the new ideas of women's liberation were beginning to reach them. At first Kerala women activists were unwilling to call themselves feminist as they were not "against men" and, as activist Nalini Nayak wrote, "the women libbers that we had come across in our country struck us as very middle-class and Western." But as wife beating, rape within marriage and the meaning of women's work were added to the problems of women fish vendors as topics of their monthly meetings, the women began to feel themselves changing, admitting that "a growing feminist consciousness is itself such a liberating process that it cannot but begin to influence and change all processes with which women interact."[5]

March 8 began to be celebrated as Women's Day; men began to be involved in the discussions of the secondary place of women. Then, in 1986, women of the fishing community joined in a demonstration in Trivandrum against rape of women during a police rampage in a central Kerala village, and did so under the banner of the "Coastal Women's Front." This became the name of their new organization.

For women, it was easy to link their concerns with rape and social and family violence to the opposition to new mechanized trawling. The capitalist transformation of fishing involved not simply mechanization and commercialization, but the treatment of the sea as a resource to be "mined," in contrast to the traditional view of it as a powerful, nurturing, yet potentially dangerous goddess to be propitiated. Resistance to the increasing drinking and domestic violence associated with the growing commercialization helped to produce an ecological perspective on developmental issues.

One of the first feminist activists to begin writing on issues of development and ecology was Gabriele Dietrich, connected with the Kerala women, who wrote in 1988 that

> ... it took quite a few years during the women's decade to realise that it was not a matter of a share of the cake but that the cake itself was a wrong concept. What was required was rice, chapatis and ragi, not cake. It was the very production of cake which destroyed the production of staple foods. It was the rush after the cake itself which enhanced poverty and marginalisation of women. . . . Women's rights are threatened from two ends. On the one hand, religious revivalism, fundamentalism and communalism are encroaching on women's free spaces. On the other hand, so-called new avenues of freedom opened up by capitalism go along with massive objectification and commercialisation of women's bodies and violent assaults on their physical and spiritual integrity. . . . Both these tendencies are connected and rooted in a development model which perpetuates and deepens poverty and marginalises women.[6]

This reflected the fact that by 1987, shortly after the formation of the Coastal Women's Association, the Fishermen's Forum itself was identifying both women's issues and ecology as crucial to building a "social movement unionism."

Similarly, the movement helped to stimulate the formation of a specifically Indian liberation theology that now was beginning to identify itself with ecological issues and the dalit movement, seeing, in the words of theologian Sebastian Kappen, that "the ecosystem crisis . . . is an invitation to theologians to return to the primitive myth of creation as generation. The growth of science, technology and industrialization has unleashed destructive forces that may, in time, make the planet uninhabitable. . . . For Christian theologians trying to find a solution to this problem the task is two-fold: discovering the divine within nature and restoring to human beings their position as children of nature."[7]

The affirmation of the "divine within nature" began to verge on the notion of Prakriti, the feminine principle that nurtured life, and was a significant step beyond Western Christian tendencies simply to treat nature as an object for the dominion of man. But there were still some crucial problems connected with women's issues.

Women, especially those of the fishing community, could not afford to simply criticize destructive "modern" development from a traditional perspective. The traditional sector itself was not an egalitarian, women-centered community: there were inequalities among fishermen, unequal boat ownership among men, and a patriarchal division of labor, men on the sea, women on the shore handling the marketing of fish. The traditional view of the sea as a capricious goddess, sometimes life-giving, sometimes nurturing, had linked the need to propitiate the goddess with binding and taming the power of women. Female chastity was the key: the beneficence of the sea was seen as dependent on the faithfulness of the women of the fishing community. This was a typical Indian way of twisting a superficial goddess-worship to a form of patriarchal bondage—and the imposition of Catholic patriarchy only intensified it.

Did an emphasis on the technological destructiveness of "modernity" mean a retreat to a patriarchal and hierarchical traditional community, in which a nurturant but capricious nature was associated with the need to repress the sexuality of women? Or was there to be a new opening? Affirming an ecological direction could still avoid some of the difficult questions of tradition, human action, and sexuality. Liberation theologists (and for that matter the women themselves) could perhaps move to a positive conception of nature as "Prakriti" more easily than they could deal with these issues. But it was a problem for all sections of the women's movement. Maharashtra peasants and Kerala fishing women found it equally difficult to challenge the value of faithfulness to a husband—known as *pativratya* and symbolized by Sita's supposedly unflinching loyalty to her husband-king Rama, but middle-class feminists also were not discussing these issues openly in India at the time.

Bihar, 1986–87: "The Politics of Cooking Rice and Lentils"

Another beginning was being made in the same year in Bihar, long considered one of the most violent, caste-ridden, and patriarchal regions of India, but fascinating to the left as a center of Naxalite-led rebellion, of the "agrarian revolution" that many expected to surge all over India. Among the young feminist activists impressed with the mass gathering at Chandwad was Chetna Gala, a member of the socialist Sangarsh Vahini group who had been working among agricultural laborers in Bihar. She had much to say about new stirrings in which women were involved.

The left organizations working in Bihar had initially given little attention to women's problems, though one of them, the Indian People's Front, had taken the lead in organizing a 1986 "national convention of women" in Calcutta. With one thousand at the mass rally, this was much smaller than western Indian efforts but did mark a new thrust in Bengal, including the unique experience for male organizers of being excluded from an all-women conference hall. The Calcutta IPF conference sparked hopes for collaboration between feminists and Naxalite-left organizations, particularly when the president of their "women's cell" declared that feminism and Marxism were not antagonistic but "complementary" ideologies, and that the "emancipation of women must be the work of women themselves."

But a real women's upsurge was hampered by the subordinated position of women in IPF's own area of strength, Bihar. Here, as researcher-activist Govind Kelkar reported, women were left out of leadership and decision-making processes: "Most of the women from political cadre families complained that they feel excluded from politics. ... In a rather challenging militant tone we were told by a woman in her late twenties, 'I am the wife of a Naxalite. My politics are the politics of cooking rice and *dal*. ... Whenever I try to relate to others or peep outside through the small opening of the door, my husband accuses me of looking for another husband.' "

Along with the "scandal factor" haunting the participation of women in public life was the failure of Naxalite-led peasant organizations to deal with issues like women's unequal wages and lack of rights to land. Yet as Kelkar noted, discussion on these questions was beginning, and in one village dalit women had ploughed and grown paddy on land seized from a landlord, though this was taken as only a temporary response to a crisis situation of the movement.[8] The new atmosphere of the women's movement was also influencing the militant Naxalites, just as it had in a different way influenced the Shetkari Sanghatana in Maharashtra, with new themes of equal rights, new ways of coming out of the home. It was after all in Bihar that the first concrete struggle on women's land rights had been taken up in 1983 by Sangarsh Vahini, and both Sangarsh Vahini and the Naxalite groups were providing a new culture of movement participation for young women.

The occasion for cross-fertilization of these movements was provided by the Bihar state itself, in a vicious police massacre of a number of poor peasants demonstrating in the small town of Arwal in 1986. In response came the strongest united mass opposition campaign in Bihar since the pre-Emergency "Bihar movement," with demonstrations, marches, and a mass gherao of the state assembly. And as Chetna described it, two main issues dominated discussions in the rural awakening campaigns in which she had taken part, the relationship between agricultural laborers and peasants, and the question of "women's liberation."

The IPF conference, which had been held in April, had ended with some tension between feminists and IPF party women, but also with a feeling that efforts to work together should continue, perhaps with a conference in North India. Then why not Bihar itself? Why not take the banner of women's liberation to the state that was the presumed birthplace of Manu, the mythical brahman lawgiver who had prescribed subordination for women and shudras, now becoming a center of a rural armed upsurge against landlord and state power?

Two earlier "national conferences" had been held to formulate "perspectives for the autonomous women's movement," but both had been in Bombay itself, organized primarily by a single group, the Forum Against Atrocities on Women, and with little involvement of women from mass organizations. Those working-class women who did come felt out of place in middle-class-dominated discussions, with hall meetings and written papers. The Calcutta conference was, in contrast, an openly party-led effort, still with its traditional format of paper-reading, but it had included a new effort to reach out to feminists and nonparty women that contrasted with the controlled platforms of other established left parties, and it had a good participation of lower-class women. Now, in the new mood of upsurge and self-confidence awakened by the Chandwad conference, it seemed possible to think in terms of grander events.

A first preparatory meeting was held in Nagpur, shortly after the Chandwad conference, in January 1987, with women from Bombay, Bihar, Delhi, Dhule, and Sangli districts of Maharashtra, dalit women from Nagpur, and a representative of the newly formed women's front of the Shetkari Sanghatana. Basic themes were worked out, and it was decided to have both three-day, small-group discussion sessions of more limited numbers and a final mass rally. Differences in orientation between party or mass organization-connected women and the Bombay-Delhi groups did not seem so much of a barrier; nor were organizers disturbed that it proved impossible to involve the "mainstream parties" of the CPI, CPI(M), and socialists, or even that some of the Naxalite organizations were too sectarian to come into a broad front. There were an increasing number of women's groups growing at the grass roots level throughout the country who were excited by the idea of a "Patna conference" conceived of as a coalitional organizational effort aimed at involving masses of rural women. For many the hopes that something new seemed about to be born, that another "awakening of women's power" might be at hand, were now extended to the volatile state of Bihar and expressed in the defiant mood of a new Urdu women's song:

> Every woman in this country is dishonored, degraded,
> With your hand on your heart, say, how can such a country be free?
> In this country, they say, there are goddesses without number—
> But not a single link of our chains could they loosen.
> Have we gained anything of honor from the veil?
> Behind the veil we remained smothered, behind the veil we burned.
> Make the veil into a flag, unfurl it everywhere,
> We will bring humanity's rule to this land!
> The power of women cannot be challenged,
> Now we resolve to take on even the form of mother Kali! [9]

Maharashtra, 1987–88: "A Dream of Restoring Matriarchy?"

For some time after the Chandwad conference there was quiet on the "peasant women's front." The Shetkari Sanghatana itself was enveloped in a wave of peasant struggles that arose in various parts of India from late 1986; in Maharashtra, the district council elections were postponed. Perhaps many were relieved, for if Sharad Patil had seen a "dream of restoring matriarchy" in the proposal for all-women's panels, to many other leftists Sharad Joshi himself seemed to represent some "mother Kali" type force of destruction. Neither the urban feminists nor the party women activists had treated political power as a women's issue before this, the former because they viewed the whole sphere as alien, the latter because, while they argued constantly for women to pay attention to politics and "join the mainstream," they also ultimately saw politics as a realm not for women but for the parties to decide.

But the issue of "women's power" was not about to go away. In late June 1987 a training workshop was called at Ambethan, with professors from Poona University, feminist activists, and Shetkari Mahila Aghadi representatives from all over the state to discuss participation in the elections which, once again, the state government was promising. The lectures not only described the structure and legal rights of the district councils and subordinate county boards, but also gave some idea of their relative impotence before the growing centralization of political power in the country, the fact that they were dependent for almost all funding on state governments. The size of a potential mass election campaign was daunting—women wanted to cover at least half the state, meaning ten to fifteen districts, with approximately fifty district council and one hundred county council constituencies in each. Now, on the background of the usual activist distaste for parliamentary politics, they were being told that the local bodies had no power; "the whole thing is a fraud."

On top of this were the obstacles women faced in coming into public life, both the downgrading of women's abilities and personal defamation, "the scandal factor"; women also admitted that some of their obstacles began right from the home: "my husband tells me, 'we'll put up any women, but why should *you* stand?'" Yet against such doubts was the excitement of challenging a sphere from which women had been totally excluded. The participants resolved to fight, and the meeting saw the formation of a "Samagra Mahila Aghadi" or "all-women's alliance" designed as a united platform.

Even more significant was the program taken up in the manifesto of the alliance. "Fighting gangster power"—the all-pervasive violence and insecurity rampant in village life—was the major justification for the campaign, but it was linked to something like the new development perspective emerging in other mass movements in which women were beginning to have an impact, such as that of Chipko or the Kerala fishworkers. The manifesto promised not the Shetkari Sanghatana program of "remunerative prices" but rather drinking water and toilet facilities, alternative sources of energy for fuel, alternatives to the exploitation of multinationals in the health industry, alternative forms of work for women rather than just the "rock-breaking" found on government employment schemes: "Through taking in hand panchayat raj women's participation in public life will increase . . . the direction of development will be seen from a women's perspective. Priority will be given to such programmes as women's health, nutrition, drinking water facilities and cleanliness. Today we see only the ferocious dance of corruption and self-interest. These will be checked and real programmes of development taken up."

The 1984 Parbhani conference of Shetkari Sanghatana had included resolutions on what Sharad Joshi called the "economic struggle"—boycotting industrial inputs to agriculture, not going to market, cultivating only for subsistence. But this was the first formal expression, within the farmers' movement, of a different direction of development.

But the hopes expressed in the meeting's final call for all political parties, "especially left and dalit parties," to come together behind the women's campaign for political power, were to be in vain. In fact women's panels could have provided an imaginative way for the "left and democratic" opposition, still fairly weak in Maharashtra, to make a mass appeal. But they did not respond. Women's political power was to them a particularly inappropriate issue to bring up in the middle of 1987, when the whole nation seemed in ferment. It was a time when the Congress government was tottering at the center and a new opposition force was emerging; in Maharashtra also, the "left and democratic" parties were engaged in their own process of political maneuvering, attempting to put together a political front to fight the ruling Congress. The big issue of debate in this effort was whether the right-wing BJP should be included in the front (most seemed to feel it was all right to include them by de facto "seat adjustments," while refusing to give any formal recognition), and the empowerment of women simply did not fit. Since Shetkari Sanghatana, the biggest mass organization in the state, was behind it, the parties had to give some response, but they saw it as a distraction, even perhaps a plot. "An attempt to split the left just at a time when a process of unity is starting!" charged Sharad Patil.

But Patil's further comment revealed something of the real dilemma behind left resistance to the scheme: "I only have one woman who's articulate enough to be a candidate." This objection—"where are we going to find that many women?"—was in fact the one most often expressed by the parties. The parties had little mass work among women and almost no committed and ideological women activists in the countryside, and they could not imagine, in the way a more fluid and open organization like Shetkari Sanghatana could, a process of absorbing women who were coming forward. Most important, they were unwilling to go against their own male cadres, who were very much aspirants for the gains even local-level office could bring.

By 1987, the euphoria generated by Chandwad was subsiding. Outside of Shetkari Sanghatana, political and feminist activists greeted the new campaigns of rural women with indifference; feminists criticized the effort as male-dominated, while left activists saw all-women panels as "too feminist." Communists refused even to discuss it, and socialists ignored a history of their parties not even sponsoring 5 percent of women candidates and saying, "but we're for equality—you should say 50 percent!" Inside Shetkari Sanghatana itself, there was sometimes subtle and sometimes open opposition, and women found themselves confronting all obstacles to going outside the home. ("Here I've been such an ideal wife," lamented one activist after being yelled at by her husband for associating with men during organizing trips; "now I know what you urban feminists are talking about!")

Nevertheless, Shetkari Sanghatana organizers went ahead and prepared lists of candidates on their own in over ten districts, but the hopes of a broad campaign in which all progressive forces united to appeal to the population with a vision of women's empowerment linked to a needs-oriented rural developmental path were vanishing. Then in February 1988 the Maharashtra government announced the indefinite postponement of district council elections. This brought the first phase of the new rural women's movement to a frustrating close.

Patna, 1988: Struggle for Unity

It was just after this that the long-awaited Patna conference was held, and this was running into similar roadblocks. "Unity in struggle" was its theme, but the sectarian and factionalism not only of parties but of some of the feminist organizations as well seemed to be the more difficult reality.

Major differences emerged in the preparatory meetings. The strongest tensions seemed to exist between the mass-movement-oriented feminists, who saw the conference as laying the basis for an emerging movement of rural women in Bihar and elsewhere, and the "autonomous" urban feminists, who laid their stress on a nonhierarchical process of small group discussion and a culturally wide-open atmosphere. Both were suspicious of others' intentions and put off by styles of behavior; feminists from Bombay got upset when IPF women coming from various states in India held a caucus of their own just before the second preparatory meeting, while IPF representatives at the Delhi meeting felt overwhelmed by the flow of words from the very articulate feminists of that city.

The issues that really became sore points were not those of "patriarchy" and "class" where rigid but clear stands could be taken, but rather organizational ones, how resolutions should be taken up, who should be included and not included in the conference "sponsoring group," and whether members of "caste-ist and communal" groups (and which exactly were these) should be excluded from the conference. Some activists felt strongly that funded organizations should not be sponsors, others who were part of such organizations insisted that their names be mentioned. These issues were resolved fairly simply, by deciding not to include any organizational names as sponsors and by deciding to exclude no one from the conference but rather accept all those who agreed with a formal "statement of unity." But they left some bad feelings.

Equally serious were the problems of infighting at the grass roots level. By

1987–88, the unity that had been seen in Bihar in 1986 had nearly vanished. The two major Naxalite groups, IPF-Liberation and MKSS-Party Unity, were at odds; a member of a third rival group explained this simply as due to the fact that the movement had become so powerful that organizations were now battling each other more than the state: landlords were "surrendering" and giving large sums of money to the groups, and the revolutionaries were "fighting over territory." Then in mid-1987 a bitter dispute erupted between Sangarsh Vahini and IPF. At the root of it was a conflict in one village between landless dalits, mobilized by the Vahini to claim the land of a huge religious estate, and backward caste peasants who felt that the land should be theirs because they had previously been its tenants; when the tenants joined the IPF and then attacked and murdered a dalit activist, a near-total split between the organizations occurred. The Sangarsh Vahini women declared they would not let this affect women's unity, but it was clear that by the time the conference was to be held in February 1988, the "unity in struggle" of the rural poor that had promised to be such a bright foundation for a new women's movement in Bihar lay in ashes.

The conference itself promised much and gave much. Eight hundred women gathered, the largest of any conference so far, and they came from all over the country, the majority of them poor rural women. The discussions on women and work, women's rights to land, violence against women, women and ecology, culture and communalism, patriarchy and struggle brought forward many new themes, and if the process of trying to sum them up and report on them in five to six major languages was exhausting, the final mass rally and march through the streets under red, green, and white banners headed by the purple banner of the conference itself brought a new sight to the citizens of Patna.

Resolutions also saw some innovations. These included several on individual atrocities, on fights on environmental issues, and for the first time a general one on women and ecology, on property rights in which it was urged that all land should be given "in joint title" to both men and women while houses should be solely on women's name, and on violence. The latter attempted to link intrafamily and state violence:

> Women face specific forms of violence: rape and other forms of sexual abuse, female foeticide, witch-killing, sati, dowry murders, wife-beating. Such violence and the continued sense of insecurity that is instilled in women as a result keeps them bound to the home, economically exploited and socially suppressed. In the ongoing struggles against violence in the family, society and the state, we recognize that the state is one of the main sources of violence and stands behind the violence committed by men against women in the family, the workplace and the neighborhood. For these reasons a mass women's movement should focus on the struggle against them in the home or out of it.

Behind all this, though, were ongoing tensions, constant eruptions in the coordinating committee, accusations of Sangarsh Vahini against IPF women, charges by feminists that the coordinating committee itself was "acting as a mafia." Issues of funding could not be seriously discussed in the group sessions; those who raised the problems of sexuality were attacked by others; and the question of violence within the movement itself was avoided, though many felt that this was as crucial a problem as that of state violence. The fact that newspaper reports wrote of "splits between Marxists and feminists" was not so serious a problem; in a way it showed the conference openness. But in the end crucial issues were left aside; the resolutions' session itself produced primarily anger and exhaustion, and finally the coordinating committee was dissolved, with the major groups declaring that they did not really want to work together.

These tensions were felt primarily by the organizers; for most participants it was a new and stimulating experience. As a group of Rajasthan women, not up to that time very political, saw it, "The Patna sammelan saw rural women holding group discussions at a national level, so far an exclusive privilege of urban academic feminists." They liked the openness of the group discussions but were bored by the long process of reporting on them and were alienated by the debates over resolutions and the conflicts between autonomous women's groups and the mass-based organizations that they felt "kept the village women out." But the mass march at the end helped to override all the negative features: "The effort to formulate and pass resolutions had left many of us feeling tense and low. The rally that followed overcame this mood, infusing us with a fresh spirit. The experience of marching alongside 12,000 women generated a heady sense of unity. . . . Marching together, we experienced the power of our numbers, a sense of joy at our coming together, and anger at our situation." [10]

The Patna conference led to no immediate new upsurge of women in Bihar itself. There was no mass or political organization ready to take its resolutions seriously as a guide to action. One small Naxalite organization working in Bihar split after the conference, with one of the charges against some organizers being that they had mobilized women for the rally in spite of an organizational decision against it. A promising organization that had arisen among tribal women in Bihar, the Jharkhand Nari Mukti Samiti, held two later meetings but could not move ahead much in the face of opposition from male leaders of the Jharkhand movement.

The IPF itself, the biggest Bihar organization among the conference sponsors, was moving toward a more conventional politics in 1988, and its national conference a little later that year had little new to offer on women's issues. Two years later a second major conference of its peasant front in August 1990 announced that all land won in struggle would be given in joint titles to men and women both. But while declaring itself to be the "first left peasant organization" to support women's land rights, the conference also rejected the idea of a "separate organization of peasant women" promising only an "autonomous movement" within the framework of the Kisan Sabha. [11]

"Women's power," then, did not seem able to move very far within a mass movement without a committed male leadership to support it, and the framework of traditional left thinking (even in its militant Naxalite form) appeared inimical to new directions. Yet the experience of Patna had clearly left some kind of ferment in Bihar; even if local Naxalite or tribal leaderships remained reluctant to movement ahead on women's issues, women in their organizations continued to press for their rights, and new, autonomous mass-based groups emerged, such as an organization of tribal women with Christian leadership in Giridh district. The Patna conference thus became a landmark for the Indian women's movement, an achievement of coalition politics that linked the fight of women against violence to mass organizing and a challenge to state power.

Bangalore, 1989: "Would the Women of This Nation Come Out and Plead for Life?"

The Patna conference's failure to give organizational direction to the women's movement symbolized the malaise of the time. Hopes had been placed in the mobilizing of rural women. Vandana Shiva had argued for a "feminist principle" of nurturance and power; Sharad Joshi had claimed that women could become a "national political force," capable of nonviolently transforming political life; Gabriele Dietrich had looked to a women-directed alternative development. All had been speaking in the context of rural women's movements, of peasants, fish-workers, tribals. Yet in this period of politics in the conventional sense, full of the potential fall of the Rajiv Gandhi government and the maneuverings of political parties, the barriers of party sectarianism, male suspicions, middle-class alienation from mass movements, even a general lack of vision seemed to signify instead the closing down of spaces for women. Instead of the "awakening of women's power," movements were facing unceasing political cynicism and above all the growing violence, both communal and caste conflict and sheer political gangsterism, that was so inimical to women.

In this context, a group of women activists from all over South Asia—India, Bangladesh, Pakistan, and Sri Lanka—met for ten days in Bangalore in February, 1989. They included women with a history of involvement with armed struggle organizations, mass movements, Indian urban feminist groups, and some of the most famous of South Asian autonomous women's organizations, such as the Pakistan Women's Forum. They took part as individuals, not as organizations; thus there was no question of establishing an organizational policy. It was, however, an occasion for deeply serious discussion on the emerging issues of feminism. Women explored not only concepts like "patriarchy" and "autonomous groups" and others that had up to then been clearly defined as "women's issues," but also ecology and development, militarism, the question of Indian hegemony in the subcontinent, culture, caste, and the new dilemmas of religious and ethnic identity. Though there was lively debate over Vandana Shiva's "feminine principle" and full-scale attack on "Western science and technology" ("why not call it imperialism?"), there was a fair measure of agreement on the emerging new perspective that some were to later call "ecofeminist":

> We uphold this "production of life" as a central concept and thus struggle not from a situation of victimisation but as defenders of organic life and of ecologically sustainable life processes. . . . It is obvious that a struggle which puts "production of life" at the center is by definition anti-capitalist, anti-imperialist and critical of mechanistic solutions which modern Western science and technology may try to offer as panacea for the ecological breakdown of the planet. It is also profoundly different from the development concepts which have been followed in actually existing socialism. . . . [It] also gets us into direct opposition to the "production of death" which culminates in the arms industry and trade, connected with the international drug trade. . . . We are therefore forced into a *new type of politics*, resisting militarisation, *upholding the common life* and expanding democratic spaces in day to day survival struggles.[12]

But there were unresolved issues. Mass organizing and politics remained controversial and were discussed only at a superficial level; there were varying attitudes toward the family and toward religion and spirituality; issues of cultural and ethnic identity were left unresolved. And again there was the problem of violence, not only that of state power, but that of the oppositional movements themselves.

This was troubling partly because feminists had always identified with the left. Particularly in India, where the tenacity of the Naxalite effort to build a force based on the rural poor made them romantic heroes to so many, an endorsement of violence seemed to provide the distinction between paternalistic Gandhism and the dividing line in the Communist movement between "revisionists" and "revolutionaries."

On the other hand, many feminists who focused on male violence also rejected mass movements altogether, seeing in them a subtle violence of bureaucratization and domination. Some questioned the very notion of "women's power": didn't the concept of *stri shakti*, with its reference to sometimes bloody mother goddess traditions, imply too much of an endorsement of power and violence? Wasn't it too readily being picked up by conservatives who could twist it to see women's ability to endure all kinds of oppression as a symbol of magnificent power? Didn't Hindu nationalists have a tradition of appealing to mother goddesses? Wasn't it a Rajput defender of the sati-murder of Roop Kunwar who had said, "Sati is shakti, the power that upholds the universe"? And wasn't the related theme of *virangana*, the historical tradition of heroic women queens who had taken up arms against one or another invader or oppressor, simply an endorsement of feudalism as well as warfare? Could the question of empowerment be separated from that of violence?

By 1988–89, the need to do so was compelling. Empowerment was on the agenda; even the spokesmen of governing parties were talking of giving representation to women in legislatures and local boards, while conversely women involved in mass movements were being forced into the political sphere to win any demands. But not only was conventional left politics useless for empowering women to deal with wider social and political issues; even the politics of the "revolutionaries" was becoming an obstacle to their needs. The heroism of guerrilla warriors, ready not only to kill but themselves to suffer torture and death in pursuit of their aims, retained a compelling quality, but it did not mean an ability to move beyond conventional left ways of thinking in other respects. Violence in revolutionary movements was correlated with the continuing subordination of women in these movements. Further, the "liberation struggles" on India's periphery were associated with religious fundamentalism and with reversion to traditions of keeping women shielded. It was becoming unclear what the once-popular image of the woman with a gun in her arms and a baby on her back really meant: was it, after all, liberatory?

The question was brought up at Bangalore in particular by the Sri Lanka representatives, both Tamils and Sinhalese: their nation was currently being torn apart by the Indian army, sent as a "peace-keeping force" but increasingly acting as an occupation army, and by the depradations of both Tamil and Sinhalese guerrillas and the Sri Lankan army. Some of the women taking part in the Bangalore workshop had been involved in both Tamil and Sinhalese liberation organizations, and the whole experience had been shattering.

Questions were raised by, among others, Rajani Thiranagama, a Tamil then active in a Jaffna human rights group that was challenging not only Indian atrocities, but the violation of human rights, including rapes of women, by the Tamil guerrillas as well. Rajni was coauthor of a just-published book, *The Broken Palmyra*, a powerful and heartbreaking account of the gloomy Sri Lankan situation, exposing the hypocrisy and casteism of the Indians, the morbid chauvinism of the Tigers (the dominant Tamil guerrilla force), and the brutality of the Sinhalese army.

The Sri Lanka situation had a particular poignancy not only because of the problem of Indian hegemony but also because of the evident degradation of a "national liberation movement" that women had once admired as a basis for revolutionary change. "Killings of comrades were justified so easily," remembered those who had been involved in such guerrilla groups; "not having the correct line . . . being a 'danger' to the movement . . . all kinds of human feelings could be considered 'betrayal.' " *The Broken Palmyra* had outlined how the association of women with these "human weaknesses" were linked with continual subordination even in guerrilla groups, which they joined in great numbers. Rajani felt that the turn to guerrilla warfare among the Tamil youth had cut off possibilities of open mass struggle and left the entire community demoralized and passive, unable to resist oppression. Women activists in Sri Lanka from the Tamil "Mothers' Front" to joint peace efforts of Tamil and Sinhala women, continued to seek alternative forms of struggle. But their future was uncertain.

The Bangalore workshop ended with the formulation of a series of position papers and vows to maintain a network; Rajni returned to Sri Lanka and then to

London for a special medical course. But unlike most other Tamil Lankans of the time, she chose to return home in spite of her pessimism about the future of her country and fears for her friends and herself. On September 12, shortly before going back, she wrote to one of the workshop participants her gloomy feelings about the development of "narrow nationalism" and the apathy of the broader community in the face of a crescendo of mutual slaughter.

> Within this context, the question of "armed" struggle has taken for me a vicious turn. For a person who had always considered armed struggle the axis of a revolutionary struggle, this question is painful and overhauling. The enormous brutalization and deterioration that has been brought about by guns—states that have militarized entire communities—narrow nationalist slogans that have sanctioned any killings—Is it a time when we can ask, organize for space for democratic mobilization, for letting children—our young boys—be free not to hold guns, but produce subsistence for the communities? . . . Would the women of this nation come out and plead for life?

Nine days later, shortly after returning to Sri Lanka, Rajni was shot down on the university campus, only 100 yards from her home, by unidentified guerrillas. Many suspected the Tigers but were afraid to say so openly. There was a protest march and meetings—unusual events in a community dominated by fear—and representatives of the Indian and Pakistani groups who had been at the Bangalore meeting also attended in solidarity. But the event was a shock. Gabriele Dietrich wrote:

> *We will*
> *affirm*
> *the preciousness*
> *of life:*
> *no more*
> *atrocities*
> *not even*
> *our own*
> *there must be*
> *an end*
> *to slaughter.*
> *They can*
> *bump off*
> *a few of us*
> *but not all*
> *if we are*
> *many*
> *you paid*
> *the price*
> *for nurturing*
> *fearlessness*
> *in all of us.*

The Bangalore workshop endorsed a perspective of alternative development, and its discussions deepened debate on issues of cultural-religious identity and violence within movements for change. But for the moment, hopes for nonviolent, nurturing change seemed to be overwhelmed by the traumas of movement and state violence.

Amraoti, 1989–1991: Women and the "Mainstream"

At the same time, though Sharad Joshi had claimed after Chandwad that "women might become the mainstream," by 1989 hopes for this seemed to be fading in Maharashtra also. The two major campaigns announced at Chandwad, the mass march to Delhi and the district council election campaign, had both come to naught. Women instead seemed to be absorbed in the general campaigns of the Shetkari Sanghatana, especially the large-scale rallies and anti-indebtedness campaign of 1988. When a meeting of the Mahila Aghadi in January 1989 declared that there was little scope for struggle on "women's issues," but rather women should "independently" take part in Sanghatana campaigns, many feminists said "I told you so"—that nothing real for women was coming out of it all.

Yet women, especially those at the village level, continued to press forward. The representatives' meeting of the women's front might reject the possibility of separate women's struggles, but a subsequent regional meeting in Vidarbha (the strongest center of the movement) planned demonstrations symbolically to "take control" of government offices in every district in protest against the failure to hold elections, and they succeeded in pushing an anti-alcohol campaign on the organization. Alcoholism was a heartfelt issue of poor women everywhere, connected as it was with male irresponsibility toward the family and with wife-beating. Left leaders had always opposed campaigns against it as divisive, and so did Sharad Joshi. But women pressed the issue, and the Shetkari Sanghatana took up a campaign to close down liquor shops in villages that drew massive and enthusiastic participation.

A series of district-level women's melavas of the Shetkari Sanghatana were held in early 1989 to discuss issues of women's subordination and inaugurate the campaign to close down liquor shops. At the same time, women and men, this time at the village level, took another step forward. The district council elections were postponed, but a series of *gram panchayat* (village council) elections were held throughout the state. The Shetkari Sanghatana gave an official call to fight party factionalism in such elections, with no mention of women's political power. But in seven villages, one after another and taking inspiration from hearing of similar attempts, peasants decided to put up "all women panels." Though the united women's political platform, the Samagra Mahila Aghadi, had died a still-born infant, the idea of women's political power was alive. Five of these panels won, and in two others villagers succeeded in electing a majority of women on the panchayat. In a country where in most cases women could hardly go to the village square, where those who were supposed to be appointed as "women members" on the panchayats usually never went to meetings but simply gave their signature to whatever the men passed, this was an unprecedented achievement.

Recognition of the issue of women's political power now began to come from the very top. Electoral politics require popular appeals to mobilize support. In the surge of farmers' movements in national-level politics, the opposition tried to consolidate its base by appealing to the nonparty peasant organizations, and every political party gave support to remunerative prices and the write-off of peasant debts. Along with this, women's political representation was becoming an issue. The Rajiv Gandhi government had appointed in late 1987 a commission to formulate a "National Perspective Plan" for women. When this was finally released, along with the usual rhetoric of the need to "incorporate women in the mainstream" of development, it took up an old idea of giving political reservations for women. The NPP suggested 30 percent reservation in local self-government bodies, and when Gandhi attempted in 1989 to win popular support with new "turn to the villages" electoral promises, he incorporated the 30 percent suggestion. This new reality of a potential reservation of seats for women in local bodies now forced both traditional left parties and women's organizations to deal with the issue.

But both feminist and left women were dealing with the issue of political power in a mainly reactive way, responding to this proposal of the NPP as they responded to other government initiatives. In contrast, the Shetkari Sanghatana as an organization had never wasted much time in responding to government initiatives, and the women shared the same outlook: the question was to formulate policy for the movement and then to organize to achieve it, which might mean putting pressure on the state and might mean simply going ahead to implement a program on their own. The Sanghatana's annual conference had been held at Nanded in March; now a second women's conference was being planned by the Sanghatana for November. What was to be its theme?

The growing violence of religious fundamentalism was becoming an issue for Shetkari Sanghatana as well as all sections of the women's movement, and this meant fighting the BJP and Shiv Sena, currently moving toward a political alliance in the state, aiming for capturing power, provoking riots against Muslims and against dalits. Sharad Joshi's strong attacks on the Shiv Sena were an important example of an issue where he could get support from women to override other leading activists who preferred a policy of compromise with the politically powerful Hindu fundamentalists.

Basic women's issues were also coming to the fore. The Chandwad session itself had passed two other important resolutions about which nothing had been done. One was on property rights, which evoked a good deal of skepticism about the readiness of peasant proprietors to hand over land to women; no action was immediately taken, while Joshi reminded his critics that "independence was not won in a day either." The other was that of women's work, as agricultural laborers and in peasant families (including not only "domestic labour" but agricultural processing work): this was unrecognized by official statistics (heavily uncounted in censuses, for example), not included in methodologies calculating the cost of cultivation of crops, and underpaid as wage work.

Property rights became a central issue in a national debate in 1989, provoked mainly by *Manushi* editor Madhu Kishwar. Madhu was an organizational iconoclast warring with both the "Marxist" and "feminist" trends of the women's movement, ready to explain in detail why she was "not a feminist," skeptical of the claims for achievements of women in mass movements. But she had been an associate of the Shetkari Sanghatana from the beginning. In 1988 she awakened a new controversy with an article, "Rethinking Dowry Boycott," that critiqued women's movement practice in a way parallel to Sharad Joshi's Chandwad challenge to get away from the negative task of dealing only with atrocities and get down to basics. Madhu later explained,

> My experience was that my boycotting dowry wedding did not bring any change in dowry practices in my social circle. . . . By talking to and listening to numerous women, I found that women did not think that merely getting married without dowry, all else remaining the same, would alter their powerless position for the better. In the absence of any better option, many women I spoke to even perceived dowry of being of some limited benefit to them, given their dependent situation, lack of fundamental rights, overall disinheritance and lack of control over assets.[13]

Since most women's organizations, especially in cities like Delhi, had centered much of their activity on fighting dowry, and since the fiery blaze of "dowry deaths" was taken even at an international level as the major symbol of women's oppression in India, the article raised a storm. It was attacked as being in some way supportive of the dowry system. But Madhu's main point, of course, was that dowry was more an effect of women's powerlessness than a cause, and that it was not usually the main factor in the brutalization and murder of women after marriage. Property rights, she argued, had to be taken up if women were to go ahead at all.

On this background study camps, organizing meetings, and discussions were being held in preparation for the Amraoti conference of the Shetkari Mahila Aghadi. Fighting communalism, getting recompense for the exhausting work of rural women, and gaining property rights for women now became the new themes. The debates took place on a background of renewed turmoil in which women were playing a major organizational role.

October 1989 saw women going en masse ticketless on the train to Delhi, in a climax of the post-1986 upsurge of the farmers' movement that ended in the split that took place during the Boat Club rally in Delhi on October 2, 1989. It was after this that the last of the preparatory camps for the Amraoti conference took place, with a broad-ranging discussion for a basic manifesto and for various resolutions. Out of a discussion on both women's work and property rights came a new suggestion: eventually a basic resolution on the tangled question of inheritance rights would be formulated, but in the meantime, as a first step, members of Shetkari Sanghatana itself should take the decision to give rights over land to the women of their families. This was to be called the "Hingoli program" after the name of the town where the meeting was held.

Then, just before the conference, Rajiv Gandhi suddenly declared elections. In the midst of growing oppositional turmoil and growing communal riots in North India provoked by aggressive Hindu right forces, the Amraoti conference now took on directly political overtones: what was Shetkari Sanghatana's election stand going to be? For the press and other representatives of the "broader public," this, not women's rights, was the overriding issue.

But Amraoti itself, held just three years after the Chandwad conference, showed the progress of women in the organization. There was much less media attention and practically no representation from other women's organizations, but women were much more in the forefront, and there was a significantly larger proportion of peasant women themselves in the mass rally. Resolutions covered issues not only of property and land rights, with Madhu Kishwar as a featured speaker, of political power, of agricultural laborers' wages, and of the anti-alcohol campaign, but also of communalism with women resolving to bar the entry of communal organizations into the villages. The basic policy statement, beginning with the claim that a peasant organization that fights for "the reward of our sweat" should be basically a women's organization "because the main sweat that falls on the fields is that of peasant women," was a development of the Chandwad position rewritten partially by the women themselves after their preparatory meetings:

> "Reward for our sweat" has been the slogan of the peasant movement. The drops of sweat that fall in the fields are primarily those of peasant women. . . . From the time of the first surplus in agriculture an era of looting began. . . . The method of looting went on changing; the looting system endured. The loot that goes on today is with a minimum of weapons but the reign of the goondas in the villages and dadas in the cities continues. The insecurity outside the household is today the greatest obstacle in the path of women. . . . The struggle of women is not a struggle of women against men, but of a nonlooting system against a looting system.

But how to fight the "looting system"? The document reaffirmed its faith in mass movements, but for the present the farmers' movement itself, along with its women, was being forced into the electoral arena. Sharad Joshi took the occasion of the Amraoti conference to declare an eleven-day fast as part of the implementation of the women's fight against communalism, but refrained from announcing the policy of the Sanghatana toward the elections. The second mass conference of peasant women thus ended in ambiguity. On the one hand, women were taking up grass roots campaigns on fundamental issues of property and power; on the other, they were being dragged into the vortex of national politics in a year of transition and growing communalism and violence.

Vitner, 1989–1991: Toward "Freeing the Goddess"

Amraoti began a process of giving women fundamental rights that was to culminate in the "Laxmi Mukti" campaign for "freeing the goddess," but a period of intense and ultimately frustrating "mainstream" political participation had to intervene before this really took off.

The dilemma of the Sanghatana, in regard to the elections, was simple. As a mass organization antagonistic to parliamentary politics but unwilling to put its faith in "revolutionary violence," it was basically against the ruling party and committed to supporting candidates in a way that would forward peasant interests. It was, at one level, the natural ally of the left-democratic parties. But this meant that it was also liable to be taken for granted by them, and in the heady days of 1989, when the fall of Congress looked like more and more a reality, the parties were ready to take up issues of mass movements, but not to yield them any political space.

The crux was the issue of communalism. The Sanghatana was threatening no support if parties allied with the BJP and Shiv Sena in Maharashtra; the left-democratic parties were making an unadmitted alliance of "seat adjustments." This meant, for instance, that even while Janata Dal leader Mrinal Gore (the only state-level woman party leader) was railing against the Hindu right-wing, ex-socialist Madhu Dandavate (later to become finance minister) was calling a special meeting to agree to withdraw two candidates of the JD in favor of the Shiv Sena if they in turn would withdraw their candidate in his constituency. The fact that the JD candidates sacrificed were his wife and a young Muslim activist only added to the poignancy of the deal. Few found very much to question in it: these were the days in which the fall of the Congress seemed near, days of hard political realism, and even respectable Marxist journals were editorializing on the need for "opposition unity."

But unity with the BJP-Shiv Sena was not acceptable to Sharad Joshi. In the middle of his fast (which women supported with a one-day "mass fast" in thousands of villages), a special executive meeting was held to decide policy, and over the opposition of most of his lieutenants, Joshi got his way. For the 1989 parliamentary elections, the Sanghatana generally supported candidates of the left and democratic parties. But in nine cases where seat adjustment deals had left only Congress or BJP-Shiv Sena candidates to choose from, the Sanghatana supported the Congress. This caused an uproar and distressed Sanghatana activists who found themselves gleefully invited to campaign for the party that they had opposed for so many years. But Joshi had made his point: the battle against communalism was not to be sidelined.

What to do next? Maharashtra state assembly elections were scheduled for February 1990, and this time, the Hindu fundamentalists were aiming at state power, at "waving the saffron flag over the assembly hall." In December, a massive 900-strong "executive" meeting of the Sanghatana was held, and now long-standing pressures from activists to participate directly in elections were overwhelming. It was not simply a matter of individual political ambitions, it was also that they had for nearly ten years worked for opposition parties that they saw as betrayors. "If Congress is 'number one enemy,' and Shiv Sena is the 'greatest danger,' then Janata Dal is number two enemy. We should stand ourselves!" In yielding to the pressure, Sharad Joshi broke a ten-year organizational policy against parliamentary participation. But he did so with a major condition: that the Sanghatana, standing on Janata Dal tickets, should build up "Progressive Democratic Front" (PDF) of JD and the left parties to oppose both Congress and the BJP-Shiv Sena alliance in Maharashtra, ensuring that the PDF had candidates in every constituency so that no bargains could be made with the Hindu parties. And 30 percent of candidates should be women.

In "entering" the Janata Dal, Shetkari Sanathana thus solidified the PDF as an independent front of left and democratic parties with many more women candidates than previously. With left and democratic parties and mass movements, including the workers' movement under Datta Samant coming together, a wave of enthusiasm was generated. A strong anticommunal link to the democratic anticaste traditions of Maharashtra was given when the Sanghatana organized a tour of twenty districts in January, not directly on the elections but on the thought of Phule and Ambedkar, propagating anticaste ideology and attacking the Shiv Sena ferociously. Then men and women of the Sanghatana plunged with fervor, if not funding, into the actual election campaign. Posters and speakers attacked both Congress gangsterism and Hindu communal brahmanism, as Joshi vowed in campaign speeches that "we will not let the state treasury fall into the hands of criminals!" The Sanghatana had ten of its thirty-five official candidates from the women's wing—a higher percentage than any other organization in India and the only one that came close to matching the promises being hurled into the air of "30 percent" or "25 percent" tickets.

Yet in the end the electoral experience proved traumatic. The Sanghatana activists were, after all, political novices, buoyed by the glamor generated by their movement and with unreal expectations of victory. Reality showed that organizing powerful movements was different from winning elections. In an election campaign fought on a larger and more expensive scale than ever before, with massive advertising, videos, electric boards, cinema stars, constantly blaring campaign vehicles, the parties of the PDF, including the Shetkari Sanghatana, were heavily underfinanced and overwhelmed by the muscle-power, money, and electoral machinery available to both Congress and the Hindu rightists. Even worse, the PDF had no discipline, no program of its own, and there was mutual betrayal by member parties of the PDF in practically every constituency.

Only five Shetkari candidates won, including one woman (who turned out to be the only woman MLA of the PDF). This was not, after all, so bad for a movement organization (it was comparable to IPF performance in Bihar and equal to both Communist parties in Maharashtra itself)—but it was much less than they had come to expect. A post-mortem meeting expressed a good amount of demoralization; "We had an awfully expensive training session in politics," as one activist put it; and the winning woman legislator, who had been a reluctant candidate to begin with, said, "I cried when I filed my nomination papers and I cried when I got elected." Joshi himself used grim analogies of the Shetkari Sanghatana's electoral participation as a "kamikaze action," preventing a Shiv Sena-headed "united opposition" coming into control of the Maharashtra state assembly, but at great cost.

The Sanghatana's participation in and influence on the PDF had been a major part of a broad national process in which the Janata Dal leadership was swinging away from compromise with Hindu rightists. But it had also been demoralizing, especially to women, who now began to doubt whether they could really do anything with "100 percent panels" in district council elections. Activists, who had been involved in one campaign after another for nearly two years, were exhausted. The year 1990 turned out to be a year in which Sharad Joshi was involved in Delhi, in the work of formulating a document that was to be a hoped-for national agricultural policy of the government, but in which no mass campaigns of the Sanghatana itself could be organized in Maharashtra. "We need a new direction, a new beacon, new methods of struggle" now became a theme in Sanghatana meetings.

It was women (and men) at the base of the Sanghatana, in its far-flung village, who began the process of providing this. In Vitner, a small village in Jalgaon district on the banks of the Tapi river, one of five that had elected an all-woman panchayat, an energetic local activist, Indirabai Patil, motivated villagers to go ahead in taking up the question of land rights for women, and 127 men of the village split their holdings to put legal shares in the name of women of their families. In the preparatory discussions at Amraoti, there had been a debate about whether legal land ownership was really useful, and it was finally decided that the first step in giving women property rights would be to assign instead the *income* from a fixed share of the land. The Vitner peasants intervened in giving women legal ownership—and this became the official policy of the Sanghatana. In 1990, in a period otherwise marked by lack of Sanghatana activity, the mass campaign of giving land rights to women was taken up under name of "Laxmi-Mukti." Laxmi is the goddess of wealth, and women are popularly described as the Laxmi or "wealth" of the household. The Sanghatana's imagery implied that this represented an enslavement, the binding of "women's power," and that peasants were to act collectively to lift these bonds. A village was to be regarded as having achieved "Laxmi Mukti" if over one hundred landholders (or over two-thirds in a very small village) turned over land rights to women.

By the middle of 1991, over three hundred villages had done so. In most cases these were small, remote villages, off the main roads, easily ignored by the press and even feminists in the cities who tended to dismiss the whole campaign and the action of villagers in initiating it. Women were on their way not to "entering the mainstream," perhaps not to "become" it as yet, but they were beginning to transform it.

Calicut, 1991: "Creating Space for Women"

A new perspective was emerging in the women's movement, which posed challenges to traditional Marxism *and* "traditional feminism" in ways that went beyond simple posings of "class and caste" or "class and gender." Notions such as the "feminine principle" and "stri shakti," which were increasingly being debated, had some profound implications. On one hand, the idea of the "feminine principle" challenged traditional Marxism by posing the nature-maintaining, subsistence-based rural peasant woman against the male industrial worker who embodied the "proletarian vanguard"; on the other, it questioned the feminist tendencies to locate violence in the family, in the relations of women against men, by stressing the "feminine "principle" as something that men and women both could unite around. The notion of *stri shakti* similarly implied not so much a separate women's movement as the leading role of women in various popular movements, helping these movements to transcend some of their own limitations. As with the slogan "the liberation of women and men through the awakening of women's power," it was a significant departure from the tendency of both urban feminists and party women to depict women as primarily victims.

By 1990, in the context of a traumatic political transformation in India, both slogans were beginning to have a new reality, as women moved toward acquiring political power and property at the grass roots level, affirming as they did so the life of their community, proclaiming a rejection of communalism but without overriding traditional cultural-ethnic identities. As the Bangalore workshop showed, new perspectives were also emerging in discussions among feminist intellectuals in the region.

But these did not immediately translate into overall strategy for the women's movement as such. As the summary of the Bangalore discussions had noted, the movement had been weakest in regard to mass mobilization:

> As was pointed out in the report on the feminist movement, it is not "women's issues" proper which bring women on the road but survival issues like land, water, forest, housing, work. There has been a gap between feminist campaigning on women's issues and such structures of mass organizations which emerge in survival struggles, especially struggles for control over basic resources of survival. Mass mobilizations and organization of women as seen in Shetkari Sanghatana or in movements like Women's Voice or Pennurimai Iyakkam (both movements of slum dwellers) or in the fish workers movement

along the Kerala coast are therefore of wider significance. Linking up the insights of feminist theory with the demands, struggles and forms of organization of such movements will be vital in order to make any headway in strategizing—which the present meeting failed to achieve.[14]

The "gap" noted in the Bangalore discussions could not be resolved at meetings like Bangalore itself because these were, after all, not movement conclaves, though almost those present both considered themselves "feminists" and had some organic linkage with mass movements. The problem was that the women's movement as such was giving no organized articulation to the new perspective. The movement was still dominated by "traditional Marxists" connected with the parties and "traditional feminists" in the urban-based organizations, and these were the most alienated from the new developments.

The urban feminists, in particular, were in a period of gloom and frustration, feeling an organizational weakness that was far removed from the promises of "women's power." They were planning a new "national conference" to be held in late 1990, but after the tensions and splits of the Patna conference were doing so without any efforts to have coalitions with mass-based organizations and party women's wings.

Contradictions between the feminist groups and the party-connected women seemed if anything to be growing. In 1989–90 the biggest Communist party, the CPI(M), was itself implicated in some notorious rape cases. In Maharashtra, where peasant activists in a tribal region near Bombay had been engaged in over a decade of murderous infighting with an independent organization known as the Kashtakari Sanghatana, a young Kashtakari woman was gang-raped by tribal men of the CPI(M). The CPI(M) leaders stonewalled on the issue, though angry demonstrations in Bombay aroused wide support. Then in West Bengal itself the brutal rape and murder of three women social workers and the driver of their van in the CPI(M)-controlled area of Bangala caused a nationwide shock, evoking a symbol of the gangster-influenced degeneration of the Left Front government. A remark of the leader of the West Bengal women's organizations that "such things have happened and do happen" did not help matters; feminists began to see even the women activists of the party as corrupted by partisanship and power.

On top of this, the left parties themselves, which earlier had projected such an image of domination to the smaller feminist organizations, were now growing weaker in regard to patriarchal-capitalist and communal forces. In the ferment of the 1989–1991 elections, most women's organizations were paralyzed. No specific overall demands were projected on the national level, in spite of localized efforts to do so, and parties were putting up fewer women candidates than ever before. The percentage of women MPs and MLAs was dropping, and those who were elected included such defenders of Hindu orthodoxy as Vijayamata Scindia, the aristocratic BJP leader who had the questionable distinction of being one of the major national defenders of *sati* and Uma Bharati, the saffron-clad fanatic famous for her diatribes against Muslims on videocassettes. In spite of the fact that women's liberation organizations, whether "autonomous," party-linked, or mass-organization-linked, opposed communalism as antagonistic to the interests of women, it appeared as if the Hindu religious fronts were doing better than the left parties at expressing themes of *stri shakti* and attracting teams of militant young activists and propagandists. The faces of screaming women at Ayodhya began to provide haunting photographic imagery.

It was no wonder, then, that many urban women activists looked with cynicism on politics and the proposal for 30 percent reservations. They felt, according to one activist of Bombay's Forum, that the increase of women political representatives would simply go along with the marginalization of women's issues (which they continued to define in terms of domestic violence, rape, amniocentisis, etc.), and they feared a growing authoritarianism of Indian politics:

> The democratic space available for women to struggle has itself been shrinking not only in India but in the subcontinent as a whole. Fundamentalism and revivalism threaten to engulf our country. . . . [and linking themes of family planning and a call for a common civil code with the aim of attacking the Muslim community in a] horrifying and fascistic perspective. . . . This is the shape of the future, at least the immediate future, for our country. This is indeed the central question that faces the women's movement here today.[15]

On this background of pessimism, planning went forward for the "fourth national conference" to be held in Calicut, Kerala, at the end of December 1990. Initiative was taken by Bombay women, and there was no major attempt to involve mass women's organizations, even in Kerala. Not only were the CPI(M) women thoroughly alienated, but the independent and feminist Coastal Woman's Association, the biggest nonparty women's organization in Kerala, was also attacked for its doubts about the conference. The Kashtakari Sanghatana women, initially involved into conference organizing, fought with many of the Bombay organizers over what they considered a crude method of dealing with the rape issue. But organizing went ahead, on a larger scale than any earlier meetings, with a budget of Rs 150,000, and an orientation that focused on expressive activities.

"The main aim of coming together," stated the brochure for the conference, "is to create space for women to express their ideas, experience and feelings . . . by verbal expression or through songs, play acting, paintings, humor, tableaus or any other creative forms of expression." The argument behind this was that whereas the Patna conference had emphasized verbal dialogue, the Calicut conference in contrast was giving scope to more varied forms of expression. But in fact, in the context of the growing communal tensions in India, rising trends of violence, and the crisis affecting the parties of the left, many of India's feminists were feeling a need for "space" out of a mood of frustration and despondency.

In spite of this beleaguered mood, the Calicut conference was a success. Over two thousand women attended the three-day program, and though the final rally was no bigger and the numbers were still small by the standards of mass movements, for most participants it was inspiring and invigorating. Women came in good numbers from NGOs in the South and states like Rajasthan and Gujarat, and while they sometimes complained of elite dominance, they found the openness of the meeting and its festival atmosphere a major achievement. As a Tamil participant put it, "The country is seething with communal hatred. . . . We in the women's movement have to establish the ethos of cultural pluralism, mutual respect and promote sisterhood. Our singing, dancing and experience-sharing is one such effort in this direction." [16]

Calicut, however, did not bring any new perspective for the women's movement: discussions on violence, the media, work, national planning policy, and ecology went over old themes; the "especially volatile" session on women and politics focused on the well-worn question of "our troubled relation with the left," concluding with the stereotypical expression of a need for a common political program. While all endorsed the necessity of fighting communalism, many who had been the most active at the local levels disagreed with the organizers' arguments that a March 8 program on this it should be a "woman-only" affair. ("After all," said one, "We've been taking the lead, but we need all the help we can get!") Madhu Kishwar, who for some time had been arguing for fighting communalism by appealing to the Hindu religious tradition itself, joined to her critique of "Westernized" feminism the comments that there was too much "networking" and too little work; that few were using the "political space that really matters," that is, their own neighborhoods: "For effective work against violence, whether at the domestic level or of the kind witnessed during riots and massacres, we need to have localised community based work. . . . We have not prepared the ground for such mobilization even in our own immediate neighborhoods, leave alone city wide. Yet we are constantly involved in holding 'national' level conferences and workshops." [17]

But this stab at the urban feminist groups missed one point. "Networking" might be a supplementary activity, but some kind of linkages were needed to help the activists who were fighting communalism and other forms of oppression at local levels; this meant providing material and ideological resources as well as summing up and learning from the wide variety of ground-level experiences. What traditional radicals did through "party" and "organization," the feminists called "networks." The Calicut conference began in isolation, but it was an important step in building these.

The concern for "networking" that supplemented the rather negative orientation of "creating space" was more open to new issues and perspectives, less sectarian. The networks were getting broader, beginning to link more and more women from both the urban and rural mass women's organizations as well as those in different social movements. The toiling women who were becoming part of these networks were also increasingly coming from a position of strength, with struggles behind them, with a growing political and social sophistication, thinking on their own, learning forms of empowerment and achievement in small and large campaigns. As networking linked them not simply with middle-class activists and party-organization leaders but also with each other, in increasing discussions, exchange of experiences, and participation in common campaigns, the dominance of a few well-placed individuals lessened, and the thrust of the women's movement itself deepened.

Conclusion: The Direction of "Women's Power"

The "awakening of women's power" was not a matter, as for traditional revolutionaries, of "capturing state power." Nor could it be seen in parliamentary terms, though both rural women's organizations and middle-class activists got involved in national and parliamentary politics in the late 1980s. But the process that began with the Chandwad women's conference of Shetkari Sanghatana did seem to be unleashing a new dynamic. Women in all kinds of mass movements were coming out, bringing their specific problems forward, and in helping to extend the concerns of the movements they were also broadening the range of issues they saw as their own concerns. By the end of the decade, women could no longer see themselves simply as participants in traditionally conceived "revolutionary" movements or as helpless victims who required only to be "integrated into development." A new kind of movement, new methods of organizing, and a new direction of development were affirmed.

What was the "awakening of women's power"? The period following Chandwad saw several interrelated developments. First, there was a growing seriousness among feminists generally about evolving effective political strategies, based on essentially nonviolent mass movements rather than on either electoral politics and lobbying or armed guerrilla struggle. This meant also that fundamental issues of women's subordination, such as property rights and political power, were being taken up in contrast to simply a negative effort to fight atrocities at the individual level. Second, a new attitude to religion/ethnicity/culture was developing, distinguished both from the preindependence uncritical acceptance of the "Sita-Savritri" ideal of Hindu tradition and from the full-scale rejection of religion as unilaterally "patriarchal" by many 1970s feminists; women were exploring alternatives and sources of strength within their culture. Third, there was a growing questioning of the nature of "development" itself and an evolution of a new model in which rural women were at the center.

A Shetkari Sanghatana story, that of the Sita temple in the village Raveri in Yeotmal district, can illustrate some trends. The temple itself was unique; even Rama temples are rare in Maharashtra villages. In its story, Sita, pregnant and cast off from Ayodhya by Rama, had settled in Raveri and after her childbirth had gone to beg wheat from the villagers. They refused to give it to a woman who had been abandoned by her husband, and in anger Sita cursed the villages that no wheat could be grown there. Indeed, said peasants, no wheat had grown in the village until the new hybrid varieties came in. "Sita had to leave Ayodhya after Rama left her because she had no place of her own; the 'Laxmi-Mukti' campaign is one to give rights to all such Sitas" was the way Sharad Joshi had promoted the campaign. Now the peasants of Raveri could redress the mistakes of their ancestors by giving legal land-rights to women! [18]

Sita has been the most important symbol of Indian women, taken by traditionalists as the epitome of chastity and husband-worshipping loyalty; the fact that she was sent away by Rama on the merest suspicion made her also one of the original "abandoned women," easily identified with by Indian women deserted or divorced by their husbands in the modern period for little or no cause. For that matter, the contemporary TV version showed a modern "updating" of patriarchy when it had Sita herself plea to Rama to send her away, feeling perhaps that his own action would appear too crude. But village women have had different traditions of Sita: ballads praising her as superior to Rama, or describing her as defying Rama, refusing to go back, raising her children on her own. Sharad Patil, interpreter of ancient myths and epics, argued that she was *bhumikanya Sita*, the "daughter of earth," symbol of the fertility goddess, that the last episode in the epic where she disappears into the earth was a return to her mother, and that the basic meaning of the Ramayana was the triumph of patriarchy over matriarchy.

The Raveri story can be seen in this context, showing Sita as a goddess linked to agriculture, rejected by male peasants in an expression of patriarchy, but capable of levying a curse on subsistence crop production even when she is defeated and subordinated. Notably, Green Revolution production seems to have even defeated her power to curse! In this respect, the campaign for women's land rights, whose small but geographically widespread steps were first taken by the men and women of the Shetkari Sanghatana, represented in the modern period a collective move toward the empowerment of women, toward reversing the ancient enslavement. By 1991 the connection of this with a new direction of development could be seen as Shetkari Sanghatana adopted an official policy of farming with as little use as possible of expensive external inputs such as chemical fertilizers and pesticides. As part of this "new direction," described by Sharad Joshi as the "direction of the kingdom of Bali," the lands held by women were to be called the "Sita lands" and farmed in an updated traditional manner, with local inputs and with an orientation to providing the subsistence needs of the household. Women in the farmers' movement were thus linked with an important new ecological direction taken by the movement as a whole, as they had been linked with a growing push for alternative development in other social movements of the period.

10

The Search for Alternatives

THE TREND of "women's power" coming forward in mass movements was not only part of a growing challenge to the path of development represented by both the Indian elite and the models of socialism of the traditional left; it was also a challenge to the methods Marxists had come to think essential for revolutionary social change. Feminist activists were grappling with the question of revolutionary violence and its relation to the violence they confronted in all spheres of life, with the murder of Rajani Thiranagama exemplifying this dilemma. In the process, they were identifying with a model of nonviolent but militant mass popular action for change. In India nonviolence had been associated with Mahatma Gandhi and through Gandhian influence had been largely inherited by the environmental movement, but in the dalit movement also, Ambedkar had identified himself firmly with nonviolent action, linking it with his posing of Buddhism as an alternative to Communism, while the farmers' movement, while disassociating itself from Gandhian religiosity, affirmed an allegiance to nonviolence as a strategy, not as a "principle." All these movements used a wide variety of militant, law-defying strategies of action but distinguished themselves from strategies based on "taking up the gun."

Yet nonviolence was increasingly under pressure in India, and although the new social movements held to it as a movement method, more and more discontented youth seemed ready to take up the gun, and guerrilla struggles were becoming more pervasive then ever before in the country's history. In Kashmir, the long-existing Jammu and Kashmir Liberation Front (JKLF) found its general policy of independence and "Islamic socialism" being challenged by fundamentalist and pro-Pakistani guerrilla organizations as both grew in the face of state repression. In Assam the nonviolent but militant "Assam movement," having impotently come to power in the government, was superseded by the underground United Liberation Front of Asom (ULFA), which aimed at independence through armed struggle. In Tamilnadu the Liberation Tigers of Tamil Eelam (LTTE) were outfighting or at least standing off both the Sri Lanka government and the Indian "peacekeeping" force and slaughtering rival liberation groups in the process. In Punjab the Khalistani guerrillas continued to hold sway in the countryside; in the northeast Nagas, Mizos, Manipuris (Meiteis), and others maintained an armed presence in coalition with similar groups in minority regions of Burma.

The situation in India by the late 1980s seemed to have gone far beyond what journalist-political scientist Selig Harrison had once described as "India's most dangerous decades," but by this time the public had seemingly become inured, and the military machine of the state could keep resources flowing from turmoil-stricken areas. In the context of the growing crisis of socialism and the increasing fundamentalist tone to the movements, they also could not catch hold of the imagination of youth throughout India.

There was one internal guerrilla struggle that did, however, project a different image, and that was the "People's War Group" (PWG). This was the biggest Naxalite group still clinging to an armed struggle orientation, and while IPF-"Liberation" was taking its dalit landless laborer base in Bihar into the political sphere through the mediation of open political fronts, PWG was mobilizing a similar base, though with a stronger tribal component, in Andhra and the mainly tribal bordering areas of Maharashtra (Gadchiroli) and Madhya Pradesh (Bastar district). Whereas the IPF was moving toward more conventional left politics not only in the electoral sense but also in its policies of concentrating a mass movement against price rise and for the "right to work," the PWG continued to struggle for land as the central revolutionary goal.

PWG heroism had a strong appeal to the youth of Andhra, and even its late 1980s tactics of fighting state repression through the kidnapping of low-level (and occasionally high-level) bureaucrats actually won some admiration from sections of the rural masses who normally experienced these as oppressors. By 1989 the PWG and its related mass organizations were forcibly banned from holding open meetings but had developed a solid base in the rural areas of many Telengana districts. During the elections they surreptitiously supported Congress against N. T. Rama Rao, who had stepped up policies of repression against them after originally praising them as "patriots." When Congress came to power in the state, they were rewarded by a new policy of relaxed police pressure, and their mass fronts came strongly into the open with a series of mass demonstrations, rallies, cultural programs, land seizures for the rural poor, and bandhs on issues of the peasantry (such as provision of electricity and remunerative prices) and the "backward classes" (support for the Mandal Commission).

PWG, then, was on the upsurge by 1990. Its famed dalit singer, Gadar, was drawing crowds of hundreds of thousands in Andhra and impressive showings in other parts of India. Its village squads were asserting themselves, running people's courts, collecting money from businessmen, forcing government bureaucrats to register land in the name of the landless, erecting impressive monuments to fallen martyrs. Yet the world had moved a long way from the "new left upsurge" of the original Naxalite movement, and in the era of the "fall of communism" in Europe and the proclaimed triumph of liberalism and consumerism, even the rural masses in Andhra itself were putting a different stamp on the movement.

The localized successes themselves were demonstrating the way in which new questions were being raised. Take the issue of land. "Agrarian revolution," giving land to the landless, had always been the central plank of Naxalite and other Communist programs, and the PWG had undoubtedly seen its sponsoring of struggles on issues of crop prices and reservations as secondary, tactical maneuvers. The land program was central: they had been organizing struggles around it on a low-key basis for decades, and now they took it up openly in thousands of villages.

Problems immediately became apparent. First was that of availability of land. Taking land only from "big landlords," leaving aside the "rich peasants" who might have had a few extra acres but were not to be antagonized at this time, yielded relatively few acres per village. Noting that a few thousand acres in five districts represented a "modest" overall achievement, PWG sympathizer Balagopal argued that "the scare this has created among the exploiting classes is less a measure of the achievement than an indication of the impossibility of a peaceful solution of the land question."[1] But this begged the question of the availability of the land, at a time when some scholars were wondering if (at least by normal farming methods) the possibilities of land reform were getting "exhausted," that there was simply not enough land to satisfy all the landless. And the "land question," in the era of environmentalism and the issue of farm prices, was revealing itself as more than that of giving land to people; it was also one of what was to be done with the land once it had been won.

For instance, a December 1990 *Times of India* article, "Madiga Mallaiah Inherits the Earth," described the joy of an old dalit when given an acre of land. Estimating at first that with a crop of groundnuts he could make Rs. 5,000, his imagination begins to soar: the PWG had promised water and pumpsets, "in which case he could grow anything he wished! Chillies! Tomatoes! Cotton! Rs. 30,000 a year!"[2] Mallaiah's dreams of prosperity had many illusions behind them, but they showed the deep penetration of development ideology. The PWG armed squads seemed to be thinking along the same lines.

To this can be added the fact that in contrast to the thousands of acres of excess land being taken over, in Khamman district tribals under PWG leadership had gained control of 80,000 acres of what was classified as "forest lands."[3] This was simply an acceleration of what was happening throughout India's forest areas, as tribal peasants desperate to manage their livelihoods seized lands for cultivation, under the leadership of Naxalites, of groups such as Jharkhand Mukti Morcha, or on their own. But forest land seized or excess land given in small amounts to landless low castes raised immediately the issue of how the land was to be cultivated: in the late 1980s, in contrast to earlier periods, occupiers were confronted immediately with either getting absorbed into "Green Revolution" developmentalism and dependence on inputs and the market or formulating some really effective alternative. Traditional subsistence agriculture, without political and technological support, and measures to restore the environment that had made it possible in the past, was no longer a viable prospect, and both peasant awareness of the ambiguities of GR technology and the environmental critique were becoming widespread enough to make left programs of simply "providing inputs" look a bit dated. The PWG leadership may well have considered that this was not an immediate problem because of their expectations of a renewed state onslaught, but the logic of their movement was leading them in new directions.

The logic of people's aspirations in a new era was operating at another level too, and that was among the boys joining the armed squads. It seems clear that throughout India at this time, village youth were becoming less and less enthusiastic about working the land at all; even the Maharashtra Shetkari Sanghatana's 1990 election postmortem brought forth many arguments that young people were simply not concerned about prices, that they wanted only to get away from the villages or get jobs. In Andhra too, while the aged Mallaiah got land, his grandsons were very likely getting guns. A *Frontline* article argued that the "'Rambo' culture is spreading . . . if not the easy money, the aura and power that a gun-toting Naxalite has these days is perhaps too tempting for the young villagers, the unemployment problem being what it is."[4] This was undoubtedly too cynical, because for the low castes in particular, the question of power within the village was one of dignity and identity itself. Nevertheless it pointed to problems, especially for the women who ordinarily claimed neither guns nor land. There were complaints that the armed squads were deciding many cases of family and sexual relations brought before them in quite conventional and male chauvinist ways, there was a frustration with the infighting among the various Naxalite groups, and there was some disgust with the violent retaliation used against suspected informers.

Whether its new collective access to land and power was temporary or not, it is clear that the PWG, most "fundamentalist" of Naxalite groups, was by 1990 being confronted with the new dilemmas of development and changing aspirations of the rural poor.

"Take Up the Red-Green Flag"

> Take the fantasy out of your daydreams
> what will happen
> from simply waving the red flag
> over the many colors of reality
> in showing the way to violent revolution
> take care of your own existence
> comrade.

Prabhakar Gangurde's poem, expressing a new dalit self-confidence in challenging Naxalite claims to revolutionary purity, was also a critique of the "monocolor" character of Indian communism, its tendency to ignore "nonclass" issues.

Politics is strongly color-oriented in India. Banners, flags, armbands, caps, often entire uniforms are used to express a political orientation. The rise of religious fundamentalism has been linked with saffron; the hegemony of Marxism over antisystemic movements has been reflected in the predominance of red. Women at the Patna conference expressed their specific identity with a purple banner, while historically the dalit movement was the first to take up an alternative color, using a blue flag.

Green came first to India not as the color of environmentalists but as a symbol of the peasantry. The Jharkhand Mukti Morcha had used a green flag; it was also used by most of the new peasant organizations as well as by politicians like Devi Lal of Haryana, aspiring for recognition as peasant spokesmen. Attempts to "combine colors" also appeared but without much success. The early Jharkhand movement was marked by the mixture of red and green, but later Jharkhandis rejected this policy of alliance with workers and by implication with Marxists for "green-only." Conversely, there were proposals at IPF's second conference in Calcutta for a red-green flag to symbolize its worker-peasant base, but this was rejected for "red only" out of a fear of weakening proletarian vanguardism. The Shetkari Sanghatana expressed a combined orientation in a red badge and a flag half-green, half-white with the red symbol at its center (and, as a woman activist said, "the red represents the blood shed by those martyred during the movement"), but this was never practically embodied in a worker-peasant alliance. The difficulty of color combination was indicative both of party sectarianism and the single-issue orientation of the new movements.

But there was one organization that from the beginning consciously used a red-green flag, built worker-peasant unity, and by the late 1980s was moving to give a new meaning to "green" itself. This was the Chattisgarh Mukti Morcha (CMM), based among low-caste and tribal peasants in Madhya Pradesh. Like the JMM, it represented a combination of mine workers and the surrounding peasantry articulated around a regional autonomy demand; it differed in being focused around the charismatic leadership of a single individual, Shankar Guha Niyogi.

In 1977 nearly 10,000 workers left a CPI-led union in the iron ore mines supplying the huge public-sector Bhilai steel plant in protest against the party's lack of militancy during the Emergency and its refusal to protest the jailing of their leader, Niyogi. In the post-Emergency tumult, militant strikes of their newly formed Chattisgarh Mines Shramik Sangh (CMSS) resulted in two incidents of police firing that left numerous workers dead. But beyond militancy, CMSS also sought to be a kind of "social movement union" with efforts to fight drunkenness among workers (by, for instance, turning over their paychecks directly to their wives) and organizing a union-run hospital.[5] Then in 1979 Niyogi and the worker-activists made their major political thrust with the formation of the CMM, centered around the demand for a separate Chattisgarhi state: "This campaign will incorporate the programs of revolutionary trade union activities, boycott of alcoholism, the peasant and land questions, the question of the price of forest produce, the question of educational and health services, struggles against every type of oppression, especially against the oppression of women."[6]

This was how Niyogi put it in 1982, and it already involved efforts to unify the working class movement with the women's movement and the price issues raised by farmers' organizations (Niyogi in fact joined rallies with Sharad Joshi and took part in the Kisan Coordinating Committee). A separate Chattisgarh Mahila Mukti Morcha was formed in 1980, and although it apparently had only a shadowy existence after that, a number of strong working-class women activists did develop with the CMSS. The movement also sought to project a new cultural identity for Chattisgarh in the celebration of a nineteenth-century tribal chieftain–freedom fighter, Vir Narayan Singh. Politically, it was becoming one of the few movement forces in this economically and politically backward central Indian state.

By the late 1980s the peasant base of the CMM was pushing in even newer directions. Chattisgarh, once considered a "rice bowl" of Madhya Pradesh, was becoming drought-prone, pushing migrant labor out to Nagpur and beyond. Fighting a series of splits and setbacks, the CMM organized a September 1989 workshop at Raipur that brought together four hundred participants, mainly workers and peasants, to discuss the need to formulate and fight for alternatives in all areas—land, agriculture, water, forestry, industry. And a fifty thousand-strong rally on October 2 put forward a wide-ranging program of concrete cultural and economic developmental measures, including the construction of small "stop dams" as opposed to large dam projects, repairing small ponds, stopping the mechanization of iron ore mines, raising the price of paddy, using local languages rather than Sanskritized Hindi in the schools, and opening hospitals and technical training institutions.[7]

"What has development meant to us? Bhilai steel plant is a national showpiece—and it has grabbed all the water from the peasants!" This was a period in which "alternative development" was becoming a slogan in the environmental movement. The concrete experiences of Chattisgarh workers and peasants were showing them the exploitation and marginalization created by the dominant model, and leading them to combine the insights of diverse social movements. An article on the Raipur rally in the *Economic and Political Weekly* tried to contrast its "workers and peasants" to the "kulaks" gathered in the big farmers' movement rally on the same day at Delhi, which had ended in a split.[8] But for the Chattisgarhi poor, the prices of rice and forest produce were issues along with drought and the monopolization of water by industry; the accumulation of capital symbolized by Bhilai was linked to the marginalization they were suffering.

"Alternative development" from below was taking on new meaning and becoming a major organizational threat to the ruling elite of the backward state of Madhya Pradesh.

Mukti Sangarsh: "The Whipcord of the Peasants"

The Chattisgarh peasants had argued for small "stop dams" instead of large irrigation projects. But dams built by peasants themselves as a part of a movement to eradicate drought were a threat to state-capitalist exploitation of people's labor and resources, as shown by the saga of a peasant struggle in Maharashtra that actually did center around the building of a small dam.

The organization leading the struggle, Mukti Sangarsh, short for Shoshit Shetkari Kamgar Kashtakari Mukti Sangarsh ('Exploited Peasants', Workers', Toilers' Liberation Struggle'), had grown in southern Maharashtra following the 1982 textile strike. This region—Sangli, Satara, and Kolhapur districts—had a history of radical democratic movements, ranging from Phule's early Satyashodhak movement to a peasant uprising against brahmans and landlords in 1920, to an underground "parallel government" formed during the climax of India's freedom fight from 1942–1946. After independence its Krishna river valley area became a center for Maharashtra's most famous cash crop, sugarcane, and for the impressive cooperative sugar factories that arose in the fields to process cane for peasants and accumulate power and wealth for local bosses. So strong was this base that the Shetkari Sanghatana never managed to penetrate the region. Yet discontent gradually accumulated also, and it was channeled by drought and the textile strike.

Mukti Sangarsh had two roots. One was in these struggles of the local peasantry, historically and directly in recent upsurges led by activists of the Peasants' and Workers' Party such as Raosaheb Shinde and Sampatrao Pawar, who had brought peasants with bullock carts full of cane to blockade roads in protest over the refusal of a local factory to process the cane. The textile strike and the decades of experience of peasant workers with Bombay life were part of this process. Indeed, this engaged them in the developmental ideology and its critique, for it was a habit of Bombay workers to invest in small projects in their home villages; now, with their long sojourn at home during the strike, the continuing backwardness of the villages was impressed upon them.

Another base of Mukti Sangarsh was the new questioning among young Marxist activists. In Maharashtra, reactions against Leninist centralism and party sectarianism had not taken the extreme antiorganizational form seen in Bengal. Rather, "new" organizations grew up that sought to reconcile a Communist or socialist thrust with emphasis on new issues. Among these was the Shramik Mukti Dal (SMD), founded in 1980 partly as an offshoot of the Magowa group joined by activists of cultural and street theater groups. The name, which means "Workers' Liberation League," was conventional, and so was the firm "class" line of interpreting Indian society as capitalist-dominated. But added to this was a strong emphasis on patriarchy, caste, and culture. Very rapidly, SMD activists working in Bombay, Belgaum, and Sangli districts began to take ecological issues quite seriously, while a group of tribal activists from the old Shramik Sanghatana in Dhule who joined it as a counterweight to CPI(M) added their own emphasis on adivasi values and culture. From the beginning, significantly, the organization never built a functioning "democratic centralist" structure—which gave it a laxness but at the same time help prevent it from splitting as it began to experience the buffetings of changing perspectives and new experiences. "We're too loose to split," as activist Shriharsh Kanhere put it.

Bharat Patankar, a leading SMD activist, went from the Bombay textile areas to work in rural Sangli and played a leading role in the formation of Mukti Sangarsh. Relatives, including his mother Indumati, an old freedom fighter, cousin Jayant Nikam, and wife Gail Omvedt, also became active. But there were other important "outsiders" in the movement: there were Joy and Mani, one from a poor Kerala Christian family, the other from a Delhi-based family of government employees, social-work graduates who transferred from an NGO to this resolutely antifunding group. There was also Gauri, a woman activist from a poor Calcutta family, and her friend Jogin Sen Gupta, a wandering offspring of the 1960s Bengal upsurge who spent long periods in Kasegaon, recovering from psychological depression, studying medicine, reading anthropology and politics, developing an enthusiasm for hunter-gatherer societies, and discussing contemporary feminist revolution.

Economic struggles of Mukti Sangarsh were centered around government work schemes (Maharashtra's famous rural job program, the Employment Guarantee Scheme), including demands to set up more projects as well as for providing facilities for women and child care. But from the beginning the perspective was not simply of "drought relief," a common theme of popular struggles of the time, but *eradicating drought*, restoring the fertility of the soil, replenishing the land. Though many of the SMD-connected organizers started with the framework of "class divisions among the peasantry" that led them to try to build agricultural labor unions and only then form "alliances with the middle peasantry," none of these took off, and the Mukti Sangarsh movement instead developed, after the textile strike, as an "all-peasant movement," though with an emphasis on the poor and on issues of equality.

The input of peasant experience pushed this process forward. In a 1984 *vidnyan yatra*, peasants and agricultural laborers argued with young urban science students about the earlier "plentiful rainfall" in their area. They joined in a Mukti Sangarsh campaign to survey rivers and wells in the taluka, with findings (hundreds of dried-up wells) that made it clear that the then conventional "development" activity of digging wells to help farmers resist drought and share in Green Revolution benefits had inherent limitations as water tables fell; that only an alternative that restored ground water could solve problems. Out of the survey came a booklet, *Shetkaryaca Asud* (Whipcord of the peasants), named after Phule's old polemic and putting forward proposals for numerous village-based reconstruction projects—small dams, percolation tanks, etc.—and low-water-using cropping patterns. It was a kind of embryonic "people's plan" for the area and was used as the basis for an October 1985 conference on "Drought Eradication."

At the same time, SMD networks connected Sangli peasants with a wider political environment. Campaigns on the Bhopal issue, on the Mathura and other rape cases, an anticaste "Phule-Ambedkar Vichar Yatra" organized in 1984, performances by Bombay street theater groups, visits to Dhule, Chattisgarh, and elsewhere were among many activities. In August 1985 a women's Stri Mukti Sangarsh was formed, and its policy of autonomy gradually began to be realized in practice as it expanded activities to cover talukas of Sangli and Satara districts that were outside the scope of Mukti Sangarsh itself. In October 1985 peasants proclaimed their new relationship to the "world of knowledge" when they demonstrated at the local university at Kolhapur with the demand that either the university do research on drought "or we'll go into the library and do our own research." One of their songs on drought mocked the "rock-breaking" work of the government relief schemes, contrasting the glitter of city life and the useless store of academic knowledge:

> Pick and shovel, iron platter,
> We're paving the taluka with roads.
> Drought is hanging on our backs . . .
> The storage of knowledge at the university,
> the colors of disco are growing
> and drought is hanging on our backs . . .

It was on this background that Bharat Patankar was writing his reassessments of the Communist movement, looking at the issues raised by the new social movements and arguing for the generalization of Marx's recognition that the working class could not simply take over the existing state and use it for its own purposes but rather had to construct a new form of state: it was not only necessary to have collective ownership or "working-class control" of the political system; the entire industrial system had to be reconstructed and not simply taken over for "socialist" development. This meant dealing with the full range of ecological insights:

> As a result of our experiences in movements, our discussions with men and women, our relationship with workers, the knowledge about new movements in America and Europe and our ideological orientation certain basic perspectives have emerged. The existence of humans on this earth is neither one-sided nor is it isolated from the rest of nature. Humans share an interlinked and collective existence with the atmosphere, water, rain, trees, jungles, rivers,

hills, other animals, birds, insects, worms, germs, the sun, the moon, the solar system and so on. Those components live in a symbiotic and harmonious balance existing in nature. At the same time there are also relations which may prove mutually destructive. Human society can advance only on the basis of all these realities and the healthy development of the interrelationships. If "development" ignores this close relationship and instead destroys it, it will eventually serve to destroy humankind along with nature.[9]

"Eradicating drought" thus led to a whole realm of what might otherwise be called "socialist construction." The central slogan of the early days of the movement posed the radical goal of abolishing drought as such against the "relief perspective" embodied in the EGS work schemes: *khadi amhi phodnar nahi, rasta amhi sandnar sandnar nahi, dushkal ghalavlyashivay rahnar nahi*—(we will not break rocks, we will not lay roads, we will not stop without throwing away drought!). It was in a sense a challenge to the traditional left practice of simply mobilizing people during drought for relief, and to the current slogan of "right to work" as a panacea for the poor. Strikingly, it was taken up most enthusiastically by the women of Stri Mukti Sangarsh and generalized from their local antidrought struggles to larger joint activities of the women's movement.

"If Peasants Build Their Own Dams, What Would the State Have Left to Do?"

Balawadi and Tandulwadi in 1986: two villages of drought-stricken Khanapur taluka. Twenty miles away, below the plateau, the Krishna River runs its course through lush fields of sugar cane in the center of Sangli district, foundation of the power and wealth of the "sugar barons" and the gaudy promises of Green Revolution development. But the fields of Balawadi and Tandulwadi were cracked and barren, its river the Yerala dry for eleven months of the year. Now the peasants of the villages had little to do but work on the "rock-breaking" EGS schemes they despised or get occasional jobs such as working for the contractors who were mining sand from their dried-up river bed.

Mining sand! Now that was an irony—making profit out of drought. The peasants, who had been involved in the struggles and alternative planning efforts of Mukti Sangarsh, mulled this over in their late-night discussions. They were also becoming aware of what these changes were doing to village social life: replacing the normal rhythms of agriculture by flows of cash from meaningless labor, flows too easily convertible to drink rather then food. As some pointed out, mining the sand could itself have a negative effect on the soil's absorptive capacity. "If we could get water for our fields . . . "

"If we could build a dam . . . " We, peasants and agricultural laborers themselves? This was unheard of. Who would design it, who would provide expert help? Above all, where would the money come from? Then the two problems came together: before them was the answer. The sand mining was but one instance of the way that wealth that rightfully belonged to the villages, from the products of peasant labor to the resources of the land, was extracted to serve the chain of contractors, businessmen, bureaucrats, and leaders who fattened on the misery of the poor. Why should sand belong to the state to let officials auction it to contractors at high profit? Why not to the people themselves? "Give us the rights to the sand and we will build a dam!"

This was the beginning of a four-year-long struggle. Finding "expertise" to design the dam was not so difficult, for K. R. Datye, a noted engineer from Bombay, had already developed an association with projects based on local initiative. Nor was it difficult to convince the peasants about "equal water distribution": the principle water from the dam should be used for ecologically sustainable agriculture and distributed on an equitable basis that included shares for women and landless labor.

The obstacle, of course, was the state. On the one hand, there were the interests of contractors and bureaucrats, from irrigation department engineers to the main officials of the district, all those involved in tapping the flow of surplus. They stalled, either by raising technical objections or by simple government fiat, giving the sand out in auction rather than government permits, ignoring Mukti Sangarsh agitations, moving to punish the peasants involved by various kinds of bureaucratic harassment. It was also clear that the very idea of peasants building their own dam as part of a people's movement went against something built into the very heart of the political system. It is reported that in the state cabinet discussion of the issue—after a mass demonstration in which peasants brought their bullock carts to the heart of Sangli city—one minister said, "But if peasants build dams, then what will the state have left to do?" Another joked, "The peasants should build their dams, we can't afford it." Behind the joking was an element of seriousness: development was something done *by* the experts and the state *for* the people. It is striking that objections raised by "mainstream" Communists to such alternative movements was along the same lines: "Why should you get into building dams? That's the work of the government."

The peasants chose as a name for their dam the Bali Raja Memorial Dam. Bali Raja, it may be recalled, was the king idealized in peasant culture who had been "sent under the earth" by the brahman boy Waman. In southern states like Kerala, the major postharvest festival, Onam, was celebrated supposedly to commemorate his returning to Earth for a day of happiness and plenty; while Maharashtrian peasants still used the slogan *ida pida javo, Balica rajya yevo* (let troubles and sorrows go and the kingdom of Bali come), Bali had been taken as the major symbol of the oppressed shudra-dalit peasantry in Phule's interpretation of the Aryan-brahman conquest. The story was given a thrust against the current exploitative state-industrial society, and women of Stri Mukti Sangarsh took this up when, in 1987, they held a ceremony as part of an agitation for drinking water for villages to "hang Waman in effigy" as representing the deceptive, repressive state and its bureaucrats.

In this way the effort of peasants to build a dam developed into a broad popular movement directed against the contemporary state. Indeed, the fact that a proposal for a small dam irrigating nine hundred acres in two villages had to be fought all the way up to the state government level showed how such issues were threatening some basic economic interests. Against these the Sangli peasants built alliances, with left and democratic parties in the district, with workers in Bombay, with middle-class sympathizers in Pune, with local students and professors who provided support committees and voluntary labor in "national service scheme" camps, even getting the help of Shetkari Sanghatana's Sharad Joshi to initiate government discussions (characteristically, he expressed his support for the idea that peasants should control local resources like sand and forests—and his skepticism about the viability of the plans for equal water distribution).

When by 1990 the dam was nearly completed, Mukti Sangarsh moved to another level to confront a larger scheme already planned by the government with a people's alternative. A medium-scale irrigation project (worth Rs 300 crores) to lift water from the Krishna River to irrigate the drought-prone talukas of Sangli had been on the drawing board for years. Ironically (or perhaps not), this "development" proposed to give water to only 8 villages fully and 22 partially, out of 108 water-starved villages in Khanapur taluka. Backed up by the Bali Raja experience and experiments they had carried out on ecologically sustainable, needs-oriented, biomass-based agriculture, Mukti Sangarsh made an alternative proposal that would provide minimum water to all families of 60 villages, enough to irrigate three acres each in a plan providing fodder, fuel, grain, vegetables, and fruit trees that could be used to earn some cash. And they organized consciousness-raising *padyatras*, poster exhibits, conferences, *rasta rokos*, and other demonstrations over their demands.

In spite of local harassments, the campaign went on. Mukti Sangarsh had from the beginning adopted the slogan of the textile workers: "Who says they won't give it? We won't stop without taking it!" and for the Ganpati religious festival in 1990 they showed their feminism and emphasis on popular action with an exhibit on a Wardha woman who had single-handedly whipped the district collector during an independence day ceremony in protest against the refusal of the government to do anything about the grabbing of a small plot of land. The Sangli collector slapped a defamation case against them; efforts to hold a "people's court" on the Takari scheme in May 1991 were banned on the excuse that it was whipping up tensions during elections. Leading activists were arrested. "How can we negotiate with them?" queried the collector, "they've got 'struggle' in their name!"

Local Naxalites occasionally charged that the nonviolent mass struggle of such groups as Mukti Sangarsh, and of the environmental movement in general, was that of "eunuchs." At one level their campaigns seemed all low-key compared to the murders, kidnappings, and armed defiance of the state going on in parts of Andhra, even in the forests of eastern Maharashtra, not to mention Punjab and Assam. But the struggles were confrontational mass struggles and there was a growing confidence among activists that they were on the right path, even if it was taking them in directions that had earlier been stigmatized in the left movement as "Gandhian." The "kingdom of Bali," after all, was not necessarily to be won by the methods of Chanakya.

"The Primary Terrain of Resistance"

Lying behind all of these new movements to formulate and practice alternatives was a process of popular assertion. By the late 1980s this was expressed not only in urges to be a part of the apparent prosperity and undeniable glitter of capitalist development, but also in a rejection of its marginalizing processes and a quest to transcend them. There was in fact, argued Jogin Sen Gupta, one of the people's theorists of the period, a "primary terrain of resistance," the "fundamental" movement that was an effort by toiling people to build new forms of cooperation and new democratic control in the process of their daily lives.

Jogin had been a participant in the 1960s' Bengal upsurge, and like so many of this generation, he was alienated by the sectarianism and infighting of revolutionary left politics, which led to mutual murders as each organization tried to establish its hegemony, laying the whole movement open to state repression.

> Communist parties became fetishes. . . . In 1972 . . . I was already shattered by this problem. We joined the movement to help each other to live in "anti-capitalist" ways, to become more human, to struggle against the forces of dehumanisation. In 1968–71, to my horror, I saw the opposite happening inside the movement. Manipulation, empowerment, utilisation was dominating our behavior towards each other. And this made us so petty and blind that we managed to destroy the whole movement in Bengal. So I too, as so many of us do now and then, turned to *Capital* to find an explanation. I found nothing! Thus Marx not only fails to go to the roots of this "fetish" but today most of the old Marxist-Leninist movements have become fossilized, fetishes in the world. Rather we are living in an era when people are successfully struggling against those! Only after I got a chance to learn from the insights of the "new movements" since 1960s could I understand how Marx relates to our needs.[10]

Young activists of Jogin's type stayed out of Communist parties and organizations, but continued to take part in movements, in people's science in Bengal, in workers' and nationality struggles in Jharkhand, in rehabilitation efforts in Bhopal. Jogin wandered among them, a nomadic activist, participating in campaigns and holding endless discussions with activists. Like many, he discovered first feminism and then the new model of human history expressed in "indigenous people's movements." These provided basic themes of his understanding:

My antihistory teachers tell me that capitalism is only the third counterrevolution that has hit humankind.... After a few million years of free and egalitarian existence, the first, patriarchal counterrevolution hit us only ten to thirty thousand years ago. It is called the Neolithic Revolution by intellectuals conned by civilization. This dealt a crushing blow to the "production for enjoyment" mode of life, put women as the breeders, and started the ball rolling. This could not go far as the free people were too many and too strong then. Then came the Second, the Statist counterrevolution.... Patriarchy took off with the state, and together they launched a powerful assault on the free people. Within three thousand years they dominated the globe. Growth of "private property" was only another basic aspect of this process. It was neither the main nor central to the growth of civilization. On this soil started the Third, the industrial counterrevolution that made mincemeat of the world. It flew the flag of private property originally. It was a leap as well as a continuation of the "civilization." In only three hundred years its momentum has brought us today ten minutes from a very real hell!

Taking "patriarchy" as primary implied for Jogin, just as for feminists, the thesis that underlying all forms of domination and exploitation were oppressive relations of daily life, "deeply hidden in the subterranean spaces of human relations and fossilized into perfectly 'normal' conventions," as he put it. It implied also that the beginnings of the fight against oppression lay in practices of cooperation and resistance in daily life.

Problems of human relations—man-woman relations, sexuality, family, relations with comrades—were questions troubling not only Jogin but a large collection of diffuse left circles throughout the country. Sometimes their search was interpreted in terms of sexual freedom; often the fascination with "feminism" was quite compatible with ignoring the basic insights of feminism about such material realities of daily life as participation in housework; sometimes the hatred of "patriarchal organization" led to a disturbing irresponsibility in organizational matters. But the broad process of rethinking was creating a new activist subculture in India, a widespread network of young men and women who continued to be involved in people's movements, who attempted to break through sectarian barriers, theorizing some of the new social movements from a basis of participation rather than that of an institutionally based elite trying to affect them. Their reflex reaction against discipline was frustrating to many, but their concern for change made them a part of the ferment of the period.

To Jogin, the fate of "Communist" societies in Eastern Europe, so disturbing to traditional Marxists, was a sign of hope. Vanguard parties, while proclaiming their effectivity, had in fact led the opposition movements into the trap of trying to oppose an exploitative system by creating organizations and societies in the image of the oppressor; that these were now getting shattered was a sign of a wide and deeply based popular upsurge, rooted in new processes of democratic assertion at the very base.

It would have been really quite depressing if the "free world" was not getting a worse beating by the democracy movement—from Africa to Latin America! Militarism is the worst form of plunder and domination. So the peace movement is a struggle for socialism. Autocracy—whatever be its color—stands for curbing the bottom peoples' right to associate, assert and build up their power. So a movement against authoritarianism—whatever be its color—is building up people's capacity for socialism. Thus, instead of the label, we look for the contents, and instead of looking for the "pure" and full-fledged form, we look for the ingredients and pieces, we find Socialism emerging as a deep global tradition. . . . Strangely, it was when the black sun— the rampaging monster of global militarism was the highest, the sixty-year-long relative defeat and paralysis of humanity started breaking up.

Jogin was insisting that the new movements were basically liberatory, and that their loose interconnections were much more fruitful than the traditional vanguard ways of organizing. "In the 1960s, enormous areas of activism and their interconnections became 'visible,' " as women, tribals, blacks, colored, lower castes, peasants, gays, and lesbians fought their battles and found new ways of collaboration.

Thus we had a world where African tribals were able to collaborate with Latin American tribal-peasants and European workers, women and peace movements! Alliance leading to strengths and wisdom never before available to the bottom peoples. The forms of its expression were of course as varied as the people—Christian socialism, feminism, pacifism, indigenous liberation, proletarian socialism, even "scientific socialism." But all were collaborating in defending humanity, to build up respect and power and democracy of the oppressed.

The contemporary era was seen as one in which "the nonvanguardist, predominant informal peoples' cooperation-based strivings" have "saved the world—by breaking the Nuclear cold war tension centre in Europe, by overthrowing the worst of the despotisms and militarisms in the 'third world' and the 'socialist bloc.' " Not vanguardist tendencies, but informal networks; not armed "liberation struggles," but popular upsurges; not the purely political, but the daily-life-based cooperative practices were the keys to the future. This process of cooperation and democratic action by ordinary people in everyday life was, according to Jogin, the "primary" social movement, the force behind the others:

First and at the largest terrain of resistance was the ordinary people with their ordinary acts who started to claw onto the stage of history . . . the power of the global establishment lies in its ability to interconnect, intensify all different modes of inequalities, distorted cooperations—between classes and communities, men and women, down to households and interpersonal relations. Similarly, the movement for communism consists of the opposite—the intersupport, cooperation, practically and in changing our desires, against all those toxic practices.

In this view, the new era of the 1990s was one in which capitalism continued to survive, but its militarist forms had suffered a major setback. The "new carrots of capitalist hegemony," the lure of consumerist democracy, continued to operate, but a major step forward had been taken—by actions of the masses that outran, and had barely been theorized by, the parties and organizations of the left that claimed to represent them. If the weapons of the state were the percolation of power and privilege and the stabilization of hierarchies to co-opt democratic initiatives, the movements in contrast should support people's actions to reduce the power of the state and of the control of resources by a small minority, and work at the same time to reduce unequal access to power and wealth among the people themselves. That this process was already going on, that it lay behind the upsurges that upset the traditional left, that were producing the new social movements and shaking established regimes, was one of Jogin's major arguments.

"Alternative Technological Horizons"

The masses "clawing their way onto the stage of history," the leaping forward of women, dalits, tribals, and peasants expressing their identities and fighting their exploitation in the new social movements were all phenomena of the 1970s and 1980s. Behind them, it could be argued, were some important technological changes, that is, changes in the very forces of production themselves.

Technology has often been viewed in negative terms, as both patriarchal and oppressive, by many in the women's movement and the environmental movement. Yet there were ways in which some of the new technologies were providing the material base for the new movements.

Communications technologies, for example, made possible a widespread awareness, reaching to even remote villages through radios and television, video and cinema, of the kind of new consumer goods and life-style made possible in the cities and centers of "civilization." Transportation technologies made it possible for people to do something about this: where villages had, say at the time of the Russian Revolution, been genuinely isolated and only the working class had a collective life in huge factories and urban centers, now it was a realistic campaign for hundreds of thousands of peasants from all over a state or even the country, to crowd on trains or hire trucks to stage rallies in massive numbers. Guerrillas could ride on bicycles or motorcycles and communicate with walkie-talkies; "liberation" movements could circulate videocassettes. Village women getting Rs 50–200 a month as "honoraria" for nursery school teaching could go without-ticket to Delhi to press their demands; tribals could gather for popular festivals.

People were planning their struggles as excursions also. "You want to organize women to fight communalism?" queried one peasant met on a train on his without-ticket way to the big farmers' rally in Delhi: "Just plan huge rallies and let them travel all over the country." He himself was part of a group of twenty-three village men and women, mostly caste Hindus but including one or two dalits and Muslims, that had taken off for Delhi "with a detour through Varanasi," combining their struggle with sightseeing. Indeed, probably every mass agitational campaign in this period assumed that those involved in marches, demonstrations, suffering the discomforts and willing to endure even clashes with the police would also be taking the opportunity to do what they could of the low-caste Indian's version of tourism. Their ability to go long distances, as well as coordinate actions, was in crucial ways related to technological developments.

One of those involved in practicing and theorizing technology at this time was K. R. Datye, the Bombay engineer who had designed the Bali Raja dam. Datye, then in his sixties and working at the time as an independent consultant, had been interested in alternative development since the 1950s when he had had a fascination with the Gandhian *gramdan* (village gift) movement and with Mao's cooperatives ("but they didn't have the technology for decentralization then; we do"); he had also been a sympathizer of the post-1960s' rural movements in Maharashtra.

Now, as these movements themselves began to be concerned with alternative development, he started to take a leading role in formulating its technological foundations. A number of younger ex-movement activists began to work in his organization, the Centre for Applied Systems Analysis in Development (CASAD), including Suhas Paranjpye, the former Magowa-Shramik Sanghatana activist who had authored the controversial Marathi version of *Capital*. CASAD began to carry on experiments in wasteland development, based on low water and chemical input-using biomass production, and it began to formulate plans for the actual material production (crops, building materials, poultry, and animals) of tribal villages and gradually whole districts. The idea was to link an agriculture based on "low external inputs" (substituting organic matter and animal manure for chemical fertilizers, local seeds for HYVs, using only small amounts of water) to building and construction that could minimize the use of energy-expensive manufactures through the mixture of biomass inputs.

In 1988 Datye and his colleagues produced a document called "Alternative Technological Horizons"[11] that extended these principles to visualize an all-India economy based on low-energy-using, sustainable agriculture but capable of supporting a population of 1,200 million. It noted,

> In setting up infrastructure, a complete or partial substitution of materials is feasible: steel by fibers, enhancement of cement strength by addition of colloidal silica from biomass sources; reinforced earth structures, . . . replacement of petrochemicals from biomass sources and so on. Through such replacements, both the material and energy inputs into the infrastructure building are drastically reduced and the use of locally produced (biomass) or locally available (earth, stone) materials is increased. . . . The overall cost of infrastructure can be significantly reduced, while increasing local employment. Thus bulk import and transport of materials like steel and cement is reduced. . . . There is an

inverse relationship between transportation needs and communication, so that as the level of communication increases, the need for transportation reduces. Urban commuting will reduce as services and even industrial work can operate through a communication network in the future. With these materials it is possible to build small dams, storages, ponds, tanks, buildings, roads, towers and so on, so that infrastructure building can be undertaken at a local level.

This meant precisely that the type of village-centered and decentralized society being depicted as an alternative to traditional socialism by the new movements was not a backward-looking utopia that stood in opposition to modern technology; rather, it could build on some of the most far-reaching technological developments themselves:

> It is simultaneously necessary to speculate about future lines of development. These point to an increasing use of polymers, carbon fibers from polymers, ceramic precuriers from biomass materials, high strength ceramics replacing iron, steel and other materials and so on. It is our belief that a strong base of biomass production, renewable energy and decentralized industrialization can pave the way for decongestion of cities, dismantling of centralized industries, productive and skilled rural employment along with an end to environmental destruction and a more benign and harmonious collective social life.

Technology, after all, represents in the Marxist paradigm the "new forces of production growing in the womb of the old society," held back by old relations of production. In fact, the new technology itself was pointing forward to a new model of socialism. In a follow-up paper, the CASAD group critiqued both capitalist systems and the planned societies "where the inertia of large bureaucracies hampers improvement of physical and social infrastructure." More important, where traditional Communists were simply asserting that the lessons of the "fall" were those of the necessity of democratizing socialism, that it was not a question of plan *or* market but of "popular control" or "workers' control," what was being projected here was a different model of the production system that was to be controlled.

The new technology, according to CASAD, made possible a socialist society far different from the large-scale collectivism of industrial-based "traditional socialism." It was also one that converged with the "generalization of property" projected at some points by the farmers' movement, though it insisted more strongly on seeking ways to equalize the existing hierarchical village structures. The bulk of the population, in Datye's projected society of 1,200 billion, would live in dispersed habitats, producing mainly for local markets, with the basic needs of food, clothing, and shelter provided by local industries. There would be substantial property in common lands that produced wood, biofuel, fodder, and biofertilizers, and in common workplaces with tools and equipment, fish culture ponds, poultry, nurseries, and so forth, but the "dominant mode of production," according to the paper, "will be commodity production by small farmers and small industries." It was also asserted that for the Third World this was not only a *realistic* model but one made *necessary* by the degradations of current development:

> For the developing countries, the alternative technology paradigm offers the prospect of achieving reasonable consumption levels and rapidly creating adequate infrastructure within a time span of twenty years. This corresponds to energy availability of 1,330 kg.CR per capita. Effectively the consumption level would correspond to that of European society before the second world war. Energy use in developed countries was then around 5,000 kg.CR per capita, but the energy efficiency was lower due to a lot of waste in transportation and defense-industry production. How the developed world will achieve the transition to an equitable and sustainable society is another matter which is outside the purview of this paper, which addresses mainly the problems of the Third World.

The paper did not address problems of political strategy; it continued to be a problem of the CASAD group, which tended to see its small groups of people employed in or connected with alternative development experiments as basic cadres for change. Nor did it deal with the question of exploitation, the relation of surplus extraction to destructive overcentralized technology. But in posing the nature of technology in the way it did, it was providing a powerful weapon for people in the movement dedicated to alternative development. It was not simply a kind of "middle way" between the wholesale rejection of modern technology expressed by many of the neo-Gandhian environmentalists and its uncritical adoption by the traditional Marxist left in the name of "strengthening the nation"; rather, it pointed to the future in offering a new kind of enrichment of human life, not just survival in the face of destructive development. "Technology has the potential for creating the material basis that can sustain the struggle against oppression and exploitation" was its proclamation.

"Clawing onto the Stage of History"

At one end of the chain was the technological base of changes in daily life and organizational life; at the other end were new creations in community and culture. Jogin had written of new movements and new actors leaping onto the stage of history, clawing their way into positions of actors. For many of India's oppressed and low-caste poor, the aspiration and reality of becoming historical *actors* was something new in their lives. More than almost any other society, it seemed that the poor and downtrodden in India were "represented" by others; due to poverty, lack of education, and the rigid social hierarchy, leaders of almost all movements tended to be both upper class and upper caste; many were of people, whether Communists or Gandhians or otherwise, who had sacrificed much for the revolution as they saw it, whose contribution to movements was irreplaceable. But it was very easy to slip into controlling movements, and people were beginning to be skeptical of leaders. A poem by a young tribal activist called "Stage"—referring to the rally platform on which leaders sit—captures the mood:

> We didn't go onto the stage
> Nor were we called
> With a wave of the hand
> We were shown our place. . . .
> They kept on telling us of our sorrows
> Our sorrows remained ours
> They never became theirs
> When we asked a question
> They told us to shut up,
> Or else . . .

The author of "Stage" was a Bhil (one of the largest of the groups classified as "scheduled tribe" in India, with nearly five million scattered through the adjoining districts of the states of Maharashtra, Gujarat, Rajasthan, and Madhya Pradesh), Waharu Sonavane, frail and asthmatic, but a leader of the Shramik Sanghatana movement in Dhule district since its beginning. By the 1980s he was emerging as a poet, writing in Marathi and Bhilori and leading in the formation of a cultural group, the Adivasi Sahitya Sammelan (sahitya sammelan, or "literary gathering," was the common term for such cultural platforms). For Waharu, the problems of tribals ranged from their open exploitation as workers and agricultural laborers to the assaults on their original life as peasants and forest gatherers resulting from environmental destruction to the question of their very identity among the masses of Indian people.

Scheduled tribes or "tribals" had by the twentieth century become a clearly demarcated category, and they were becoming known in radical circles as "adivasis," meaning "original inhabitants." Yet perhaps more than any other group, the question of *who* were tribals, *who* were "adivasis," what their place was in relation to the masses of toiling people (dalits, shudras, or bahujan samaj, workers, peasants, etc.), was enmeshed in dilemmas. These were complicated by the fact that in most of India, the groups classed as "scheduled tribe" had a much lower rate of education than any other, were much more removed from what was generally called the "mainstream" of national life. The inevitable consequence was that although throughout recent history they had revolted against exploitation many times, the radicals who led many of their movements—whether Communists leading peasant revolts or, in more recent times, environmental activists protecting the destruction of tribal culture by big dam projects—were overwhelmingly nontribals and upper castes.

Who was an "adivasi"? Clearly they were related to the "indigenous peoples" of the world, but when their first representative testified before a United Nations committee on this issue in the early 1980s, the Indian government delegate protested that the majority of people in his country, and not only those who were "scheduled tribes," were indigenous. This obviously represented the self-interest of the ruling elites of India—but on the other hand, it was a fact that the "adivasi" representative was a Maharashtrian brahman. It was also a fact that a large section of those classed as "tribals" preferred different names for themselves: thus the Nagas, Mizos, Khasis, Garos, and others of the northeast called themselves "hill peoples," while leaders of the Jharkhand movement such as Ram Dayal Munda apparently preferred to talk of the "Jharkhandis" as inhabiting an area that had seen the mixture of the different races of India, Aryan, Dravidian, Austro-Asiatic. In both cases, people saw their movements in "ethnic-national" terms more than as "tribals."

What, then, was the relation between "adivasis" and the forests? It was true that these were groups who had historically inhabited the forested and hilly regions; but few were actually food gatherers and hunters—most practiced some form of cultivation, usually shifting cultivation combined with other means of living off the forests. On the other hand, this was perhaps only a quantitative difference, since "caste Hindu" peasant communities also had in many areas a crucial social and economic reliance on the forests (and everywhere on "grasslands" or "commons"). And while "tribals" were prominent in environmentalist protests, there were also many who listened to the argument that their communities needed industrialization, that "keeping them in the forests means keeping them in the Stone Age." Did adivasis really have a "special relation" to the forests? Especially when so many of them seemed to be involved in cutting down trees (or moving into patches left deforested by the forest department itself) to get land for cultivation?

One thing was clear: that "adivasis," like other peoples of India, wanted the right to decide themselves, that all movements invariably involved some demand for local control. Thus Waharu Sonavane had helped (with other Bhil and Pavara tribals of his area, with peasants from Sangli, and with working-class and middle-class activists from Bombay of the Shramik Mukti Dal) in organizing an Adivasi-Jungle Parishad, or "adivasi-forest conference," in 1986. This passed a whole series of resolutions on deforestation, drought, and water management, but the cutting edge, as far as the Indian state was concerned, stated,

> The monopoly held over the forests by the Forest Department (and the authority of its officials such as the rangers) should be abolished. Control over the entire forest should be distributed among the villages spread in the forest areas. The responsibility of maintaining and developing the forests should be given to these villages. The production of fruits, vegetables, herbal medicines etc., should be under collective ownership of these villages. Permission can be given to cut trees when they are the right age but other trees should be left standing. The government should give all necessary help for planting trees. Primary economic aid should also be given. The government should merely check whether the maintenance and expansion of forests is going on.[12]

These demands not only echoed all tribal-area agitations for autonomy; they were basically equivalent to the suggestion put forward by environmentalists Anil Agrawal and Sunita Narain that villages as a general principle should have control over the "commons,"[13] and to the arguments of Mukti Sangarsh in Sangli that the primary control over water and resources such as sand should be at the village level. They presaged major statements that were to come from both the farmers' movement and the environmental movement in 1990 calling for village ownership or "community control" of lands, forests, and other natural resources.

Were "adivasis" then really so different from other peasants? By 1990 Waharu was giving an answer to this. Giving the presidential speech for the "fifth Adivasi Sahitya Sammelan," he drew on the "non-Aryan" thesis of Jotiba Phule, arguing that adivasis were part of the original community of native inhabitants, enslaved by conquest. But added to this were insights arising from nearly ten years of discussion on history and culture in Shramik Mukti Dal circles, drawing on a wide mixture that varied from insights on hunter-gatherer societies of wandering activists like Jogin Sen Gupta to the reading of India's most eminent historian, the Marxist D. D. Kosambi. Thus, where Phule had paid no specific attention to "tribals," simply naming "Bhils" along with other castes of the *bahujan samaj* as part of the oppressed section ("mahars, mangs, bhils, kolis . . . kunbis, dhangars, malis," the list might run), Waharu made an important distinction:

> The struggle between the original adivasis, the tradition of the Indus civilization, and the tradition of Indo-European language speakers began to be transformed into a compromise. . . . On the basis of violence and aggression, a strong alliance of brahmans and a handful of rajas took one after another adivasi tribe under their control. They made them into slaves and disarmed toiling peasants paying taxes to rajas, and settled them in villages for stable agriculture to increase their kingdoms. Between the sixth century B.C., that is, the period of Buddha, and the fifth to sixth centuries A.D., a defined balutedari (occupational) caste hierarchy was established. Most free adivasi tribes became toiling castes giving surplus to rajas and brahmans and looking on each other as inferior. That was the brahman-dominated feudal society! This society had the capacity to slowly transform adivasi tribes and communities into castes and absorb them in the hierarchy but at lower levels. We were those who faced all this but remained outside!

"We were those who remained free": this was Waharu's theme, and he went on to argue it was because of the resistance of the free adivasi tribes that those absorbed in the caste hierarchy as exploited peasants and artisans could retain what limited autonomy traditional caste panchayats offered them. Theirs was a history of resistance and revolt, ignored by the cultural and social elites who had defeated them with violence and cunning:

> Inspired by determination Ekalavya made his guru out of an earthern statue and became more skilled in archery even than Arjun! Dronacharya himself

could not endure the skill of adivasis. By breaking Ekalavya's thumb under the name of *gurudakshina* that generation of adivasis was suppressed. Adivasis' history has been filled with blood. But that Dronacharya was a villain is not seen in literature, not found in history.

To Waharu, therefore, Rama was simply the leader of the Aryan aggression of his time. He saw one of the deepest threats to adivasi culture in the "Rama culture" of the day, promoted by TV and the cinema and the active efforts of Hindu fundamentalists to impose brahmanic marriages and life-styles on tribals. Attacking all forms of "Hinduization" or "Christianization," he argued for the uniqueness of adivasi culture with its central values of community solidarity and relations of nonhierarchical "friendship" among all, young and old alike, contrasting with the tight kinship hierarchy of caste Hindu society. "Laughing" over the "furor over love marriages," he stressed the natural and spontaenous nature of love relations among the adivasis.[14]

These themes left unanswered questions as to how adivasis were to maintain their identity as a "free people" in an industrial age, in the face of the very power of the onslaught of environmental destruction, on the one hand, and the pull of the commercial culture and Hinduization/Christianization, on the other, when educated tribals were adopting "middle class" life-styles and imposing a Hindu/Christian-style dominance over their women. Waharu's arguments also raised objections that they were romanticizing adivasi life; just as Vandana Shiva could be accused of ignoring important differences (as well as hierarchies, inequalities, and exploitation) in pre-British Indian society, so the idealization of an adivasi model ignored considerable differences within and between different tribal communities. But from another point of view "idealization" is simply model-creating, and Waharu was putting forward a model of adivasi community life that was a powerfully argued assertion of community pride, of the argument that "tribals" were not simply objects to be "brought into the mainstream" or turned into "proletarians," but that they had something of their own to contribute to the whole process.

It was at cultural forums in particular that such issues were discussed. Cultural activity as a crucial part of all movements involved both conflict with the state and the important process of self-assertion, self-action by lower-caste and specially oppressed sections. A wave of street theater sprang up in the 1980s, with independent dalit and women's groups intermingling with left party-connected groups. Some cultural activists became more famous than party leaders. Gurcharan Singh toured the Punjab with his Naxalite-linked group, a continuous voice opposing terrorism and communalism, trying to promote the unity of different Naxalite factions. Safdar Hasmi of a CPI(M)-connected group in Delhi became a famous martyr of the movement when a performance of his was attacked by thugs in 1988. A whole wave of resistance, relatively nonsectarian, arose in response to his murder. Finally, there was Gaddar of the Andhra

Peoples' War Group, a magnificent performer out of the dalit folk-theater tradition; his tours drew massive audiences throughout India once the PWG came out into the open in 1990, marked by revolutionary fervor and conflicts with the police when the state tried to ban his performances.

But there were also problems, illustrated by the fact that independent (though left) artists and performers confronted party domination; that they criticized party-connected street theater performances as simply "a dramatization of their party study groups"; that a leading activist of the Andhra Dalit Mahasabha had complained about Gaddar himself that "the party won't let him sing songs of Malas and Madigas; they only want him to sing red flag songs." These were old debates. The fact remained that for the large majority of dalit, adivasi, peasant, and women artists, cultural programs were not so much a means of spreading revolutionary culture as searching, debating, coming to grips with their own identities, their own history, and from this basis working out in a collective process their relations to one another, to the entity known as "India," and to strategies for change. It was an often complex but exhilarating process.

The dalit movement in Maharashtra had not only grown out of the energies of young poets but had continued throughout the two decades to be nourished in its *sahitya sammelans*, scenes of both expression and cultural debate. This had been true for all groups; from the broad but brahman-dominated Marathi Sahitya Sammelan at one end of the political spectrum to the Revolutionary Writers' Association of Andhra, the first open mass organization of Naxalites, active since 1970. In all these cases, annual conferences or "gatherings" organized not only poetry reading, story reading, and drama performances, but also workshop discussions on the political and social issues facing the people.

In many areas at least, such "sammelans" could not be held to any kind of sectarian line; they were becoming platforms of debates among groups. What was the relation of dalits and OBCs, for instance? What about women's liberation? How should religious fundamentalism be fought? These questions were discussed, not in political meetings only, but on cultural platforms.

This had its own dynamic. Dalit literature, in Maharashtra, inspired not only "adivasi literature" to assert its independent identity; it was also followed, spontanously, by a trend of "rural literature," mainly based among the nonbrahman or *bahujan samaj* peasant masses. Young poets and writers of different trends intermingled, discussed their identities, their exploitation, their relationship with each other. By the late 1980s, a *Dalit-Adivasi-Gramin Sahitya Sammelan* or "Dalit-Adivasi-Rural Literatures" organization had emerged: the first concrete organizational platform bringing together the "Untouchables, Tribes, and Sudras" about whose unity Ambedkar had been so pessimistic. The first conference of this united group was held in a tribal area in Dhule district; the second in a kunbi-maratha-dominated peasant area in southern Maharashtra under the auspices of a democratically run (about the only case of which this could be said) sugar factory and with poetry reading and debates attended by

5,000-10,000 peasants at a time sitting through night and day sessions. The questions of Rama (communalism), the depiction of women in literature (women's liberation), and whether there was such a thing as a "nonbrahman aesthetics" (i.e., was the caste contradiction real or should one only speak of the aesthetics of the poor or was aesthetics universal) were among the topics of debate.

Boys and girls taking up the pen to write of their lives and their ideas for the first time, young people from the poor and oppressed gathering in the thousands to listen enthralled to their leaders *and to each other* on the vital issues of the day; a new song of freedom, a new self-confidence: this was the cultural movement. Like the rising force of *stri shakti*, it represented a creativity growing among the most exploited sections at the base of society, capable of transcending the gloom and stagnation of traditional forces for change, with a growing self-confidence:

> *don't worry about me*
> *now I have awakened*
> *I am moving in blazing sunlight*
> *come*

Whether women's power or adivasi and dalit identity, technological alternatives or cultural assertion, the established powers dominating Indian society and its state had a tremendous ability to survive apparently unscathed. Yet the late 1980s saw even this survivability challenged, with the rise of an alternative politics that shook hitherto secure hegemonies even more than the Naxalite movement of the 1960s. Once more, even as traditional socialism was crashing in Eastern Europe, the new social movements of India were mounting their challenge, and a full account has finally to turn to the political sphere.

11

The Rise of Alternative Politics

FAR FROM the villages and small towns where "alternatives" were being enacted, symbolizing the very opposite of the earth-linked processes of "women's power," were the broad plazas, tree-lined avenues and Mughal halls of Delhi, home of India's bureaucracy and center of the aspirations of every politician. Delhi was the very symbol of corrupt and cynical game-playing with the people's anguish, brutal and violent, wealthy, patriarchal, brahmanical, "India" as opposed to "Bharat" in the terminology of the farmers' movement. For the new social movements, there was little so despised as this power center and the parties that gathered around it. In return, Delhi repaid the movements by ignoring them, attacking them, or overromanticizing and trivializing them.

Yet, in the late 1980s, the new movements were irrevocably pulled into the political sphere. It was a period in which the world was going through the momentous changes leading to the "fall of socialism" and the swing to a market economy in countries that had for decades represented the only alternative to an exploitative capitalist system. In India itself, in the much modified version of state-controlled development that I have called "four-anna socialism," the political system went through parallel violence-marked convulsions climaxing in 1991 in the final loss of Congress political hegemony, the establishment of Hindu communalism as a political force, and the opening up to the international economy. The new social movements were drawn into this process. They played a major role in it, and in the end their failure to supplant the murderous developments with a different logic—and in turn, the failure of the left parties, traditional agents of change, to represent the movements—left the way open for the return of establishment power after a period of popular upsurge. Not only did the process parallel in time the events in Eastern Europe, its dynamics were in many ways the same.

"Matters Will Have to Be Settled in the Streets"

It took only two years for Rajiv Gandhi's yuppie hopefuls of the twenty-first century to come into political crisis. A renewed imbroglio of violence and state repression in the Punjab, the ravages of drought, and unprincipled maneuvering in the Congress party itself awoke renewed political instability. Then came Bofors, the arrow that was to pierce the Achilles heel. In early May 1987, Swedish radio announced the discovery of a scandal involving the payment of millions of dollars in kickbacks by their Bofors company for a weapons contract to unnamed Indian middlemen who were high in Congress circles. It sent shock waves throughout the nation. Rajiv Gandhi immediately denied it ("Sweden has confirmed that there was no middleman and no money was deposited in Swiss banks," he told an incredulous Parliament), and the Congress issued a statement with its usual rhetoric blaming a "sinister move by the forces of imperialism . . . through a calculated campaign of calumny" aimed at "the destabilization of our political system." [1]

But this could not hold back the storm. With only a small band of companions, with no party machinery at his command, V. P. Singh, an ex-minister who had resigned some months earlier on the corruption issue, became the center of a gathering political whirlwind. A popular response, spontaneous and unprecedented, created a new opposition. In Singh's first major 50,000-strong public rally in Muzzafarnagar in western U.P., his procession over the 120-kilometer route from Delhi was mobbed by crowds shouting slogans of "*gali gali mein shor hai, Rajiv Gandhi chor hai*" (every alley shouts, Rajiv Gandhi is a thief) and "*V. P. Singh sangarsh karo, ham tumare sath hain*" (V. P. Singh fight on, we are with you).

The new leader was significantly different from Jayaprakash Narayan, leader of the pre-Emergency opposition. Unlike "J. P.," a committed Gandhian socialist out of electoral politics for years, "V. P." had been a life-long Congressman, with little political philosophy of his own, with a reputation for honesty but identified indeed with Rajiv Gandhi's liberalization program, and with no nationwide mass base. His later interviews show him constantly speaking for change but with little program for change, talking of his "natural allies" in the left though ready to make his own deals with the right, adopting the slogans of left parties and movements but above all thinking in terms of social forces and political constituencies and ways to mobilize these.

Without a political machinery of his own, V. P. gravitated toward the new social movements, professing a "nonpolitical" orientation that fit in well with the mood of cynicism toward politics as such. He set up the Jan Morcha (People's Front) as a professedly nonpolitical, struggle-oriented body, with a dalit politician as its convenor, and began to associate himself with movement leaders like Sharad Joshi and Datta Samant. The Morcha was not for elections, but for campaigning on issues of national importance, he said: "We want to give organizational shape to the feelings agitating people today." [2] His speeches began to center on the problems of workers, farmers, "social justice" for low castes (meaning the implementation of reservations in government service as recommended by the Mandal Commission), and the fight against communalism, corruption, and the "sell-out" to imperialist capital. V. P. projected an almost poetic image of uncertainty, insisting that he had no political ambitions, that he was consulting with friends about what to do, that he wanted "issue-based politics" and not "hero-worship." So what if his ideas were more utopian than practical: "Sometimes some madness is needed in politics. Had I been practical I would not have resigned. . . . The ultimate goal is to find a way out of the impasse in which the country finds itself today." [3]

In turn, the new movements and many of their leaders responded. The fact was that in spite of their hatred of politics and suspicion of the centralized state, the movements were pulled into the political sphere, simply because the Indian state was so powerful, so much at the center of the exploitative and oppressive machinery weighing on people's lives. Whether they were challenging big dams and development projects, the domination of the bureaucracy by high castes or low prices for agricultural products, activists had to confront the state.

The plunge toward politics, however, took varying forms for the different movements. The farmers' movement had most consciously acted as a political pressure group for a long time; now with V. P. emerging as a charismatic but in ways vulnerable leader, Sharad Joshi decided to associate with him. He was a last-minute speaker at the Muzaffarnagar rally, winning wide applause when he attacked the exploitation of peasants and concluded that they "are looking for a new Mahatma Gandhi to lead a second independence struggle." Joshi later qualified his enthusiasm, arguing that he was getting access to masses in North India in exchange for bringing V. P. to farmers' rallies in West India, saying that V. P. was being supported to achieve "a balance of power between thieves." Nevertheless, he was coming to feel in these days that a major upheaval was taking place in the political system, that all parties were "splitting into Bharat and India" factions, that some kind of turning point was at hand.

Environmental and women activists, on the other hand, had been resolutely outside of politics, antagonized by the very processes of large-scale mobilization, hierarchy, and strategy that seemed required to operate even as pressure groups. Except for the drive for local political power, the women's movement by and large remained so. But by the late 1980s the environmental movement was confronting the biggest development projects, such as the Narmada and Tehri dams, that were backed not only by local business and political interests but national-level ministries and international bodies such as the World Bank. Within the movement, the kind of moral and spiritual appeal represented by figures such as Baba Amte, with his letter writing to Indira Gandhi, began to give way to the organization-building methods and struggle orientation represented by Medha Patkar, new leader of the struggle against the Narmada dams and the first woman to head a mass movement in India.

The anticaste movement, finally, had always been directly political, placing the drive for political power at its center and concerned to organize political parties representing the low castes. In the 1980s there was a brief rise to prominence of these parties, in particular Kanshi Ram's Bahujan Samaj party and the Bharatiya Republican party headed by the grandson of Ambedkar. But in the end, this "political" orientation only seemed to make the anticaste movement the most co-optable, for it had no major mass leaders or organizations outside of politics itself to remain as independent pressure groups.

As far as the politicians were concerned, co-optation remained the name of the game. With the political parties discredited, the new left-centrist opposition leaders moved to make a name for themselves by appearing as representatives and leaders of movement issues: Devi Lal, the Haryana patriarch, projected himself as a "peasant leader," with his followers wearing green turbans; Maneka Gandhi, widow of Indira's younger son Sanjay, took up the cause of animal liberation to come into politics as a radical environmentalist; and while dalit and backward caste politicians Ram Vilas Paswan and Sharad Yadav sought to be spokesmen for these constituencies at an all-India level, V. P. Singh himself began to take up the cause of the anticaste movement, which was simmering in north India where he had his main popular base, making the slogan of "social justice" a shorthand for giving jobs and power to dalits, shudras, and Muslims.

If this was in fact deflection and absorption of the movements, in the turmoil of 1987 it still promised a new kind of politics. It proved capable of attracting even the radical left. Vinod Mishra, leader of the CPI(ML)-"Liberation" group, wrote in an article entitled "Matters Will Have to be Settled in the Streets" that

> The crisis we are witnessing in 1987 is different from that of the 1975–76 period in many ways, the most notable difference being that while the post–74 J.P. movement had an antiworking class overtone and looked at democracy merely as a structural phenomenon—leaving the working class and Left forces immobilised in the process—this time certain structural questions have been raised about our economy, big capital is being identified as a major target, and as a result there are prospects of the working class and Left forces playing a far greater role.[4]

The influence of the farmers' movement and shudra castes was not to the liking of the established left. The impending agitations of the Jan Morcha, wrote Inder Malhotra in *The Times of India*, were "a sure recipe for unleashing economic chaos and discontent," since "equal emphasis on more remunerative prices for farmers, higher wages for the workers, and stringent curbs on inflation" was inconsistent. Once more the specter of the kulak was dangled: "In reality it is the rich and middle peasant, the sole beneficiary of the green revolution and deeply conscious of his political clout, who is being wooed by every contending political group."[5] There was much editorializing about the "rise to power" of the "affluent OBCs" of north India—yadavs and kurmis of Bihar, jats of Western U.P. and Haryana. Bhabani Sen Gupta described the elite's disdain for these social forces massing behind V. P. Singh:

> There is to be sure, a lot of fear behind the sneer. There is fear that the so-called backward classes and harijans will make a determined bid for power at the national level and thus put an end to the elitist rule that has prevailed since 1985. . . . Girilal Jain [editor of the *Times of India*] has gone to the length of suggesting that only Brahmans can hold India together, while one of his columnists finds in the cohorts of Devi Lal tribes and groups condemned by the British as "criminals" and therefore capable of "criminalizing" the political process. . . . Devi Lal is nothing short of an apparition. He would bring the jats, gujars, ahirs—the narods—to power in Delhi; with them will come the mobilised peasants of the entire Hindi belt and the politically mobilised dalits of Rajasthan and Maharashtra. They will rampage the imperial superstructure built in forty years of independence, with the glitter of five-star hotels and the feasty social and political culture of the English-speaking elite.

Sen Gupta concluded that "those who ruled over the poor and humiliated them for centuries will sooner or later be ruled by them if India continues to be democratic. It is silly and dangerous to take an apparitional view of the vast majority of our people."[6]

Yet the turmoil of 1987 gave way to a round of political party formation in 1988 that had the effect of sidelining the movements and ensuring that the "rule of the poor" would again be postponed. The Jan Morcha never did lead any agitations. Instead, V. P. Singh yielded to pressure from the left political parties and contested a by-election in Allahabad in July 1988. His victory confirmed his leadership over the political process at the expense of his movement orientation. Then came the period of party formation. In September the National Front (NF) was formed in Madras, bringing together the disparate regional parties and leaders, seeking in effect to give representation to the anti-north India, anti-Delhi regional autonomy sentiments growing in so many parts of India. And in October the core of the NF, the "Janata Dal," was founded, bringing together old socialists in the Janata party, the north India peasant and low-caste Lok Dal, the Congress (S) remnant and V. P. Singh's Jan Morcha.

The program of the new Janata Dal combined old left and new movement issues. It promised for the movements 60 percent party tickets to dalits, OBCs, and minorities, implementation of the Mandal Commission recommendations, remunerative prices and the increase in the share of agriculture in plan allocations to 50 percent; for the parties there was right to work and legislation for rural workers, and keeping the public sector as the "anchor" of development. The program ended with a kind of equivalent in Gandhian language to the promise that the proletarian dictatorship would lead to the withering away of the state, in an eloquent but incomprehensible formulation that "We must move from the colonial heritage of being a state-centric nation-state to a community-oriented state system for becoming a communitarian democracy of the dreams of Gandhi."[7]

Disillusionment was quickly expressed. "A year ago," said Sharad Joshi, "V. P. appeared to be the man who could have created a national movement offering us an alternative in the real sense. He was prepared to fight on issues." Instead, said the peasant leader, "V. P. has regressed from offering a national alternative to a political one."[8] Young activists of his organization had a more agricultural comparison: the new party, they wrote in an editorial in the bi-weekly *Gyanba*, "is like a new hybrid seed come into the market to fool the peasants."

Nevertheless, the ability of the politicians to co-opt and deflect the social movements was in part a result of the weaknesses of the movements themselves, particularly of the farmers' movement and environmental movement as they geared up agitations in 1988–89 to show their mass strength and challenge Delhi itself.

The Farmers' Movement Storms Delhi

The recovery of the farmers' movement after its 1984 setback began, following the Chandwad session, with a massive Shetkari Sanghatana cotton growers' agitation in eastern Maharashtra that saw 30,000–40,000 arrested in *rasta rokos* and *rail rokos* and four killed in police firing. It ended with a quick compromise with the chief minister. At the same time, new areas of struggle emerged in Gujarat and western U.P. Yet the latter brought unexpected difficulties.

In Gujarat, a state swinging in a conservative direction throughout the 1980s, a BJP-led peasant front had won a strong base in drought-afflicted North Gujarat on demands for lower electricity charges and higher prices. Nonparty organizations in south Gujarat, the Khedut Samaj and the Kisan Sanghatana, contacted Sharad Joshi at the end of 1986 and built a coordinating committee in coalition with the BJP peasant front and then slowly and with some degree of success worked to outmaneuver it ("I was horrified," reported Joshi, "to see so many peasants wearing saffron"). But the Gujarat organization remained relatively weak, and the problems of unity between middle-caste farmers and low-caste, often tribal laborers daunting.

U.P. presented a different problem. This was jat territory, dominated by the powerful clannish peasant caste that had traditionally been able to rally other middle- and lower-caste sections around it, but that had less of a history of social reform and stronger tensions with dalit agricultural laborers (primarily chamars) than was the case in Maharashtra or even Karnataka and Punjab. It had provided a base of support for the opposition to Congress ever since 1967 and had produced one "peasant" hero as a short-lived prime minister, Charan Singh. In January 1987 a police firing on peasants demonstrating against raised electricity rates killed three in the small town of Shamli, and a new clan leader, Mahendra Singh Tikait, emerged to revitalize the Bharatiya Kisan Union. Huge rallies and demonstrations were organized, a new show of strength in the highly strategic rural areas surrounding Delhi itself.

Sharad Joshi attended the Shamli rally, and like the Gujarat peasant organizations, Tikait's BKU became part of the Interstate Coordinating Committee (ISCC). But there was trouble from the beginning. Part of it was at a personality level. Tikait was the very image of a peasant patriarch, hookah-smoking and whimsical, encouraging his followers to call him a "mahatma" but flanked by a cohort of armed bodyguards, Joshi, in contrast, a retired United Nations official concerned with ideology, capable of a sophisticated articulation and strategy. Tikait saw Joshi as a wily brahman infiltrating the peasant movement, Joshi saw Tikait as a crazy and casteist leader. Behind these were regional cultural differences: "You have to talk of Ram or Krishna in every breath; you can't speak scientifically as we do of surplus and exploitation," remarked Maharashtra peasant youth who had gone in a small group to one of Tikait's rallies, describing the cultural backwardness of the U.P. farmers as well as the greater prosperity of the region seen in the food supplied to the peasants occupying Meerut city. "They *are* rich peasants!"

A struggle for leadership ensued. Tikait had the unshakable support of U.P. jats, the section of the all-India peasant movement that held the keys to Delhi; Joshi had the equally unchallengeable loyalty of Maharashtrian peasants. They struggled for the support of the leading activists of other state organizations. Tikait agreed to the ISCC decision to organize a massive united rally in Delhi in January 1988, heralded as bringing five million peasants to the capital, united around four central demands: higher prices, freedom from debt, a minimum twenty-five rupees wage for agricultural laborers, and protection from drought. It was to be a kind of peasants' magna carta, to be won by invading Delhi itself.

Then in September 1987 Tikait walked out of an ISCC meeting on the grounds that Joshi was "becoming political" in supporting V. P. Singh. Joshi repeated his argument that the support was aimed only at maintaining a balance of power in which no government would be strong enough to repress the movement; Tikait in fact was playing his own games with politicians. But it made no difference. The projected Delhi rally was called off, and instead Tikait held a massive sit-in of his own, called a *kisan panchayat*, in Meerut from late January to early February 1988. Later in October he stormed Delhi itself, and fifty thousand peasants occupied the Boat Club, the historic center of political rallies, forcing a planned Congress rally to shift, and emblazoning the peasant presence into the minds of the capital residents. "You can begin to see why this community of farmers has managed to take a blasé capital city by storm," wrote one correspondent in describing the sports and games, the peasant political discussions, and a new phenomenon in Delhi: streets around the Boat Club were safe for women.[9]

Sharad Joshi initiated a campaign on indebtedness, justifying it as a focus to unite the struggles of peasants growing a wide variety of crops. Debt was in fact a major means of controlling peasant production and their integration into capitalist agriculture. The role of indebtedness to moneylenders in the "formal subsumption" of the peasantry to capitalism had been described for nineteenth-century India by Marxist scholars, but the progressives of the twentieth century only talked of the need for "making credit available" to the rural poor. It took a German feminist, Veronica Bennholdt-Thomsen, to point out that just as peasant labor (like women's domestic labor) contributed to capitalist accumulation, debt to banks and credit societies helped keep them subordinated: "In agriculture the subordination of small producers through credit mechanisms has become the predominant form throughout the world in the last forty years.... The profit realizes itself in the sphere of inputs and outputs and not in the actual production process.... The living labor power of the peasant family is absorbed through repayment by working." [10]

Peasants struggled against this subordination, but unequally; as many studies have noted, it was the rich peasants who most successfully managed to evade repaying their loans. Most left analyses took this as a sign of the exploitative nature of rich peasants, but the poor peasant repayment of debt was a sign not of their virtue but of their political weakness. Now the farmers' movement proposed to remedy this weakness by a collective campaign to refuse repayment. This was called *karz mukti* or "liberation from debt," and it was organized through mass bankruptcy petitions filed in the court backed up by refusal to pay when government officials came around. The Shetkari Sanghatana's *karz mukti* petitions were themselves political documents that argued that peasant bankruptcy was due to the fact that "the state itself depends on a policy of holding prices down to keep agriculture at a loss."

With the North India peasants taking their cause to Delhi, with the Shetkari Sanghatana making the issue of debt into a major national campaign, the farmers' movement was on the upsurge. But its two most powerful leaders were at odds. Tikait argued for an all-India vanguard, "one organization, one flag, one leader"; Joshi, in contrast, upheld the "federal" structure of the Interstate Coordinating Committee. After an inconclusive organizing tour throughout India, Tikait finally marched into Joshi's center at Ambethan in July 1989, his gun-bearing guard forced to remain outside, and agreed, once again, to a united Delhi rally.

Initially planned for September, the long-awaited rally was postponed again at Tikait's insistence, and finally scheduled for October 2, Gandhi's birthday. There was little time for formal preparations, no postering, no campaign. But the word went out, and peasants from all over India massed in their hundreds of thousands on trains and buses to besiege the capital. At least seventy-five thousand went from Maharashtra, which was also the state with the only sizable contingent of women. The Zhelum Express from Pune, filled with peasants from Western Maharashtra, was so crowded that, as activist Chetna Gala reported, "even in first class you could hardly find a place to put your feet. But we told people—you were warned, don't travel at this time, peasants are going to Delhi!" Five

THE RISE OF ALTERNATIVE POLITICS 265

times the ticket collector forced peasants off the train, and five times they sat on the tracks to enforce their right to ticketless travel.

Here, only a month before, Devi Lal had held his "birthday rally" to demonstrate his political base among the peasantry. The October 2 farmers' movement demonstration was even larger, and this time locally mobilized trucks and ticketless travel in the trains replaced the fleets of centrally organized trucks sent out from Delhi. But it was to end in a final rupture in the farmers' movement that represented its second major defeat.

By noon on October 2 the Joshi and other leaders reached the dais, but there was no sign of Tikait. When he finally did show up, he marched in with his armed guard and began shouting for the leaders to come down: "This is a panchayat—we shouldn't sit above the people." Though on other occasions he had no objections to rally platform, the rhetoric appealed to the nonhierarchical mood of the new movements and fit with the informal behavior cultivated by Tikait, sleeping, smoking the hookah at various places in the center of the crowds. Shetkari Sanghatana women were the first to respond, surging forward with slogans of unity and arguing with Tikait, "We're ready to accept your leadership too, if people decide; but this is not the way." The call for unity began to affect some of the BKU men, enraging Tikait: one photographer caught a dramatic shot of him beating some of his own men. But others began shaking the platform. Joshi jumped down (later news reports had it that he was pushed) and in the tension of the moment felt a minor heart attack coming on—he had been suffering an ongoing heart condition and bad health since an attack in 1985. He went off to a hospital, later explaining, "If I had had a heart attack there, it would have been bloodshed."

As it was, the scene dissolved into chaos. The angry Shetkari Sanghatana boys were confused. "We are disciplined," said their future president later; "whatever the insults to our leader, we don't move a hand unless the word comes." But with Joshi gone, the second-rank leadership was immobilized. Finally a call was given to withdraw to the other side of the huge grounds, and the Shetkari Sanghatana did so, resulting in a divided rally and one in which large numbers of peasants simply walked away in frustration. In the aftermath, the reformed Kisan Coordinating Committee maintained the allegiance of most of the state units and voted to expel Tikait, but the damage had clearly been done. The split in the farmers' movement stood for all to see.

Rumors in Shetkari Sanghatana circles had it that Devi Lal (who had his own alignment with Tikait on caste grounds) had instigated Tikait to provoke a split. The end result in any case was clear. Peasant demands were placed in center-stage, but the weakened and split peasant organizations themselves could not directly represent them. When the V. P. Singh government came to power after the 1989 elections, Sharad Joshi was named as head of a powerful Standing Advisory Committee on Agriculture assigned the task of formulating a new national agricultural policy. But Devi Lal, now the most visible "peasant spokesman," became deputy prime minister.

In this way the upsurge of the farmer's movement in 1987–89 broke upon the stones of the Delhi fortresses; yet as it did so, new directions blossoming within it began to be seen. At the "top" level there was a movement toward the formation of a total agricultural policy that was to be in fact a kind of manifesto for alternative development; at the grass roots, peasant women in Maharashtra took steps toward political power and property rights.

Narmada Activists Declare War

While the farmers' movement was gearing itself to "storm Delhi," the environmental movement was taking a major plunge into the political sphere with a challenge to the building of a series of big dams on the Narmada River. Up to this point, environmental struggles had been organized on a local basis, with all-party coalitions and committees linked to informally structured intellectual networks whose ideology of "grass-roots-ism" rejected mass politics as alien. "Think globally, act locally" was not itself an Indian slogan, but the spirit was there, in the orientation to locally rooted, small-scale alternatives. Yet it was the state and large capitalist forces, Indian and international, that were imposing environmental destruction. The way in which the very logic of their situation forced environmental activists into politics and into confrontation with the state was seen most clearly in the struggle over the Narmada project.

In March 1986, a few months before the peasants of Sangli district began their struggle to build the Bali Raja memorial dam, and about the same time as Dhule tribals were organizing their "forest-adivasi conference," two activists crossed the Narmada River dividing Madhya Pradesh and Maharashtra, their boat capsizing in the process, to contact tribals on the Maharashtra side whose villages were due to be submerged by the Sardar Sarovar dam. Achyut Yagnik, a Gujarati heading an NGO in Ahmedabad working with dalits and tribals, and his then-colleague and employee Medha Patkar proceeded to organize the beginnings of village-level committees, then hiked over the hills to Shahada where they met Shramik Sanghatana activist Waharu Sonavane, and finally went to Dhule to call social activists together to form a Narmada Dam Evictees Support Committee.

In 1986 the Rajiv Gandhi image was only beginning to tarnish; he was at the time calling leading environmentalist Anil Agrawal to talk to his cabinet on ecological issues. In Maharashtra a left-led Committee of Dam and Project Evictees organized, only three months later, a big demonstration in Bombay on the slogan "first rehabilitation, then the dam." While most of its leaders were still supporting developmental projects, many were rethinking issues of environmental degradation and deforestation, and demands for justice in "rehabilitation" were in fact militant enough to halt many dams in this period. The early organizing over Narmada dams had also taken place from this perspective, whether among tribals in Maharashtra or in the Nimad valley in Madhya Pradesh, where a Congress-backed agitation in 1979–80 had fought to lower the height of the dam.

The new struggle against Narmada dams also began in this way. In April the Sardar Sarovar project received its environmental clearance from the central government. By this time Medha Patkar had broken away from Yagnik and begun to form the Narmada Bachao Andolan (NBA or Save Narmada Movement), based on committees in the three states (Gujarat, Maharashtra, and M.P.) where villages would be flooded by the dam, but also drawing in a large number of urban-based environmental organizations and activists. The NBA was strongest in Madhya Pradesh, where rural women were mobilized for the first time and dalits, tribals, and caste Hindus brought together in a movement; though the fact that the Congress and the BJP were the only political parties in this part of the state made local support problematic.

Then a new radicalism emerged. Through 1987–88 as the NBA began to mobilize agitations, attempt to organize workers on the dam site, and generate publicity, it gradually endorsed the perspective of not simply seeking justice for the evictees and workers but of opposing the dam as such: a full-scale, total radical environmentalist opposition to the Narmada project. This was linked to the rise to predominance of Gandhian social worker Baba Amte. In a July 1988 meeting of environmentalists in his eastern Maharashtrian leprosy center, the Anandwan Declaration Against Big Dams was adopted, taking up the rhetoric of opposition to big dams as such. Shortly after this Medha Patkar was won over to his position in a meeting in Bhopal. Then Baba himself staked a claim to leadership of the movement by first calling meetings in April and June 1989 in Anandwan to issue a document projecting a "Green Front," and then dramatically shifting to a small village in the area to be flooded by one of the dams, Narmada Sagar. He would never return to his Anandwan home, he declared; from here he would not move, staying until his death if necessary by *jal samadhi*, "suicide by water," a term with a religious ring to it. Soon he was being projected in the media as the heart of the struggle; in the words of an American correspondent, his "name alone has become a singular war-cry for grass roots environmental movements."[11]

All of this involved problems.

The Narmada Valley project was the biggest and most prestigious of the government's major irrigation projects. It was huge, including 30 big dams (the biggest being Sardar Sarovar in Gujarat and Narmada Sagar in M.P.), 135 medium projects, and over 3,000 minor projects on the river and its tributaries. Together these projects, it was estimated, would submerge 325 million acres and displace 300,000 people. The Sardar Sarovar project alone was estimated to cost Rs 9,000 crores (slightly over $5 billion; by 1990 this estimate had gone to Rs 14,000 crores); it had been planned from 1947, its foundation stone laid by Nehru in 1961, and it was expected to irrigate 1.8 million hectares in Gujarat plus 75,000 in Rajasthan and generate power for three states, giving irrigation to

2.5 million villagers and drinking water to 29.5 million. In turn it would submerge 37,000 hectares, displacing 100,000 villagers in 248 villages, the largest number of these in Madhya Pradesh.[12] The figures were dazzling, the promises bright, the numbers involved immense.

So were the interests behind it. Power was of course crucial for industry, and Gujarat and Maharashtra provided the strongest base for Indian capitalism, with much of M.P. industry also controlled by Gujarati businessmen. They had built up "Narmada" as a prestige project for Gujarat over four decades, using emotions heightened in the 1980s by the ravages of drought and the fight for survival of the rural poor. In one sense every irrigation project involves a conflict of interest between those in the "catchment area" whose lands are to be submerged, and those in the "command area" who look forward to increased irrigation and prosperity. In the case of Sardar Sarovar, practically the whole of Gujarat was being projected as the command area (without much justification in actual plans for the distribution of water, which were inequalitarian and inefficient) and the dam was taken up as a "national" cause. Politicians began to grab on to Narmada as the "pride of Gujarat."

On the other hand, Narmada had become a worldwide environmental symbol, one of the biggest of the "big dams" ravaging the environment, destroying the culture and livelihood of indigenous peoples, and spearheading the tyranny of destructive industry. As the NBA began to oppose the dam as such, it could tap an impressive national and international network, drawing in groups like Lokayan and the Kothari family, getting regular access to newspaper publicity, tapping a reservoir of idealistic middle-class youth for activists. But even as this was happening, the potentialities of building a broad mass-based oppositional coalition were vanishing.

Most of the activists connected with radical environmental platforms like those of Baba Amte were neo-Gandhian intellectuals or radicalized middle-class youth, without much experience or instinct for real organizing among the people; the groups they were linked to were funded NGOs, not organizations with a mass base. There were a significant number of the latter, many left-led, working on rehabilitation of project evictees. But none of these had a policy of full-scale opposition to dams: even when activists were convinced, the fact that they were dealing with masses who still had hopes in developmental projects (even immediate victims nearly always said, "we're not against the dam as such.") led them to moderate their stand. NBA activists argued that their shift of perspective had grown out of their realization that a ecologically sustainable rehabilitation of all evictees was simply impossible. But many found this unconvincing, and even those who felt that the dam as such would have negative consequences disagreed with the rhetoric of the movement and felt that the romanticism of the opposition, linked with the projection of paternalistic Gandhians like Baba Amte, was no substitute for strategy.

The total oppositionist perspective developing in the NBA was rejected not only by Gujarati activists like the Sangarsh Vahini group in Rajpipla, which was active in finding lands for rehabilitation, but also by Maharashtrian groups; not only by left-party-dominated organizations like the Committee of Dam and Project Evictees, but also by ecologically oriented radical groups such as Shramik Mukti Dal. The SMD, with its work on environmental issues among middle-caste peasants in Sangli and tribals in Dhule, argued that the movement should unite both evictees and proposed peasant "beneficiaries" of the project and that to build a wide mass coalition capable of confronting the powerful interests behind the dam, it had to win the support of a significant section of Gujarati peasants. But this required going beyond rhetorical slogans to deal with the concrete issues of accountability, rehabilitation, and water distribution. SMD activists were also told, however, "If you don't agree, don't work."

The fact was, though, that a large number of mass rural-based organizations were opposed to NBA policy. In Gujarat, Gandhians working in tribal areas and the farmers' movement were enthusiastically supporting the dam. In Maharashtra, the Shetkari Sanghatana remained uninterested in an issue "dividing the peasantry," while dalit activists saw environmentalist opposition to development as a romanticization of village life designed to keep low castes and tribals "in their place." Peasant leaders criticized environmental activists as "urbanites who don't understand anything of agriculture," and anticaste organs attacked the movement as "brahman-led." In turn, the rhetoric of the movement often seemed designed to alienate people, by posing the issue as one of victimizing "tribals" for the narrow self-interests of "rich cash-crop farmers" and "apartment dwellers" of Gujarat. Little way was found to forge links between peasants and tribals on both sides of the issue, and at the time, only the women's movement, in both the Patna and Calicut conferences, seemed to be supporting antidam movements. As the movement was forced to show its mobilizing force in the growing political turmoil of 1989, it was doing so under the burden of a top-heavy leadership without mass organization, with a romantic image that could capture media attention but had little strategy to gain mass backing.

Nevertheless, under the lead of the NBA the first major mass rally of the environmental movement was planned at the M.P. town of Harsud, designed to be flooded by one of the dams. This brought together a coalition of over one hundred environmental and tribal organizations, and promised an attendance of a hundred thousand to be the biggest environmental rally in history. The big day saw a gathering of public figures, film stars, Gandhian patriarchs like Amte and Sunderlal Bahuguna and the saffron-clad Swami Agnivesh, famous for his work with "bonded laborers." Politicians (among them Maneka Gandhi) were barred from sitting on the stage, and tribal women danced in the streets at the final rally.

But the Harsud rally was as much a crisis for the environmental movement as the Delhi Boat Club rally was for the farmers' movement. The twenty-five thousand who came did in fact represent the largest crowd ever for such a gathering, and Harsud saw the founding of the first national-movement-based environmental organization presenting some kind of total alternative perspective, the Jan Vikas Andolan (Movement for a People's Development). But for purposes of political power it was not enough; politicians used to actual crowds of hundreds of thousands gave little weight to twenty-five thousand and could well assess the situation as one in which environmentalism had some middle-class base, a lot of "stars" and strong localized support on some issues in some areas, but was otherwise a negative factor that could cost them votes among a majority still sold on "development," on jobs to be had in polluting factories or prosperity to be gained through unhealthy Green Revolution technology. The moral image of Gandhian leaders such as Amte meant nothing to them, particularly when other well-known Gandhians of Gujarat were on their side and industrialists supporting the dam could finance huge rallies of their own evoking equally potent religious and political symbols. At the same time, the style of rapid organizational formation, media-blitz, and dominance of "stars" (whether of the Gandhian or cinema tradition) alienated many who had been attracted to the grass-roots orientation of environmentalism. Thus, Rajni Bakshi and Smitu Kothari wrote in the *Lokayan Bulletin* that "the rally left many disappointed, for it did not reflect our own limitations on breaking out of the more prevalent and conventional modes of expression. . . . For six long hours [it] was dominated by speeches from a high perched covered platform . . . more reminiscent of a party rally. . . . Was this inevitable in a meeting of this scale?" [13]

The political outcome of Harsud had some similarities to that of the farmers' Boat Club rally. The new V. P. Singh regime appointed Maneka Gandhi as state minister for environment, perhaps one of the most radical people in the world to hold such a position. But she had little real power and was overshadowed by more powerful ministers committed to carrying through the Narmada project. Consequent agitations saw many visits to Delhi, meetings with V. P. Singh, and negotiations with all kinds of political leaders, but no change in policy on Narmada.

Yet the Harsud rally did mark a kind of turning point for the anti-Narmada campaign. It was followed not only by increasing talk of "people's development" and "alternative development" in movements throughout India, but also a turn to grass-roots struggle led by Medha Patkar. "Narmada activists declare war," one newspaper headlined in late 1989 as a series of demonstrations and fasts were held.[14]. These began in Maharashtra, then led to a march, or *jan sangarsh yatra* (people's struggle campaign) into Gujarat that was stalled at the border by police and mobilized citizens. Baba Amte's van stood at the head of the march, and publicity first centered on him, until Patkar grabbed the initiative in early 1991 by going on a "fast to death" with six other activists, including two poor tribal women. This could win no concrete results and was called off, but only after twenty-two grueling days. Then NBA activists retreated into the villages scheduled to be flooded by the dam, declaring a boycott of elections and of all government officials, with a new slogan of political self-sufficiency and decentralization: "our village, our rule."

The "save Narmada" movement had taken its first plunge into practical politics not with a perspective of building a political coalition and mobilizing a mass force behind it, but instead as a romantically depicted force linking oppressed tribals with an ideologically motivated middle class, united around the charismatic figure of Baba Amte, threatening Gandhian-type sacrificial immolations in the flooded villages, all without much effect. Even as its image of heroism grew, the mass social base supporting a challenge to the Narmada project seemed to be shrinking; even as international pressure mounted, the large mass of opinion in Gujarat continued to support the dam. The "war" declared by environmental activists seemed lost.

Yet by 1991 a change could be seen. Gradually, as the activists on the banks of the Narmada continued to take up one militant struggle campaign after another, the varying concrete possibilities of alternatives for Narmada irrigation and rehabilitation began to be more thoroughly discussed, and the process of dialogue began to pull in peasant organizations, engineers and technicians, even some party activists. Themes of struggle symbolized by Patkar, rather than the appeal to sentiment symbolized by Amte, began to take predominance. The fact of getting thoroughly based in a rural area, not just as securely paid NGO activists or city dwellers visiting in periods of agitation, was producing its own results.

Along with this, new perspectives were getting expressed in the environmental movement, and environmental issues were gaining an increased cogency at the national level. One sign of the latter was that the Commissioner for Scheduled Castes and Scheduled Tribes, B. D. Sharma centered his 1987–89 official report around the issue of eviction and human rights, focusing on Narmada. The report itself went much beyond the usual discussion of atrocities and the reiteration of the need for land reform to give a constitutional justification for basic rights—right to life, right to entitlement (meaning not just "right to work" but work for proper remuneration), right to means of production and right over resources. It endorsed Sharad Joshi's division of "Bharat and "India" and emphasized the linking of agricultural wages and prices, but it added that to the organized/unorganized sector division had to be added a "third tier" of the most exploited, comprising the bulk of Scheduled Castes and Scheduled Tribes, which Sharma called (in an unfortunate choice of words) "Hindustanva." About the Narmada struggle he wrote,

> So far people's movements against displacement were sporadic and more or less isolated. Moreover, displacement itself was accepted as inevitable and the affected people would just beg for some relief. In the Narmada struggle people from all parts of the country facing the backlash of development have come together and are raising perhaps for the first time the question of constitutional rights. And this issue has not been raised only at the conceptual level for the sake of an argument or debate; instead it is backed by people's own understanding and their resolve. That is not all. As the real nature of issues has become clearer, questions are being raised about the concept of development itself.[15]

At the same time as Sharma was making these formulations for the environmentalist intellectuals and the government bureaucracy (from which he was shortly to resign to work on issues like Narmada), the activists involved in the Jan Vikas Andolan were moving to a new analysis in a "working perspective" adopted in early 1991. Whereas earlier statements on the "politics of environment" such as that of the Second Citizens Report (1984) had linked environmental destruction to the failure of centralized planning, the nature of modern industry and the "consumption of the rich," the Andolan went a step further to make the question of control of resources central: "Behind our exploitation of nature often lies our exploitation of each other. By taking away the traditional rights of millions of tribals and small and marginal farmers from subsistence use of natural resources . . . the benefits are derived at the cost of enormous suffering to the affected population and massive overuse and degradation of the surrounding resources."

"Community control" of natural resources was projected as the linchpin of the solution. Thus, environmental activists, sparked by the NBA, were raising, along with the critique of industrialization and modern technology, the "Marxist" question of property rights—but in contrast to the traditional left, they were giving the "Green" answer: decentralization.

With the anti-Narmada campaign, the environmental movement had taken a giant leap on to a political terrain. Throughout the rise and fall of the V. P. Singh regime, in a period when the Communist alternative was disintegrating, it was this campaign that posed the question of a new vision of development at the level of popular consciousness. The constant militancy of those engaged in direct battle on the banks of the Narmada was forcing a dialogue in which more concrete formulations of the nature of exploitation and environmental destruction, as well as the assertion of popular power from below as opposed to enlightened state intervention from above, began to replace the originally vague and romantic slogans. Out of this, backed up by new experiments in agricultural production and struggles such as that for the Bali Raja peasant-built dam, the themes of "alternative development" began to take shape in the oppositional movements in India.

The Mandate of '89

Much of the Indian political elite had been inclined to see the social movements behind V. P. Singh as a kind of spectre. But the real demon was represented in the forces of Hindu communalism that were on the upsurge. More than the left, the Hinduist forces seemed able to identify issues that appealed to mass instinct and find innovative ways of campaigning on them. On the left, there was a clear "movement-party" split: the movements organizing the masses on new issues and with new forms of struggle, but relatively disarmed in the realm of politics, while the parties continued to articulate traditional rhetoric but maintained their electoral domination. On the right, however, a potent "movement-party" combination seemed to be growing.

Spearheading the Hinduist upsurge was the Vishwa Hindu Parishad, which now began to step up its campaign for rebuilding the temple of Rama in Ayodhya. With sadhus and swamis in the forefront, a nationwide campaign for bringing consecrated bricks to the town from villages all over the country was organized to climax just before the scheduled elections. It was accompanied by vicious anti-Muslim rioting through much of North and Central India, with some of the worst carnage seen since the riots at the time of independence, thousands killed, shops and businesses razed to the ground, and places of worship leveled to have the saffron flag of militant Hinduism placed on them. The worst massacre took place at Bhagalpur in U.P.: "Dead bodies inside walls, large patches of blood on the floor and walls of plundered homes, jagged ruins of houses which were torched, corpses in hyacinth filled village ponds, twisted remnants of utensils and bicycles in the debris of fire, a red plastic doll in the rubble, refugees in relief camps. . . . The haunting images of Bhagalpur inspire pessimism, hopelessness, desolation. And, admittedly, fear in the pit of the stomach."[16]

The suave and sophisticated politicians of the BJP did not hesitate to identify their party with the VHP and with the rabid, Maharashtra-based Shiv Sena, proclaiming with new confidence an ideology of "positive secularism" that attacked the "pseudo-secularism" of the left and the Nehruvian Congress, claiming that only Hinduism represented India's ancient and liberal cultural traditions and that only a pride in Hinduism could provide a foundation for nationalism. The BJP moved into the 1989 elections with a growing confidence, and a skill in combining the tempo of "mass" agitations with the scheduling of elections. Feeling incapable of defeating the Congress on its own, the nervous National Front opposition—even to some extent the CPI(M) in Bengal—cautiously moved to de facto alliances and opportunistic seat adjustments with it in constituencies throughout the country.

The 1989 elections thus marked the ambiguity of the Indian political crisis. A new opposition was taking shape with the National Front, Janata Dal, and left parties, including even one Naxalite force, the IPF, and it was borrowing themes from the social movements, as talk of decentralization, of social justice for backward castes, and promises of remunerative prices and debt relief for peasants dominated political manifestos. The Congress itself attempted a "turn to the villages" in promising a new dynamism for village self-government and 30 percent reservation for women. But little of this was more than the politicians replaying their populist games in the 1980s context. It was haunted with the shadow of the rise of communal forces, the Hindu rightists making their claim for political power in North India and a resurgence of Sikh and Muslim separatist forces in the Northwest. Electoral violence, shooting of candidates, "booth-capturing" by gangsters who simply marked illegal ballots en masse became widespread phenomena. Even the advertising campaign of the Congress seemed to express the fears of the elite, with gruesome depictions of torn-apart dolls, snakes, and scorpions that professed to show an opposition aimed at breaking the country into fragments.

On this background of fear, in an international context in which "socialism" was crashing to the ground, the voters of India cast their ballots for change in the ninth Lok Sabha elections. In what later commentators would call the "Mandate of '89," they voted against the ruling party in almost every part of the country. They voted for the various opposition parties in the mostly Congress-ruled North, and for the Congress in the opposition-ruled South. The only states in which a ruling party got the majority of parliamentary seats in 1989 were Maharashtra (Congress) and West Bengal (the Left Front)—but the Left Front in turn lost to a Congress-led opposition in Kerala. The final result was that no party could claim a clear majority: of 525 seats in parliament, the Congress had 192 but few prospects for alliances, while the Janata Dal had 143, the BJP and its allies 92, and the Left Front 52 (most of these from CPI(M) in West Bengal). Smaller progressive regional and movement parties like the Jharkhand Mukti Morcha (3), the Bahujan Samaj party (3), and the pro-Khalistani faction of the Akali Dal (11) also scored. A Naxalite was elected to parliament for the first time, from the IPF in Bihar.

The Janata Dal/National Front was now the only acceptable political front to head the government, but it required the support of the Left Front on one side and the BJP on the other to maintain a majority. The support was offered by both, and accepted. V. P. Singh was chosen as the new prime minister, but though he was the only Janata Dal leader with a popular mandate, it took hectic maneuvering and a deal with Devi Lal to defeat a last-minute challenge by Chandra Sekhar. The new government was thus a regime elected on a mandate of change and with social movement backing, but it was also a fragile coalition government marked by factionalism, maneuvering, and clashing political ambitions from the very beginning. As the new government began its work, riotous demonstrations shook many cities in Northern India as high-caste youth began a protest over the coming implementation of the Mandal Commission. It was a prelude of the storm to come.

An Alternative Politics?

The new government began, almost unexpectedly, in an atmosphere of hope. In spite of its lack of a majority, it took steps in new directions. There were signs of fulfilling promises made to peasants with the implementation of the promised debt relief up to Rs. 10,000 and the appointment of the committee for a new agricultural policy; there was Maneka Gandhi as a minister of environment; there was the prominent position of dalit minister Ram Vilas Paswan as well as the imminent implementation of the Mandal Commission.

Fears aroused by BJP political gains (an *Illustrated Weekly* article had headlined them as the "Real Victors") receded a bit when subsequent assembly elections produced a Janata Dal-Left victory in Bihar and a narrow Congress victory in Maharashtra. Then Mulayam Singh Yadav, one of the two new backward caste chief ministers in the North, arrested a Shankaracharya (one of four Hindu "high priests") on his way to Ayodhya and announced he would do the same to any others who tried to destroy the mosque. Fragile as it was, this government was not only moving ahead in some new directions, but it also seemed more capable of taking firm stands against fundamentalism than the Congress with its massive majorities.

But the real dissidence emerged in regard to programs for change. Measures for debt relief and higher agricultural prices were attacked consistently by the bureaucracy, the capitalist press, and many left intellectuals; there was a spreading fear about the reservations issue. While Maneka Gandhi's concern for animals and trees made good press copy, they aroused exasperation if not hostility among the main powerholders. There was disagreement within the government itself on all these issues, and there was no single concerted policy put forward by the new movements or the left from outside the government. In the end, it was not so much the threat of communalism from the right, as the simple lack of perspective for change in the political leadership itself, that represented the real failure of the V. P. Singh regime.

The year 1989 was one in which alternatives were being put forward. At the grass roots level the varying social movements headed toward the adoption of a totalistic perspective. The Kerala fishworkers were spearheading a "Protect Waters, Protect Life" march in the middle of the year along the coasts of India, with women playing a major role, linking the sea with the water needs of the peasants and the people, confronting police repression to challenge nuclear power plants. Mukti Sangarsh was generalizing its campaign on the Bali Raja dam in western Maharashtra to talk of an overall policy of equal water rights and ecologically sustainable water use in the context of a model of "alternative development"; Chattisgarh Mukti Morcha was bringing peasants and workers together in Central India to debate alternatives; engineers and technicians were formulating concrete policies for housing and feeding the population through biomass-based production. The Narmada Bachao Andolan was condemning the destructiveness of current World Bank and state-banked policies and calling for a "people's development," and moving to demands for local control. All of these were becoming "political" in the very general sense of representing a coalition of the poor and exploited that linked local issues to a wider perspective on international processes of exploitation and destruction, and the means of overcoming these.

At the same time, much more financially and institutionally powerful, the trend toward economic "liberalization" was becoming increasingly prominent with more and more businessmen and intellectuals calling for change, complaining of stagnation, of the corruption of officials, the weight of the bureaucracy. Their influence was reflected in a new industrial policy aired by the government.

The traditional left parties had little to say in this situation. In a period of ideological battering, when the CPI(M) governments in Kerala and West Bengal were themselves working to attract private investment, proposals for further nationalization were not on the agenda; "agrarian reform" remained mostly an empty slogan. The clearest direction the parties could formulate for change in the contemporary Indian context was the slogan "right to work." The Communists, the socialists within Janata Dal, a large number of NGOs, and IPF once it settled down to becoming a new vanguard and not a platform for "alternatives" all took right to work as a central theme for mobilizing the poor and as a strategy of development. The left had always used the slogan, and it seemed a good progressive counter to the growing appeal of fundamentalism and "extremism" for unemployed and disillusioned youth. Yet, from the perspective of even traditional socialism, let alone that of the new social movements, it had severe limitations.

"Right to work" implied that the cause of Indian poverty was that people did not work when in fact (at least outside the offices) they normally worked too hard for miserable returns; and it identified "work" as wage-earning. It had, in fact, somewhat of an industrial society image behind it, in contrast to the discourse of the peasant and environmental movements, which spoke instead of rebuilding villages, restoring the land and forests and providing the basis for a full human life in a rural, mostly non-wage-earning agro-industrial economy. It was statist, in committing the state to provide employment, without giving any indication of the structure of the economy that might do so. Worse, when planners or experts came down, in practice, to the brass tacks of how any guarantee of work would be implemented, they came to a vastly expanded version of the "employment guarantee schemes" that had indeed played a progressive role in states like Maharashtra but that were hardly socialist panaceas. Instead of a vision of a new economy or community life, of a truly liberating development, the slogan at best preserved a slender hope for a job in the organized sector and at worst condemned one to breaking rocks and building roads.

If "right to work" was what the traditional left was offering as an alternative, "decentralization" was a major theme of the new, neo-Gandhian socialists. These were given an opportunity when the government reconstituted the Planning Commission, bringing in neo-Gandhians Rajni Kothari and Ela Bhatt under L. C. Jain as deputy commissioner. With new energy, the planners adopted an approach paper entitled "Toward Social Transformation" that picked up the theme of right to work by arguing that the developmental process would be organized around the commitment to create employment for all, modifying this with the Gandhian-environmentalist perspective of "democratic decentralization" and "integrated local area planning" to be carried out by local panchayats.

But this turned out to be only a version of "four-anna socialism," a more Gandhian version of the usual radical rhetoric. While there was much talk of local panchayats, there was no recognition of local *rights* or *powers*, no economic basis projected for decentralization; instead, constant references to "transfer of resources" to local bodies made it clear that surplus was to continue to flow to the center and then downward. Sections on agriculture stressed the expansion of irrigation, developing the productivity of agriculture in arid and semiarid zones, and providing employment, all with hardly a mention of "remunerative prices" and within the overall perspective that the way to agricultural prosperity was to provide 50 percent of investment for rural development and make more efficient use of resources by "reducing linkages and by better targetting and delivery." The agricultural program, in other words, was that of Devi Lal, not Sharad Joshi, that is, one that relied on the control over agriculture by bureaucratic forces.[17]

The most radical alternatives were in fact put forward by Sharad Joshi's Standing Advisory Committee on Agriculture (SAC), representing the only direct intervention of "new movement" politics in the sphere of the government. If it was the Narmada Bachao Andolan that placed the slogan of "people's development" in public consciousness, the "national agricultural policy" could claim to be the most concrete high-level formulation of an alternative development. The policy, which was worked out over a period of six months and was designed to be an official policy of the government, began, like the eighth plan approach paper, with an invocation of a Gandhian model of development: "The Gandhian talisman would be the natural reference point. How do the most deprived and the most oppressed see things? What is their vocation? Why is it that despite long hours of back-breaking work they find it impossible to eke out a living? This brings us to the essence of all process of development—application of labour to land, in brief, policy as regards agriculture."[18]

In contrast to the approach paper, the policy itself linked broad proposals for land regeneration, increases in productivity, and political decentralization to the issue of exploitation of labor in agriculture.

The main instrument for a village-centered economic development was to use remunerative prices, in Joshi's terms, to leave the surplus generated in agriculture largely in the hands of the peasants. Prices were to be set high, and the major factor in achieving this was a high valuation of agricultural labor, both hired and peasant family labor. Up to now the "cost methodology" of the government's Commission on Agricultural Costs and Prices had calculated prices by attributing a cost for hired labor at existing wage rates (which were low and varied regionally) and for male family labor at the level of an "attached laborer" ("bonded laborer," in other words) in each region; female family labor was valued at only a small fraction of this since official statistics and popular thinking consistently undercounted women's labor. This effectively made the state an exploiter of peasant labor directly, and agricultural labor indirectly, at the existing low wage rates. The SAC proposed to break with this completely by setting a minimum wage of twenty-five rupees (equivalent to the entering pay of a soldier) and evaluating all labor (hired, and male and female peasant family labor) at this rate.

Along with this a target rate of a 6 percent growth in agriculture was set, and it was proposed within two decades to raise the standard of living in agriculture to that of the lowest levels of the organized sector. Both assets and control of income were to be given to rural women. Specific goals were also proposed for broad changes in agrarian production: within two decades, the proportion of those dependent on agriculture was to be reduced from 70 percent to 50 percent; one-third of land currently cultivated would be relieved from exhaustive plough cultivation and restored to grassland or forest. Finally, there would be a concerted effort to replace chemical by natural fertilizers, and fertilizer subsidies would be dropped. Arguing that subsidies for chemical fertilizers actually subsidized the fertilizer industry rather than the peasants, the SAC policy stated that any subsidies should be at the point of consumption and not that of production.

Finally, in a section on panchayat raj, the SAC took up in very specific terms the theme of decentralization and popular control that was emerging from movements all over the country:

> The panchayat . . . would have the ownership of the entire land vested in them as also specific lands allotted as common, grazing, forests or agricultural lands for their exploitation as such. In many tribal villages shifting cultivation is a fairly common practice. If proper attention is paid for regeneration of the forests, shifting agriculture by itself is not an undesirable practice. While allocating the area of control to the tribal panchayats, the area allocated should be extensive enough to permit continuation of the practice.[19]

The bureaucratic and press reactions to the various official policy proposals were revealing. The new industrial policy was attacked from a "socialistic" perspective by Chandra Sekhar and the left, but there was little real debate. The Planning Commission proposals were generally welcomed, though without great enthusiasm, while "right to work" issues brought forth some subdued debates, critiques, and expressions of support. The SAC proposals were by far the most controversial. There was strong and subtle resistance from the bureaucracy throughout, and as some themes were leaked out to the press they were roundly denounced: "Farm plan boon for kulaks," "Farmers' gain at consumers' expense," and "Hike in foodgrain prices will check industrial growth" were typical headlines of news stories.[20] Left intellectuals were brought in to defend the policy of low crop prices, and the objections of an "Expert Committee for Review of the Methodology of Cost of Production of Crops," headed by C. Hanumantha Rao, who had been a prominent opponent of higher crop prices for decades, were used to mobilize intellectual resistance. The Hanumantha Rao committee argued that costs should evaluate farm labor at actually existing wage rates instead of a legal minimum wage, on the grounds that the farmers did not normally pay their laborers the minimum wage—continuing to use the "kulak" specter without ever mentioning that the labor rates included not only hired labor but peasant family labor as well. In addition, every expert testifying before the committee argued that it was impossible to replace more than 10 percent of NPK chemicals by biofertilizers.

The bureaucrat attached to the committee, the "member-secretary," gave a dissenting note in December 1990, using the rhetoric that the committee was neglecting the "poorer sections of the farming community." The goals of reducing land under cultivation, reduction of the porportion of population dependent on farming, and giving land and income to women were attacked as "lofty views [which] can merely raise false hopes and damage government credibility." He also claimed that the cost of high support prices and other proposals would be an unbearable Rs. 25,000 crores (about $10 billion) per year—a figure that, looked at a bit differently, could be taken as the amount of surplus extracted from agriculture through low pricing.[21] This dissension and a subsequent seminar of "agricultural economists" set up by the government paved the way for scuttling SAC's proposal and putting forward a hastily drafted and thoroughly watered down agricultural policy statement in March 1991. The latter was welcomed by the Federation of Indian Chambers of Commerce and Industry and by most newspaper editorials, and denounced by Sharad Joshi as a "meaningless collection of phrases."[22]

The debate over agricultural policy was showing some strange lines of division. On one side were Sharad Joshi and the farmers' movement, calling for political *and* economic decentralization; on the other were those arguing for keeping prices low and promoting agriculture through government investment focusing on major irrigation projects and a Green Revolution technology including fertilizer subsidies. Devi Lal was the "farmers' representative" for this approach, but behind it stood the bureaucrats and capitalistic interests, and for that matter most of the presumably progressive planners and "experts." If we decide to use the term "kulak" to describe a system of inequalitarian, ecologically destructive agriculture, then the debate posed the "kulak lobby" versus the farmers' movement.

More important, though the SAC proposals were finally put to death under the Chandra Sekhar regime that succeeded the V. P. Singh government, neither V. P. Singh himself nor the "peasant spokesman" Devi Lal gave any particular attention to the actual alternatives being formulated for agricultural development by their official government committee, let alone any other movement alternative proposals. The new government had ridden to power on the wave of the new movements and of general popular disgust with the Congress regime, but it seemed unable and unwilling to formulate serious alternatives. It fell, not in defending an alternative politics, but in the waves of corruption and factionalism and the murderous dialectics of what Indians were beginning to call the "politics of Mandal and Mandir," that is, of the Mandal report and the Rama temple (mandir), the tensions generated by drives for caste justice and religious fundamentalism.

The Flames of "Mandal and Mandir"

Factionalism in the V. P. Singh government came to a head in July and August. A hostile press focused on Devi Lal, who had succeeded in identifying farmers' issues not only with his plans for five-star hotels with village-style restaurants and calls for appointments of peasants' sons as ambassadors, but also with the corrupt dynasty of his family, with the politics of gangsterism and patronage. Demands for his resignation grew. Then, in a late July interview to *Illustrated Weekly*, he unloaded himself in earthy peasant language, including a reference to V. P. Singh as "spineless." [23] This proved the final straw, and Singh asked for his resignation. Devi Lal gave it, but struck back by organizing a massive peasant rally in Delhi, trucking in hundreds of thousands of peasants, and winning the support not only of Singh's constant opponent Chandra Sekhar but also of such jat-belt movement leaders as Mahendra Singh Tikait and even Kanshi Ram, responding to Devi Lal's appeals for "harijan-kisan unity." Tikait repeated his slogans that a "peasant" should be the one raising the flag at the Red Fort on independence day (i.e., as prime minister), and Kanshi Ram attacked the "brahman-bania-thakur" combine.

V. P. Singh's response to this challenge was to pick up the one social movement issue that did not require a major political reformulation of the process of development: he announced the implementation of the Mandal Commission report. This unleashed the storm.

Urged on by their elders, by the press, professors and parents, students took to the streets. A desperate campaign for the defense of a claim to organized-sector jobs (its casteist character revealed when Delhi students protested by depicting their future as being only that of rickshaw drivers and flower and vegetable sellers) was painted as the defense of equalitarian values. Eminent upper-caste social scientists who had made their scholarly reputations on studies of caste and community now found themselves trying to outdo Marxists in talking of "economic" realities and asserting that caste did not exist outside the political arena. M. N. Srinivas predicted the transformation of the "brain drain" into a flood if upper castes were barred from higher-level jobs; Arun Shourie used the front pages of *Indian Express* to write as if merit would be dead in India once a few percentage points in exams would no longer be the deciding criteria for jobs; and the newspapers and magazines day after day featured in full color the massive demonstrations in northern cities.

V. P. Singh was attacked as never before, as a self-interested politician who was rendering the fabric of the country's existence to create caste vote-banks for his political survival. The rhetoric of the "antireservation movement" used the language of building an egalitarian caste-free society, insisting that it was not against reservations for the "really downtrodden and deserving," the scheduled castes and tribes, but that the "rich peasants" and "affluent OBCs" had no right to them. The term "Mandalization" came to mean splitting or fracturing the country, just as demands for regional autonomy or separate states for, say, the Jharkhandis or Gorkhas had been countered as antinational and separatist. The whole propaganda against reservations for low castes illustrated the way the elite had come to see its position and power as dependent on a centralized, unitary, "caste-blind" bourgeois order.

The real horror started when self-immolations began to occur. Many of the deaths may have been suicides that would have taken place anyway. But there was no denying that perhaps over two hundred desperate upper-caste boys and girls, often the children of lower-middle-class families who had seen education and jobs as their way forward and now found a chasm appearing under their feet, were ready to commit the most painful form of suicide over the issue. There was also no denying that the deaths and the agitations in general were highly localized in cities and in northern India, and that the publicity given to them was provoking a contrary reaction from large sections of lower castes throughout the country. Many Bengalis, Tamils, and others also saw the uproar in terms of the Hindi belt elite trying to maintain their domination of the country.

The Mandal Commission was not fragmenting the country, but it led directly to the fall of the government. The BJP, the party most threatened by the split in "Hindu" votes caused by caste divisions, decided it had to act to divert the issue—in a kind of repetition of the way proreservation forces in Gujarat in 1985 had been diverted into Hindu-Muslim rioting:

> The centripetal forces of Hindu society ... would have received a body blow had Singh been allowed to implement the Mandal report. Till that stage, the BJP had decided not to place its campaign on the Ramjanmabhoomi issue on an aggressive mode. Certainly there was no question of bringing down the National Front government on this issue. But Singh's overnight love for Mandal changed all that. Advani felt that his party had little option but to brazenly whip up Hindu emotions over the temple issue and remained undeterred by the trail of blood his campaign stirred up. He perceived that the very survival of Hindu society was sought to be challenged by Singh.[24]

Advani thus organized a *rath yatra* or India tour in a van shaped like the chariot of Rama, urging a massive assault on Ayodhya on October 30 to demolish the mosque and build the temple through "direct action." It provoked scores of riots, leaving over five hundred Muslims dead, but dozens of Hindus killed in firing by a police force instructed to protect the mosque no matter what. Advani himself and many other leaders were arrested, and the BJP carried out its threat and withdrew support for the V. P. Singh government.

In the face of loss through a no-confidence vote, maneuvering began among the politicians. Chandra Sekhar and Devi Lal took the lead in organizing a small break-away Janata Dal faction to form a new government, supported by the Congress party and many businessmen, who were much happier with a Chandra Sekhar-Congress combination. Among those who joined Chandra Sekhar's

Samajwada Janata party (Socialist people's party) were Maneka Gandhi, irritated by Singh's lack of support for environmentalism, and Mulayam Singh Yadav, frantic to save his minority ministry in U.P., which would have fallen without Congress support.

So ended the second major attempt at a change from Congress rule in India. A wave of social movement agitations, particularly by peasants and tribals on environmental and farmers' movement issues, had played a major role in defining the issues confronted by the Indian people; they had begun to move toward concrete proposals for alternative development, and they had, in 1989, forced some of their demands into the manifestos of parties. But the movements were sidelined by the politicians. By the late 1990s, communal and anticaste issues were dominating Indian politics. On the one hand loomed the rising aggressiveness of the BJP. On the other, peasant issues along with the environment and women (let alone any socialist program of the traditional left) were now ignored, and while V. P. Singh was adopting the major issue that had been brought forward by the anticaste movement in the last decade, he was doing so in the absence of a program for structural change.

In taking up the issue of the Mandal Commission proposals for reservations, V. P. Singh was emphasizing that it was not simply a matter of employment but of bringing low castes to power: "The greater debate is not about government jobs.... The point is of share in the decision making and share in the power structure. In fashioning the country's destiny, do you have a share? ... Even after half a century virtually, the deprived sections have not received the benefits flowing from the government. Unless they become a party to decision making in the power structure, they remain deprived."[25]

This was adopting a major theme of the anticaste movement, that "we must become the rulers of the land." But the earlier revolutionary leaders of this movement—Phule, Ambedkar, Periyar—had called for low-caste power in the context of an all-around socioeconomic vision of change, though their visions varied. In the new uncertainties of the 1980s, V. P. made no effort to adopt any concrete overall program. Perhaps the North Indian context he was familiar with encouraged a limitation of vision—Bihar and U.P. had little of the revolutionary democratic trend of an anticaste movement among the middle castes, such as had been seen in the southern nonbrahman movements. In any case, V. P.'s "social justice" was an anticaste movement from a politician's perspective.

But it was still radical enough to upset the elite. It had a major progressive feature in posing the need for the unity of dalits, backward castes, and minorities. It also produced some immediate political gains. Independent dalit politicians such as Kanshi Ram or Prakash Ambedkar lost much of their prestige for their hesitancy in supporting the government; through the Mandal Commission issue, V. P. Singh was capturing a powerful dalit and backward caste base. By the end of 1990, he was touring India, usually in the company of the fiery Ram Vilas Paswan, drawing unprecedented crowds in Maharashtra, Tamilnadu, and Kerala.

A reporter described a massive Pune rally on the death centenary of Jotiba Phule:

> Dhondiba, a backward-caste farmer from Sangli who had waited in the
> blazing sun for four hours to hear V. P. speak . . . angrily told this correspon-
> dent, "For centuries we have been dehumanized and oppressed. When V. P.
> Singh announced one little step in our favour it could not be tolerated by the
> Brahmanical parties. . . . V. P. Singh has sacrificed his gaddi for our sake, now
> we must stand by him." Seventy-five-year old Savitribai of Pune was attending
> the meeting. . . . .Why had she, despite failing vision, ill health and arthritis
> made it a point to come? Savitribai answered, "I have come to see and hear V. P.
> Singh. He belongs to the same caste as me. I am a dalit and I consider V. P.
> Singh a man of my caste because he has stood up for us, spoken of social
> justice for us." [26]

An alliance between "left and democratic forces" now had a different and
more hollow core. V. P. Singh continued to assert the firmness of his solidarity
with the Communist parties, whose cadre networks seemed indispensable in light
of the Janata Dal's own disastrously fragmented party machinery. The CPI and
CPI(M), in turn, endorsed his leadership out of fear of Congress and the
fundamentalists, and in the hopes of making a challenge for power in Delhi,
rallying behind the National Front regardless of its lack of overall program,
regardless of their own reluctance on Mandal Commission proposals.

But radical Communists and movement leaders were now becoming totally
alienated from the developing National Front/Left Front alliance. The IPF, the
only major section of Naxalites participating in the electoral process, decided to
go on its own in Bihar, arguing that without "an emphatic qualitative improvement in the well-being and social standing of the overwhelming majority of
working people," reservations were meaningless and would result in "only a
readjustment of the ruling classes' social base." [27] In Maharashtra, Shetkari
Sanghatana withdrew from its linkage with the Janata Dal to insist only on the
defeat of communalism; in Karnataka the Rayatu Sangh, already alienated from
Janata forces, proclaimed itself as an independent party, setting up candidates on
its own in many constituencies, often fighting for the same base as the Janata
Dal; in U.P. Mahendra Singh Tikait flirted with the BJP. Women and enviromen-
tal activists found even less than before to attract them to the NF/Left alliance.
Thus, when the Chandra Sekhar government fell in March 1991, and parties
geared themselves up for new elections, they did so not only amid a general
popular atmosphere of cynicism and exhaustion, but also with the major forces
for change in India sidelined.

Impasse

In spite of V. P. Singh's claims that the National Front's slogan of "social
justice" could mobilize the forces for change, the dominant features in Indian

politics by 1991 seemed to be the growing violence and forces of disintegration. In the outlying regions, armed underground fighters in Punjab, Kashmir, Assam, and other parts of the Northeast were on the offensive, and in the rest of the country it was militant Hinduism that appeared to be the fresh, if dangerous, political force. *Far Eastern Economic Review* journalist James Clad was only one of many who saw India as heading "toward a Hindu Raj," commenting that the BJP "is riding a surge in support that shows no sign of slowing. . . . Most of all, the BJP gives the impression of knowing what it wants and how to get it." [28]

The BJP's ideology was gaining increasing respectability among the elite throughout the country, even in left strongholds such as Kerala and West Bengal. Prominent recruits came into the party, retired high-level bureaucrats and military men, ex-maharajas, sportsmen, and film stars, and more funding than ever was available as a large section of India's capitalists were ready to see it as an effective alternative ruling party to a discredited Congress. In the meantime, out on the streets and dusty roads, the troops of militant Hinduism were keeping the issue of the temple alive, proclaiming ceremonies for the "martyrs" killed at Ayodhya, circulating inflammatory, hate-filled casettes, organizing tours of vitriolic speakers on Hinduism. A huge rally of the VHP in Delhi in late March filled the massive lawns of the Boat Club with saffron and was proclaimed to be the largest in history. Fears expressed by feminist activists that the "democratic space was shrinking" were shared by a large section of India's progressives.

As the reluctant cadres of political parties geared themselves up for the second major parliamentary election campaign in less than a year and a half, trying to find a way to mobilize funds and voter enthusiasm, the voters themselves faced a historically new situation. Previously the Congress, with its socialist rhetoric and conservative practice, had been the center of India's "dominant party system," facing an opposition comprising those to both the right and left of it, partly united and partly at odds. Now, for the first time, three clearly defined political fronts, each with a distinct central slogan, appeared in the political arena. The Congress offered "stability," hoping frustration with the factionalized efforts at change in the last two years would turn people back to it; the BJP laid its hopes on militant Hinduism and on the backing of a growing army of sadhus and swami, maharajas and bureaucrats; and the V. P. Singh-led alliance of the National Front and left parties made a claim for the support of the exploited and low castes with the slogan of "social justice."

With Communists, socialists, dalits, regional parties, and anticorruption democrats, the National Front-Left alliance should have been able to mobilize a popular appeal. "There is a new alignment of forces taking place," claimed V. P. Singh in an interview to *Frontline*; "now the National Front and the Left axis are the forces of change." [29] The dalit-OBC combination was in fact disturbing the high-caste elite and promising a realignment of social forces, especially in North India. The NF-Left Front alliance was consistently underrated by the press, as election results were to show (see table 11.1), and underfunded by the bourgeoisie, who

Table 11.1
1991 Election Forecasts and Results
(seats)

	Congress	BJP	NF/Left
Predictions:			
Sunday	310	83	81
India Today	233	155	105
Frontline	224	140	115
The Week	277	100–110	95–115
Actual Results	225	123[a]	127

Source: Sunday, June 2–8, 1991.
a. BJP actual total includes four seats for the Shiv Sena.

much preferred either the Congress or the BJP. Yet in spite of its low-caste and working class base, its popular appeal was now lackluster. Singh's crowds during the election campaign were noticeably less enthusiastic than before; even Rajiv Gandhi, newly "mingling with the masses," was winning more popular acclaim. The basic problem remained that no matter how much they claimed to represent working class and popular forces, none of the parties or political leaders of the NF-Left alliance had any vision of the real dynamics of the new capitalist era; there was little difference between their manifestos and those of their opponents, no radical new economic program. This revamped "left and democratic alliance" was a force for change without a direction for change, other than seeking to bring the traditional toilers of the varna system, or some of them, into the existing arenas of power and prosperity. While this was enough to thoroughly alarm India's holders of bureaucratic power, without a new socialist vision it was unable to overcome the cynicism and indifference now pervading the Indian electorate.

And as the grueling summer went on, campaigning for the election that no one really wanted was again marked by growing violence, especially in U.P. and Bihar where this time almost all political parties not only were hiring gangsters to back up their candidates and capture voting booths but were even sponsoring them as candidates. In Punjab, where elections were ultimately postponed, Khalistani terrorists were murdering candidates; in Andhra the Peoples' War Group was attacking or threatening attacks on campaigning parties, and the ULFA boycott appeared to herald the same threat for Assam.

Then came the shocking climax: on May 21 evening, after the first round of voting, Rajiv Gandhi, campaigning in a town near Madras, was brutally murdered along with a dozen bystanders, his body torn apart in a suicide bomb tied to the body of a young woman linked with the LTTE or Tamil Tigers. Indira Gandhi had been assassinated by Sikh bodyguards as revenge for the massacres caused by the attack she had ordered on the Golden Temple to checkmate Bhindranwale, whom her party had in the very beginning helped to build up. Now her son was murdered by killers who had been given training in India by the Gandhi-led governments themselves from 1983 through 1987. Rajani Thiranagama and the coauthors of *The Broken Palmyra* had noted that

> The LTTE is the product of a brutal world; a world where great leaders, men whose education and maturity entitle them to know far better, routinely use deceit and mass murder as legitimate forms of action. . . . The RAW cannot claim moral superiority over the Tamil militant groups. The fight against terrorism will be futile as long as the world's leaders play with terror when it suits them. The impressionable young minds of the LTTE were moulded by the cynicism and duplicity they encountered in their dealings . . . with the TULF, the Tamil elite, and the Sri Lankan and Indian authorities.[30]

The grown-up Tiger, offspring of powerholders in South Asia, had turned to devour its parents. The Congress, which had interfered and maneuvered in neighboring countries even while shouting "national integration" and raising the bogey of the "foreign hand" for every challenge to its own dominance, now found itself orphaned. So strong had the habits of dynastic rule become that the inside men of the party—the high-level clique around Rajiv who came to be described in the press as the "coterie"—proposed the name of his Italian-born widow Sonia Gandhi as Congress president; it was even clear that had his daughter Priyanka been three years older and eligible for electoral office, she would have been tapped. But Sonia, quite wisely, refused, and instead P. V. Narsimha Rao, an old-guard brahman from Andhra, was settled on as party leader. The final rounds of elections were postponed until June 12 and 15.

When they were over, an apathetic electorate (a 51 percent turnout was the lowest since the early 1950s) had rendered a mixed verdict. Congress, with 224 seats of 541, was the biggest party, though without a parliamentary majority. But in spite of a considerable "sympathy vote" (made clear in the much better performance of the Congress in the constituencies that had gone to the polls after the assassination), it could only get 37.3 percent of the vote, lowest since 1977. The BJP had made significant gains, with 119 seats and 23 percent of the vote, but 50 of its seats had come from U.P., the state most affected by the Ayodhya confrontation and the politics of defection. Outside of this, it received a setback in the three states where it had ruled the assemblies for two years and in Maharashtra, where it had been hoping with its Shiv Sena ally to grab for power.

The "politics of Mandal" had been salient only in Bihar and U.P., and partly in Orissa (where the anti-Mandal faction of JD chief minister Biju Patnaik lost out). In the rest of the country the Janata Dal could barely establish its existence. In several cases this was linked to its new distance from large sections of peasants: the BKU was alienated due to the exclusion of jats from the Mandal Commission and its confrontations with the U.P. state government; and Shetkari

Sanghantana and the rest of the Kisan Coordinating Committee were alienated due to Singh's failure to support the new agricultural policy or to give peasant issues any significant role in the campaign.

The Communists won in West Bengal but lost in Kerala once again, while the regional parties fared at best moderately: the Telugu Desam recovered partially, the DMK, tarred with its association of the Tigers, was thoroughly rejected in Tamilnadu; the Assam Gana Parishad also made a poor showing; even Biju Patnaik, the Janata Dal leader who had grabbed headlines prior to the elections with demands for state autonomy and praise of Naxalites, was rejected.

Yet the alliance of Janata Dal, the left parties, and the regional parties as a whole got 135 seats, making it second as a political front only to Congress, letting some analysts find hope in the fact that those who had stayed with the "mandate of '89" were by and large endorsed by the voters.[31] Further, the "sympathy wave" had given the Congress around 9–10 percent of the vote; without the assassination, the party would have had its lowest vote in history. Indeed, a region-by-region assessment of the effects of the assassination argued that the National Front/Left combine would actually have come out on top, with a total of 181 seats, while the INC and its allies would have gotten 174 and the BJP would have been only around 129![32] The suicide-bomber Dhanu and her Tiger colleagues appear, in the end, to have done a significant favor for the Indian ruling elite, which still found the Congress the best party to represent its interests.

The overall result was what the Indian press called a "hung parliament," no party with a clear majority. With the government facing a growing balance of payments crisis and "unpopular" belt-tightening economic decisions in the air, a new era of instability seemed inevitable. But none of the opposition parties trusted the mood of the voters to shake up the political scene—the last election had been unpopular enough and none had an effective alternative economic program to offer. Power was again in the hands of a fragile but ever-ready Congress.

Narsimha Rao became prime minister and an economist favorable to international finance circles, Dr. Manmohan Singh, was picked as finance minister. He immediately announced devaluation of the rupee and the seeking of a new IMF loan. Thus, after an election characterized by slogans emphasizing caste and religious issues, and accompanied by growing violence linked to regional-national separatist movements, India plunged into a process of radical economic change similar to the new capitalist orientation of all the ex-socialist countries. A prime minister and a finance minister who had never been elected, heading a party that could claim support of only about 18 percent of the electorate, were implementing economic measures never discussed during the campaign. But there was little popular resistance. In spite of Narsimha Rao's obeisances to the Nehru tradition as the only alternative to "fascism," in spite of the continued attempts of the elite to cling to the Nehru dynasty, the Nehru model was as discredited in India and being discarded as surely as state socialism was crashing in Europe. "Four-anna socialism" was coming to an end, but with the social movements still politically sidelined and the left-democratic opposition unable to find a substitute vision, Indian politics had come to an impasse.

Demise of the Nehru Model

Arguing that the "dividing line between politicians and criminals [has] disappeared," *Manushi* editor Madhu Kishwar wrote following Rajiv Gandhi's assassination, "Forty years after independence, the peoples of India have no illusions left about this system's capacity to deliver social justice. . . . Disaffection against the government is universal. It has hardly any defenders left. . . . This disaffection is spread across all classes, segments, and regions of society. Whether in a village *chaupal* or in urban elite drawing rooms, the theme that dominates conversation is the incompetence, corruption and tyranny of the bloated government machinery." [33]

This assessment of the current political-bureaucratic system was indeed shared by all sections, from the "man in the street" to the woman in the fields, from flashy news magazines like *India Today* to the leftist commentators writing in serious journals like *Economic and Political Weekly.* "Sordid, bloated, corrupt, tyrannous, parasitical, gangster-ridden, sanctimonious" were only a few terms used for the existing political-bureaucratic system. All agreed that it had ruined the economy and done nothing to fulfill its continual promises to the poor. Nearly all also agreed that the current changes were radical, if not revolutionary, in spite of Narsimha Rao's efforts to assert that the "Nehru model" was not being forsaken.

But Marxist and Gandhian intellectuals were still inclined to defend what Rajni Kothari had called the "liberatory" role of the original independent Indian state, what socialist H. K. Paranjpe described as an "effort to build up India as an independent, self-reliant, socialist, decentralized, and people-oriented economy." Leftist defenders of "four-anna socialism" were now arguing that if it had gone wrong, it was because it had somehow been taken over by the small privileged section who had used electoral office and bureaucratic privilege only to gain power and wealth, and it was these who were now attempting a final coup by jumping into the world economy. They viewed the whole prospect with gloom, expecting the complete domination of capitalism and consumerism, and predicting that it would be the poor who would pay. [34]

But to activists of the new social movements, the system had been not simply flawed but exploitative and destructive in its very beginnings; there was nothing of genuine self-reliance or decentralization in it; rather than "people's power," it had been based on elite domination, with paternalism the central characteristic of even the Gandhian saint-figures who talked of village traditions. Its bloated bureaucracies were inefficient and parasitical; its scientists, engineers, and technicians were living off the people rather than trying to create anything new or engage themselves in renovating the dusty world of village life; "socialism" was only its legitimizing myth. They saw its demise as having been forced on the elite, not chosen by it, and saw in this demise certain kinds of new openings.

There was no denying that the left was in a mood of gloom and that large sections of the working class, including the urban poor, were feeling new pressures as jobs and state-supported welfare schemes were threatened. Yet others welcomed the cracking of the bureaucracy. There were dalit intellectuals to argue that "Ambedkar would have welcomed devaluation," while environmental activists pointed out that the World Bank would now put pressure against many big dam projects, because it had no concern to finance top-heavy, bureaucratically bloated projects that were also politically costly, and because the Indian government no longer had any leverage to force it to do so. Finally, Sharad Joshi hailed the new era of "efficiency and competition" involved in the free market and argued that the peasants' fight for remunerative prices was to a large degree won, mainly because the state no longer had power to hold prices down. So what if the new liberalization meant that food prices would rise as primary products became India's most successful exports? So what if much of India's outmoded and inefficient industry could not compete at all? So what if organized-sector jobs were endangered? Such industry and employment had been bought off the sweat of peasants and laborers who had gotten only misery, drought, and displacement in return for the surpluses they produced. The changes just might provide new opportunities to the majority of the exploited who had had precious few opportunities in the previous regime.

What exactly was going on?

Long-term political trends could be clearly traced. The irrevocable decline of Congress hegemony, the rise of a party representing the forces of militant Hinduism to a position as largest single opposition party, the increasing predominance of regional parties based in different states, and the stabilization/stagnation of socialist-Communist votes (see table 11.2)—these were some of the changes that climaxed in the 1989–91 period. There was also a significant, though fragile, coming together of socialists, Communists, and regional parties in a "left and democratic" front opposing both the Congress and the BJP-led Hindu rightists, an alliance that posed the possibility, if not the reality, of a political platform for a democratic socialist vision. Beyond these were other significant features not seen in the electoral statistics: the cynicism of the population about their political leaders, the growing salience of armed struggle politics, not only in peripheral states but also in central India where youthful Naxalite guerrillas were beginning to roam more and more at will, and new demands for radical "decentralization," "autonomy," and "alternative development" that the political forces were reluctant to articulate.

Immense changes had taken place in a country that had given the world Gandhian nonviolence and that had had a mass independence struggle led by one of the most deeply based of any non-Communist Third World ruling party. But

Table 11.2
Percentage of Votes by Major Political Forces

	Congress	BJP and allies[a]	Socialists/Janata[b]	Communists
1952	45.0	6.1	16.4	3.3
1957	47.8	6.8	10.4	8.9
1962	44.7	6.4	9.5	9.9
1967	40.8	9.4	8.0	9.4
1971	43.7	7.4	3.4	9.8
1977	34.5	41.3[c]		7.1
1980	42.7	19.0[d]	9.4[d]	8.7
1984	48.1	7.4	12.3	8.4
1989	39.5	11.8	17.9	9.3
1991	37.3	21.2	11.6	10.4

a. Includes Jana Sangh, Hindu Mahasabha, and Ram Rajya Parishad in 1952–62, and Shiv Sena in 1989–91.
b. Socialist party and Kisan Mazdur Praja party (1952), Praja Socialist party and Socialist party (1957, 1962), Samyukta Socialist and Praja Socialists (1967, 1971), Bharatiya Lok Dal, etc., Janata party and Lok Dal (1984) and Janata Dal (1989, 1991).
c. Janata party (1977 and 1980) includes the Jana Sangh plus the Socialist and Lok Dal forces and dissident Congress.
d. In 1980 the Janata party split, though both used the same name, into a mainly BJP and a mainly Socialist–Lok Dal party.
Source: Singh and Bose, *Elections in India Today*, July 15, 1991, p. 41, and Abhijit Sen and C. P. Chandrasekhar, "Verdict 91," *Frontline*, July 6–19, 1991, p. 105.

the crisis of Congress rule in India and of the political-economic system it represented was not simply a ploy of a bourgeoisie and "middle class" grown aggressive and powerful enough to junk the system that had tried to provide for development for the poor; it was primarily a result of the contradictions of that system and the social opposition it aroused.

Capitalism in the contemporary era was a massive machine of accumulation utilizing surplus accumulated from nonwage (small production, subsistence production, even surviving unfree forms) as well as wage labor and benefiting from the low pricing of natural resources and raw materials. During colonial rule the Indian subcontinent had occupied a central place in this machine of capital accumulation, while imperial traditions dating back to Mughal times and earlier provided an indigenous framework for the colonial state which administered the empire. Both this state and the imperial framework as a whole provided opportunities for the Indian bureaucratic and commercial elites to spread through much of the Third World during the colonial period.[35] Thus, the Indian national movement fought the imperial state, but its leaders also saw themselves, consciously or not, as its heirs, and with independence they took it over. The "Nehru model," with its socialist rhetoric and elitist practice, was attractive to so many for this reason, and in spite of themes of Gandhian "decentralization," neither the Gandhians nor the Marxists working in the bureaucracy or in political parties had any methods or vision for really generating popular power from below.

With independence the high-caste Indian elite and bourgeoisie put itself at the head of an essentially exploitative system, seeking to control its surpluses, justifying this with the ideology that these were being used for "development," and adding a heavy element of statism to the effort to promote fossil-fuel-based centralized industrialization. This suited bureaucrats and businessmen alike, but it could not lead to an egalitarian society. With a democratic framework—one major gain of India's history and the nature of its independence struggle—explosions were bound to come. Ambedkar had threatened these explosions at the time of independence itself; the state was not hijacked by "new middle classes" or greedy capitalists seeking to expand into the world market, it was eaten away from within by internal contradictions and so forced to yield to the pressures from without. There was no "socialist revolution" taking place, but what was happening in 1991 was also not a capitalist consolidation.

It took four decades for the processes to work themselves through. Indian mechanisms of political rule used not only considerable resources of police suppression but also an upgraded "brahmanic" ideology and a sophisticated party mechanism of patronage and co-optation for managing discontent. The state defined itself as "secular and socialist," certainly not as "capitalist" or "brahmanic." But, secularism was interpreted not as the separation of the state from religion, but as the equality of all religions, and state patronage to religion meant a heavy bias in favor of brahmanic Hinduism, in the media, in school texts, in the continuing patronage of swamis and "god-men" by leading politicians; the process was designed to stifle but if necessary incorporate low-caste discontent. It succeeded in projecting the image of a "Hindu majority" that was benign and secular for some time, but lay the ground for its fundamentalist shadow. "Socialism," in its turn, meant not the rule of the toiling masses, but a large state sector coupled with benefits and schemes for the poor, all managed by the upper castes and coexisting comfortably with a rapacious bourgeoisie and an increasingly affluent upper middle class: a "four-anna socialism," linked to caste domination.

Political parties helped to preserve this system. They served not as platforms to represent the masses but as collections of leaders or "bosses" who mobilized their constituencies by the dispensing of patronage through all the "projects," "schemes," and "benefits." At the center the Congress effectively managed, for three decades, a hegemony based on populist appeals to the very poor combined with the solid backing of the upper-caste intelligentsia and support of business interests; opposition parties also worked within the same framework, managing it only with a little more initial honesty when they came to power. The dispensing of patronage functioned mainly to demobilize the oppressed; those who weren't rendered quiescent could be repressed. The system remained intact and its inequalities grew.

"Divide and rule" was an important aspect of ruling: dalits versus the poor of "other backward castes," different ethnic groups posed against each other, peasants versus agricultural laborers, peasants in command areas of dams versus peasants in catchment areas of dams, workers dependent for jobs on polluting factories versus the rural poor seeing these as sucking out resources—all could be set against each other. Central to this strategy was dividing wage workers from peasant and other commodity producers, with left intellectuals taking a lead in convincing the youth who provided cadres for all parties and organizations that wage workers were the only really socialistic and democratic force. "Four-anna socialism" meant a fundamentally negative attitude toward the largest section of the exploited, the peasants.

An unreal picture of the countryside was fostered by Marxist and Marxist-influenced intellectuals, whether it was a Cambridge seminar arguing that political democracy was no good for India because it allowed the domination of "the miniscule rich landowning kulaks with hundreds of thousands of small farmers in their thrall," or the Rudolphs characterizing 2.5–15-acre landholders as "bullock capitalists" who could only have a "centrist politics," or an Andhra leftist analyzing the consolidation of Congress dominance as a result of the "persistence of the large strata of landowning poor peasants [that] weakened the Communist base." [36] This assumption that the politics of the largest section of exploited Indian toilers was at worst feudalistic and at best that of a capitalist status quo helped to keep the countryside demobilized by leading the young activists of the left parties and organizations to ignore the grievances of the peasantry. The discourse on caste, which accepted the oppression of "harijans" but focused on all "caste Hindus" as perpetrating this, also helped to blunt any real mobilization of the oppressed castes. "Communists have never gone to the rural areas" became the constant and largely valid theme of both the dalit and peasant movements.

And when revolutionary youth in the late 1960s under the name of "Naxalism" turned to the rural poor and began to talk in new ways of "people's power," they did so with a militarism that left them open to brutal state repression. More importantly, their ideology left them with few major differences in perspective and demands from the "revisionist" parties they criticized. Naxalite organizations survived and even grew, but they attracted fervent cadre and mass support, not so much because they offered an alternative vision of development, but because they offered alternative and apocalyptic methods. Large sections of activists and organizations—shown in the example of IPF—continued to retrace their steps to try to become a renewed left vanguard. The difference between the remaining Naxalite groups and the "liberation fronts" in places like Punjab and Kashmir with their ideologies of religious fundamentalism became increasingly one only of degree.

Those left out of radical organizing attempts found their own way, in regional-nationalist upsurges that increasingly took on the garments of religious

Table 11.3
Voting in 1991 Parliamentary Elections

	Total Seats	Congress	BJP and Allies	National Front and Left
Andhra Pradesh	42			
Seats won		24	1	15
% Vote		44.6	9.4	38.7
Bihar	54			
Seats won		0	5	42
% Vote		22.6	17.6	47.4
Gujarat	25			
Seats won		5	20	0
% Vote		41.6	50.6	3.8
Haryana	10			
Seats won	9		0	1
% Vote		38.9	10.6	18.1
Himachal Pradesh				
Seats won		2	2	0
% Vote		46.2	42.8	7.0
Karnataka	28			
Seats won		21	4	0
% Vote		42.1	28.0	20.3
Kerala	20			
Seats won		16	0	4
% Vote		49.2	4.6	44.9
Madhya Pradesh	40			
Seats won		27	12	0
% Vote		45.3	41.9	4.7
Maharashtra	48, one countermanded			
Seats won		37	9	1
% Vote		48.6	28.7	17.6
Orissa	21			
Seats won		12	0	8
% Vote		43.7	9.9	39.6
Rajashtan	25			
Seats won		13	12	0
% Vote		44.2	41.1	6.9
Tamil Nadu	39			
Seats won		39	0	0
% Vote		60.7	1.6	30.1
Uttar Pradesh				
Seats won		5	50	23
% Vote		18.6	32.9	23.7
West Bengal	42			
Seats won		5	0	37
% Vote		37.0	10.7	48.2

Source: V. B. Singh and Shankar Bose, *Elections in India: Data Handbook on Lok Sabha Elections, 1952–80* (New Delhi: Sage 1984) and Abhijit Sen and C. P. Chandrasekhar, "Verdict '91," *Frontline*, July 6–19, 1991, p. 106.

identity, and in the new social movements. It is not surprising that a bitter hostility to all political parties pervaded these; if parties were "bourgeois" or "revisionist" to Naxalites, to those who took part in the social movements they were representatives of a brahmanic, patriarchal, urban, ecologically destructive system. Movements thus worked primarily as agitational pressure groups, seeking to organize the protests of hitherto ignored sections. But by the mid-1980s the limitations of being simply pressure groups were clear. Social movement activists were enticed into politics, and as the Congress system hit its second major period of crisis, the parties appealed to the issues of the movements for support. This climaxed with an increased salience of movement issues in the 1989–91 period, promises of implementation of reservations for backward castes, of remunerative prices, of 30 percent reservation for women in local governing bodies. The movements made a turn "toward Delhi," and V. P. Singh emerged as an opposition leader largely in association with them.

The National Front/Left alliance, however, did not have the vision to become a political platform of alternative politics. Quite aside from the factors of institutionalized socioeconomic interest that made the politicians what they were, the framework of traditional left thinking made it impossible for them to adopt an alternative vision. The "left-democratic" political leadership appeared fossilized. Even in methods of organizing, the parties of the alliance could not match the cleverly worked out campaigns of the Hindu right, let alone the innovative agitations and struggles of the new movements. Their revamped slogans had little appeal. How, after all, could "socialism" appeal to a peasant majority when it was identified with policies that kept food prices (and peasant incomes) below world market prices, when the "liberalization" the leftists feared had its initial impact in the raising of crop prices? How could it appeal to environmentalists when it was linked to defense of an ecologically destructive industrial development? Or to dalits and OBCs when it was so evidently designed to be under the management of an upper-caste intelligentsia? There were inherent and unresolved contradictions between the socialist visions the Indian left had represented, their heritage of sacrifice and struggle for the interests of the exploited, and their political-ideological framework; yet few of their leadership and cadres seemed ready to do any serious rethinking of that framework.

By late 1990, under pressure from factional leaders in his own government and growing dissidence, the best V. P. Singh could do was adopt the least structurally disturbing of the new movement issues, the "Mandal commission" demand for representation of the low caste majority in public services and educational institutions. This proved sufficient to arouse a ferocious backlash from the educated children of the high-caste elite, but it could not build a firm alliance of the exploited.

The National Front/Left alliance not only failed to become a platform of a new, alternative socialism comprising issues represented by the movements; it did not even try. The result left the political system in a condition of seemingly permanent instability, in which a surviving Congress now headed the turn to a more "liberal" economy and a Hindu rightist party waited in the wings, stirring up the communal cauldron, dipping into movement issues, preparing to govern while the Communist parties became more and more demoralized and the Janata-socialist center seemed to go on splitting. The new social movements could not go ahead with the political parties as they existed, and they were not capable of replacing them. By 1991 the movements were also experiencing a political impasse and seeking new directions.

"In the Direction of the Kingdom of Bali"

The dalit movement faced the 1990s in a state of confusion. Political leaders were never so discredited, including the leaders of the new movement organizations who had gone into politics. There seemed by 1991 to be a renewed wave of atrocities, many centered around the vicious backlash by the poor of middle and low castes against the limited signs of dalit advance, and quite often in reaction to village relations between dalit and caste Hindu young men and women. Many questioned if justice would ever be won and doubted the very possibility of unity between dalits and OBCs.

Yet the other side of "atrocities" was the ever-widening circle of dalit and low-caste militancy and claims for equal honor as human beings, as well as the readiness of youth of all castes to step outside the boundaries of an outmoded social system, at personal levels as well as political. There was increasing discussion and ferment of thinking among grass roots activists as well as the growing low-caste intelligentsia, and the growing salience of "Ambedkarism" —rediscovering his political strategies and economic thinking, which talked of limited state intervention and ownership in the framework of political democracy—possibly provided greater flexibility for dalit activists in adjusting to the new complexities of world capitalism.

The women's movement was showing more concern than ever about effective political strategies, although this was not yet matched by an increase in political capacity. Yet in spite of contradictory visions and often sectarian quarrels, both community-based work and "national conferences and networks," which had been posed against each other by Madhu Kishwar, were going on with vigor, while signs of new trends in sexual mores, quite outside of feminist circles, in all sections of Indian society, indicated both possibilities and ambivalences of breaking through patriarchal/caste bondages. In rural areas, new themes of "women's power" represented an assertion at the grass roots.

Within the environmental movement, the slogan of "our village, our rule" given by the Narmada Bachao Andolan and the calls for community control of natural resources represented a new turn to the village; at the same time the increasing international visibility of the movement was shown when it won the prestigious Right Livelihood Award (sometimes called the "alternative Nobel

Prize") in 1991. Medha Patkar announced that the money would be used not for antidam organizing but for funding searches for development alternatives, and when questioned about the propriety of "taking foreign funds," she replied that it was Manmohan Singh who was making the biggest attempts to do so.[37]

Between world fame and village roots were victories being won? The Gujarat government was still stonewalling on Narmada, but the Narmada project authority itself was forced to finance a prestigious international seminar on big dams, and K. R. Datye, invited to give a paper for it, gave a considered argument for the total revision of the project, scaling down the dam height, taking up new forms of water distribution and energy generation, and concluding that since "restructuring of the economic system is on the agenda of the nation," there was no reason not to consider stopping construction of projects.[38] A concurrent campaign organized by Anil Agrarwal and Sunita Narain of the Centre for Study of the Environment seemed on the verge of getting government approval for a total revision of rural development schemes. The "bourgeois state" had hardly vanished, but options seemed to be opening up. Vandana Shiva, writing of the dangers of corporate and state "globalism," at the same time posed the possibility of taking the next step, moving to "democratizing the global," linked to the reassertion of people's power at the local level: "*Every* local community, equipped with rights and obligations, constitutes a new global order for environmental care."[39]

Finally, while the major organizations of the farmers' movement remained split after the "assault on Delhi," apparently unable to mobilize as in the past and even more alienated from the political parties, its activists were not disheartened. Sharad Joshi, who had always opposed subsidies and was scornful of all the statist programs for development of Indian agriculture, was moving in a new direction. The Shetkari Sanghatana, the leading ideological organization of the farmers' movement, was now taking a stand for carrying on agriculture with as little use of destructive chemicals and fertilizers as possible. There was no need, its leaders agreed, to focus energies on political agitation for the present because the government no longer had the power to hold down prices; prices would rise and farm products could become India's most successful exports because they were much more competitive than the inefficient, high-import-content manufactured goods; peasants could even "save the nation" by earning foreign exchange—but only if they could produce without high import-content petroleum-based industrial inputs and do much of the primary processing themselves.

Joshi described this turn toward a modified form of natural farming as the "economic struggle," and he put it in terms of a new developmental path, the "direction of the kingdom of Bali." With his abhorrence of fixed ideal utopias, Joshi redefined the ancient peasant utopia, "the kingdom of Bali" (or "Baliland"), as a "direction" and not a "system," a direction in which human labor used the means of production gathered from nature and energy to produce more day by day, but in such a way that the wealth of tomorrow would not be destroyed by the production of today and that the growth of human freedom would be assured. Rejecting the idea that a society completely free from exploitation and injustice "could ever descend on the earth," he stated instead that neither caste nor class nor gender should be a cause for being deprived of a share in economic development.[40]

It was of course a utopia, but a very cautious one with a strong ecological overtone, as well as specific references to women, those most victimized by overcentralized industrial development—and women were central to these new programs of Shetkari Sanghatana, with the campaigns for getting land continuing and women in the new village councils now being linked to programs for collective, sustainable development. Turning ancient Indian traditions against the Hindu fundamentalists, the Sanghatana and its women's front proclaimed that the lands given in women's name in the Laxmi-Mukti campaign to symbolically "free the goddess" would be called "Sita lands" and would be farmed for household consumptions, with natural, local, and low-cost inputs. Women would also contribute to the building of a "self-reliant Sita" temple in the village of Raveri. This was only part of the way in which many women's organizations were turning to programs of alternative agriculture, and it represented the "material base" of a growing "ecofeminist" trend in the women's movement.

In one form or another, the movements were focusing their energies on trying to build concrete alternatives of their own making, beginning from the villages, testing the possibilities of a transformed economic and political arena. There were political uncertainties and the continuing threat of religious fundamentalism and gangster-state violence; there were fears of new economic insecurities due to the IMF-induced liberalization and the specter of the "license-permit raj" being replaced simply by backward capitalist profiteers. The brutal murder of Chattisgarh Mukti Morcha leader and alternative development pioneer Shankar Guha Niyogi in September 1991 symbolized these fears for many. But overall, while the left parties and intellectuals gloomily saw the period as one of retreat, the movements saw new openings. *"Ida pida javo, Balica rajya yevo"* had been the saying of the Maharashtrian peasants, echoed in its movements—a term for the search for a liberated, socialist society. The 1990s represented a new stage in the search, as the false alternatives of the past were being cleared away.

Conclusion

THE NEW social movements, particularly when they show some mass power, have been seen in largely negative terms by most of the Delhi left intellectual elite. For example, Utsa Patnaik, an expert on "class differentiation among the peasantry," says:

> The ideology of the capitalist landlords, moreover, forms a hegemonic ideology in rural areas particularly where democratic mass movements have been weak. The ideology expresses itself in anti-industrialism, against state intervention, in an assertion of the "traditional" values of pristine "Bharat" against the modernizing efforts of the centralised state in industrializing "India" and carries with it both anarchist and reactionary elements, bears a family resemblance to the agrarian radicalism in interwar Japan. . . . It carries within it the potential for fascisization of the Indian policy.[1]

A specter is indeed haunting Delhi. It has been doing so for some time, in the form of the peasant-as-kulak, the peasant-as-OBC, and the peasant as obstacle to "development." It has been seen in the subdued but unrelenting intellectual opposition to the demands for "leaving the surplus in the villages" raised in the form of the "New Agricultural Policy," in the hysteria unleashed over the declaration of implementation of the Mandal Commission report, in the refusal of left intellectuals to see a critique of industrialism as anything other than backward-looking. The object of Utsa Patnaik's anger in the above passage is the farmers' or new peasant movement, and I have been using the term "farmer" rather than "peasant" for convenience, to emphasize that their demands have to do with the marketplace and state; there are as yet no distinctions between "farmer" and "peasant" in Indian languages and most cultivators are to some extent involved in the market. But Patnaik cannot use either term, because they would require from a Marxist at least some favorable consideration, and so she denotes what she describes as "capitalist landlord." The most interesting fact, however, is not simply that peasant radicalism is seen in such negative terms, but that it is now seen as radicalism. Earlier, for Barrington Moore and as recently as the Rudolphs, peasants were seen as a source of stability, of "centrist" politics. Now, by political theorists such as Utsa Patnaik or Achin Vanaik,[2] they are increasingly looked upon as destabilizing and radical, even though the biases of these scholars lead them to see this "agrarian radicalism" as right wing and reactionary.

While Patnaik is writing about the farmers' movement, the critique could have been even more clearly directed at the environmental movement—equally a peasant movement, I have argued—for it is more explicitly anti-industrial, hostile to the central state, expressing itself in terms of "traditional" values. For that matter, it would be appropriately directed at Gandhi himself.

The fact is that both the farmers' movement and environmental movement have positive assessments of many aspects of modern technology; their radicalizing use of traditional symbolism looks not backward but forward to a less exploitative as well as "sustainable" community, and they have been as strongly opposed as the left parties to the only force in the country that can legitimately be called "fascistic," Hindu fundamentalism.

It is true that there is a broad opposition to the type of "industrialism" that has taken place and that the movements do indeed direct themselves against "the modernizing effects of the centralized state." They are in a sense "anarchistic"; as Anjan Ghosh has put it, "the rhetoric of the new social movements is laden with the vocabulary of decentralization, plurality, autonomy, and participation."[3] This is true even for the farmers' movement, which he does not consider, while sections of the anticaste movement are also increasingly talking of decentralization and autonomy for communities in India. It is also true that the new movements tend to use what might be called "traditional" or "populist" symbols drawn from Indian tradition perhaps more than the "old" working-class movement has done. But the point is that it is only from a centralist and statist perspective that a decentralizing thrust is seen as "reactionary" and "anarchist" in a stigmatizing sense; and it is only from a particular interpretation of secularism that any reference to community identity is seen as "traditionalism." Finally, it is only from a particular interpretation of "class" and "economic exploitation" that the farmers' movement is seen as "rich peasant" (or "capitalist landlord"!), and that the women's movement, anticaste movement, and environmental movement are seen as dealing with "nonclass" issues.

The political crisis in India is also a crisis in comprehension and articulation of the struggles that are going on. Politics remains at an impasse because as yet there is no political formation that is expressing the direction that is implied in the thrust of the new social movements. In spite of aspirations to represent the "forces of change," the National Front/Janata Dal/left combine led by V. P. Singh represents quite standard politics, with no clear program aside from the "social justice" plank. The political parties, notably the parties of the left, are still responding to the themes of the new movements, co-opting and displacing rather than representing them. Nor have the new social movements themselves as yet presented an effective alternative program or a new powerful political platform. And so, in spite of the astounding political change involved in the end of Congress hegemony, the country is drifting. Yet beyond the "single-point programs" dialogue is growing, and there are clear trends toward a new ideological-political formulation of a decentralized, ecologically sustainable form of socialism. If to many this is a specter or a dreamlike wraith, to others it is the reinvention of revolution.

"On the Ruins of Earlier Antisystemic Movements"

"We stand on the shoulders of giants" has been taken to be a paradigm of how science moves forward. In regard to the antisystemic movements, however, it almost seems as if the relationship between old left and new left can be better characterized in terms of clambering over ruins, slipping and sliding over rocks; in the words of Anjan Ghosh again, "the new social movements are built on the ruins of earlier antisystemic movements."

These are harsh words, and incomplete, for the new movements have also in many ways grown out of the old. But the growth has been at times a painful one. There has indeed been tension and hostility, as shown in the way a left intellectual like Utsa Patnaik can characterize the rural situation, so much that it has frequently seemed that the new movements and "Marxism" are at odds. Indeed, there are common features behind the crisis of socialism in the "postrevolutionary societies" and the relationship of the Marxist left in India to the new movements, so that if one accurately understands why the first has happened, one can then understand and in a sense compensate for the hostility in the relations of the latter. Then one will be in a position to understand the deep interlinkages that do in fact exist between "old" and "new" movements, Marxism and the ideologies that often seem to be put forth in contradiction to Marxism.

In any case, there is a good deal of debris of conventional interpretations to be cleared away before an analysis of the new social movements begins.

What has hampered analyses of India's new social movements is a lack of detailed and accurate research; a lack of studies of the relations of exploitation against which they protest; and a serious in-built bias in the Indian (and much of the foreign) intellectual world regarding both. Characterizations of the farmers' movement, for example, as "kulak" or "capitalist landlord" seem to be made in a vacuum, from libraries in Delhi or Bombay, or for that matter Berkeley, without live contact with the movements, with little experiential knowledge of the rural areas that have generated these movements or the stands that the movements have taken over a period of time. In an opposite but equally devastating fashion, many environmental movements are romanticized as protests of "victimized tribals" without having the basic issues they are raising taken seriously. Both responses stand as barriers to understanding by intellectuals just as they have raised barriers to communication and joint action among activists.

This study, while based on fairly extensive experience and familiarity with the literature, obviously has its limitations; my direct experience is uneven, and in particular I know more about movements in Maharashtra than elsewhere. Still, I will outline some major issues and try to make some generalizations about the new movements that can at least serve as a basis for carrying forward our understanding.

First there is the question of definition. I have argued, for reasons given in the introduction, that the concept of "new social movement" does delimit a genuine empirical phenomenon. While many would now agree with this, few would include the particular movements I have taken here. This question of which movements are "new social movements" is not an innocent one. Part of the debate is political. Since among progressives "new social movements" are now a phenomenon admitted to have insights to contribute to a movement toward socialism, excluding some movements (e.g., the farmers' movement) and defining others in particular ways (e.g., seeing the anticaste movement as only a "dalit movement") has the function of allowing the excluded sections to continue to be depicted as part of the "enemy camp."[4] There are more direct questions of analysis. For instance, the *Seminar* issue on "new social movements" takes up five movements—women, ecology, science, health, and civil liberties; along with almost all other recent discussions, its editor Ramchandra Guha excludes the farmers' movement and anticaste movement and then goes on to criticize the position of Frank and Fuentes that the movements mobilize hundreds of millions of people throughout the world:

> This is emphatically not the case in India. Compared to class-based struggles—the trade union movement, peasant movements of the Sharad Joshi/Mahendra Tikait variety, and Naxalite-led movements of landless labourers and tribals—the popular support enjoyed by the new social movements is negligible. Where the latter score, perhaps, is in their incisive analysis of those aspects of poverty and oppression—ecological degradation, subordination of women and so on—that are given short shrift by the class-based movements. Some observers have optimistically suggested that the new social movements are on the verge of *replacing* classical movements as the major force for social change in the modern world. However, given their limited social base, perhaps a more appropriate role would be one *complementary* to the more powerful class-based movements. The moral vision of the new movements may be compelling, yet they are by no means a substitute for the existing organizations of peasants and workers. For in India, struggles in the factory and over land and its produce are as important today as at any time in the past.[5]

First the farmers' movement and anticaste movement (both of which mobilize as massively in India as any of the traditional "old" class movements and now have provided the major themes for equally big mobilizations of politicians) are excluded from the category, and then the "new" movements are contrasted with the "old" in terms of moral versus economic, small-scale versus mass; in the process the anticaste movement is left in a vacuum, and the way in which a Marxist perspective considers the farmers' movement (which struggles over the "produce" of land) as a "class movement" is not theoretically confronted. The new movements are shown their place, "complementary" but "by no means a substitute."

In contrast to this position I would assert—following Chhaya Datar's thesis on the women's movement—that all the new movements are involved in "redefining exploitation," that all have clear economic aspects. Similarly, the movements are obviously political, though in different ways than traditional parties, and though the political sphere is a problem for all of them, not just the "small" women's and environmental movements. They all are putting forward what Guha calls a "moral vision," and they are not "complementary" but are confronting the guiding vision of the old movements head-on.

So I begin by defining the movements as being those against particular forms of exploitation not recognized in traditional class analysis. These movements are coming to the fore now, it appears, on the one hand these forms of exploitation have intensified (in varying ways) with the particular development of modern capitalism, and on the other because the traditional left has been able to give no solution to them or has offered no real understanding of their situation. It is on this basis that I have distinguished four major movements; this is not to say that there are not others.

We must obviously distinguish "organizations" from "movements" and note that while there are some organizations that are clearly organizations *of* a particular movement (e.g., most of the groups classified as "autonomous" women's groups, the Dalit Panthers), there are many others that are involved in struggles around issues representing different movements (e.g., the Jharkhand Mukti Morcha, Chattisgarh Mukti Morcha), while some organizations by definition overlap movements (e.g., the Shetkari Mahila Aghadi).

There are some problems of classification. In particular there is the question of classifying what are often called "nationality" movements, essentially movements of peasant-based ethnic groups for varying degrees of autonomy, since so many of them express and organize struggles over themes of the movements (in particular ecological destruction and "looting" of the peasantry), are related to the caste dynamic of Indian society, and certainly are part of an overall push for decentralization. There is also a question that might be raised regarding "adivasi" movements; there is certainly an "adivasi" identity, but it is perhaps premature to speak of a "movement"; what scholars have talked of "tribal movements" are more often seen by their protagonists as "ethnic-nationality" movements. Much of the emerging "adivasi" identity issues also can be looked at as part of the "anticaste" movement (adivasis plus dalits plus bahujan castes). In the future, adivasis will themselves give a clearer answer to this question.

In spite of these questions, the classification given is adequate to allow some preliminary generalizations about the movements, their mass base, leadership, and organizational forms, their economic and political aspects and perspectives, their involvement with Indian history of "identity" issues, and their dialogue with Marxism.

India's New Social Movements

The movements described here all had their origins in the early 1970s; strikingly, 1972 represents a founding date for many of their important organizations: the Dalit Panthers, the first farmers' organizations in Punjab and Tamilnadu, SEWA, the Jharkhand Mukti Morcha, the All-Assam Students' Union. Why 1972? The mid-1960s had seen the major crisis around the world of postwar capitalist development; it resulted everywhere in a "new left" upsurge. If one looks more closely, one might see not only the crisis of the old model, but also the development of the material and human base for new movements—new forces of production, new transportation and communication technologies, the reorganization of the world division of labor bringing peasants to the cities (and often to the cities of the European-north American center) and the cities to the peasants. The "primary terrain of resistance" in daily life of people would also show new capacities for assertion and new forms of resistance and struggle.

In the initial period, traditional Marxism remained hegemonic, at any rate among the intellectuals who analyzed the upsurges and the educated middle classes who provided so many of their cadre. In India the crisis was reflected first in the Naxalite movement, which combined orthodox Marxist-Leninist language with what many saw (with a good deal of validity) as "ruralist anarchism" and took the form of armed struggle as the revolutionary means of breaking through the stultifying parliamentarianism of the mainstream Communists. After this challenge was crushed, the Indira Gandhi-led Congress returned to power in 1971 on a renewed program of "socialist" rhetoric. The antisystemic thrust of the toiling people was then expressed in the form of new social movements and of regionalist, sometimes separatist, linguistic-national movements. While the ethnic-nationality movements tended toward armed struggle and aimed at the seizure of political power, the new movements as such were single-issue, oriented toward nonviolent action, posing themselves primarily as pressure groups, and above all suspicious of all political parties and the male/high-caste/urban elites who guided them.

The movements drew on much of the same mass base (and the same base as earlier antisystemic movements in India had), that is, a wide section of rural and urban toilers. This was a divided, pluralistic, diverse, hierarchized section. (So, for that matter, was the "working-class movement" in the nineteenth century and today at a world level: wage laborers in manufacturing have encompassed a wide range of people, hierarchized and divided in race, language, gender, and nationality;

those who have been most active in organizing have quite often represented a better-off section compared to nonwage laborers—slaves and serfs in the early period, subsistence producers, commodity producers—whose labor has also contributed to the accumulation of capital.) The movements are sometimes described as "multiclass" because of this, but the term does not capture the complexity of their divisions. Sharp polarizations are not to be found (even in caste terms, it is frequently difficult to pinpoint who is OBC, and who is scheduled caste, who is tribal); in economic or "class" terms, the majority of toiling families combine wage labor, petty commodity production, and subsistence production in varying mixes.

There were differences in the bases of different movements, but less than might be expected. The anticaste movement began with a more dalit and urban base but spread to the rural poor and, as OBCs began to get more involved, to wider sections of the rural poor, to encompass many of the same sections involved in other cases in the "farmers' movement." The farmers' movement was of course more rural, but even this had its share of small-town (or even city) educated boys and girls from village origins—if not Bombay, it could have a presence in Nasik, Amraoti, or even Pune. In the villages the anticaste movement had its center in the dalit areas, the farmers' movement in the "caste Hindu" village; dalits were on the whole poorer, but many rural middle castes were as poor, and the greater role played by upper-middle-caste and richer villagers in the farmers' movement was perhaps matched by the greater participation of low-caste employees, students, and teachers in the anticaste movement. The environmental movement, in turn, was more heavily based on tribal and peasants in more "backward" egalitarian regions, but it also had its share of caste Hindus, and more commercialized regions and better-off peasants threatened by development projects were also involved in resistance movements.

What I am arguing here is that conventional ways of looking at the movements in "class" terms have to be considerably rethought, and that they all are essentially movements of exploited sections in the same way that the "working-class movement" has been a movement of the exploited. To take the most contentious example, the farmers' movement as such mobilizes a slightly better-off section than is involved in agricultural laborers' organizations, and there is, just as obviously, a conflict of interest (which takes varying degrees of intensity in different areas of India) between laborers and wage-paying peasants. But "agricultural laborers" do not represent a movement, but a section of the "working-class movement," the poorest, least organized, and most exploited section. The section of nonagricultural "unorganized workers" is economically comparable to the mass of those mobilized in peasant movements (statistically their incomes are higher), while organized industrial workers as a whole are significantly better-off; such workers (the Bombay textile workers or workers at the Patalganga area in the Konkan awaiting expected campaigns of the Shetkari Sanghatana) have always spontaneously expressed their urge for a "worker-peasant" unity. Finally, the farmers' movement does include participants, sympathizers, and mobilizers who are much better-off than this poor majority, who can be classed as "capitalist farmers" or "rich peasants" (or nonagriculturalists) and the like; but even this section, excluding perhaps 2 to 3 percent of farming households, are worse-off economically than the office workers (bank employees, government employees) who are normally considered part of the "working-class movement," and who certainly are encompassed in the slogan "*ham sab ek hai*" (we are all one). In this sense, it is not true that the farmers' movement mobilizes a "richer" section.

Of course, the farmers' movement can be clearly differentiated from the working class movement and classed as "nonproletarian" or "petty bourgeoisie" from a particular class perspective. But there are many who argue that this perspective represents an analysis not in the interest of the proletariat (industrial working class) as such but of the last groups within what I have above depicted as the "working-class movement"—white-collar workers and the highest section among them, the intelligentsia, or what some have described as a "coordinator class."[6] I am not yet prepared to argue this point of view, but I am prepared to argue that a preliminary for determining these "class questions" is to have a firm grip on the empirical facts on which to test them, and so far beginning with a conventional "class" perspective has prevented this.

What about the leadership of the movements? With a caveat about the difficulties of separating "leadership" from "base" in fairly informally organized movements, some generalizations, again, can be made. The leadership, in all cases, is more urban, "higher" in class and caste terms, certainly more educated. Of course there are obvious differences: the dalit movement has dalit male, urban, educated leaders; women activists are overwhelmingly upper caste, urban, educated women, and so on. But aside from this there is little difference, and there is also little difference between this leadership cadre and that of traditional left organizations. Put another way, just from looking at who sits on the stage, one can find little to distinguish the leaders at an IPF conference from those at a farmers' rally: they are both predominantly male, upper and middle caste, and physically taller and healthier than the masses mobilized. It is not obvious qualities but a framework of analysis that says one is "proletarian" and the other is not.

Indeed, what the movements have been bringing forward is the central question of who is really "proletarian" in the sense of being the most oppressed, and being at the advance point of efforts to change the system of exploitation.

Finally, let me note some aspects of the way the movements are organized. The movements I have discussed here are not localized grass roots organizations, but movements that have an all-India reach and regional/national organizational forms. Yet these have some unique features. In all cases, there are indeed very localized groups, functioning at the village or neighborhood level, which operate usually on an informal basis, though there may be imposed hierarchical structures (e.g., government-registered mahila mandals or unions). These are coordinated or articulated in different ways.

In the case of the anticaste movement there are both statewide organizations of various types and two political parties (the Bahujan Samaj party and the Republican party factions) and one semipolitical organization (the Dalit Panthers) that claim "all-India" status and that do have organizational links beyond the state level. The women's movement has had two national "coordinations": the loose but still very real networks that link the feminist groups, and the united platforms that link the women's wings of the left (Communist and Janata Dalsocialist) political parties. More recently, growing networking has begun to link both groups and the mass-movement-connected women's groups. The farmers' movement has a clear structure: regional associations linked in a national "federation" (and even though it has gone through two splits, this makes it still fairly united by Indian standards). Finally, the environmental movement has had the loosest structure: local committees with state-level or national organization so far provided only in loose networks. Only in the last two years have organizations like the Jan Vikas Andolan emerged to try to provide a more formalized wider coordination or serve as political platforms.

Economics of the Movements

The main difference between the new movements and the most typical of what one might think of as "old social movements," that is, the working-class movement, is that organization on wage issues and conflicts of toilers with those who exploit them directly as owners of property play a relatively small role. It is largely for this reason that their characterization as "social" frequently is interpreted as being noneconomic or "nonclass."

Wage struggles have gone on, and the movements have related to them (accepting them, trying to organize them) but not taken them as central. For example, agricultural labor organizing has been related to the dalit movement (it was central to Naxalite organizing in Bihar and Andhra, for instance, although these organizations do not define themselves as "dalit" or "anticaste" movements), but the movement as such has been more oriented toward gaining entry into better-paid organized-sector jobs, that is, to the demand for reservations. Similarly, the women's movement has quite often made the demand for "equal wages for equal work," especially for women agricultural laborers, but there has been no direct organizing on the issue. The farmers' movement has also come to include a fairly high demand for legal minimum wages for agricultural laborers (while many of its individual participants continue to come into conflict with their own laborers over that issue) and in doing so at least serves to legitimize laborers' demands and perhaps weaken resistance—but it has not taken up this as an organizing issue. Again, environmental movements such as the Narmada Bachao Andolan have been involved with attempts at workplace organizing of contract laborers on the dams, but this has been relatively rare.

To put all this another way, the movements have not been trade union movements in any basic sense. In fact, many of their activist-theorists would argue that taking working-class organizing on wage issues as a basis for socialist transformation has had little to show in the way of results. The organized working class in the West is solidly incorporated in the system; indeed, winning of union gains is normally analyzed even by classical Marxists as a factor pushing capitalist development forward, by forcing accumulation through development of the forces of production rather than simply increasing the rate of labor exploitation. Clearly, wage organizing can bring limited (though important) gains in standards of living for the work force, but it does not change the system, as was recognized even before the "new social movements" came along.

There are obviously other forms of economic struggle, and these have been much more important, even central, to the movements. The most important economic struggle for the traditional left understanding of a peasant movement is land reform gaining and maintaining control of individual means of production. But strikingly, in India, after the tenants' movements of the preindependence period, this has not taken place so much in the sense of taking excess land from big private landowners; dalits, adivasis, and other landless have most frequently gained land by encroaching on "forest" or "waste" lands and fighting the government for rights to maintain it. This has gone on even without organizations to support it (at what I have referred to as the "primary terrain of resistance," part of daily life struggles), but they have been taken up by local "agricultural laborer" unions, organizations calling themselves "peasant" or "toilers' " organizations, dalit or adivasi organizations as such, often Communist- or socialist-led, but also often within the framework of environmental, anticaste, and other movements. At times, dalit claims to village "commons" have come into conflict with "dominant caste" peasants' claim to it, but more frequently both have attempted to gain control of land "belonging" to the state. At the same time, the main thrust of all mass-based environmental movements is to assert the community's control over local resources and to resist the state's appropriation of their property. That is, in regard to "property," the movements have most frequently centered around individual and community efforts to reappropriate property from the state.

The basic economic demand of the anticaste movement has been for reservations for jobs in government service, and while most Marxists see this as essentially "middle class" and hence are uncomfortable about supporting it, to the extent that community-caste membership is a real factor in determining access to resources, even lower-class members of excluded communities benefit economically.

The central economic issues for the women's movement have been those of breaking the monopoly of control over property by male family members, whether these are "bourgeois," peasant, or worker, and of gaining rights to "maintenance" (alimony) in the case of divorce. Much more than the wage issues, these issues of inheritance and divorce rights have provided themes for action by women's groups.

Finally, the basic economic demand of the farmers' movement has been for higher prices for agricultural products. This demand implies that the relations between peasants as petty commodity producers and the buyers/appropriators of their products are relations of production and exploitation. But its direction against the state reveals the centrality of the political sphere in Third World societies (in all capitalist societies?) in managing exploitation and even in imposing itself as a direct exploiter.

All of these areas of economic struggles, in fact, force one to widen the analysis of relations of production and exploitation. The most common theme is that their economic struggles are directed against the state, rather than against the holders of private property; that is, the "decentralizing" or "antistatist" thrust, is economic as much as political. One recent theorist of world capitalism who understands this is Immanuel Wallerstein. He sees a link between a decentralist political thrust (emphasizing democratic participation, resisting the power of the central state, emphasizing "eroding the state" rather than attempting to take state power, etc.), and a decentralist economic thrust (which involves retaining "local" control over surpluses):

> I am thinking rather of attacking the flows of surplus at another point, at the point of their production. Suppose that antisystemic movements concentrated their energies everywhere . . . on efforts defined as retaining most of the surplus created. One obvious way would be to seek to increase the price of labour, or the price of sale by the direct producers. . . .[Capitalists] spend a considerable amount of their worldwide political energy on the politics of pricing. . . . The movements cannot afford their close links to the states, even to the regimes they have struggled to bring to power. Their concern must be how at each point on very long commodity chains a greater percentage of the surplus can be retained. Such a strategy would tend over time to 'overload' the system, reducing global rates of profit significantly and evening out distribution. Such a strategy might also be able to mobilize the efforts of all the many varieties of new social movements, all of which are oriented in one way or another more to equality than to growth. . . . An emphasis on surplus retention by the producers, that is an emphasis on greater equality and democratic participation, far from being utopian, could be devastatingly effective.[7]

Wallerstein is putting his arguments in terms of prescriptions, yet it can be argued that in fact it is a description of much of what the movements have been doing, with peasants fighting for retention of the surplus through higher crop prices or debt relief, or resisting the ongoing extraction of their land and forest resources for state-sponsored "development" programs. Working-class demands also gain a place in this perspective; so in a sense do daily-life oppositions to "sacrifice" for distant goals. The "antistatist" orientation so attacked by Utsa Patnaik finds its strategic justification here. But if Wallerstein's point defines the implicit thrust of the "economic" and "not-in-my-back-yard" struggles, the overall vision, ideology, direction, and model of a new society have not yet attained a political articulation.

Eroding the State

This is not easy. Since, even in economic terms, the movements are directed more against the state than against the holders of private property, they have of necessity been led to become "political" in the more narrow sense of dealing with the questions of state policy and electoral politics. Yet they have not been political in the conventional sense. When they operate politically they have done so in different ways from the traditional political parties—with more informal structures, more charismatic leadership, a "one-point program" stress. Their focus of organizing has been quite different from efforts to "capture political power," the direct assault on the state made by earlier antisystemic movements. The antistate thrust of the new movements, with its inherent distrust of electoral politics and political parties, has not meant an "antipolitical essence," but rather an effort to redefine political action, to find ways of reconstructing politics. These efforts have not yet been strikingly successful, and "politics" has remained an extremely problematic sphere for all the movements.

The dalit and anticaste movement, with its stress on gaining a share in political power, has been the most highly political in the conventional sense; from beginning to end it has thrown up political parties that have generally been part of the left-democratic (antiCongress, anti-Hindu rightist) spectrum. Yet the most interesting organizations in the recent period (the Dalit Panthers, the Dalit Sangarsh Samiti, the Andhra Dalit Mahasabha) have been more nonpolitical. At the same time, the most effective political party of the last decade, the Bahujan Samaj party, is almost more of a "movement" than a party: organized around one charismatic leader and with no political program in the normal sense except for that of dalits, OBCs, and minorities coming together to take power, BSP saw its foundational organization, BAMCEF, undergoing a split on grounds that it was "premature" to form a political party.

The women's movement has in many ways concentrated on making demands of the state (for laws against amiocentisis or sati, giving welfare benefits to poor women) or in dealing with the state in regard to atrocities against women. Yet "politics" has remained a problematic sphere. Networks of feminists, on one hand, and the party-connected women's organizations on the other still dominate the national coordination of the women's movement; as yet the newer mass-organization-linked women's groups have achieved no separate coordination or "national" reach. Of these, the feminists have tended to be antipolitical; the party women have been constantly urging that women must take part in politics but only under the leadership of the party, thus leaving women's organizations as such nonpolitical. Thus, until recently, in regard to electoral politics feminist activists or women's groups have simply supported a "left-democratic opposition" or tried to exert an independent presence by separate campaigning, "charters of demands," and so on.

Outside of these "traditional feminists" and "traditional Marxists," there has been a broad trend from below and from outside of the existing organizations of women going directly into politics. This has been seen in the fights for village and district council representation, begun on a spontaneous basis and carried on most vigorously by the Shetkari Mahila Aghadi. But there has also been for some time a growing sentiment among women at all levels that, if it were at all possible, a "women's party" would be a nice thing. The announcement in Delhi of such a party, or Mahila Dal, at the time of the 1991 elections, though not a very serious effort, is an indication of the sentiments involved.[8]

The farmers' movement has been more directly involved from its beginning in "political" life than has been the women's movement or the environmental movement, in the sense of attempting to have an effective strategy to influence the policies and holders of state power and being in a position to do so; at the same time it has been suspicious of all political parties. Its experiences exemplify the political dilemmas of the new social movements. Its power as a "mass" movement has led to direct political pulls; aspiring politicians have sought its support, and ambitious activists have been attracted to politics. Yet attempts to participate directly in electoral politics (formation of political parties by the Tamil leaders and later the Karnataka leaders) have had little success; "movement strength" does not easily translate into electoral political strength.

Sharad Joshi, the dominant theorist of the movement, thus argued that the Shetkari Sanghathana should remain as a pressure group or movement and act in elections to maintain the political conditions (balance of power) that would make pressure-group politics effective. This was the justification given for opposing Congress steadily for nearly a decade while maintaining the position that "all political parties are those of India" (i.e., antipeasant). This strategy was broken in 1989 under intense pressure from activists to stand directly for elections. The Shetkari Sanghatana chose to do so not by contesting as a party on its own but by taking tickets of the Janata Dal. Shetkari Sanghatana MLAs of Janata Dal functioned after the election as an effectively autonomous group, but the result as a whole was unsatisfactory. It not only tied Shetkari Sanghatana to Janata Dal, but it was demoralizing to the organization when far fewer candidates won than the enthusiastic activists had expected.

The dilemma exists for all of the new movements described here. The environmental movement has also found the results of trying to act as a pressure group unsatisfactory, and the 1989 and 1991 national elections saw first an independent "environmental" candidate and second a renewed thrust at trying to exert influence from without and organizing specifically environmental electoral platforms on a modest scale.[9]

In other words, there is a logic of political involvement that is acting in the same way for all the movements, with unsolved dilemmas. The fact is that the movements, whether the Shetkari Sanghatana, women's organizations, environmental organizations, or whatever, find their "natural" political place with the "left and democratic opposition," that is, the National Front/Left combine, fighting both Congress and the Hindu rightists as clear enemies. But it seems that this very fact limits their ability to exert pressure and leads the NF-left to take their support for granted, giving only nominal concessions to their demands while maintaining a conventional form of politics. At the same time, as ties with the left-democratic front become clear, their "autonomous" status, which is important to their mass following, is compromised. As a result, the movements finally seem to be forced into the position where they have to have a political front of their own—even to exert pressure within the democratic-left opposition. But (aside from all the other questions of electoral fund-raising, compromise of movement demands, etc.), direct "politics," which requires an overall perspective, necessitates a transcendence of their existence so far as single-issue movements. In other words, the movements now seem to be faced more and more with the need to generalize and coordinate their demands as part of an overall political perspective for the transformation of society, and this requires a truly integrated unification of the insights and political programs of the various social movements. This has as yet barely begun.

Reimagining the Community, Reinterpreting History

At one level, much of the focus of the new movements is on "community" rather than "class," even when their demands are economic; and it is in their relation to traditional symbols of the Indian community/nation that their differences from both the dominant nationalism and the left and working-class movements stand out. Their radicalism with regard to the traditional symbols of India is one of the things that makes them "new."

Here the dalit movement has been, in some ways, in the vanguard, setting the tone for looking at Indian history as beginning not with the Aryan invasion but with Mohenjo daro and even its early tribal inhabitants. Rama is not simply ignored (as even Phule had done) but strongly attacked; rakshasas such as Bali Raja and Ravana are looked to as representatives of their own powerful past; Shambuk and Ekalavya, figures of the defeated tribals and dalits in the epics, are taken as heroes.

The women's movement also is "new" in this sense compared to the main women's organizations of the colonial period. Then the dominant organizations like the AIWC functioned within a framework of accepting idealized interpretations of the Vedic, Aryan, Hindu past. Now the movement rejects an identification with the "Sita/Savitri" symbolism of the loyal Hindu wife. Many feminists reject religion altogether as inherently "patriarchal," while most of those who do look to religious-cultural traditions are seeking the more countercultural themes. A swing to identification with "one's own cultural tradition" especially by the *Manushi* group in the last few years (the tenth anniversary number of *Manushi* in 1989 focused on women *bhakti* saints) has been controversial among feminists—but even this identification, which reflects some of the realities of a North Indian localization, specifically rejects values like *pativratya* and has focused on contesting the meaning of Rama put forward by the fundamentalist organizations, criticizing the militaristic and aggressive interpretation given by the Hindu fundamentalists.

The farmers' movement also looks to a large extent to "countertradition" symbols. There are again important regional differences, with organizations in more "Hinduistic" states such as Gujarat and U.P. reflecting greater traditionalism in their rhetoric, but the Shetkari Sanghatana identifies with Phule and Bali Raja, very "anti-Hindu" heroes, and it has strongly contested the Brahmanic and anti-Muslim interpretation given to Shivaji by the Hindu rightist tradition. A similar thrust appears to exist in the case of the farmers' organizations in Karnataka and Tamilnadu.

The environmental movement in many ways has the strongest "Gandhian" element in it and thus tendencies to idealize pre-British history, and sometimes Hindu symbolism. Here also, however, such themes as Bali Raja (for the Mukti Sangarsh movement in Maharashtra), Ekalavya (for a movement for water rights in Bihar), and other tribal symbols provide important points of identification. Again, where traditional "Hindu" symbolism is used, it is more often that of the "mother goddess/prakriti" symbolism, which has, arguably, pre-Sanskritic and non-Brahmanic roots.

There is an inherent pluralism in this symbolization of the traditional community and community heroes/heroines of the various social movements. But it would be inaccurate to say that it is a return to an essentially Hindu pluralism; it works within a new framework that is, more than ever, being defined by the activities of castes and communities that have been traditionally low in the hierarchy and on the peripheries of the country. In the process of their assertion on the cultural as well as political and economic spheres, two identifiable trends can be discerned operating in all the movements, one a liberal Gandhian or Lohiate one that continues to define itself as "Hindu" but stresses the pluralistic, open, even "feminine" aspects of "Hinduism"; the other deriving ultimately from Phule, which attacks Hinduism as such. Gradually the second trend seems to be gaining predominance. What is going on can be said to be a process of reinterpreting Indian history, redefining the communities, reimagining the country itself. It is a new, as yet incomplete, cultural dynamic in which the center of gravity is shifting to antibrahmanic and non-Hindu identifications.

To many who are uncomfortable with the battlefield of cultural symbolism, or who see in it nothing but the "identity politics" pervading the social movements of many Western countries, the use of traditional symbolism is a sign of backwardness; thus to Utsa Patnaik the posing of "Bharat" versus "India" can only be antimodern. In part this is a reflection of the traditional Marxist idea that the proletariat is a "naked" class, stripped of any of its social history, created out of the wreckage of the old society and totally immiserated, "with nothing to lose but its chains," nowhere to go but forward. From this point of view, communalism can only be opposed through a secularism that stands in opposition to community identity. If these preconceptions are rejected, then we can understand why the movements can refer *both* to the past ("Let the kingdom of Bali come") *and* to modern class-type slogans of struggle ("We don't want alms but the reward of our sweat"; "Who says they won't give it? We won't stop without taking it!").

It is a mixture that was expressed in a song, actually written decades back, by a woman activist of a fairly traditional Communist party, the Lal Nishan party of Maharashtra. The song ends,

> The final class war has not yet come to Bharat; when it does
> It will be neither the Kauravas nor Pandavas
> But the long-neglected Ekalavya who will take
> Up bow and arrow to establish his state. [10]

Rethinking Marxism

The new movements have attacked Marxism on so many points that it may seem out of order (or, conversely, an act of intellectual imperialism) to describe them as having an effect of restructuring Marxism. For example, Sharad Joshi's occasional claims of being a Marxist—in spite of rejection of "class struggle, the labor theory of value and the proletariat as vanguard"—has been taken as simply a gimmick, with many quite reasonably likely to ask, "What's left?"

What is left? All the movements have been concerned to stress exploitation and contradiction (some sections of society living off the labor and benefiting from the enslavement or poverty of the rest); they have all seen this as historically created; they have all projected the possibility of the establishment of a nonexploitative—casteless, nonpatriarchal, nonlooting—sustainable society. They have all seen themselves as somehow fighting to create this.

Along with this, many of their activists and leaders have described themselves as "Marxists," as the "true Marxists" or the "real proletariat," however much orthodox Marxists may reject this as unscientific. Among the masses mobilized in the movements, "Marxism," "communism," and "comrade" represent identities that for all their ambivalence still carry the heritage of the militant resistance to oppression. This is why, for instance, angry youngsters of the Dalit Panthers could rail against Communists "for not being *really* Communist" (i.e., they have not reached the villages, they perform pujas, they give dowries for their daughters' weddings). This is why, again, an older peasant of the Shetkari Sanghatana could say, when explaining why threats against Sharad Joshi's life by a Congress boss had helped them mobilize more people for their demonstration, "We can take him on, we've got a lot of Naxalites among us!" In other words, the statement that the movements are arising "on the ruin of earlier antisystemic movements" reflects only a part-truth; they are arising out of them, and they are not yet forgetting this history.

This adds up to a good deal, particularly considered in terms of the explicitly prosystem characteristics of many "pressure group" movements elsewhere, or in contrast to the mobilization in terms of religious identities expressed by current fundamentalist revivals. This is not to say that there are not anti-Communist trends in the movements, or that they do not include many quite conservative elements which, if they had their way, would lead to reincorporation in the system. (This after all was also true of old social movements.) But on the whole, the movements have taken "Marxism" not as an enemy to be destroyed, but as a fallen entity to be reformed, and they have carried on often angry dialogues with it.

Once this is understood, the fallacy of an "end of history" perspective shows itself not only as an ideological claim, but as a desperate attempt to recoup a situation that is not as bad as many of those still within traditional left frameworks believe. The dialogue, however, has to be taken more seriously by larger sections of those following the Marxist tradition than it has been.

The movements, in this ongoing dialogue, critique various, often quite different aspects of traditional Marxism.

The anticaste movement until recently has taken much of the economic analysis of Marxism for granted, while simply arguing for the necessity of considering the separate reality of "caste." This has frequently led to the oversimplifications of the various *additive* formulas of "caste and class," "economic and social" struggles, and so forth. With these, "caste" is given a superstructural or idealistic interpretation, so that ideological tendencies in the anticaste movement have sometimes veered to idealism or racism (as in the stress on "non-Aryan" or "Dravidian-black" racial identities). Yet the main trend in the movement (going back to Ambedkar; Phule's economic analysis has not yet been much taken up) has stressed economic factors also, in taking the fight to be against both "brahmanism and capitalism," for instance. As the impulse to an overall perspective analyzing exploitation grows, the "economic" factor itself is beginning to be reexamined, and activists coming out of a broad Communist movement, such as Sharad Patil and Bharat Patankar of Maharashtra, Dev Nathan of Bihar, and Kancha Ilaiah of Andhra, have begun to put forward new analyses, stressing the material reality of caste and linking with analysis of other factors such as gender.

The women's movement for some time, like the anticaste movement, has put its theoretical stress in "additive" terms, that is, "class and patriarchy," without questioning very much the conventional interpretation of class relations. Most women activists in both the "autonomous feminist" groups and the party women's wings still seem to function within this framework. Yet the problem of dealing with women's work—in particular unpaid domestic labor—forced some new thinking quite early, and this has now been articulated with the emergence of an "ecofeminist" trend involving a wide number of women activists—from Chhaya Datar and Gabriele Dietrich to the most well-known, Vandana Shiva. At the same time, Shiva's articulation of the "feminist principle" that sees the united action by women and men to transform society in a "feminist" (ecological, participatory) direction finds its echo in themes of *stri shakti* within the women's movement connected with the Shetkari Sanghatana and other rural organizations. Here one finds a groping toward a genuine "historical materialism" for women.

The two directly peasant-based movements have more explicitly challenged the economic conceptualizations of traditional Marxism. This has been done differently by the farmers' movement and the environmental movement. The farmers' movement, most notably as articulated by Sharad Joshi, has announced itself as "economistic" but not a "class movement," has argued that the accumulation of capital takes place not primarily through the control of private property and the exploitation of the wage labor of factory workers but through the looting of the peasantry backed up by force. Its central demand for higher prices for agricultural products is seen as linked to the abolition of poverty because it will keep the surplus in the villages and prevent centralized accumulation of capital. "Communities" or "systems" rather than classes defined in terms of private property are seen as objects of exploitation. This calls either for a drastic reinterpretation of the concept of "class" or dropping it to talk only of "economically exploited group," and gives a different basis for analyzing the role of force and violence (and indirectly, the state) than simply seeing it as protecting a system of production based on private property. At the same time, the nature of a different kind of economic development from this centralized form of capital accumulation has rarely been outlined.

Conversely, the environmental movement has spoken more of environmental destruction rather than exploitation in conceptualizing the type of development and system it is fighting, and has tended to see "consumerism" rather than a particular material production system as its cause; the question of capital accumulation has hardly been considered. But this is the movement that has most clearly expressed the need for an "alternative development" that would be decentralized, ecologically sustainable, based on renewable resources, and clearly different in its organization of production from that of industrial capitalist or "statist" society.

Obviously there are other gaps in all of these: The anticaste and women's movements have not addressed each other's issues, and neither has yet gone very far, collectively, to analyze the problems of the peasantry and nature. In the farmers' movement, the issue of women's exploitation has recently been taken up, but the question of caste remains neglected (except in the "traditional Marxist" sense of fighting it as a form of "division of the peasantry") while, in general, ways of overcoming inequality within the village are neglected. The environmental movement has also remained single-issue, not dealing with the question of caste-community exploitation (reflecting the ambiguity of much of its relations with Hinduism) or confronting the economic issues that trouble the peasantry or the working class for that matter. And in spite of the new ecofeminist trend, the movement as such has rarely confronted theoretically or practically, the oppression of women.

The life-span of all of these movements, in fact, as movements conscious of a separate identity, stressing their autonomy in theory and action, has for the most part been quite short; only the anticaste movement, arguably going back to Ambedkar, Phule, and others, has a long history. Indeed, in many ways the "crisis of Marxism" at a theoretical and practical level may be the key factor in opening new doors. The habits of dependence, of taking theoretical frameworks for granted, are strong; few are ready or able to question radically or think anew at a fundamental level unless forced to do so. Now world events themselves are forcing rethinking, while at the same time the gradual spread of education to wider and wider sections of the exploited populations the world over, the expansion of the reach of communication create the possibilities for new people to come forward. If nations and peoples can avoid major disasters, the future decades promise to be interesting ones, ideologically and politically.

Reinventing Revolution

Finally, are the new movements "revolutionary"?

The term has been taking something of a beating lately. The movements, which started in a period that seemed only a partial setback for orthodox revolutionary movements—indeed, one in which the Vietnam War was being won and revolutions did emerge in new countries of Latin America—have come to a climax in a very different period, marked by Tiananmen Square, the loss of electoral power by the Sandinistas, the shockingly rapid fall of Communist parties in Eastern Europe and the Soviet Union, and the drift of these countries to an unabashed capitalism. For many it is a period not only of the "crisis of Marxism" but the "crisis of socialism" itself; leftists in much of Europe and North America appear to be in gloom, and bourgeois ideologists are proclaiming the "end of history."

Yet it is worth remembering that there were others for whom the nature of the "socialist" or "postrevolutionary" regimes itself represented a foreclosure of real revolutionary possibilities. For example, James Scott argued in 1985, in his widely admired study of the Malaysian peasantry, *Weapons of the Weak*, that peasant revolutions have only brought to power, in "a more coercive and hegemonic state apparatus. . . . new ruling groups whose plans for industrialization, taxation and collectivization are very much at odds with the goals for which peasants had imagined they were fighting." Scott concluded grimly that this is true of workers as well, that neither peasants nor workers are able to envision any "new plan for the reorganization of society" and that "if revolution were a rare event before the creation of such states, it now seems but foreclosed." [11] Within this context, the incredibly rapid fall of what seemed such effectively hegemonic states has opened many doors that were closed and brought a renewal of history for the masses of exploited people of the world.

The new movements described here have, it is true, been focused on single issues. They have frequently refused to describe themselves as "socialist" and have very often been resistant to grandiose terms such as "revolution." They also, like movements throughout history, contain diverse elements, conservative as well as radical, self-seeking as well as idealistic, and, it may be said, a seething variety of "nonantagonistic contradictions" that are not always pleasant. Yet they have been explicitly antisystemic in their ideologies, looking towards a casteless, nonpatriarchal, nonlooting, sustainable society; they are involved, in their own view, in inherent conflict with the current social order. They are analyzing the current situation and causes of exploitation and oppression in new ways ("rethinking Marxism"), constituting a new interpretation of Indian society and history ("reimagining the community"), and seeking new modes of action to effect change.

In the process of organizing, their songs still echo the aspirations for the creation of a new society of equality and freedom, traditionally known as "socialism." They proclaim the resurgence of the oppressed and historically defeated: Ekalavya will rise again, the reign of Bali Raja will come, Kali Mata will rise. They proclaim the rule of the poor, the liberation of peasants and workers. Caution and pessimism coexist with aspiration and hope; thus Sharad Joshi will in one moment repeat his claims that "there is no utopia; we only move from one flawed society to another" and in the next moment proclaim the "year of independence of the peasantry" while the annual conference of Shetkari Sanghatana takes as its slogan "*ida pida talnar, balica raja yenar*," changing the verb form of the Marathi slogan to read "sorrows and troubles *will go*, the kingdom of Bali *will come.*"

Is there a process of revolutionary change going on? Listen to those who are disturbed by the process. A recent article by India's best-known establishment sociologist, a strong opponent throughout of reservations for lower castes as represented in the Mandal Commission, concluded that overall India is "living in time of revolution." For M. N. Srinivas this includes a caste revolution of "shifting dominance" (lower castes challenging the higher ones at all levels), a "feminist revolution" that is leading to distintegration of the traditional family, and a revolution of "runaway ethnicity" challenging the nation-state as it has been known: "It is not understood that what the country is undergoing today is not a crisis in one of its distant corners but several kinds of crises, all structural, and all occuring simultaneously, and which are, let us be clear about it, threatening India's very existence as a single political entity. The situation is qualitatively different from the previous crises and this fact should be grasped firmly." [12]

The gloom and negativity with which Srinivas interprets this has to be itself reinterpreted: in particular, his stress on the violence of the current situation, that "India has moved from a period in which many important changes occurred by and large nonviolently in its polity, economy, law and society, to a period of extremely rapid and violent change," [13] is overdone. The poor have always experienced a good deal of violence, and the violence that is publicized in the press, categorized in official statistics, and perceived by the middle classes is not a good indicator of the actual situation. Against the gloom of the intellectuals stands what so often seems the amazing, undefeatable optimism of the poor and exploited, coupled with an ironic message to the left intellectuals, as expressed in the poem of the dalit writer Prabhakar Gangurde,

> *Now I have awakened,*
> *I am moving in blazing sunlight.*
> *Come . . .*
> *You won't come with me*
> *you won't embrace me.*
> *I have tiger claws scattered*
> *all over my body;*
> *they won't pierce you.*
> *If they pierce you it is*
> *certainly not for your sacrifice*
> *comrade.*[14]

Notes

Introduction

1. S. Gopal, ed., *Selected Works of Jawaharlal Nehru*, second series (New Delhi: Teen Murti House, 1985), 3:135. Nehru also served the longest of any prime minister to date.

2. Dhananjay Keer, *Dr. Ambedkar: Life and Mission* (Bombay: Popular Prakashan, 1971), p. 415.

3. Lloyd I. Rudolph and Susanne Hoeber Rudolph, *In Pursuit of Lakshmi: The Political Economy of the Indian State* (Bombay: Orient Longman, 1987).

4. Atul Kohli, *Democracy and Discontent: India's Growing Crisis of Governability* (New York: Cambridge University Press, 1990), p. 388.

5. See also Francine Frankel, *India's Political Economy, 1947–1977: The Gradual Revolution* (Princeton: Princeton University Press, 1978); Francine Frankel and M.S.A. Rao, *Dominance and State Power in Modern India: Decline of a Social Order*, 2 vols. (Delhi: Oxford University Press, 1989); Zoya Hasan, S. N. Jha, and Rasheeduddin Khan, *The State, Political Processes and Identity: Reflections on Modern India* (New Delhi: Sage, 1989); Utsa Patnaik, *Peasant Class Differentiation: A Study in Method with Reference to Haryana* (Delhi: Oxford, 1987); Pradhan Prasad, *Lopsided Growth: Political Economy of Indian Development* (Bombay: Oxford University Press, 1989); Ranjit Guha, ed., *Subaltern Studies*, 6 vols. (Delhi: Oxford, 1972–90); Terry Byres, "Agrarian Structure, the New Technology and Class Action in India," in *Sociology of "Developing Societies": South Asia*, ed. Hamza Alavi and John Harriss, (London: Macmillan, 1989).

6. Willem van Schendel, *Three Deltas: Accumulation and Poverty in Rural Burma, Bengal and South India* (New Delhi: Sage, 1991); Olle Tornquist, *What Is Wrong with Marxism? On Capitalists and the State in India and Indonesia* (Delhi: Manohar, 1989).

7. D. N. Dhanagare and J. John, "Cyclical Movements Toward the 'Eternal'," *Economic and Political Weekly*, May 21, 1988.

8. André Gunder Frank and Marta Fuentes, "Nine Theses on Social Movements," *Economic and Political Weekly*, August 29, 1987.

Chapter 1

1. Quoted in Sumit Sarkar, *Modern India, 1885–1947* (Delhi: Macmillan India, 1983), p. 268.

2. V. I. Lenin, *The Awakening of Asia: Selected Essays* (New York: International Publishers, 1963), pp. 7–8.

3. Quoted in Sarkar, *Modern India*, p. 69.

4. M. K. Gandhi, *Hindu Swaraj*, in *The Moral and Political Writings of Mahatma Gandhi*, ed. Raghavan Iyer (Oxford: Clarendon Press, 1968), 1:209, 214.

5. Ibid., p. 213.

6. Ibid., p. 257.

7. Quoted in Ramchandra Guha, *"Chipko:" A Grassroots Perspective on the Environmental Debate* (United Nations University, February 1987), p. 18.

8. Cited Ibid., p. 17.

9. Gandhi, *Hind Swaraj*, pp. 232–33.

10. *Dr. Babasaheb Ambedkar: Writings and Speeches*, (Bombay: Government of Maharashtra, 1979), 1:352.

11. Preface to *Gulamgiri*, in *Mahatma Phule: Samagra Wangmay* (Complete writings of Mahatma Phule, Marathi), ed. Dhananjay Keer and S. G. Malshe (Bombay: Government of Maharashtra), pp. 72–73.

12. For an account of this little-known formation of a peasant woman's organization in the 1930s, see Kapil Kumar, "Rural Women in Oudh, 1917–1947," in *Recasting Women: Essays in Colonial History* ed., Kumkum Sangari and Sudesh Vaid (New Delhi: Kali for Women Press, 1989), pp. 336–69.

13. K. Murugesan and C. S. Subramanyan, *Singaravelu—First Communist in South India* (New Delhi: People's Publishing House 1975), p. 176.

14. G. Adhikari, ed., *Documents of the History of the Communist Party of India* (New Delhi: People's Publishing House, 1974), 2:591–629.

15. *Documents of the History of the Communist Party of India* (New Delhi: People's Publishing House, 1978), 3A:150–51.

16. Murugesan and Subramanyan, *Singaravelu*, p. 83.

17. A. J. Syed, ed., *D. D. Kosambi on History and Sociology* (Bombay: University of Bombay Department of History, 1985), p. 73.

18. David Washbrook, "South Asia, the World System and World Capitalism," *Journal of Asian Studies* 49, 3 (August 1990).

19. Gyanendra Pandey, *The Construction of Communalism in Colonial North India* (Delhi: Oxford University Press, 1990), p. 210ff.

20. Ibid., p. 235.

21. From *Discovery of India*, cited in Ibid., pp. 241–2.

22. Ibid., pp. 253–54.

23. Stree Shakti Sanghatana, *"We Were Making History" : Women in the Telengana People's Struggle* (New Delhi: Kali for Women Press, 1989).

Chapter 2

1. Cited in Francine Frankel, *India's Political Economy, 1947–1977: The Gradual Revolution* (Princeton: Princeton University Press, 1978), p. 14.

2. Ibid., p. 15.

3. Ibid., pp. 16–17.

4. Lloyd I. Rudolph and Susanne Hoeber Rudolph, *In Pursuit of Lakshmi: The Political Economy of the Indian State* (Bombay: Orient Longman, 1987), p. 51.

5. Olle Tornquist, *What Is Wrong with Marxism? On Capitalists and the State in India and Indonesia* (Delhi: Manohar, 1989), pp. 94–105.

6. Pradhan Prasad, *Lopsided Growth: Political Economy of Indian Development* (Bombay: Oxford University Press, 1989), p. 89.

7. Jayant Lele, *Elite Pluralism and Class Rule: Political Development in Maharashtra* (Bombay: Popular Prakashan, 1981), describes "High Marathas" as holders of political

power, but much of his data is only for "Marathas" as a whole, and he himself at times uses this conceptualization.

8. Song by Jaysingh Mhaske, Sangli district, Maharashtra.

9. All-India Debt and Investment Survey, *Statistical Tables Relating to Disposition of Land Held and Area and Value of Irrigated Land Owned by Rural Households as on June, 1979* (Bombay: Reserve Bank of India, 1978); Centre for Monitoring the Indian Economy, *Basic Statistics Relating to the Indian Economy*, vol. I: All-India (Bombay, 1987), table 9.1; P. C. Joshi, *Land Reforms and Agrarian Change in India and Pakistan*, Reprints from Studies in Asian Development, no. 1.

10. On landholding, see the National Sample Surveys, especially the All-India Debt and Investment Surveys of 1971–72 and 1981–82. National Sample Survey Organization, 37th Round, January–December 1982, no. 318, *Assets and Liabilities of Rural and Urban Households* (New Delhi: Department of Statistics, July 1985), pp. 17–18. These also give the Gini coefficient ratios; see All India Debt and Investment Survey, *Assets of Rural Households as on June 30, 1971* (Bombay: Reserve Bank of India, 1976), p. 39, table 2.5 and All-India Debt and Investment Survey, *Assets and Liabilities of Rural and Urban Households as on 30 June 1981* (Bombay: Reserve Bank of India), table 1.1.1, p. 5. See also Debesh Bhattacharya, "Growth and Distribution in India," *Journal of Contemporary Asia* 19, 2 (1989): 155.

11. For the dominant view see Terry Byres, "Agrarian Structure, the New Technology and Class Action in India," in *Sociology of ('Developing Societies'): South Asia*, eds. Hamza Alavi and John Harriss (London: Macmillan, 1989), pp. 50–53; see also V. G. Rastyannikov, *Agrarian Evolution in a Multiform Structure Society* (London: Routledge and Kegan Paul, 1981).

12. V. M. Dandekar, "Agriculture, Employment and Poverty," in *India, Rebellion to Republic: Selected Writings, 1857–1990*, ed. Robin Jeffrey (New Delhi: Sterling Publishers Private Ltd. 1990), p. 243–44.

13. N. Krishnaji, "Land and Labour in India: The Demographic Factor," *Economic and Political Weekly*, May 5–12, 1990; Maria Mies, *Patriarchy and Accumulation on a World Scale* (London: Zed Press, 1985), "Capitalist Development and Subsistence Production: Rural Women in India," *Bulletin of Concerned Asian Scholars*, 11, 1 (1980); *The Lace-Makers of Narsapur: Housewives Produce for the World Market* (London: Zed Press, 1984); and *Indian Women in Subsistence and Agricultural Labour* (Geneva: ILO, 1986) (assisted by Lalita K. and Krishna Kumari).

14. Cited in Mohan Ram, "The Telengana Peasant Armed Struggle, 1946–1951," *Economic and Political Weekly*, June 9, 1973, p. 1028.

15. This is given in the important statement of 1975, published ten years later in a Naxalite-linked theoretical journal; P. Sundarayya, "Why I Resigned from GS and PB," *Marxism Today* 1, 2 (November 1985).

16. George Katsiaficas, *The Imagination of the New Left: A Global Analysis of 1968* (Boston: South End Press, 1987), p. 58.

17. John Roosa, "The Punjab Crisis: Fallout of the Green Revolution," September 1989, ms.

18. Ranabir Samaddar, "Revolution Created or Revolution Destroyed?" *In the Wake of Marx* 2, 3 (July 1986): 12.

19. Ibid., p. 19.

20. Partha Mukherjee, "Naxalbari Movement and the Peasant Revolt in North Bengal," in *Social Movements in India*, ed. M.S.A. Rao (New Delhi: Manohar, 1978) 5:43.

21. Samaddar, "Revolution," p. 15.

22. Ibid., pp. 19, 21.

23. Mukherjee, "Naxalbari Movement," p. 49.

24. Kanu Sanyal, "Report on the Peasant Movement in the Terai Region," *Liberation* 2 (December 1968).

25. Samaddar, "Revolution," p. 20.

26. Mukherjee, "Naxalbari Movement," p. 52.

27. Jogen Sen Gupta, "An Optimistic Interpretation of Current World Events," 1990, ms.

Chapter 3

1. The following account is from Prahlad Chandavarkar, "Pantherca Janma" (Birth of the Panthers, Marathi) in *Dalit Panther* ed., Sharan Kumar Limbale (Pune: Sugawa Prakashan, 1989), pp. 24–49.

2. Cited in Barbara Joshi, ed., *Untouchable! Voices of the Dalit Liberation Movement* (London: Zed Press, 1986), pp. 77 and 83; translations by Jayant Karve and Eleanor Zelliot, and Jayashree Gokhale-Turner.

3. B. R. Ambedkar, "Untouchables or the Children of India's Ghetto," in *Writings and Speeches* Vol. 5, comp. by Vasant Moon (Bombay: Government of Maharashtra, 1989), pp. 115–16.

4. Limbale, "Samyak Kranti" (All-round revolution), in *Dalit Panther*, p. 3.

5. Sudhakar Gaikwad, cited in ibid., pp. 45.

6. See my chapter on "Ambedkarism" *Dalits and the Democratic Revolution* (New Delhi: Sage, forthcoming).

7. Translated by Jayant Karve and Eleanor Zelliot, in *An Anthology of Dalit Literature* ed. Mulle Ray Anand and Eleanor Zelliot, (New Delhi: Gyan, 1992) p. 53.

8. Arun Sinha, "Class War in Bhojpur," *Economic and Political Weekly*, January 7, 1978.

9. Sinha, "The Awakening in Bhojpur," *Frontier*, December 24–31, 1977, p. 6.

10. Ibid.

11. Praveen K. Chaudhry, "Agrarian Unrest in Bihar: A Caste Study of Patna District, 1960–1984," *Economic and Political Weekly*, January 2–9, 1988.

12. Anonymous, "Agrarian Movement in Jehanabad," *Economic and Political Weekly*, May 19, 1986. There were also conflicts between the different Naxalite organizations, climaxing around 1988–89, described in reports of both, in reports of civil liberties organizations, and in Dev Nathan, "Agricultural Laborer and Poor Peasant Movement in Bihar: Nature of Resistance and Problems of Strategy" (Draft Paper for Research Project on Terms of Political Discourse in India, 1990) and "Violence in Jehanabad" in *PUCL Bulletin* 10, 7: (July 1990).

13. Dev Nathan, "Agricultural Labour and Poor Peasant," p. 13.

14. Ibid., p. 14; see their documents, for both the 1988 IPF Conference and the earlier party conference of the CPI(ML), cited in chapter 7.

15. "Slogan War in Karnataka," *Times of India*, December 13, 1973.

16. See V. Laxminarayana, "Post-Independence Dalith Movement in Karnataka," report for ICSSR, 1989.

17. Ibid., p. 10.

18. V. T. Rajshekhar, *Dilemma of the Class and Caste in India* (Bangalore: Dalit Sahitya Academy, 1984), pp. 6, 10, 15.

19. Ibid., pp. 10, 21.

20. Atyacar Virodhi Samiti, "The Marathwada Riots: A Report," *Economic and Political Weekly*, May 12, 1979.

21. See, for example, R. S. Morkhandikar, "The Background," *Economic and Political Weekly*, August 26, 1978, and my "Class Struggle or Caste War?" *Frontier*, September 30, 1978.

22. Shantaram Pandhere, "Marathwada Vidyapith Namantar Andolan" (Marathwada University renaming movement), Marathi; seminar paper on Dalit movement in Maharashtra, Shivaji University, Kolhapur, February 1989.

23. *Oppressed Indian*, January–February 1978, p. 12.

24. Sharad Patil, "Should 'Class' Be the Basis for Recognizing Backwardness?" *Economic and Political Weekly*, December 15, 1990.

25. See Gail Omvedt, "The Twice-Born Riot Against Democracy," *Economic and Political Weekly*, September 29, 1990, and Francine Frankel and M. S. A. Rao, *Dominance and State Power in Modern India: Decline of a Social Order*, vol. 1 (Delhi: Oxford University Press, 1989), appendices.

26. Marc Galantar, "Who are the Other Backward Classes," *Economic and Political Weekly*, October 28, 1978, n. 59.

27. *Oppressed Indian*, November 1983, p. 4.

28. *The Mandal Commission Report*, chapter 13, Recommendations, 13.5.

29. Arun Sinha, *Economic and Political Weekly*, April 22, 1978.

30. Ruth Glass, "Gujarat: Divided and Degraded," *Frontier*, January 1, 1982, p. 7.

31. Upendra Baxi, "Reflections on the Reservation Crisis in Gujarat," in *Mirrors of Violence: Communities, Riots and Survivors in South Asia*, ed. Veena Das (Delhi: Oxford University Press, 1990); Achyut Yagnik and Harshad Desai, "The Wages of Populism: The Second Anti-Reservation Agitation," *Lokayan Bulletin* 3,2 (1985).

32. "Class, Caste and Reservations," *Frontier*, January 21, 1986, p. 5.

Chapter 4

1. Song by the dalit poet Daya Pawar.

2. See *People's Democracy*, April 29, September 2, October 7, 1973; February 17, April 28, September 29, 1974; January 19, April 13, 1975; and *Times of India*, September 26, November 10, 27, 1973; January 17, 24, February 24, 1974.

3. *People's Democracy*, April 13, 1974.

4. Gail Omvedt, Chetna Gala, and Govind Kelkar, *Women and Struggle: A Report of the Nari Mukti Sangarsh Sammelan, Patna 1988* (New Delhi: Kali for Women Press, 1988), p. 9.

5. Letter in *Manoman* (Marathi), July 1990.

6. Godutai Parulekar, "Stri: He Jokhad Kevha Zugarnar?" and response by Durga Bhagwat in *Stri* (Marathi magazine), June 1973.

7. Manifesto of the Progressive Organization of Women, in *Stree Vimukti* (Hyderabad, 1975).

8. *Towards Equality: Report of the Committee on the Status of Women in India* (New Delhi: Government of India, 1974).

9. Resolutions of the Trivandrum Conference, in *Social Scientist* (January 1976): 69.

10. *Times of India*, October 20, 23, 29, 1975.

11. Olga Tellis, "Women's Emancipation and Class Struggle," *Economic Times*, February 27, 1976; "Marxist Cobwebs," *Economic and Political Weekly*, February 21, 1976; "Marxist Cliches to the Fore at Women's Conference in Kerala," *Times of India*, January 12, 1976; and Jessica Jacob, "Women's Conference: Rhetoric, Anger, Fellowship," *Femina*, January 30, 1976.

12. The then anonymous writers were two Indians (Wandana Sonalkar and Chhaya Datar), two American women (Carol Brown and Gail Omvedt), and a prominent Sri Lankan Marxist-feminist, Kumari Jayawardene.

13. *Janwedena*, December 8, 1975; Mahila Samata Sainik Dal, "Jahirnama" (Manifesto), in *Marathwada*, April 1, 1975.

14. "Declaration of Socialist Women's Group," in *Reaching for Half the Sky* (Bombay, 1985), p. 98.

15. Report of Workshop on Women, Bombay, July 2–8, 1978; *Feminist Network* (Cyclostyled bulletin), no. 1.

16. See Nandita Gandhi and Nandita Shah, *The Issues at Stake: Theory and Practice in the Contemporary Women's Movement in India* (New Delhi: Kali for Women Press, 1992), which defines patriarchy in terms of "the control of men over women's labour, fertility and sexuality" (p. 16). While all those in the new movement considering themselves "feminists" agreed on the special subordination and exploitation of women involved in the concept of "patriarchy," not all agreed with the tendency to see men, as a group, as the exploiter.

17. "Declaration of Socialist Women's Group," p. 102.

18. Chhaya Datar, *Redefining Exploitation: Towards a Socialist Feminist Critique of Marxist Theory* (Bombay: ISRE, 1981), p. 144.

19. Radha Kumar, "Contemporary Indian Feminism," *Feminist Review*, no. 33, (August 1989): 24.

20. Report of Workshop on Communications Network at the Conference on Perspective for the Women's Movement, December 1985.

21. Report on Shalinitai Patil and women's rally, *Maratha*, May 7, 1975.

22. Tarabai Deshmukh, "Striya va Grampanchayaticya Nivadnuka" (Women and *gram panchayat* elections) (Marathi), *Bayja* (August, 1978).

23. *Satyashodhak Marxwadi* (October–November 1978).

24. Gabriele Dietrich, "Women's Struggle for Housing Rights," *Economic and Political Weekly*, October 17–24, 1987.

Chapter 5

1. K. C. Alexander, *Peasant Organization in South India* (New Delhi: ISI, 1981), pp. 131–35; Marshall Bouton, *Agrarian Radicalism in South India* (Princeton: Princeton University Press, 1985), pp. 275–94; Claude Alvares, "The Peasants Rehearse the Uprising," *Illustrated Weekly*, February 24, 1985.

2. Nirmal Azad, "Recent Farmers' Agitations in Punjab," *Economic and Political Weekly*, April 26, 1975; Sucha Singh Gill and K. C. Singhal, "Farmers' Agitations: Response to Developmental Crisis of Agriculture," *Economic and Political Weekly*, October 6, 1984.

3. G. S. Bhalla and G. K. Chadha, "Green Revolution and the Small Peasant: A Study of Income Distribution in Punjab Agriculture," *Economic and Political Weekly*, May 15, 22, 1982, p. 871.

4. Ibid., p. 831.

5. Pramod Kumar et al., *Punjab Crisis: Context and Trends* (Chandigarh: Centre for Research in Rural and Industrial Development, 1984), tables 16 and 17.

6. Teekayem, "The Punjab Peasantry—I," *Frontier*, May 30, 1981.

7. Ibid., June 20, 1981.

8. Vandana Shiva, *The Violence of the Green Revolution: Ecological Degradation and Political Conflict in Punjab* (Dehra Dun, 1989).

9. Bouton, *Agrarian Radicalism*; Alexander, *Peasant Organization*, pp. 135–36.

10. Ibid. Alexander's more recent assessment, however, recognizes the limitations of organizing only agricultural laborers. See "Caste Mobilization and Class Consciousness: The Emergence of Agrarian Movements in Kerala and Tamilnadu," in Frankel and Rao, *Dominance and State Power in Modern India*.

11. Azad, "Recent Farmers' Agitations," p. 705.

12. Kwon Ping, "Revolt of the Landless Peasants," *Far Eastern Economic Review*, January 12, 1979.

13. Bouton, *Agrarian Radicalism*, pp. 287–88.

14. "Immediate Agrarian Programme," adopted at Fourth All-Party Congress, January 1–5, 1988.

15. V. M. Dandekar and Nilakanth Rath, "Poverty in India," *Economic and Political Weekly*, January 2, 9, 1971; Sanjib Baruah, "The End of the Road in Land Reform? Limits to Redistribution in West Bengal," *Development and Change* 21, 1 (January 1990).

16. Alexander, *Peasant Organization*, pp. 118–31, 167–89.

17. Dalip Swamy, "The Kanjhawala Agitation," *Frontier*, October 21–28, 1978; see also Anjan Ghosh, "Caste Idiom for Class Conflict: Case of Kanjhawala," *Economic and Political Weekly*, February 3, 1979; Brij Mohan, "Khanjawala Agitation," *Times of India*, March 4–5, 1979.

18. Studies of the "commons" have been many, but for the general argument about keeping the commons under collective control rather than giving it to individual poor families, see Anil Agrawal and Sunita Narain, *Towards Green Villages* (New Delhi: Centre for Science and Environment, 1989).

19. See J. Kishan Rao, "Remunerative Farm Prices and Terms of Trade Between Agriculture and Industry" in *Peasant Farming and Growth of Capitalism in Indian Agriculture*, ed. Y. V. Krishna Rao (Vijayawada: Visalandhra Publishing House, 1984), pp. 412–13.

20. Indradeep Sinha, "Why Remunerative Prices for Agricultural Produce?" in ibid., pp. 396–97.

21. M. V. Nadkarni, *Farmers' Movement in India* (Ahmedabad: Allied Publishers Private Ltd., 1987), p. 155.

22. Vinod Mishra, introduction to *Report from the Flaming Fields of Bihar* (Calcutta: 1986).

23. See "Farmers' Agitation," *Economic and Political Weekly*, June 1978; *Times of India*, April 19, 1978.

24. Indradeep Sinha, *The Changing Agrarian Scene: Problems and Tasks* (Revised version of General Secretary's report to the 22d National Conference of All-India Kisan Sabha) (New Delhi: People's Publishing House, 1980), pp. 105–6.

25. See Kwon Ping, "Revolt of the Landless Peasant."

26. Nadkarni, *Farmer's Movement*, pp. 96–97.

27. Olga Tellis, "Nasik's Farmers Demand Justice," *Sunday* December 1980; see also "A Belligerent 'Bharat,' " *India Today*, December 1–15, 1980, and "The Angry Farmers," January 16–31, 1981.

28. See Nadkarni, *Farmer's Movement*, pp. 111–12, and *Times of India*, November 22, 1980.

29. "A Belligerent 'Bharat.' "

30. "The Angry Farmers."

31. *Times of India*, April 2, 12, May 13, 1981.

32. *Times of India*, January 3, 11, 1982.

33. See Kai Friese, "Peasant Communities and Agrarian Capitalism," *Economic and Political Weekly*, September 26, 1990, and articles by Ghansham Shah and D. N. Dhanagare in *Seminar* 352 (December 1988), issue on "Farmers' Power." Khedut Samaj leaders contest Shah's characterization of their organization as patidar-based.

34. Interview, Dr. Shivaswami, *Mazdur Kisan Niti*, September 16–30, 1981.

35. See Dipankar Gupta, "Country and Town Nexus in Agrarian Mobilisation" in *Economic and Political Weekly*, December 17, 1988.

36. Cited in Alvares, "Peasants Rehearse the Uprising," p. 17.

37. Gupta, "Country and Town Nexus," p. 2693.

38. Sunil Saharasabudhe, "Peasant Movement and the Quest for Development," in *Peasant and Peasant Protest in India*, ed. M. N. Karna (New Delhi: Intellectual Publishing House), p. 152.

39. Alvares, "Peasants Rehearse the Uprising," p. 17.

40. Ibid., p. 19.

41. Sharad Joshi, "Balancing Act," *Illustrated Weekly*, January 7, 1990.

42. John Roosa, "The Punjab Crisis."

43. "Has Bharat Declared War on India?" *Business World*, July 16, 1984, p. 39.

44. Ibid.

45. Baljit Malik, "There is Still Hope," *Illustrated Weekly*, April 29, 1984.

46. Gill and Singhal, "Farmers' Agitation," pp. 1730–31.

47. Roosa, "The Punjab Crisis," pp. 91–92.

Chapter 6

1. Cited in K. Suresh Sharma, *Dust Storms and Hanging Mists* (Calcutta, 1966), preface.

2. Nirmal Sengupta, "Class and Tribe in Jharkhand," *Economic and Political Weekly*, April 5, 1980, p. 669.

3. Ibid., p. 667.

4. Amit Roy, "Second Phase of Jharkhand Movement," *Frontier*, May 9, 1981, p. 4.

5. Sengupta, "Class and Tribe," p. 668.

6. A. K. Roy, "Jharkhand: Internal Colonialism," *Frontier*, April 17, 1982, p. 6.

7. Interview, *Sunday*, March 11, 1979, p. 23.

8. R. N. Maharaj and K. G. Iyer, "Agrarian Revolution in Dhanbad," in *Fourth World Dynamics: Jharkhand*, ed. Nirmal Sengupta (Authors Guild Publications, 1982), pp. 178–79.

9. Radha Kumar, "Will Feminist Standards Survive in Jharkhand?" in ibid., p. 209.

10. Maharaj and Iyer, "Agrarian Revolution," in ibid., p. 127.

11. "Struggle in Singhbhum," *Frontier,* September 1979; see also "Singhbhum: Exploitation, Protest and Repression," *Economic and Political Weekly*, June 2, 1979.

12. A. K. Roy, *New Dalit Revolution*, ms., 1980, p. 3.

13. Ramchandra Guha, *The Unquiet Woods: Ecological Change and Peasant Resistance in the Himalayas* (Delhi: Oxford University Press, 1989).

14. Cited in Vandana Shiva, *Staying Alive: Women, Ecology and Survival in India* (New Delhi: Kali for Women Press, 1988), p. 69.

15. Kumud Sharma, Balaji Pandey, and Kusum Nautiyal, "The Chipko Movement in the Uttarkhand Region," in *Rural Development and Women: Lessons from the Field* (Geneva: ILO, 1985), pp. 189–90.

16. Sunderlal Bahuguna, *Chipko: A Novel Movement for the Establishment of Cordial Relationship between Man and Nature* (Delhi: April, 1980), pp. 7–8.

17. Cited in ibid., p. 71.

18. Sharma et al., "The Chipko Movement," p. 190.

19. Shiva, *Staying Alive*, p. 70.

20. Ramchandra Guha, "Will the Real Chipko Please Stand Up?" *Seminar*, June 1987.

21. "Political-Organisational Report of the CPI(M-L)," *Documents of the Fourth Congress*, Delhi, January, 1988), pp. 19–20.

22. Quoted in Shiva, *Staying Alive*, pp. 76–77.

23. *The Hindu*, June 10, 1984, in *Kerala Fisherman's Struggle* (Bangalore: ISI Documentation Centre, 1985).

24. S. Kappen, "Towards Radical Christianity," *Negations*, no. 11, cited in ibid.

25. John Kurien, "Trawling and Bans: Economics and Politics" (Travancore: Centre for Development Studies), in ibid.

26. Thomas Kocherry, "Fishermen Struggle for Survival," *Vigil India*, August 30, 1984, in ibid.

27. Quoted by Kappen, "Towards Radical Christianity."

28. Gabriele Dietrich, introduction to study by Nalini Nayak, 1990.

29. Ibid.

30. O. V. Vijayan, "Cry the Beloved Country," *Lokayan Bulletin* 2,2 (November 1984).

31. B. B. Vohra, "Protecting the Land: Reviving Our Forests," *Times of India*, August 7 and 8, 1984.

32. PPST *Bulletin*, (December 1980): 4.

33. Anil Agrawal, "Politics of Environment" in Centre for Science and Environment, *The State of India's Environment 1984–1985: The Second Citizens' Report* (New Delhi, 1985), p. 366.

34. Ibid., p. 374.

35. "A Statement on Scientific Temper" (Bombay: Nehru Centre, July 19, 1981), published in *Mainstream*, January 1981.

36. *Social Scientist* 10, 1 (January 1982).

37. PPST *Bulletin* 2, 2 (November 2, 1981).

38. Ramchandra Guha, "The Alternative Science Movement: An Interim Assessment," *Lokayan Bulletin* 6,3 (1988): 8.

39. Ibid., p. 18.

40. "Naxalism in the Nineties," *Frontier*, Autumn Number 1990.

Chapter 7

1. Peter Waterman, "Reflections on Unions and Popular Movements in India," ms., June 1980, p. 15.

2. Bipin Chandra, "Marxism in India," *Journal of Contemporary Asia* 4,4 (1974).

3. Ibid., p. 462.

4. Suman Katre, song of the Lal Nishan party.

5. Chandra, "Marxism in India," p. 479, n.3.

6. Those who did make an effort to broaden analyses included Hamza Alavi and Harry Cleaver, but their articles were, notably, not included in the Indian collection on the debate. See *Agrarian Relations and Accumulation: The 'Mode of Production' Debate in India*, ed. Utsa Patnaik (Bombay: Oxford University Press, 1990).

7. Harry Cleaver, "Internationalisation of Capital and Modes of Production in Agriculture," *Economic and Political Weekly*, March 27, 1976.

8. Arvind Das, Fernando Rojas, and Peter Waterman, "The Labour Movement and Labouring People in India," ms., The Hague, Institute for Social Studies, December 1980, p. 5.

9. Zoya Hasan, S. N. Jha, and Rasheeduddin Khan, *The State, Political Processes and Identity: Reflections on Modern India* (New Delhi: Sage, 1989).

10. P. Sundarayya, "Why I Resigned from the GS and PB," *Marxism Today* (November 1985).

11. *Indian Express*, September 6, 1989.

12. See Documents of the 7th Congress, 1982.

13. Prakash Karat, "Action Groups/Voluntary Organisations: A Factor in Imperialist Strategy," *The Marxist* (April–June 1984).

14. K. Balagopal, *Readings in the Political Economy of Agrarian Classes and Conflicts* (Hyderabad: Perspectives, 1988), p. 46.

15. See Communist Party of India (Marxist-Leninist), *Documents of the Fourth Congress*, Delhi, January 1988.

16. Indian People's Front, "Political-Organizational Report," Delhi, Third National Conference, March 1988, pp. 23–24.

17. *Manifesto of the Indian People's Front with Postscript*, adopted at the Third National Conference, Delhi, March 20–23, 1988.

18. Draft of postscript for the IPF Manifesto, cyclostyled manuscript, March 1988.

19. *Manifesto of the Indian People's Front with Postscript*, pp. 14–15.

20. Bharat Patankar, "The Bombay Textile Workers' Strike of 1982: The Lessons of History," *Bulletin of Concerned Asian Scholars* 20, 2 (1986).

21. As argued by Hub van Wersch, "Bombay Textile Strike 1982–83: Workers' Views and Strategies," Ph.D. diss., University of Amsterdam, 1989.

22. Quoted in ibid., p. 116.

23. Bharat Patankar, "Communists and Politics," *Frontier* (September, 1984).

24. Patankar, "India: Transcending the Traditional Communist Movement," *Race and Class* 26, 3 (Winter 1985).

Chapter 8

1. Rajni Kothari, "The How and the Why of it All," *Voices from a Scarred City, Lokayan Bulletin* 3,1 (January 1985).

2. Ibid., pp. 14–15.

3. P. B. Mayer, "Congress(I), Emergency(I): Interpreting Indira Gandhi's India," in *India: Rebellion to Republic*, ed. Robin Jeffrey et al. (New Delhi: Sterling Publishers, 1990), p. 406.

4. Ibid.

5. *Far Eastern Economic Review*, April 22, September 16, 1972; September 24, 1973.

6. James Manor, "Anomie in Indian Politics," *Economic and Political Weekly*, Annual Number (May 1983): 727.

7. Cited Francine Frankel, *India's Political Economy*, pp. 545–46.

8. Ranjit Guha, "Indian Democracy: Long Dead, Now Buried," *Journal of Contemporary Asia* 6,1 (1976).

9. Ibid., p. 53.

10. Javeed Alam, "Political Articulation of Mass Consciousness in Present-Day India," in *The State, Political Processes and Identity*, ed. Zoya Hasan, pp. 238–39.

11. S. Dutt, "The Assamese Psyche," *Frontier*, April 5, 1980.

12. Amalendu Guha, "The Cudgel of Chauvinism," *Economic and Political Weekly* (October, 1980): 1707.

13. Utsa Patnaik, "Some Aspects of Development in the Agrarian Sector in Independent India," *Social Scientist* 16,2 (February 1988): 37–38.

14. Pritam Singh, "Two Faces of Religious Revivalism," *Shackles and Women*, special Punjab issue (May–August 1986).

15. Quoted in ibid., p. 28.

16. Utsa Patnaik, "Some Aspects of Development," p. 39.

17. "Militant Revivalism," *India Today*, May 11, 1986.

18. Javeed Alam, "Political Articulation of Mass Consciousness in Present-Day India," pp. 241–47.

19. Achin Vanaik, *The Painful Transition: Bourgeois Democracy in India* (London: Verso Books, 1990), p. 144.

20. Frankel, *India's Political Economy*, p. 510.

21. Prabhat Patnaik, "A Perspective on the Recent Phase of India's Economic Development," *Social Scientist* 177, 16, 2 (February 1988): 11.

22. T. Ninan, "Rise of the Middle Class," in *India: Rebellion to Republic*, ed. Jeffrey, p. 332; and Jeffrey, "The Perils of Prosperity," ibid., p. 380.

23. Ninian, "Rise of the Middle Class," p. 333; Kalyan Chaudhuri, "Left Front's Ten Years in Power," *Economic and Political Weekly*, July 25, 1987.

24. Joan Mencher, "Changing Agriculture, *Economic and Political Weekly*, February 2, 1991.

25. *Lokayan Bulletin* 3,6 (1985): 5–8.

26. Rajni Kothari, "The Rise of People's Movements," *Social Action*, 40,3 (July-September 1990), p. 235.

27. See the debate in *Lokayan Bulletin*, 1986.

28. Kishore Saint, "Development Cooperation and the Development-Environmental Crisis," *Ifda dossier* 70 (OctoberDecember 1990).

29. *Dalit Voice*, November 16–30, 1984.

30. *Times of India*, December 29, 1984.

31. *Times of India*, January 7, 1985.

Chapter 9

1. Vandana Shiva, *Staying Alive*, pp. xvii–xviii.

2. The most thoughtful criticism is found in Govind Kelkar and Dev Nathan, *Gender and Tribe: Women, Land and Forests in Jharkhand* (New Delhi: Kali for Women Press, 1991).

3. Chandwad *Manifesto*, adopted November 11, 1986.

4. "The Uprising," interview with Rajni Bakshi, *Illustrated Weekly*, January 18, 1987.

5. Nalini Nayak, *A Struggle Within the Struggle* (Trivandrum: GEO Printers, n.d.), pp. 40, 47, 52–53.

6. Gabriele Dietrich, "Development Debate/Models and Gender Implications," *Lokayan Bulletin* 8,1 (January–February 1990).

7. Sebastian Kappen, in *Illustrated Weekly*, August 12, 1990.

8. Govind Kelkar, "Peasant Movement and Women in Two Bihar Districts" (New Delhi, 1988), pp. 95–96.

9. From an Urdu song by Kamla Bhasin.

10. "On the Women's Movement," a report compiled by a group of women working in Rajasthan, in *Lokayan Bulletin* 6,3 (1988): 65–66.

11. *Janmat*, September 5–9, 1990, pp. 10–11.

12. Gabriele Dietrich, "On Conceptualisation," a summing up of the conference, in *Pressing Against the Boundaries*, Report of an FAO-FFHC/AD South Asian Workshop on Women and Development, draft, 1991, pp. 53–54.

13. Madhu Kishwar, "Toward More Just Norms for Marriage," *Manushi* 53 (1989): 3.

14. Dietrich, "On Conceptualisation," p. 54.

15. Anita Abraham, "Autonomous Women's Groups and 30% Reservations," in *Getting a Foothold in Politics*, ed. Vibhuti Patel (Bombay, SNDT Women's University, 1991), pp. 42–43.

16. Vibhuti Patel, "Reaching for Half the Sky," in *Newsletter* of the Research Center on Women's Studies, Summer 1991.

17. Madhu Kishwar, "Ways to Combat Communal Violence: Thoughts on International Women's Day," *Manushi* 62 (January–February 1991): 7.

18. *Shetkari Sanghatak*, February 1991.

Chapter 10

1. K. Balagopal, "The End of Spring?" *Economic and Political Weekly*, August 25, 1990.

2. "Madiga Mallaiah Inherits the Earth," *Times of India*, December 9, 1990.

3. Balagopal, "The End of Spring?"

4. *Frontline*, May 15–25, 1990, p. 22.

5. Peoples' Union for Democratic Rights, *Repression of Miners' Movement: Report of a Fact-Finding Committee* (Delhi, 1981).

6. Shankar Guha Niyogi, "Chattisgarh and the National Question," *Nationality Question in India* (Hyderabad, 1982), p. 115.

7. "The 'Other' Peasant Rally," *Economic and Political Weekly*, December 2, 1989.

8. Ibid.

9. Bharat Patankar, "Notes on Bhopal and the People's Science Movement," 1985.

10. Jogin Sen Gupta, "An Optimistic Interpretation of Current World Events," manuscript, 1990.

11. Forthcoming in revised form in *Capitalism, Nature, Socialism*.

12. See "Resolutions of the Adivasi-Jungle Parishad, Bhute-Akaspur (Dhule District, Maharashtra)," translated from Marathi, *South Asia Bulletin* 6,1 (Spring 1986).

13. Anil Agrawal and Sunita Narain, *Towards Green Villages* (New Delhi: Centre for Science and Environment, 1988).

14. Waharu Sonavane, *Adhyakshiya Bhashan: Pachave Adivasi Sahitya Sammelan* (presidential speech, 5th Adivasi Sahitya Sammelan, Marathi) (Thane: Nelson Mandela Nagar, 1990).

Chapter 11

1. *India Today*, May 15, 1987, p. 39.

2. *Indian Express*, September 12, 1987.

3. *Times of India*, September 9, 1987.

4. Vinod Mishra, "Matters Will Have to Be Settled in the Streets," *Voice of Alternative*, September 1987.

5. *Times of India*, October 15, 1987.

6. Bhabani Sen Gupta, "A Different Script,"*Economic and Political Weekly*, October 29, 1988.

7. *Frontline*, October 29–November 11, 1988.

8. *Indian Express*, November 13, 1988.

9. *Indian Express*, November 11, 1988.

10. Veronica Bennholdt-Thomsen, "The World Bank and the Small Peasantry," in *Women: The Last Colony*, ed. Maria Mies et al. (New Delhi: Kali for Women Press, 1989), p. 56.

11. Mark Fineman, "Frail Hero Stands in the Way of Progress," *Minneapolis Star and Tribune*, March 5, 1990. See also the document *Assertion of the Collective Will of Environmentalists: Green Front* (Anandwan, July 1989).

12. *Indian Express*, January 31, 1990.

13. Rajni Bakshi and Smitu Kothari, "On Sustaining 'Grand' Events," *Lokayan Bulletin*, September–October 1989.

14. *Times of India*, December 9, 1989.

15. *Report of the Commissioner for Scheduled Castes and Scheduled Tribes, Twenty-Ninth Report, 1987–89* (Faridabad: Government of India Press, 1990), p. xviii.

16. S. N. M. Abdi, "When Darkness Fell," *Illustrated Weekly*, November 26, 1989.

17. Government of India, Planning Commission, *Toward Social Transformation: Approach to the Eighth Five-Year Plan*, May 1990.

18. The SAC's proposal was in fact published at the expense of the farmers' movement itself only a year later; see *National Agricultural Policy: Views of the Standing Advisory Committee, July 1990* (Jallandar: Government Printing Press, 1991).

19. Ibid., p. 49.

20. R. K. Roy, "Farm Plan Boon for Kulaks" and "Farmers Gain at Consumers' Expense," in *Times of India*, July 14 and July 25, 1990; Ila Patnaik, "Hike in Foodgrain Prices Will Check Industrial Growth," *Times of India*, July 23, 1990.

21. "Panel Member Challenges Draft Farm Policy," *Business and Political Observor*, December 11, 1990.

22. *Economic Times*, January 9 and March 17, 1991.

23. Pritish Nandy, "The Taming of the Tau," *Illustrated Weekly*, July 29, 1990.

24. S. Balakrishnan, "The Chosen One," *Illustrated Weekly Weekend*, January 12–13, 1991, p. 16.

25. "We Are the Forces of Change: Interview with V. P. Singh," *Frontline*, February 16-March 1, 1991, p. 29.

26. *Sunday Observor*, December 2, 1990.

27. *People's Front*, January 1991, p. 4.

28. James Clad, "Towards a Hindu Raj," *Far Eastern Economic and Political Review*, September 20, 1990.

29. *Frontline*, February 16–March 1, 1991, p. 128.

30. Rajni Thiranagama, et al., *The Broken Palmyra*, p. 178.

31. Prabhu Chawla, "Betrayers of '89 Mandate Punished," *Indian Express*, June 23, 1991.

32. Abhijit Sen and C. P. Chandrasekhar, "Verdict '91: Going Behind the Figures," *Frontline*, July 6-19, 1991.

33. Madhu Kishwar, "The Assassination of Rajiv Gandhi," *Manushi*, 1991.

34. See, for example, Rajni Kothari, "State and Anti-State," *Economic and Political Weekly* Special Number (November 1991); Vinod Vyasulu et al., "Towards a Political Economy of the Economic Policy Changes," *Economic and Political Weekly*, September 21, 1991; H. K. Paranjape, "New Industrial Policy: A Capitalist Manifesto," *Economic and Political Weekly*, October 26, 1991; K. S. Krishnaswamy, "On Liberalisation and Some Related Matters," *Economic and Political Weekly*, October 19, 1991, for representative discussions.

35. For important recent discussions of the colonial state and India in the imperial framework, see David Washbrook, "South Asia, the World System and World Capitalism," *Journal of Asian Studies* 49,3 (August 1990) and the section on "The Colonial Transformation" in *Sociology of "Developing Societies": South Asia*, eds. Hamza Alavi and John Harris (London: Macmillan, 1989).

36. British Marxist Fred Halliday was a main organizer of the Cambridge seminar, which tried to hold up Deng's China as a Third World model; see *Illustrated Weekly of India*, November 9–15, 1991; Lloyd and Suzanne Rudolph, *In Search of Lakshmi*; and G. Ram Reddy, in Frankel and Rao, *Dominance and State Power*, 1:281.

37. "Award Won't Finance Dam Struggle: Medha," *Times of India*, November 30, 1991, and *Sakal*, November 30, 1991.

38. K. R. Datye, "Sustainable Development Alternatives and the Large Dam Controversy," December 1991.

39. Vandana Shiva, "The Greening of the Global Reach," *The Illustrated Weekly of India*, October 12–18, 1991.

40. "Balirajyaci Disha" (The Direction of the Kingdom of Bali, Marathi), *Shetkari Sanghatak*, October 21, 1991.

Conclusion

1. Utsa Patnaik, "Some Aspects of Development in the Agrarian Sector in Independent India," *Social Scientist* 177 (February 1988): 37.

2. Achin Vanaik, *The Painful Transition: Bourgeois Democracy in India* (London: Verso, 1990), pp. 83–84, 107–9, and postscript; Vanaik seems to see the "agrarian bourgeoisie" as the source of "endemic instability" but holds back from defining the "decentralist" thrust as radical/anarchistic in the way Patnaik does; since the "agrarian bourgeoisie" is a bourgeoisie, his logic leads to the implication that it ultimately has no basic contradictions with the industrial bourgeoisie, and thus a decentralist thrust is not necessarily a threat to the bourgeois democracy of the system and the territorial integrity of the country; in other words, the hegemony of the industrial bourgeoisie and thus of the Congress party must reassert itself.

3. Anjan Ghosh, "Civil Liberties, Uncivil State," in "New Social Movements," *Seminar* 335 (March, 1989): 35.

4. This appears to be why Vanaik, for instance, discusses the "new peasant movement" in a separate heading, under "Rural India," rather than in his section on "New Social Movements"; Ibid., pp. 195–209.

5. Ramchandra Guha, "The Problem," *Seminar* 335 (March 1989): 15.

6. Michael Albert and George Hahnel, *Unorthodox Marxism* (Boston: South End Press, 1980).

7. Immanuel Wallerstein, "Development: Lodestar or Illusion," *Economic and Political Weekly*, September 24, 1988.

8. "Mahila Dal to Field 400 Candidates," *The Hindu*, April 10, 1991.

9. See "One More Party in AP Fray," *Economic Times*, April 9, 1991; "Environmental Issues May Figure in Poll Campaign," *The Hindu*, April 10, 1991; and "Eco Group's Call to Political Parties," *The Hindu*, April 11, 1991.

10. Song by Suman Katre, LNP.

11. James C. Scott, *Weapons of the Weak: Everyday Forms of Peasant Resistance* (New Haven: Yale University Press, 1985), pp. 29, 350. It is interesting that while Scott himself pinpoints the problem of a "coercive and hegemonic state apparatus," and although he shows quite clearly the role of state pricing for Malaysian capitalism, his study also does not deal with this kind of relationship and with the poor peasants' attitudes toward the state and its officials.

12. M. N. Srinivas, "On Living in a Revolution," *Economic and Political Weekly*, March 30, 1991, p. 835.

13. Ibid.

14. See p. x.

Gail Omvedt received her Ph.D. in sociology at the University of California, Berkeley. As an activist, writer and teacher she has been a participant observer for three decades in many of the movements described in this book. Her many publications on India include the books *Cultural Revolt in a Colonial Society: the Non-Brahman Movement in Western India 1873-1930* and *We Will Smash This Prison: Indian Women in Struggle.*